UNDERSTANDING SOUND TRACKS THROUGH FILM THEORY

UNDERSTANDING SOUND TRACKS THROUGH FILM THEORY

Elsie Walker

OXFORD
UNIVERSITY PRESS

OXFORD
UNIVERSITY PRESS

Oxford University Press is a department of the University of
Oxford. It furthers the University's objective of excellence in research,
scholarship, and education by publishing worldwide.

Oxford   New York
Auckland   Cape Town   Dar es Salaam   Hong Kong   Karachi
Kuala Lumpur   Madrid   Melbourne   Mexico City   Nairobi
New Delhi   Shanghai   Taipei   Toronto

With offices in
Argentina   Austria   Brazil   Chile   Czech Republic   France   Greece
Guatemala   Hungary   Italy   Japan   Poland   Portugal   Singapore
South Korea   Switzerland   Thailand   Turkey   Ukraine   Vietnam

Oxford is a registered trademark of Oxford University Press
in the UK and certain other countries.

Published in the United States of America by
Oxford University Press
198 Madison Avenue, New York, NY 10016

© Oxford University Press 2015

Library of Congress Cataloging-in-Publication Data
Walker, Elsie M., 1975–
Understanding sound tracks through film theory / Elsie Walker.
    pages cm
Includes bibliographical references and index.
Includes filmography.
ISBN 978–0–19–989630–1 (hbk. alk. paper) — ISBN 978–0–19–989632–5 (pbk. alk. paper)
1. Sound in motion pictures.   2. Sound motion pictures.   3. Motion pictures—Aesthetics.
4. Motion pictures—Sound effects.   I. Title.
PN1995.7.W36 2015
791.4302′4—dc23   2014016766

9 8 7 6 5 4 3 2 1
Printed in the United States of America
on acid-free paper

for Jim,
who I always want to hear,
and who always hears me

CONTENTS

PART V: QUEER THEORY

ACKNOWLEDGMENTS

First, I thank Norm Hirschy, for his clarity, efficiency, and kindness as editor for Oxford University Press. I also thank the anonymous readers who read my original book proposal and chapters for Oxford University Press, and who provided invaluable suggestions. I am extremely grateful to Andrew Westerhaus for his meticulous copyediting, as well as Kate Nunn and Molly Morrison for working on the book in production. I thank all my colleagues at Salisbury University, Maryland. I am especially grateful for my friends and colleagues in the Fulton School of Liberal Arts who have encouraged me and offered great advice: Brenda Grodzicki, David T. Johnson, T. Ross Leasure, April Logan, Loren Marquez, Nick Melczarek, Nicole Munday, Maarten Pereboom, and Judith Pike. My heartfelt gratitude, also, to Becky Pauly (West Chester University), and to the composer Peter Dasent. I give special thanks to all my film students at Salisbury University, especially the students in my course on sound tracks: they have inspired me far more than I think they can possibly know. I thank Ron Sadoff and Gillian Anderson for being terrific mentors, especially as they welcomed me into the *Music and the Moving Image* community. I thank the great teachers who fostered my love of music from a very early age: Margaret Crawshaw, Colin MacMillan, Sue Radford, Kathy Shelhart, David Sidwell, and Sally Swedlund. Thank you to Michael Hattaway for being the most perfect PhD research supervisor I could have had, and who influenced me throughout my writing this book without his even knowing it. I thank the first inimitable teachers of my life: my father, for inspiring me to learn, write, and teach with passion in all things; and my mother, for showing me how to be ever mindful of detail and ever appreciative of empathy. (And Dad, although you died while this book was in production, I want you to know that your enduring presence helped me finish it.) I am grateful for the support I have from my families in New Zealand, America, and the United Kingdom—including my families by blood, marriage, and friendship. I thank my daughter Charlotte Hope, and my new baby Dorothy Jane, for being the best motivation I could ever have to finish this book, *and* to make it count. Finally, I thank my husband, James Burton, whose love made this book possible in the first place: "You know I dreamed about you, for 29 years, before I saw you."

UNDERSTANDING SOUND TRACKS THROUGH FILM THEORY

GENERAL INTRODUCTION

*So, you're expressing something and you're hoping that somebody else
will listen. Maybe there's a message in it. The message in it is not gonna
be something that Western Union can carry, but it's gonna be a message.*
—David Raksin, composer for *Bigger Than Life* (Duffie [1988] 2008)

*Cinema overall is 70% sound. Because your ears are far more developed
than your eyes. You cannot stop yourself hearing, even if you put your finger in your ears, you still hear. Because it goes through the cheek bones
and everything. But eyes are. . . you can shut your eyes and that's it.*
—John Currie, sound designer for *Ten Canoes* (Starrs 2009, 249)

In 1988, the prolific film composer David Raksin hoped we might
be listening to his scores. In 2009, the independent sound designer John Currie asserted
that we have no choice but to hear cinema. The contrast between these perspectives parallels a sea change in scholarly approaches to sound tracks over the last several decades—
overall, there is a collective shift from making readers aware that cinema must be heard,
to finding new ways for readers to understand the aural elements of cinema.

In 1987 Claudia Gorbman published one of the most influential works in soundtrack
studies: *Unheard Melodies: Narrative Film Music*. It was the first book to focus on film
music within contexts of contemporary film theory, and this set it apart from earlier
works by critics and practitioners.[1] As Kathyrn Kalinak explains, *Unheard Melodies*

---

[1] As Kalinak points out in her review of Gorbman's book, the first wave of critics and theoreticians of
film music emerged in the 1940s. One key influence on *Unheard Melodies* is Hanns Eisler and Theodor
Adorno's *Composing for the Films* ([1947] 2007), an important treatise on creating scores that challenge
the ideological norms of Classical Hollywood. Though numerous other anecdotal, instructional, and historical books on film music preceded Gorbman's book, hers was the first to analyze film music in relation

came out at a time when film music was "yet to be absorbed into the mainstream of writing on cinematic history, theory, and criticism" (1988, 56). Kalinak herself has done much to challenge the visual bias of film scholarship: her book *Settling the Score: Music and the Classical Hollywood Film* (1992) is another key work, especially as it explores the enduring conventions of Classical Hollywood scoring.

The surge of new attention to film sound tracks since the 1990s is overwhelming, so much so that we can only cite a few important examples here: *Sound Theory, Sound Practice* edited by Rick Altman (1992), *The Sounds of Commerce* by Jeff Smith (1998), *Changing Tunes: The Use of Pre-existing Music in Film* edited by Phil Powrie and Robynn J. Stilwell (2006), *The Spectre of Sound: Music in Film and Television* by K. J. Donnelly (2008), and several books by Michel Chion, including Gorbman's English translations of *Audio-Vision: Sound on Screen* (1994), *The Voice in Cinema* (1999), and *Film, A Sound Art* (2009). Two leading journals devoted to sound tracks have also emerged in the past decade: *Music, Sound, and the Moving Image* (University of Liverpool, founded in 2007), and *Music and the Moving Image* (University of Illinois Press, founded in 2008). The latter journal is affiliated with an annual conference of the same name that brings together composers, sound personnel, graduate scholars, and professors to discuss the relationship between music, sound, and the entire universe of moving images (including film, television, video games, iPod, computer, and interactive performances).[2] The strong presence of university faculty at the Music and the Moving Image (MaMI) conference indicates that sound tracks are not only increasingly researched, but also increasingly *taught* in film curricula all over the world. In 2011 alone, more than sixty different tertiary institutions were represented at the conference.

The MaMI conference reflects a more general global awareness of the aural power of cinema. Films, in turn, seem to be increasingly created with the expectation that audiences will *hear* as well as see them. In 2013, Gorbman herself directly addressed this trend with the title of her paper: "Heard Music." Where *Unheard Melodies* is a demand for new attention to Classical Hollywood sound tracks that have all too often been neglected, and which themselves seem to dissuade conscious perception, "Heard Music" is an analysis of contemporary "background music" that self-consciously demands to be perceived, especially in the films directed by Paul Thomas Anderson.

Understanding Sound Tracks Through Film Theory is a response to the increasing emphasis on sound tracks within film scholarship and university curricula, especially

---

to theoretical trends that had transformed cinema studies (especially semiotics, Marxism, and psychoanalysis) (Kalinak 1988, 56–57).

[2] This quotation comes from the call for papers for the 2014 MaMI conference: http://steinhardt.nyu.edu/music/scoring/conference/.

as it reflects a growing expectation that many filmmakers *assume* we are aurally alert. This book follows in the footsteps of *Hearing the Movies: Music and Sound in Film History*, by James Buhler, David Neumeyer, and Rob Deemer (2010), a book designed for undergraduate tertiary courses. *Hearing the Movies* offers a comprehensive introduction to the study of sound tracks, along with providing crucial industrial and historical contexts for understanding their construction and power. *Understanding Sound Tracks Through Film Theory* builds upon this strong foundation by being written for those who are already familiar with the terminology and methodology introduced by *Hearing the Movies*, and who are interested in studying sound tracks further with regard to specific theoretical approaches. It is primarily designed for film scholars, at the upper-undergraduate, or graduate level, and beyond. But it is also written for anyone interested in challenging what Kalinak refers to as the "visual chauvinism" of much other scholarship, across many disciplines (1988, 56).

Although we have seen a great boom in critical attention to sound tracks, the presumption that film is a visual medium is still pervasive. In his recent study of complex cinematic representations of reality, tellingly titled *The Eyes Have It*, Murray Pomerance refers to film as "one form of pictorialization" (2013, 4). This is but one representative example of the enduring visual bias within film scholarship. Moreover, many of the foundational theoretical works which have inspired this book reveal a similar visual bias, and this all too often goes uncontested. Indeed, one of this book's primary objectives is to challenge the visual emphasis of many influential theoretical works by redirecting their arguments towards sound tracks.

As Anahid Kassabian has written, dominant studies of music tend to be written for those who are already musically trained and therefore able to read scores (2001, 21). Similarly, studies of sound tend to be jargon-heavy or weighed down with overly technical emphases. This book redresses the balance by introducing readers to new ways of analyzing sound tracks without requiring much formal training: anything beyond basic film and music terminology is briefly defined. There is also a select glossary of musical terms that move beyond the basics of melody, rhythm, tempo, texture, dynamics, and harmony. Even though some musical transcriptions are included, the arguments of this book are not reliant upon the reader's ability to interpret them: this is, in other words, a book for "musos" *and* "non-musos" alike.[3] Moreover, the theoretical arguments of each chapter resonate with other contemporary scholarship in music, history, politics, literature, and culture, as well as film studies.

---

[3] Here we borrow Phillip Tagg's terminology in an important article about democratically teaching sound tracks (2012).

Each chapter of this book is organized as follows:

1. First, we explore some fundamental concerns of a particular theory. This introductory section is anchored in close attention to a representative example of foundational and/or influential scholarship within that theory's history.
2. We use the representative example of scholarship to generate a list of specific questions about applying the given theoretical approach to sound tracks.
3. We then apply the set of theoretically driven questions to two specific films. The films are selected because they strongly resonate within a given theoretical context. That said, each of the two films selected in relation to a theory resonates quite differently, demonstrating the malleability of the theories and the related questions we generate from them. Each film analysis is primarily influenced by the representative example of scholarship already introduced, but also enlivened with references to contemporary examples of the given theoretical approach. We begin every film analysis with a brief plot summary before developing our approach in relation to close readings of particular scenes and sequences. Along the way, we give due consideration to historical, industrial, and artistic contexts for analysis.

This book gives most attention to the music of films because it is a necessarily selective approach to sound tracks. *Understanding Sound Tracks Through Film Theory* is also best contextualized in relation to other scholarship on film music. However, this book also breaks a dominant trend within soundtrack studies. As Stilwell points out, music is too often misleadingly segregated from other elements of sound tracks in close film analyses (2006, 48). Given that the study of sound has been such an important growth area in film studies for the last two decades, this enduring segregation is strange. Each close analysis of this book includes some consideration of *the interplay of* sound effects, dialogue, and music. Investigating how and why certain sounds work together and/or are used hierarchically is crucial for fully understanding the aural power of cinema.

Since all aural elements work together, we will open out the concept of "film musicality" beyond its literal meaning: in other words, we will apply musical principles to all the interconnected elements of film sound tracks. In the feminism chapter, for instance, we will consider the relative volume, pitch, and tempo of Lauren Bacall's speaking voice in addition to her singing one, as well as in relation to other aural elements of *To Have and Have Not* (1944). It is important to explore ways in which dialogue and sound effects are used "musically," with a sensitive ear for all aural structures. Some scholars, such as Gianluca Sergi, argue vehemently against the application of musical terms to non-musical sounds (2004, 6), for fear that it perpetuates a bias towards music at the expense of other elements of film sound. However, we shall find there is much to be gained from applying the rich vocabulary of musicology to everything we hear in cinema. Here again, we build upon the precedent of *Hearing the Movies*, a book that uses concepts of musicology to highlight the compositional intentionality of all kinds of film sound.

This book is not an effort to fix the meaning of anything we hear, but to open up possibilities for hearing cinema through various important theoretical approaches. Though each chapter places theoretical limits on how to analyze each sound track, the final section of this book is a short consideration of how all theoretical approaches might be meaningfully combined. This "coda" is followed by a series of films for "further perceiving." Like Kassabian, we shall think of the hypothetical *perceiver* of a film, rather than using the much more common term "spectator." The word "perceiver" allows for subjective impressions, along with allowing for *aural* as well as visual impact (2001, 110–11).[4]

To preview the preoccupations and assumptions of this book in more specific terms, let us consider the first three minutes of a film: *Brokeback Mountain* (2005). From the outset, the sound track of this film works in self-consciously affective and intertextual ways. Moreover, the interplay of *all* aural elements—music, dialogue (or lack thereof), and sound effects—matters.

The action of *Brokeback Mountain* focuses on two cowboys named Innis del Mar (Heath Ledger) and Jack Twist (Jake Gyllenhal) who first meet while sheepherding on Brokeback Mountain in 1963. Both men are painfully aware that their relationship is socially taboo in mainstream American society. They both marry women and start young families. But they also risk a long-standing romantic affair with each other, though it is limited to sporadic meetings over a period of almost seventeen years. The film ends after Jack is tragically killed, and though his wife describes his death to Innis as an accident, it is visually presented while she provides this explanation as a violent hate crime. This is but one example of the film's self-conscious emphasis on the power of that which is seen *in relation to* what can be heard.

Brokeback Mountain is a deeply subversive response to classical examples of the western that preceded it. It aurally recalls other westerns, just as it plays with our expectations of what its sound track "should" amplify. The very first sound of the film is wind, a common aural motif in westerns, especially in connection with vast, inhospitable landscapes. Then comes the sound of a single guitar and a lone truck winding its way

---

[4] Kassabian challenges the notion that all possibilities of interpretation may be theoretically anticipated by generally applied, psychoanalytically determined paradigms. Her work reminds us that audiences bring individualized and social histories (of gender, race, class, sexuality) and "many other axes of identity" into the movie theater (2001, 110–11). Further, unlike the theoretical spectator of traditional psychoanalysis, the "perceiver" engages (both consciously and unconsciously) with aural messages in *addition to* visual ones.

down the empty road. The guitar dominates Gustavo Santaolalla's original non-diegetic score for the film. It is an instrument much-associated with the western genre, but its usage varies widely: from traditional folk songs, to lyrical themes, to contemporary, fragmented cues.[5] That said, as Michael J. Blouin writes, Santaolalla's music is not a conventional "narrative melody" in the sense that it "does not follow traditional tension/release structure; instead, it is constructed of drawn out notes that are not seeking any familiar resolution (hence, [an] 'uncontained' quality)" (2010, 1185).[6] This distinguishes it from the music featured in more sonically conventional westerns, such as the melody-driven score by Max Steiner for *The Searchers* (1956), which we analyze in due course. This music from the opening of *Brokeback* is also distinguished from the traditional country tunes associated with heterosexual romance later in the film (Blouin 2010, 1185).[7] The music itself thus suggests a kind of generic and narrative subversiveness—it carries meaning beyond the already heard and the already familiar.

Santaolalla's guitar line is a series of fragments that are first associated with Innis del Mar, especially as he jumps out of the truck and stands alone by a cabin where his soon-to-be employer will arrive. The guitar line anticipates his own speech that is similarly hesitant, fragmented, and economical. In this first scene, though, he is the *silent* image of the quintessential cowboy, leaning against the cabin with his legs casually crossed, head bowed under a cowboy hat (see Figure 0.1).

As we see Innis this way, the fragmented line of guitar music begins to be answered by a group of harmonizing strings. However, this aural harmony fades away quickly as, all at once, our view of him is disturbed by the entrance of a freight train, its black silhouette rushing past the camera with as much aggression as its sound. Then, a second truck enters the scene: the old, stuttering, backfiring vehicle driven by Jack Twist. Jack kicks the truck when he climbs out, a futile gesture of frustration, soon overtaken by the sound of wind and the silence of the two men as they wait together. Jack eyes Innis in a somewhat suggestive way, especially as he momentarily poses against his truck (see Figure 0.2), but he says nothing.

---

[5] To cite but a few specific examples: in *The Searchers* (1956), a character named Charlie (a parody of the singing cowboy) accompanies his own traditional songs with guitar; in *Unforgiven* (1992), a haunting and lyrical guitar theme (composed by lead actor and director Clint Eastwood) poignantly reinforces the film's emphasis on romanticizing its hero despite his condemnably violent deeds; and in *Dead Man* (1995), Neil Young's improvised, distorted, and heavily reverberating music for electric guitar is a crucial example of the film's defamiliarization of western conventions.

[6] Blouin here writes of the famous main love theme associated with Jack and Innis, rather than this opening music, but his argument nevertheless applies.

[7] This same music re-enters much later in the film when Innis anticipates a visit from Jack [1:01:30–1:02:12], this time without being cut off, suggesting the possibility of their transcending circumstance (albeit tragically temporarily).

FIGURE 0.1 Innis del Mar, the archetypically withdrawn and silent cowboy.

FIGURE 0.2 Jack suggestively eyes Innis: there is no need for words.

While Innis and Jack both steal looks at each other, their mutual silence prompts us to consider that which cannot be spoken. The wind that was barely perceptible at the start of the film now "speaks" loudly in the place of words, pointing to the absence of their direct communication.

Let us pause on what the sound track has already established, even before either character has spoken a word. First, the two characters are clearly established as ironic counterparts to each other. Innis's ride through the landscape of the film is smooth, driven by another, and makes little sound. Jack's ride through the same terrain is independent, faltering, and "messy," suggesting his inability to be discrete and in control of his own presence. The film thus aurally announces their differences before we even see them. On a deeper level, the film suggests that Innis can travel through the terrain of the western without calling attention to himself too much. Innis's comparatively quiet presence relates to his fearfulness: he is a character haunted by what it means to define oneself against the "rules" of dominant masculinity, especially when he later recalls his father showing him the mutilated corpse of a gay man. Jack, on the other hand, willfully speaks out against the limitations of the world as it oppresses them, literally shouting at Innis against the backdrop of Brokeback Mountain while he insists on the possibility of their living together. Jack is much more sonically subversive than Innis, but he is also punished for it. The film amplifies his presence, but it also emphasizes the tragic cost of his aural rebelliousness.

The musical score of this opening subtly suggests a kind of yearning, gesturing towards the possibility of an "answer" that is suddenly interrupted by the *forte* entrance of the train. In being the "iron horse" that replaced horses and stagecoaches, the train alludes to the expanding world of the contemporary western. Its sight and sound also emphasizes the power of the world intruding upon Innis's space, a power that interrupts his music and the film's focus on his silently iconic power. Innis's silence is important because it initially connects him with a long line of taciturn and stoic cowboys who define themselves in terms of action more than words.[8] But the silence he then inadvertently shares with Jack suggests something more: it is a full silence that suggests an understanding between them, albeit tentative at first. In combination with the furtive glances that they steal of one another, this silence is "queer."[9] It raises the possibility of their subtextual, mutual desire within a recognizably western context.

---

[8] For more on this tradition, as well as important exceptions to it, see Kozloff (2000, 139–69).

[9] Santaolalla's score might be meaningfully discussed in relation to other queer sound tracks for contemporary films. Some recent examples (from the journal *Music, Sound, and the Moving Image*) include: Miguel Mera's explanation of the subversively beautiful music he composed to underscore the emotional truth of Salvador Dali's gay relationship with Federico García Lorca in *Little Ashes* (2009); and Todd Decker's analysis of a queer dichotomy in *The Talented Mr. Ripley* (1999) between established

Brokeback Mountain was released after seven years in preproduction, and its reputation as a "gay western" was well established before its première (Kitses 2007, 23). Thus, even its first audiences were primed to read this silence for its suggestive power. Even the wind that dominates the sound track, in place of the men's words, suggests the tumult that they come to embody within a generic context. From the outset, the sound track positions us to sympathetically perceive its gay characters—to smile at Jack's awkwardly noisy entrance, to be intrigued by the protagonists' silence, to shrink from the sound of the train, and to seize hold of those fragments of melody that suggest something hopefully, even if cautiously, different.

This analysis of just three minutes establishes several fundamental preoccupations of this book:

1. First, a challenge to the hegemony of the visual.
2. Second, an emphasis on the most heard *and* the less perceptible elements of sound: here, the subtlety of the wind motif and the absent dialogue, in addition to Santaollala's award-winning musical score.
3. A consideration of how all aural elements work interdependently.
4. An awareness of how using theoretical frameworks can deepen our understanding of why sound tracks resonate: understanding the above example entails consideration of genre studies and queer theory.
5. A belief that there is much more work to do in analyzing sound tracks, and that this area is fertile ground for genuine contributions to film scholarship. Much has been written on how *Brokeback Mountain* subverts the traditional narrative and visual implications of the western, but there is plenty more to say about its aural density.[10]
6. The assumption that sound effects, dialogue, and silences are as carefully "orchestrated" as film scores.[11]

---

classical music (associated with genuine gay desire) and popular jazz music (associated with conformist heterosexuality).

[10] See Erica Spohrer's 2009 article for but one strong example. As of December 4, 2013, there are 137 articles about *Brokeback Mountain* listed by the MLA International Bibliography, but only one that focuses primarily on its sound track. Even this example (by Blouin) gives only four pages to the film in relation to several other western sound tracks.

[11] As Sergi points out, there are often numerous personnel involved in the creation of a final sound track, including sound mixers (involved in different areas of sound effects, dialogue, and music), foley artists, re-recording mixers, music supervisors, composers, sound editors, and sound designers (2004, 183). We could also add the importance of musicians performing the composed score, and actors delivering dialogue or, equally, providing silence, as well as the directors and producers who may have controlling power over any aural dimension of the film. We will only mention someone by name (such as a composer or sound designer) where the agency behind something we hear is easily identified. That said, we will always take it as a given that every element of a sound track belongs more to a film as a collaborative creation than to any one person involved.

7. The belief that close analyses help readers hone their own skills, as well as contributing to the field of soundtrack studies (even the relatively well-established subfield of film music analysis). As recently as 2008, and despite so much attention to film music over the last three decades, Peter Larsen wrote that close analyses of scoring for "specific, individual films are in short supply" (2008, 8).

This book is organized in terms of theoretical approaches that logically follow on from each other. However, the reader may well decide to read the parts out of order: though they become exponentially more ambitious, the book is designed so that no part is contingent upon any other. Only with the coda do we assume the reader's familiarity with everything before it. This final section is an anticipation of the further analyses that will combine theoretical approaches, and it focuses upon a recent release: *Gravity* (2013). Throughout the rest of the book we focus on a wide range of films dated from the Classical Hollywood era to the present day. No matter which film is being discussed, we shall find that the visual bias in film scholarship is still strong enough that even the most canonized films provide fertile ground for new, aurally based research. This is an exciting prospect for any film scholar: from *Rebecca* (1940) to *The Piano* (1993), there is still much more to hear.

WORKS CITED

Adorno, Theodor, and Hanns Eisler. (1947) 2007. *Composing for the Films*. London: Continuum.

Altman, Rick, ed. 1992. *Sound Theory, Sound Practice*. New York: Routledge.

Blouin, Michael J. 2010. "Auditory Ambivalence: Music in the Western from *High Noon* to *Brokeback Mountain*." *Journal of Popular Culture* 43 (6): 1173–88.

Buhler, James, David Neumeyer, and Rob Deemer. 2010. *Hearing the Movies: Music and Sound in Film History*. New York: Oxford University Press.

Chion, Michel. 1994. *Audio-Vision: Sound on Screen*. Edited and translated by Claudia Gorbman. New York: Columbia University Press. Originally published as *L'Audio-Vision* (Paris: Editions Nathan, 1990).

———. 1999. *The Voice in Cinema*. Edited and translated by Claudia Gorbman. New York: Columbia University Press. Originally published as *La Voix au cinéma* (Paris: Cahiers du cinéma (Editions de l'Etoile), 1982).

———. 2009. *Film, A Sound Art*. Translated by Claudia Gorbman. New York: Columbia University Press. Originally published as *Un art sonare, le cinéma* (Paris: Cahiers du cinéma (Editions de l'Etoile), 2003).

Decker, Todd. 2012. "The Musical Mr. Ripley." *Music, Sound, and the Moving Image* 6 (2): 185–207.

Duffie, Bruce. (1988) 2008. "Composer David Raksin: A Conversation with Bruce Duffie." Accessed December 2, 2013. <http://www.kcstudio.com/raksin2.html>.

Donnelly, K. J. 2005. *The Spectre of Sound: Music in Film and Television*. London: BFI Publishing.

Gorbman, Claudia. 1987. *Unheard Melodies: Narrative Film Music*. Bloomington: Indiana University Press.

———. 2013. "*Heard Music*." Paper presented at the Music and the Moving Image Annual Convention, NYU Steinhardt School of Culture, Education, and Human Development, New York, May 31, 2013.

Kalinak, Kathryn. 1988. Review of *Unheard Melodies: Narrative Film Music*, by Claudia Gorbman. *Film Quarterly* 41 (4): 56–58.

———. 1992. *Settling the Score: Music and the Classical Hollywood Film*. Madison: The University of Wisconsin Press.

Kassabian, Anahid. 2001. *Hearing Film: Tracking Identifications in Contemporary Hollywood Film Music*. London and New York: Routledge.

Kitses, Jim. 2007. "All that *Brokeback* Allows." *Film Quarterly* 60 (3): 22–27.

Kozloff, Sarah. 2000. *Overhearing Film Dialogue*. Berkeley, CA: University of California Press.

Larsen, Peter. 2008. *Film Music*. London: Reaktion Books.

Mera, Miguel. 2012. "Outing the Score: Music, Narrative, and Collaborative Process in *Little Ashes*." *Music, Sound, and the Moving Image* 6 (1): 93–109.

Pomerance, Murray. 2013. *The Eyes Have It: Cinema and the Reality Effect*. New Brunswick, NJ: Rutgers University Press.

Powrie, Phil, and Robynn J. Stilwell, eds. 2006. *Changing Tunes: The Use of Pre-existing Music in Film*. Burlington, VT: Ashgate Publishing Ltd.

Sergi, Gianluca. 2004. *The Dolby Era: Film Sound in Contemporary Hollywood*. Manchester: Manchester University Press.

Smith, Jeff. 1998. *The Sounds of Commerce*. New York: Columbia University Press.

Spohrer, Erika. 2009. "Not a Gay Cowboy Movie?: *Brokeback Mountain* and the Importance of Genre." *Journal of Popular Film and Television* 37 (1): 26–33.

Starrs, Bruno. 2009. "Aural Auteur: Sound in the Films of Rolf de Heer." PhD diss., Queensland University of Technology. Accessed December 4, 2013. <http://eprints.qut.edu.au/29302/2/Bruno_Starrs_Thesis.pdf>.

Tagg, Philip. 2012. "Music, Moving Image, and the 'Missing Majority': How Vernacular Media Competence Can Help Music Studies Move into the Digital Era." *Music and the Moving Image* 5 (2): 9–33.

PART I

Genre Studies

INTRODUCTION

"A Semantic/Syntactic Approach to Film Genre" by Rick Altman

We begin with a comparative, genre-based analysis of two sound tracks for westerns: *The Searchers* (1956) and *Dead Man* (1995). To understand the significance of these sound tracks, we will place them within a context of genre analysis. Using Rick Altman's seminal article "A Semantic/Syntactic Approach to Film Genre" ([1984] 2012) as a starting point, we can establish some fundamentals of genre analysis with particular reference to the western.

Altman advocates a combination of semantic and syntactic approaches to genre. He explains these approaches as follows:

> We can as a whole distinguish between generic definitions that depend on a list of common traits, attitudes, characters, shots, locations, sets, and the like—thus stressing the semantic elements that make up the genre—and definitions that play up instead certain constitutive relationships between undesignated and variable placeholders—relationships that might be called the genre's fundamental syntax. The semantic approach thus stresses the genre's building blocks, while the syntactic view privileges the structures into which they are arranged (31).

To anchor this in concrete examples, Altman references the western. He cites Marc Vernet's list of semantic elements for the genre, one that includes: "general atmosphere ('emphasis on basic elements, such as earth, dust, water, and leather'), stock characters ('the tough/soft cowboy, the lonely sheriff, the faithful or treacherous Indian, and the strong but tender woman'), as well as technical elements ('use of fast tracking and crane shots')" (31–32).[1] Then, Altman cites Jim Kitses's more syntactic approach of considering how "the western grows out of a dialectic between the West as a garden and a desert (and between culture and nature, community and individual, future and past)" (32).[2] For Altman, favoring either the semantic or the syntactic approach exclusively means losing interpretive possibilities: the semantic approach rests with identifying the building blocks of genre without necessarily having *"explanatory power"*; and the syntactic approach, on the other hand, entails logical patterns of connection that resist *"broad applicability"* (33, original emphases).

Claudia Gorbman and Kathryn Kalinak have provided strong analyses of patterns within musical scoring for numerous westerns. Though neither of them explicity cites Altman, both of their approaches resonate with his semantic/syntactic approach. Gorbman surveys how Native Americans have been scored from the silent era to the 1990s, establishing how they were first cinematically associated with ominous "tom-tom" rhythms, modal or minor-key melodies, and threatening "Indian-on-the-warpath" motifs, all of which suggest "primitive or exotic peoples" (2000, 236). Gorbman also mentions a less common pattern of musically representing the romanticized Indian (as one close to nature, "the emblem of the lost Eden") through legato melodies for flutes or strings and pastoral harmonies (235). Gorbman then establishes a pattern of much stronger variety in "scoring Indians" since the end of the Second World War, citing many sound tracks that have expanded the semantic repertoire of the genre. Kalinak (2007) provides a book-length analysis of musical patterns across films directed by John Ford, highlighting the non-diegetic scoring practices that he favored,[3] along with his use of folk songs and other traditional American music. Kalinak and Gorbman thus establish many semantic elements of western film scoring, along with considering how these elements are uniquely applied and syntactically placed within specific films. Their works are important pretexts for our own semantic/syntactic analysis of two westerns, the first of which (*The Searchers*) incorporates elements of the stock Indian music mentioned by Gorbman in contrast with the music for its sharply individuated white characters, and the second of which (*Dead Man*) plays

---

[1] For the original reference, see Vernet 1976, 111–12.

[2] For the original reference, see Kitses 1969, 10–14.

[3] Though the distinction between non-diegetic and diegetic is repeatedly used in contemporary analyses of film sound tracks, we should be cognizant that the diegetic/non-diegetic worlds of a film often cross over. We shall simply use the terms to distinguish between aural information that characters in the film world can or could potentially hear (diegetic) and aural information that they cannot or could not hear (non-diegetic) in order to maintain fictional coherence. For a provocative and influential discussion of music that escapes the fixity of a solely diegetic or non-diegetic classification, see Stilwell (2007).

with expectations of what the western "should" sound like in keeping with its subversive treatment of racial politics.[4]

Many genre films self-consciously play upon expectations: as Steve Neale has authoritatively argued, the survival and development of a genre relies upon dominant patterns of repetition combined with "difference, variation, and change" ([1990] 2012, 189).[5] The determining sources of genre development are often, however, debatable. Before Altman, genre films were frequently discussed as *either* originating within audience desires ("the ritual approach") *or* being generated by Hollywood ("the ideological approach"): "the ritual approach sees Hollywood as responding to societal pressure and thus expressing audience desires, the ideological approach claims that Hollywood takes advantage of spectator energy and psychic investment in order to lure the audience into Hollywood's own positions" (Altman [1984] 2012, 30). For Altman, such positions might be irreconcilable but are still both necessarily at play in genre analysis. He argues that we should consider what films do in terms of their preestablished audiences *as well as* analyzing what Hollywood preordains the audiences "should" get. As Altman writes, "Hollywood does not simply lend its voice to the public's desires, nor does it simply manipulate the audience" (37). Further, since audiences presumably do not want to know they are being "manipulated, the successful ritual/ideological 'fit' is almost always one that disguises Hollywood's potential for manipulation while playing up its capacity for entertainment." Indeed, for Altman, the extent to which a genre is "successful" is in large part determined by its ability to combine the imperatives of the audience's "ritual values" with "Hollywood's ideological ones" (37).

We shall therefore consider what the sound tracks of two westerns reveal about their ritualistic *and* ideological values in the contexts of audience reception and Hollywood production. Though our second film, *Dead Man*, is an independent film,[6] it was

---

[4] Characters of *The Searchers* always refer to the indigenous people of America as "Indians" (except when they use derogatory terms such as "injun" or "buck"), thus denying them a clear-cut claim on the land. The characters of *Dead Man* never use the term "Native American," but the film treats them as such. The different terms are used here to emphasize the contrasting cultural politics of the two films.

[5] Both Altman and Neale's articles are included within *Film Genre Reader IV*, Barry Grant's excellent (2012) collection of genre-based readings, many others of which might be meaningfully brought to bear on the study of sound tracks for genre films.

[6] "Independent film" is difficult to define, not least because "indie cinema" has become more absorbed into mainstream American culture in recent years. That said, the term "independent film" still has meaningful associations in terms of connoting that which is potentially subversive and/or eccentric, revisionist and/or ideologically challenging, structurally unconventional and/or deliberately "raw," relatively low budget and/or (often) produced outside a major studio. All these ideas apply to *Dead Man* although it was released through Miramax, a company founded by the Weinstein brothers on "independent" principles but which become increasingly mainstream (not least through its aggressive promotion of such arthouse successes as *Shakespeare In Love* (1998) after it was bought by Disney in 1994).

nevertheless conceived in response to the mainstream westerns that preceded it. With *The Searchers* we have an example of cinema that also works in terms of logical contradictions of the sort embraced by Altman. The film incorporates numerous semantic elements of the western narrative (the lone white hero, the frontier homesteads, the Indian Chief, the showdowns between whites and Indians, and the final duel), yet all are handled in complex ways that exceed generic familiarity. The film apparently grants preconceived audience expectations but also challenges them; that is, it plays out familiar "Hollywood" conventions of the western but it also interrogates those same conventions. More particularly, *The Searchers* invokes familiar thematic oppositions (such as the essential conflict between civilization and barbarism) in order to complicate them.

The thematic tensions within *The Searchers* are most obvious in the characterization of the protagonist Ethan Edwards. Ethan is, paradoxically, both heroic *and* antiheroic, the savior *and* the savage, an icon *and* a caricature of masculinity. That he expresses racism in especially vile terms is mediated by the star power of John Wayne in the lead role. The film's contrary views on him are made explicit through camerawork and *mise-en-scène*. Ethan is sometimes shot to seem as impressively imposing as the mountains of Monument Valley, the spectacular location famously exploited by Ford. Here, Wayne looms large, even against the massive dimensions of Monument Valley. The image in Figure 1.1 connotes rugged and authoritative heroism. The visual harmony of his red shirt and the red rock behind him also communicates his oneness with and mastery of the landscape.

FIGURE 1.1 The impressively imposing Ethan Edwards.

But Ethan is also shot in menacing shadows that prompt critical or even fearful responses (see Figure 1.2). This close-up emphasizes Ethan's barely suppressed hostility and, more specifically, his revulsion at seeing several white women driven mad after their having been prisoners to Indians. Ford chose to emphasize Ethan's hatred for and resentment towards Indians to such an extent that the impact is terrifying, despite Wayne's heroic stature elsewhere in the film.

The complexity of Ethan's character and the significance of contrary responses to him in terms of the western genre, Ford's work within it, and the industrial context of *The Searchers* being a studio production of Classical Hollywood, has already been analyzed many times. What has not been yet much considered, however, is how the tensions of *The Searchers*, especially those represented in the characterization of Ethan, are repeatedly emphasized through its visual and dialogue-driven messages *in opposition to* what Max Steiner's score "says." In particular, Steiner's score repeatedly quashes those troubling moments of the film in which other narrative elements prompt us to dwell upon that which makes Ethan a most dangerous character.

To pave the way for analyzing the sound track of *The Searchers* further, consider the following questions inspired by Altman's work:

- What aspects of the sound track are semantic elements of the western?
- How are the semantic elements of the sound track syntactically arranged?

FIGURE 1.2 The menacing Ethan Edwards.

- Do different elements of the sound track (dialogue, music, and sound effects) work together to create syntactic meanings? Or, is there tension between different aural elements that yields more complex, even contrary, syntactic meanings?
- Do the semantic and syntactic elements of the sound track match other, visual elements of the film?
- What are the "ritual" and "ideological" values communicated by the sound track? In other words, how does it answer its audience's preconceived desires with regard to genre?; and how does the sound track work in relation to sound tracks of other genre films or in relation to the industrial (re)generation of filmic expectations?

  # THE SEARCHERS

PLOT SUMMARY

Along with the dominance of John Wayne as Ethan, *The Searchers* begins with some familiar semantic elements of a western narrative: as William Luhr writes, "Indians massacre a white family and the central character [Edwards] seeks retribution for this savage act." Thus, the film's exposition initially reinforces familiar syntactic oppositions, especially between "whites as the agents of civilization in the wilderness and Indians as murderous, raping savages" (2004, 82). That said, as Luhr (among others) asserts, the film thereafter problematizes its own expository foundations. The Indians take Debbie (Lana Wood), the youngest child of the massacred family, prisoner. However, after living with them for several years, she comes to identify with them as "my people." Though the Chief of the tribe, Scar (Henry Brandon), is first seen as a threatening shadow over Debbie, and therein demonized, we also learn that he has killed in retaliation for his sons' deaths at the hands of white men. Therefore, the first attack of the film is really a *"counterattack,"* even if it initially appears to be a senseless "murder-raid" as Ethan describes it (Colonnese 2004, 337). Moreover, the main character who is intent upon achieving retribution is far from heroic: driven by what becomes a pathological need for vengeance, Ethan not only mutilates the corpses of Indians, but slaughters buffalo "to promote racial extinction" (Luhr 2004, 81). Most of the film focuses on Ethan's quest to return Debbie home over a period of several years, mostly accompanied by Martin Pawley (Jeffrey Hunter), his nephew whose one-eighth Indian ethnicity repulses Ethan. Ethan is first driven by the tragedy of losing members of his family in the film's expository massacre, especially his sister-in-law Martha (Dorothy Jordan), the woman he loves. But Ethan's desire becomes much more disturbing than a quest for straight vengeance or to find Debbie. After learning that Debbie has become assimilated within Indian culture, he becomes intent upon destroying her. That such destructiveness is embodied in Wayne, *the* exemplar of Western ideology, makes *The Searchers* an especially important interrogation of the cultural politics within the genre.[7] The film ends soon after Martin kills Scar and Ethan resists killing the now grown-up Debbie (Natalie Wood) in Martin's presence. The final shots show Ethan carrying Debbie safely to a homestead of family friends and then wandering back out into the wilderness alone.

AN OVERVIEW OF THE SOUND TRACK

As Kalinak has noted, there is a surprising lack of in-depth attention to the score of *The Searchers* (2007, 158).[8] Though Kalinak's own work represents an important corrective, sustained attention to the film's music (let alone other elements of its sound track) is rare. *The Searchers* is routinely regarded as one of the most important westerns, and among the greatest films ever made. That its aural components are largely ignored reflects a broader tendency towards downplaying the importance of sound tracks in cinema studies. However, as we shall find, a full analysis of *The Searchers'* sound track is a crucial part of understanding the ideological, emotional, and tonal complexity of the film. What follows is by no means an attempt to describe all that the film's sound track does. Rather, the emphasis is on representative moments in which semantic elements of meaning are easily identified and syntactic logic may be explored. So, this case study is about applying Altman's approach to selective aural details of *The Searchers* so as to better understand the genre-based, ideological, and ritualistic work of the film. Since much of the film's dialogue has already been addressed in narrative analyses of the film, and since the film's sound effects are mostly subordinate to other aural details (as is typical of the Classical Hollywood era in which the film was made), it makes sense to pay primary attention to Steiner's musical score.

Many conventions of scoring for classical westerns are played out in *The Searchers*. In that sense, Steiner's score builds straightforwardly upon Hollywood precedents, thus having ideological value weighted in mainstream American cinematic tradition. The soundtrack also has ritualistic value in gratifying audience expectations and desires associated with the genre experience. K. J. Donnelly even goes so far as to refer to *The Searchers'* score as a "standard blueprint" for the western (2005, 75). The music, which

---

[7] For a representative analysis of the film as it dramatizes and implicates us "in the neurosis of racism," along with the paradoxical enterprise of creating an "antiracist western" (given that the genre is largely defined in "white supremacist terms"), see Douglas Pye (2004, 223).

[8] Kalinak does mention some exceptions, such as K. J. Donnelly's summary of music in the film (2005, 75).

dominates over most sound effects of the film, is comprised of many familiar semantic elements of meaning. As is typical of numerous westerns, the music that is primarily and pejoratively associated with Indians features dissonance, angular and modal melodies, and frequent inclusion of the strict 4/4 tom-tom beat (Scheurer 2008, 157). The "sinister overtones" of such music makes contemporary Native American audiences cringe.[9] It is clearly meant to communicate Otherness,[10] barbarism, and wild strength in contradistinction to what Timothy Scheurer refers to as the "four-square harmonies" and "sweeping melodic gestures" that are "typically associated with the [western] hero" (156). In *The Searchers*, the harmonious, folksy accessibility of "What Makes a Man to Wander?" and Steiner's sweeping orchestral arrangements of the traditional song "Lorena" are much associated with the protagonist Ethan. Even though he may not be straightforwardly called "heroic," the music defines and reinforces his mythical cowboy status in terms of the present *and* the past, along with defining his status in harmonious contrast to that which is primarily associated with the Indian characters.

The music of *The Searchers* resonates with patterns of Othering Indians that were established long before its production. Though some films that precede *The Searchers* attempted to musically portray Indians much more sympathetically, and even romantically (as an important example, Gorbman (2000, 240–44) analyzes *Broken Arrow* (1950)), Steiner's score reflects what was already a long-standing tradition of easily decoded, musically enforced dichotomies between white/non-white, self/other, and civilized/barbarous. In addition to the film's generic use of different types of music, Steiner's score for *The Searchers* also includes well-known songs featured in other westerns. For instance, some of the Indian music in *The Searchers* and the Irish jig "Garry Owen" are also featured in Steiner's score for *They Died with Their Boots on* (1941). Steiner often imported music across films (and across genres), and he had already used "Lorena" in *Gone with the Wind* (1939) as a waltz at a Confederate ball.[11] Steiner did, however, prefer to use his own music from scratch rather than preexisting

---

[9] Colonnese, for instance, reports such responses at a screening that he set up with his Native American colleagues at the University of Washington at Seattle (2004, 337).

[10] The term "Otherness" is loaded in terms of cultural politics. Abdul R. JanMohamed situates the term in relation to colonialist fiction and ideology: "Troubled by the nagging contradiction between the theoretical justification of exploitation and the barbarity of its actual practice, [colonialist fiction] attempts to mask the contradiction by obsessively portraying the supposed inferiority and barbarity of the racial Other" ([1985] 2006, 22). He primarily refers to literary texts, but his entire article also applies to numerous filmic representations of colonist perspectives.

[11] Kalinak also suggests Steiner would have got the idea to use "Lorena" from Margaret Mitchell's source novel in which ""Lorena" figures prominently at a Confederate ball and serves as a marker for lost love and tragedy" (2007, 165).

period music. Ford, by contrast, typically and knowingly used the associative power of well-known songs (Kalinak 2007, 167). For instance, Ford also used "Lorena" in *The Horse Soldiers* (1959) as a leitmotif for Miss Hannah Hunter (Constance Towers), "a southern belle loyal to the Confederacy" (167). Kalinak has mapped out the numerous similar cross-connections among Ford's films in terms of other songs. *The Searchers* soundtrack most memorably exploits the established power of "Bonnie Blue Flag," "The Yellow Rose of Texas," "Oh, My Darling Clementine," and "Shall We Gather at the River?" in addition to "Lorena." This also makes the soundtrack representative of Ford, a director who was so attuned to the power of preestablished music that, as Donnelly points out, he even "entitled some of his films after folk songs" (*My Darling Clementine* (1946) and *She Wore a Yellow Ribbon* (1949) (2005, 71)).

The semantic, or primary, structural elements of Steiner's original scoring for *The Searchers* are intertextually resonant in deeper structural ways as well. Steiner's music reinforces the ideological *and* ritualistic power of the film through its deep connections to many other Classical Hollywood scores, not least Steiner's own.[12] Steiner's music represents Classical Hollywood scoring through reinforcing each narrative shift but also binding scenes together, punctuating emotional changes, establishing the dominant musical material with overture-like directness at the outset, and thereafter giving pleonastic emphasis to many visual and narrative details of the film (whether through Mickey-mousing or leitmotif manipulation).[13] Although archival evidence suggests that Ford made significant cuts to the non-diegetic music that Steiner composed for the film (Kalinak 2007, 170), much of the film is still saturated in the affect of his score.[14] Indeed, Steiner's music for *The Searchers* is much fuller than the leaner approach he took for earlier Ford westerns such as *Stagecoach* (1939) and *My Darling Clementine* (1946). Moreover, Steiner repeatedly used phrases from songs chosen by Ford for *The Searchers* (notably the then-new song "What Makes a Man to

---

[12] Max Steiner (1888–1971) was one of the most prolific composers of the Classical Hollywood era. He was also among the first composers to define their careers primarily in terms of writing soundtracks. Along with Franz Waxman, Erich Wolfgang Korngold, Alfred Newman, and Miklós Rózsa, his name is often synonymous with composing for films in the studio era. Steiner's music is much influenced by late Romanticism, incorporating Wagnerian operatic structures (especially leitmotifs) and utilizing the affective power of full orchestras and rich harmonies (an approach "revived" by John Williams in the 1970s and which endures today). Steiner's most celebrated scores include *King Kong* (1933), *The Informer* (1935), *Gone with the Wind* (1939), and *Casablanca* (1942).

[13] The word "pleonasm" is used for phrases of words with the same (or similar) definitions ("true fact," for instance). Here, the term "pleonastic" applies to those moments in the film when the visual details and the soundtrack communicate the "same" message (despite being different forms of signification).

[14] Ford tended to prefer leaner soundtracks: he famously told Peter Bogdanovich "generally I hate music in pictures," except for "a little bit now and then" (Anderson 2006, 13).

Wander?"[15] and the traditional "Lorena") as leitmotifs in a structure that is also representative of Classical Hollywood. The patterns of leitmotifs provide formal cohesion and also gather in their cumulative and heavily weighted meanings. The music thus builds upon a preexisting foundation of well-known tunes *and* well-established film scoring practices. The music was also written in the postproduction period, as was typical of Steiner's process and Classical Hollywood practice more generally: ironically, this perhaps amplifies the sense of its coming from somewhere else than the rest of the film.[16]

The many familiar semantic elements of Steiner's music signify traditionalism within the generic context. The relationships among these semantic elements often *also* work towards syntactic meanings that are also traditional. The conceptual conventionality of Steiner's music does not, however, match the less conventional (and sometimes revisionist) other components of the film. Though the film incorporates many familiar semantic elements of the western, it uses them to generate great syntactic complexity that is sometimes at odds with the ritual *and* ideological familiarity of Steiner's score. Where Steiner's score often answers those expectations that audiences bring to a generic experience, as well as meeting those expectations that are repeatedly affirmed by Hollywood westerns, the *overall* impact of *The Searchers* is far from predictable in Altman's terms of analysis. The film thus makes for a particularly complex, surprising, and confrontational experience of genre, not least in relation to Ford's other work.

THE SUBVERSIVENESS OF *THE SEARCHERS*

The Searchers is widely understood as a turning point in Ford's contribution to the western, signifying Ford's "first thoroughgoing attack" on the racism at the heart of the genre (Eckstein 1998, 7).[17] This is most obviously played out through the moral corruption

---

[15] Kalinak mentions that the use of "What Makes a Man to Wander?" connects with what was a new vogue for incorporating theme songs in the 1950s. She mentions that the "phenomenal success" of the song "Do Not Forsake Me, Oh, My Darlin'" as a tie-in for *High Noon* (1952) inspired Hollywood's embrace of contemporary music being combined with classical scoring in the 1950s (2007, 163).

[16] Steiner famously composed the major leitmotif for *The Informer* in preproduction "so that Ford could film Victor McLaglen in perfect synchronization to it." Such practice was the exception to the rule, however, and Steiner himself preferred to not work in advance of a rough cut: he said "I never read a script; I run a mile when I see one" (Kalinak 2007, 162).

[17] Eckstein also notes that this was a theme to which Ford returns with more and more explicitness in his last decade of filmmaking (1998, 7). Similarly, Anderson reads *The Searchers* as a "line of demarcation" leading into Ford's later words that are comparatively "traumatic" (2006, 10) and "overtly unsettling" (11) when it comes to questioning ideology. In relation to this pattern, Anderson cites *Sergeant Rutledge* (1960), *Two Rode Together* (1961), *The Man Who Shot Liberty Valance*, and *Cheyenne Autumn* (1964) in particular (11).

of Ethan because he embodies a profound challenge to the expectations that were well established by the genre, not to mention Wayne's star persona, when the film was released. In another near-contemporary western, *Shane* (1953), the hero is violent, but justifiably so. As John G. Cawelti, argues, we can justify the hero's violence "because the [film] world is violent, treacherous and corrupt," and "the moral man is the one who can use violence, treachery and corruption most effectively" (1984, 114). Shane has been described as the "archetypal western hero" because he fights malevolent forces "for the sake of settlers," as well as "resisting the love of a married woman, and then riding off into the sunset. In his triumph, the gunfighter as savior enacts his moral code, however divergent from ordinary law" (Kupfer 2008, 104).

Shane's apparent right to administer justice beyond the "ordinary law" is much more readily acceptable than Ethan's self-appointed role of revenger. The sympathy-inspiring psychological damage to Ethan after the murder of his family members (Martha, in particular) is overshadowed by his being propelled by racist hatred to find and murder his niece rather than save her. Moreover, the main Indian character of *The Searchers* (Scar) is often read as Ethan's "dark alter ego," not least because the two men are ironically united in seeking vengeance for the death of family members, as well as their both being capable of extreme violence. Such ironic connections between Ethan and Scar constitute a deep challenge to the western as, in Eckstein's words, a "white triumphalist genre" (1998, 4). In addition, the other significant Indian character, "Wild Goose Flying in the Night Sky" or "Look" (Beulah Archeletta), is an atypically sympathetic representation of the Other: she even becomes a partial guide for Ethan and Marty in their pursuit of Scar, and is apparently killed for her role in helping them.

It is the character of Ethan, however, who represents an especially important challenge to generic expectations, not least in terms of Wayne's previous, heroic roles. We might most usefully compare Ethan with Ringo in *Stagecoach*, one who Kent Anderson describes as being "the quintessential Ford outlaw hero, an unsophisticated man who could see what needs to be done and do it. . . with a lucid determination to act, as when he simply, yet elegantly and respectfully woos Dallas (Claire Trevor)" (2006, 16). Ford clearly intended to foreground the darker elements of Ethan Edwards, defining the character in contradistinction to that brand of heroism represented by Ringo and numerous other cowboys Wayne had played before. This is reflected in the fact that, as Arthur M. Eckstein explains, Ford made many crucial adjustments to the original screenplay by Frank S. Nugent in order to place more emphasis on the most troubling aspects of Ethan's character. Though Wayne's star power is coercive enough that even Native American audiences have been predisposed to side "with" the character of Ethan,[18] the film complicates any inclination to be aligned with him. Therein, *The Searchers* problematizes a fundamental semantic element of the genre—the heroic cowboy. Eckstein summarizes Ethan's far-from-traditional role as follows:

> He shoots people in the back (and then robs them), disrupts funerals (and weddings), and views all religion with bitter cynicism. Furthermore, he desecrates the bodies of the dead (gleefully shooting out the eyes of dead Comanches or scalping them. [. . .] In short, Ethan is a grim, solitary, and forbidding figure for whom social constraints mean nothing (1998, 5).[19]

Along with the film taking risks with its protagonist, let alone Wayne's star persona, it also complicates the myth of progress associated with the western genre. In *The Searchers*, the key speech with regard to fulfilling progress belongs to Mrs. Jorgensen (Olive Carey) in response to her husband's claim that "this country's killed our boy." She speaks of being "Texican" and, therefore, "way out on a limb," but she also looks forward to a time when "this land will be a good place to live," even if that time is beyond her and her family's lifetime. This statement of faith in projected progress originally belonged to Amos (the Ethan character) in Le May's novel (Eckstein 1998, 6):[20] that the speech would be completely incommensurate with defining the Ethan of Ford's film is revealing. Instead of Ethan being the man of martyrdom,[21] courage, selflessness, righteous determination, and promises-made-good that an original trailer for *The Searchers* presents,[22] Ethan is a man of hypocrisy, brutality, and thwarted efforts. In the film, his narrative trajectory is bookended by failures: the failure to save Martha's family and the failure to have a final showdown with Scar. Through such narrative unconventionality, Luhr argues that the film knowingly undercuts and critiques the "monumental" star persona around which it ostensibly revolves (2004, 77).

---

[18] See Shively's (1992) analysis of Native American reactions to *The Searchers*.

[19] Eckstein also mentions an astonishing account from Harry Carey Jr. who, in relation to the first scene he played with Wayne in *The Searchers*, said "When I looked up at him in rehearsal it was into the meanest, coldest eyes I had ever seen. Eyes like an angry snake" (1998, 5). That Carey had this reaction even after knowing Wayne for many years is telling.

[20] Eckstein calls attention to several other differences between the film and Frank Nugent's screenplay that are of further decisive impact when it comes to de-heroizing Ethan (1998, 11–13).

[21] In LeMay's novel, Amos dies as a martyr "to the traditional heroic code." In the final attack on Scar's camp, he refuses to shoot a Comanche woman from behind for fear she might be Debbie. Ironically, she turns and shoots him instead. This difference is rightly emphasized by Eckstein (1998, 8).

[22] This is the original trailer included on the 1997 DVD edition of *The Searchers*. The example is representative of how the film was marketed in its own time as a "John Wayne" western in "theatrical trailers, print ads, and the contemporaneous half hour, promotional television show about its making" (Luhr 2004, 75).

To summarize so far, then, *The Searchers* interrogates and resists the power of well-worn formulae. By contrast, Steiner's music much more decisively relies upon convention. Before exploring tensions between the musical score and other formal elements of *The Searchers* any further, we should consider the opening of the film and its establishment of fundamental concepts. During the first three scenes, music works interdependently with visuals and dialogue to reinforce every key narrative *and* thematic point. Thereafter, as we shall explore, the relationship between music and other film elements becomes much more complex, and even *strained*. After establishing the meaning of Steiner's expository musical material for *The Searchers*, we shall delve deeper into the cultural politics of the film, especially as the score defines Ethan in contrast to the two most important Indian characters (Scar and Look). We will then consider the complexity of the film's ending with regard to its contrary narrative, thematic, and musical statements. By the end of this analysis, we will have analyzed the sound track, and Steiner's music in particular, to better understand the unique syntactic complexity of the film within a generic context.

INTRODUCING STEINER'S SCORE

The narrative logic of Steiner's music is readily identifiable within the film's first four minutes. Though the overall film will turn in on itself, complicating everything that is established in its beginning, Steiner's score stays (mostly) true to the essential meanings of the musical exposition. First, and most obviously, Steiner's music establishes binary relationships between concepts that are in keeping with the conservatism of the traditional western. As Douglas Pye has noted, the traditional western is associated with the thematic binary of civilization versus barbarism and is, in turn, associated with binaries of white and non-white, the garden and the desert, us and them, order and chaos (Pye 1975, 208).[23] Pye's analysis resonates with Frederick Jackson Turner's famous 1893 conception of the frontier as "the meeting point between savagery and civilization," a point that had been long-established in related literature before westerns were ever made but which Turner wrote just a decade or so before the genre was first represented on screen (Hall 2001, 8).[24] There is, in other words, a long-standing, fundamental, ideologically driven emphasis on the "meeting point" of extremes in the western film genre that even predates its origins.

---

[23] Similarly, Roger Bromley writes of how "the West was based upon a radical distinction between the civilized European/American and the barbaric, Native American other" (2001, 57).

[24] For a full exploration of the resonance in Tuner's work with regard to Ford's films in particular, see Redding (2007).

In under a minute of *The Searchers*, the primary distinction between barbarism and civilization is musically defined.[25] Steiner communicates this dichotomy by using readily identifiable aural oppositions: first, there is an Indian theme which features the 4/4 tom-tom rhythm with a slightly discordant, stereotypically shrill theme on brass and brass [0:01–0:14]. This music resonates with dominant practices of "scoring Indians" as documented by Gorbman in particular. The theme communicates immediate internal drama by extremes in pitch, and heavy percussion (especially through the mighty cymbal clashes), as well as intertextual familiarity. In addition, it is a startling displacement of the production company logo music that we often hear in films of Classical Hollywood. Despite the *forte* articulation of this Indian music, however, this first theme is quickly taken over by the music primarily associated with Ethan [0:23–1:33]. The power of Ethan is immediately, aurally emphasized because his music is fuller, lasts longer, and is accessible without being clichéd. Ethan's harmonious theme song "What Makes a Man to Wander?"[26] is sung by the male ensemble Sons of the Pioneers, and written by Stan Jones (a group and composer who also worked with Ford on *Wagon Master* (1950) and *Rio Grande* (1950)). We hear the song's second verse only, the lyrics of which are three questions followed by the thrice-repeated instruction to "ride away":

> What makes a man to wander?
> What makes a man to roam?
> What makes a man leave bed and board
> And turn his back on home?
> Ride away, ride away, ride away.[27]

The homophonic clarity of men's voices accompanied by violin and guitar strumming culminates in the first "ride away" sung in unison. This phrase being in unison, as well as its being repeated in harmony, emphasizes it as an imperative instruction before we even see Ethan riding into the film. The low, all-male singing "stands in" for Wayne's own low

---

[25] As Donnelly notes, "this basic opposition, or dichotomy, is evident in the vast majority of western films" (2005, 71).

[26] Kalinak connects the song "What Makes a Man to Wander?" to Ethan's translation of Scar's people, the Nawyecka Comanche, as "Sorta like round about: man says he's going one place, means to go t'other". Moreover, Kalinak favors James F. Brooks's translation of the Comanche term "Nawyecka" as "wanderer" (2007, 159). Though the film surely sets up such ironic, self-conscious, and interrogative parallels between the two men, the song is nevertheless primarily associated with Ethan.

[27] The film includes only two verses of the eight in the song. Kalinak summarizes the impact follows: "Without the frame of verse one and eight, the song is dramatically altered from a rather prosaic search for romantic love to a metaphysical search for what can never be found" (2007, 160).

speaking and singing voice. Thus, the music anticipates his riding out even as we antici-pate his first entrance. The song, then, establishes an all-too-neat anticipation of Ethan's literal trajectory that belies the deeper complexity of his inward journey and the disturbing aspects of his being a driving force in the film. The music, furthermore, anticipates the clos-ing down of (or at least riding away from) questions which the film, overall, leaves open.

Ethan's arrival is then anticipated by the first shot of the film proper: Martha open-ing the door. The visual moment, like the song "What Makes a Man to Wander?," antici-pates his leaving and the door closing at the end of the film proper. The formal neatness of the visual message, opening the door into the film, is seductively matched by the sonorous sweetness of an arrangement of "Lorena" for strings and guitar [1:34–1:57]. Martha's silhouetted image emphasizes her iconic appearance as she waits for "the hero" to return (see Figure 1.3).

Soon Ethan himself appears to spring from the spectacular landscape of Monument Valley that is spread before Martha, and us, in all its VistaVision glory. Again, the senti-ment and scale of the visual message is matched by the meaning and history built into the music.

"Lorena" (by Joseph Webster and Henry Delafayette Webster) is a sentimental song of a man longing for his now-dead love. The song reflects upon the tragic passing of time, and on the literal and figurative changing of seasons. Its lyrics are regretful. In the absence of its lyrics, Steiner's use of "Lorena" obscures the desperate and trou-bling implications of them, especially the hint at adultery in "We loved each other then,

FIGURE 1.3 Martha at the door for Ethan.

Lorena/More than we ever dared to tell" (even if such absent lyrics are registered, especially because they resonate with the unspoken love of Ethan and Martha).[28] "Lorena" was a favorite song of Confederate soldiers during the Civil War.[29] The political associations of the song, which could be especially troubling in a film that interrogates racism, are smoothed over by the romanticization of the legato and vibrato violin sound. If the score is meant to invoke the song's historical associations, it does so with tremendous sympathetic interest in the war of defeat that is now attached to Ethan. The racist ideology of the Confederacy is a buried subtext of this music (just as, later on in the film "The Yellow Rose of Texas" is used without any indication of its origins in minstrel shows).[30] Though the film does not represent the Confederacy as unproblematic—especially given that Ethan's racism may be easily connected with his being a former Confederate soldier—Steiner's music places Confederate music in such contexts that it becomes associated with cherishing and honoring nostalgia for a lost time.

So, the first use of "Lorena" in *The Searchers* matches the sentimental and nostalgic image of an iconic woman on the porch waiting for the man she loves, and her looking across the vast wilderness against which the hero gallops towards her. This iconic woman, Martha, is soon joined on the porch by her husband, her children, and even their dog, all in anticipation of Ethan's arrival (see Figure 1.4). (Though not included within the frame here, Martha's son Ben (Robert Lyden) also joins his family on the porch.)

The romance of "Lorena" in this context soon segues into a slow version of "The Bonnie Blue Flag," an "anthem" of the Confederacy [2:02–2:39].[31] This Southern anthem is typically played in a rousing manner but is here played at a "melancholic, dirge-like tempo" (Cumbow 2009). The cumulative associative power of Steiner's use of "Lorena" and "The Bonnie Blue Flag" is in their poignant evocation of weariness after a war lost. This is the musical context for the first word of the film: as we see Wayne riding towards the homestead, accompanied by the latter tune, we first hear the name

---

[28] Kalinak also emphasizes the resonance of the song in terms of this illicit love (2007, 167). As Anderson explains, Ford meant for the relationship between Ethan and Martha to be unspoken but nevertheless clearly defined for the audience (Anderson 2006, 169).

[29] Cumbow writes: "Though 'Lorena' originated in the North and was popular with both sides, its primary significance remains as an anthem for the Confederate Army. As such, it stands alongside 'Dixie' and the stirring 'Bonnie Blue Flag'" (2009).

[30] Kalinak provides a full analysis of "buried ideological meaning" of the minstrel-show origins of "The Yellow Rose of Texas" (2007, 177–79).

[31] This song "commemorates the unofficial flag of the Confederacy, a blue flag with a single white star, used earlier by the sovereign state of Texas from 1836 to 1839 and often carried by Texas Confederate cavalry" (Kalinak 2007, 180).

FIGURE 1.4 Martha's family gathers to greet Ethan.

"Ethan?" (spoken by his brother Aaron). The accompanying arrangement of "Bonnie Blue Flag" features the fullness of brass and string harmonies that reinforce the power of Ethan's approach towards the archetypal scenario of a family waiting on the homestead porch: the weight of history and the "answer" to it ("Ethan") is built into what we hear as well as what we see. That said, Ethan's name is first said as a question spoken over the music of defeat: thus the film prepares us for an unusually indeterminate hero, one who may speak of himself proceeding as "sure as the turning of the earth," and one who is romanticized as well as supported by Steiner's music, but one whose capacity for savagery will lead us to question him. The music does not, in itself, necessarily prompt such a response: however, the combination of music and Ethan's name being spoken as a question plants a seed of doubt that grows through the film.

Yet more music establishes the poignant significance of Ethan's arrival. After the elder daughter, Lucy (Pippa Scott), repeats his name to her brother Ben ("that's your uncle Ethan"), Ethan shakes Aaron's hand as a reprise of "What Makes a Man to Wander?" begins, led by cellos [2:42–2:58]. "Welcome home Ethan," Martha then says with ardent warmth. At this point we hear, for a third time, the name of the man around which everything revolves, and characters echoing each other with saying it.[32] Perhaps

---

[32] A few moments later, Lucy says "I'm mighty glad to see you Uncle Ethan," then Ben says he was going to ask what "Uncle Ethan's going to do with his saber," and then Ben says "thanks Uncle Ethan" when Ethan quickly offers the weapon to him. Martha chimes in with "let me take your coat for you Ethan," to which Aaron adds "welcome home Ethan." So, we hear Ethan's name six times in about three minutes [1:33–4:30], as opposed to three times at most for the other characters in the opening sequence. The

FIGURE 1.5 Martha turns away from Ethan.

their repetition of Ethan's name signifies their grasping for certainty in everything that "Ethan" means while they are surrounded by a wild landscape where Other voices echo. Next, just as Ethan is kissing Martha's forehead, the strings mark the moment with a *tremolo* (a rapidly repeated note with built-in sinister associations). There is the brief punctuation of an aural pause and then a stinger chord as Martha turns away from Ethan [2:58–3:01]: the sound track herein communicates Ethan's vulnerability at the moment of Martha's turn away, even as we lose sight of his face (see Figure 1.5). But Martha soon turns to re-face Ethan, literally backing into her own home so as not to lose eye contact with him (see Figure 1.6). As Martha re-faces Ethan, the opening phrase of "Lorena" returns and carries over the dissolve into the next scene [3:01–3:19].

Thus, "Lorena" is established as suggesting restoration and reassurance for Ethan: it is associated with the visual restatement of a bond that predates the film. The song's associations historicize that relationship in terms of loss, but the pleasing arrangement of it qualifies the song's built-in pathos with musical strength. Ironically, the song is reprised only long enough for the next scene to begin and it stops in suspension with Ethan lifting up the youngest daughter, Debbie, who he mistakenly identifies as "Lucy." The musical moment of suspension matches the image

---

very next sequence even begins with the young Debbie standing up at the table as Martin enters, proudly declaring "Marty!, here's Uncle Ethan," to which Martin says "Evenin' Uncle Ethan." In short, once the emphasis on Ethan's name is identified, it is impossible to miss.

FIGURE 1.6 Martha re-faces Ethan.

of the girl held in midair. This audiovisual match anticipates the climactic moment of suspension near the end of the film when Ethan will hold up the adult Debbie, intent upon destroying her but finally embracing her, accompanied by a full reprise of "Lorena" [1:55:57–1:56:15]. This is the kind of structural neatness within Steiner's score that ultimately works differently from much else in *The Searchers*, as we shall continue to explore.

INTERPRETING "LORENA"

More than one commentator has argued that "Lorena" is primarily associated with "home" (and thus family) or Martha in *The Searchers*.[33] Such readings do, however, reduce the cumulative strength of the meanings the song gathers through Steiner's scoring. If we consider Ethan's misidentification of Lucy (his pronouncement of the wrong name as he picks up the young Debbie), the music is also associated with the pathos of time lost—for Ethan, and for Martha, but also from a metacinematic standpoint (given its having been used in many other films, notably *Gone with the Wind*). In addition, and as previously mentioned, Steiner's use of the song communicates a problematic kind of nostalgia in relation to Civil War-time and the Confederacy. Finally, the song

---

[33] See Schuerer, for instance, who calls "Lorena" the "Homecoming Theme" (2008, 162). Eckstein reads the song as being "Martha's Theme" (1998, 14, 16). Kalinak reads it as signifying Ethan's brother's family, especially Martha (and, in turn, forbidden love) (2007, 167).

is associated with a moment of purification for Ethan, a moment that means redefining what "family" means as well as the return "home" that becomes (im)possible: when the film ends, we know Debbie can stay with the Jorgensen family, but Ethan is apparently doomed to continue wandering. So it is that "Lorena" has a far from straightforward syntactic meaning in the context of *The Searchers*.

"Lorena" is reused as a leitmotif many times through the film: we hear it reprised in a major key when Ethan gives Debbie his Confederate medal [7:11–7:33]; as Ethan watches Martha and his brother close the door as they go to bed on his first night home [8:49–8:59]; and when the Reverend Clayton witnesses Martha stroking Ethan's Confederate cloak in a gesture of unguarded doting and then pretends obliviousness to Ethan kissing Martha's forehead before she watches him leave [13:13–13:49]. The song recurs in a furtively tender variation for strings when the grown-up Debbie runs to meet Ethan and Marty after they have found her location [1:26:31–1:26:54]. The theme seems to drop away all too quickly, but as Debbie suddenly stops speaking the language of "her people," and tells Marty she remembers him "from *always*," their long-delayed verbal reunion is underscored by yet another variation of "Lorena" [1:27:07–1:27:30]. Thus, when in a major key, the song becomes primarily associated with moments of emotional truth, love, poignant connection, and reunion.

Fragments of "Lorena" are *also* repeated in a minor key: most memorably, when Ethan looks off towards Martha's distant homestead in anticipation of the imminent massacre there [17:14–17:23]; and when Ethan falls to his knees at the burning entrance of the shed where the bodies of Martha and her family are left [22:17–22:23]. In the latter scene, "Lorena" gets "lost" in a series of minor key phrases, emphasizing Ethan's desperation, until they lead back into a further minor-key repeat of the song as Ethan picks up the blanket the young Debbie held at the gravestone where Scar's shadow first fell upon her [22:24–23:33]. A few scenes later, Marty comprehends Ethan's potentially violent intentions towards the girls they search for (due to the girls having been claimed by "injuns"), and he seeks reassurance by saying "there's just one reason we're here ain't it?—that's to find Debbie and Lucy?" Low strings repeat the first phase of "Lorena" in a minor key after Ethan's response: "if they're still alive" [36:48–36:57]. Thus, when in a minor key, "Lorena" becomes primarily associated with Ethan's unknowable past and the sinister aspects of his character. It is also associated with dread, desperation, violence, and death.

"Lorena" thus becomes about much more than "home" or "Martha." The original tune in a major key, combined with the minor-key variants of it, bring home and threat, life and death, child and woman, past and present, love and loss, restoration and grief together.[34] Altman's writing on the semantic/syntactic logic of genre films is analogous to Steiner's use of a cumulatively powerful leitmotif system in *The Searchers*: if leitmotifs are like the building blocks or semantics of Steiner's score, we can discover unique syntactic meanings created from their inter-relations and development. Moreover, Steiner's full use of "Lorena" carries an especially important and transcendent syntactic implication: each positive contains the possibility of its opposite, but the positive *must* ultimately win.

STEINER'S MUSIC: OBFUSCATING THREAT, EMPHASIZING REASSURANCE

This essential last point is made in a different musical way in the funeral scene after Martha's family (excepting Debbie) is massacred. Mourners sing the Methodist hymn "Shall We Gather at the River?" with dirge-like flatness [23:35–23:58]. The hymn's lyrics imagine gathering at a beautiful river with the saints, and a river "that flows by the throne of God." But the hope of these lyrics is undercut by the lackluster low-pitch stagnancy of how it is sung by a small group of mourners, their heads bowed on a hill, and their bodies buffeted by wind (see Figure 1.7).

The defeated delivery of this hymn serves to stress the fatalism built into its lyrics, emphasizing that "only those who will be judged worthy by God are allowed to cross the river Jordan and be judged by him" (Kalinak 2007, 171). In addition, the Revered Clayton (also captain of the Texas Rangers) "underscores" the hymn with grim words from the Bible: "Man who is born of woman is of few days and full of trouble" (Job 14:1). Ethan is exasperated by the inaction of those around him, and the stillness of the mourners (in contrast to his manifest agitation) is ironically emphasized by the limited range and the repetitions of the hymn. In under a minute, Ethan shouts over the music: "put an 'Amen' to it. There's no more time for praying. 'Amen!'" When he then strides away from the funeral, shouting at Brad (Harry Carey Jr.) and Martin to join him, he cuts off the satisfaction of the song's final cadence. Thus, Ethan cuts off the moment of emotive closure connected with the song. However, a non-diegetic cue by Steiner gives us the final phrase of the song, bringing formal closure to the scene [23:59–24:12].

Steiner's cue to complete the funeral scene—even against Ethan's exit—is part of a pattern whereby his score obfuscates distressing or disturbing aspects of the film with sudden musical emphasis on comedy, lightness, or resolution. Indeed, in the most ideologically

---

[34] As with "As Time Goes By" in *Casablanca*, Steiner makes this song—the first phrase in particular—particularly malleable as a leitmotif.

FIGURE 1.7 The mourners sing "Shall We Gather at the River?"

problematic moments of the film, Steiner's music provides nonverbal but nevertheless insistent, and coercive, reassurance. To take but one example, there is a later scene where Brad, Lucy's fiancé, desperately says to Ethan and Martin "they [the Indians] *gotta* stop some time. If they're *human* men, they *gotta* stop."[35] Ethan's response is one of emphatic pragmatism informed by his self-professed superior understanding of what the Indian is capable of: "No. Human rides a horse until it dies, and then he goes on afoot. Comanche comes along, gets that horse up, rides him twenty more miles, then eats him." Here, Ethan's words are *pleasantly underscored* by Steiner's variation on his theme song [37:20–37:45]. The tune that unites the beginning and ending of the film with deceptive neatness belies the brutality of his claims. The song is established as being about Ethan's singular brand of heroism, rising like a mirage from the Monument Valley plains to meet his Martha. The power of this music's association with his iconic entrance thus smoothes over the violence and hatred in his words to Brad. So, the syntactic logic of the music works against the film's provocative, and therein revisionist, interrogation of extreme, generic, western ideology.

Not much later in the film, a portion of "What Makes a Man to Wander?" is repeated as orchestral underscoring right after Brad is killed by Indians (after he runs towards them for revenge on Lucy's death, a desperately suicidal act). The horror of Brad's death is thus immediately displaced by the reassurance of Steiner's music which accompanies some shots of Ethan and Marty riding on together across the sunny desert and through

---

[35] The italics reflect the original emphases in Carey's delivery.

FIGURE 1.8 After Brad's death, Martin and Ethan simply ride on through the desert and snow.

FIGURE 1.9

snow [42:21–42:42] (see Figures 1.8 and 1.9). Put simply, the men "ride away": the mission continues without Brad.

The juxtaposed images of seasons passing, reinforced by the now-familiar music, further reinforces the sense of life moving on with cyclic determinacy. Soon thereafter Ethan reassures Marty as the snow comes down over them, "we'll find 'em in the end, I promise you, we'll find 'em, just as sure as the turning o' the earth." A cut then shows

Marty and Ethan making their first return to the Jorgensen home, and Steiner's score provides another rousing, string-led variation on "What Makes a Man to Wander." This variation suggests triumph, reinforcing Ethan's sureness, as well as glorifying their return to another family awaiting them on the porch [43:50–44:47]. Their return connects with the opening of the film, and also the door closing at its end. Such patterns of circular musical neatness belie those perturbing elements of the film that work against a sense of that which is safe and familiar within the generic context.

RIDING AWAY FROM DISTURBANCE

Steiner's music communicates an even more emphatic "ride away" from disturbance, rupture, and conflict at other moments. A strident example follows the scene in which Ethan has Martin read his revised will aloud. This new will reveals Ethan's disinheritance of Debbie because, for him, her being taken by Indians and becoming one of Scar's wives is tantamount to her being "dead." Ethan thus considers only Marty his rightful inheritor, despite the latter's "mixed-blood." When Marty therefore understands him denying the life of Debbie, his entire body tightens with quick anger. Gripping a sharp knife, he speaks with trembling rage: "I hope you *die*." Ethan answers with his catchphrase, "That'll be the day," as if the moment and Martin's violent wish is nothing-above-the-ordinary.[36] But Wayne also delivers the catchphrase with a kind of dogmatic severity, as if he (and/ or Ethan), is attempting *but failing* to achieve the laconic composure associated with him long before *The Searchers*. The attempt at star-defining cool reticence is undercut by Wayne's manifest strain to affect nonchalance [1:31:55–56]. Indeed, the tightened sinews of his neck and his clenched mouth as he says "That'll be the day" convey the unsympathetic menace and discomfort that set Ethan apart from Wayne's earlier roles.[37] His use of

---

[36] Ethan uses this catchphrase ("that'll be the day") earlier in the film when the Reverend/Captain Clayton asks him whether he wants to "quit" searching, and when Brad threatens to fight him for speaking pessimistically about Lucy and Debbie's chance of survival. He says it later on when Marty wonders whether the wedding party they hear on returning to the Jorgensens' home is for them.

[37] William Luhr provides an in-depth account of how audiences of the 1950s apparently perceived Wayne's performance as Ethan as "little more than a darkened variation on his established persona" (2004, 77). Later audiences have, however, "seen that same performance as profoundly undercutting and critiquing that persona" (86). Luhr charts the contradictory behavioral tendencies in Wayne's roles—the restraint and violent power embodied by Wayne's characters in *Stagecoach, Tall in the Saddle* (1944), *Angel and the Badman* (1947), and *Hondo* (1953) (79), in contrast with the "maniacally driven and ambitious," harsh and intrusive, aggressive and dominating characters he plays in *Flying Tigers, Pittsburg* (1942), *Reap the Wild Wind* (1942), *War of the Wildcats* (1943), *Tycoon* (1947), and *Red River* (1948) (79). Whatever Wayne's roles, however, Luhr finds connections among them in terms of having "a mission evident to all" and being in command of others accordingly (79). In *The Searchers*, by contrast, Luhr finds a departure: a character not in control of a mission but "tense, troubled, often seething with rage" (79).

the catchphrase thus seems disingenuous. Moreover, the delivery of his line seems at odds with the greater confidence of Steiner's music for him.

In response to Ethan's grimly delivered catchphrase, Marty is rendered helpless, petulantly throwing his knife on the ground. The film gives us little pause to consider the importance of Martin's reaction to Ethan as a critique of betraying Debbie on racist grounds. Instead, there is soon a dissolve to the pre-wedding scene at the Jorgensen household. Full plaid skirts billow close to the camera in a traditional four-square dance to characters singing yet another Confederate song, "The Yellow Rose of Texas" [1:32:06–1:32:52]. Their rambunctiously joyful singing is supported by on-screen instrumentalists playing fiddle, double bass, guitars, and accordion. Studio publicity cites the song as being chosen by Ford for its nostalgic and sentimental conveyance of Americana (Kalinak 2007, 161). The exuberance of the musical performance and the stomping feet seem *too* determined to quickly stop our dwelling upon the previous scene, and the darkness of more besides. For just as quickly as "The Yellow Rose of Texas" takes over from a wish of death, so too does the wedding band follow the dance with a repeat of the hymn "Shall We Gather at the River?" [1:34:23–1:34:53]. As the song begins, Mrs. Jorgensen raises a handkerchief to her cheek in an exaggerated gesture of archetypal grief. She then joins the neat formation of the wedding party in anticipation of her daughter Laurie's (the bride's) arrival (see Figure 1.10).

This moment signifies Mrs. Jorgensen's luxuriating in the anticipation of her daughter's marriage and, along with that, the satisfaction of her matchmaking between Laurie (Vera Miles) and Charlie MacQuarrie (Ken Curtis). Charlie, the groom (pictured in Figure 1.10), is a buffoonish character, a parody of the singing cowboy who is ironically mismatched with Laurie:[38] he is the white male equivalent to Look, the Indian mismatch for Marty. That Charlie stands ready to be wrongly married as the hymn is resung ironically parallels the song's strange recontextualization: in this scene, the music associated with the scene of ritualized grieving is now attached to a clownish character about to marry a woman driven to accept him by desperation rather than real feeling, a potentially tragic situation that is played for laughs in the film. To reinforce the connection between these different contexts for the same music, where Ethan cut off this hymn the first time, he now arrives (with Marty) to its being resung [1:34:55–1:35:29]. This is but one example of numerous ironic parallels in *The Searchers*—a formal feature of the film that, along with the many patterns of Steiner's music, syntactically communicates the decisiveness of that which has been cyclically prearranged "as sure as the turning of the earth."

---

[38] Luhr reads how Charlie serenades Laurie in this way (2004, 90).

FIGURE 1.10 Mrs. Jorgensen's gesture of archetypal grief at her daughter's wedding.

(OCCASIONALLY) ABSENT MUSIC

Thus far we have established how the formal coherence, ideological transparency, patterned nearness, and emphasis on closure within the film's music contrasts with many other elements of *The Searchers*. There are many other ways in which competing aural and visual details of the film further emphasize irresolvable complexity in terms of syntactic meaning. Particularly memorable are those points of dramatic tension in the film at which we might typically expect music but hear none. In a film that features much music (even though, as already indicated, Ford pared down the full score supplied by Steiner), some moments of relative quiet are especially affective. For instance, there is the quiet around Ethan claiming to have lost his Johnny Reb coat when Marty asks about its disappearance. The lack of music here means that we are not prepared to later learn that Ethan used his coat to cover Lucy's body [39:55–40:06]. In the scene of Ethan shooting buffalo, some tom-tom music (ironically connecting his behavior to the "barbarism" of the Indians) builds to a dissonant climax before it drops out on Ethan's first shot [1:08:58–1:09:35]. Then, before the sound of cavalrymen interrupts the scene from a distance, there is no music to mediate the sounds of buffalo running, Ethan shooting with savage abandon, and his shouting down Marty's attempt to stop him [1:09:36–1:10:05].[39] When the cavalry bugle can be heard in the distance, Ethan's shouting is much louder

---

[39] Ironically, we later learn that the cavalry are entering after the massacre of a Comanche village—a detail that "marks eloquently the way in which Ethan's racist hatred is repeated at the institutional level in the genocidal actions of the U.S. Cavalry" (Pye 2004, 224).

than anything: "At least they won't feed any Comanches this winter. Killing buffalo is like killing injuns." The lack of music to soften his words is a marked contrast with many other scenes. Much earlier in the film, after Martha's son Ben anticipates the first murder-raid and says "I wish uncle Ethan was here, don't you Ma?," Steiner's quiet underscoring suddenly stops, leaving silence around the piercing scream of Lucy when she suddenly comprehends the imminent danger [19:28–19:30]. Soon thereafter Aaron looks out the window and, along with him, we perceive dust blowing across the prairie in a shot of fading light [19:39–19:42]. Here, the absence of Ethan is thus emphasized in the scene of an isolated scream answered by a sound of nothingness. Perhaps the absence of music thus signifies those moments beyond that which Ethan would wish to, but cannot, control.

Elsewhere, however, Steiner's music reinforces Ethan's ideological vantage point *and* his single-minded power, not least through punctuating his words and actions. It is telling that when he first meets Scar, Ethan insists "I don't stand talkin' in the wind." Much earlier in the film, Ethan's gunshots echo across Monument Valley when he shoots an "Injun" in the eyes so that the latter won't enter the spirit land and "has to wander forever between the winds." Thus, wind is not only associated with the imminent massacre of Martha's family but also with a spiritual concept of never-ending irresolution. Ethan's is a brand of heroism that evidently *expects* to be answered by the fullness of Steiner's score and not the terrifying threat of the tuneless wind.

INDIAN MUSIC

That Ethan defines himself as superior and set apart from the Indians is indisputable. For our purposes, it is equally and especially important to acknowledge the power of Steiner's music in *reinforcing* Ethan's stature. The overall film represents a profound challenge to the coercive power of the lead white character, let alone Wayne's star power, but Steiner's music repeatedly reinforces Ethan's sense of his absolute difference from, and superiority to, Scar's people. The Indian music of *The Searchers* is not only subjected to the greater power of white music in the film, its structural emphasis on dissonance, shrill melodies of narrow range, and asymmetrical harmonic progressions (notably from A minor to A-flat minor), along with clichéd musical devices such as the tom-tom beat and low "sinister" instrumentation sets it apart from the sounds of "civilization" (Scheurer 2008, 164). It is worth our dwelling on how the Indian characters are aurally defined in greater detail than the opening theme already discussed. We should particularly consider the musical material associated with the two *named* Indian characters, Chief Scar and Look, in contrast with the many Indian extras who are unnamed and uncredited for being in the film.

There are two phrases associated with Scar: an ascending three-note pattern, outlining a minor third; and a minor second (B to B-flat) that resolves on a lower fourth (F), a pattern that evokes grief or tragedy (Scheurer 2008, 164). The use of a minor key and a tritone establish and emphasize the ominous presence of Scar. In addition, Scar's very name is punctuated more than once by stinger chords or, in one scene, the sound of Ethan throwing a shot of tequila in flames. The power of Scar's presence is also more hauntingly associated with the sound of wind.

So, music *and* other aural details associate the most powerful Indian with unrest, disturbance, threat, as well as clichéd Otherness. Ideologically speaking, though, the film's most insidious aural detail is in the language of the Indians: the actors playing those identified as "Comanche" speak Navajo. As Tom Grayson Colonnese explains, "this is no small point": "It would be as if when we meet the Jorgensens, they have Italian accents, or as if the Hispanic Comanchero who finally leads the searchers to Scar speaks with a heavy Swedish accent" (2004, 340).[40] It is also worth mentioning that the traditional songs and dances depicted in the film are Navajo and not Comanche.[41] It is even more disconcerting that the Indian character with the most lines, Scar, is played by a white German actor wearing dark makeup (as pictured in Figure 1.11).[42]

Ironically, the music for the other important Indian character, Look, defines her rather differently from the rest of her people. In terms of the western genre, Look is an atypically kind Indian. She is a frumpy woman apparently inserted for some laughs, especially when she assumes herself to be traded as the new wife for Marty, but she is later treated with some compassion by the film. With such details in mind, Pye reads the character of Look as a nexus of the film's ideological complexity. For Pye, Look embodies the unresolved questions of the film as well as its unsettling accordance with Ethan's perspective at crucial moments of narrative development (2004, 225–29). Though Pye does not analyze the film's music, Steiner's cues for Look reinforce his claims, at least until her death. Look's theme is relatively sweet and innocuous, featuring the light timbre of woodwind, soft percussion (especially tambourines), and harp, and being defined by intervals of fifths and seconds: Scheurer even summarizes it as being like an innocuous Indian "version of Debussy's 'Golliwog's Cakewalk'" (2008,

---

[40] Kozloff states that "although there were more than two thousands separate Indian [*sic*] languages, [Classical] Hollywood often did not bother to get any of them right" (2000, 150).

[41] Colonnese explains that the Navajo "extras" were nevertheless happy to be involved because they needed the money even if they were going to be portrayed negatively. This practical point aside, Colonnese argues that the connotation of marginalization in the term "extras" ironically speaks to "the usual place of Indians in American history" (2004, 336).

[42] This was, as Gorbman explains, standard practice during the 1950s (2000, 239).

FIGURE 1.11 Henry Brandon, a white German, plays Indian Chief Scar.

FIGURE 1.12 Look's first scene.

164). Look's theme is first heard when we see her trying on a bowler hat traded by Ethan and Marty [1:02:10–1:02:21] (see Figure 1.12).

This scene comes from the lengthy section of the film during which Laurie reads Marty's letter and in so doing first says the name "Scar," a name punctuated by an unmissable stinger chord [1:01:30–1:01:31] that segues into a version of his sinister music (a minor second that resolves on a lower fourth). Soon thereafter, Look's music

literally takes the place of the sinister cue associated with Scar. Thus the music emphasizes comic elements of the film in such a way as to implicitly suggest that anything
disturbing can be displaced.

Though Look obviously embodies Otherness, she does not represent a serious
threat. Marty inadvertently and quite literally labels her differently. In response to misunderstanding Marty's desperation about her following him on the mistaken impression they are married (and his saying "Look, I wish I could make you understand"),
Look tells Marty that even though her name is "Wild Goose Flying in the Night Sky"
she'll answer to "Look" if that pleases him. The irony of her accepting a renaming is
compounded by the detail that Ethan authoritatively translates her Navajo words about
this as a *Comanche* statement to Marty. Look's musical theme is thereafter ironically
altered when Marty kicks her down the slope and away from his bed. The action is
reinforced by a descending scale under her theme that Mickey-mouses the tumbling
of her plump body [1:07:05–1:07:06]. This cartoonish audiovisual match reinforces
Ethan's hearty laughter over Marty's action. Moments later in this scene, the mention
of Scar returns us to a stinger chord, and low ominous strings giving way to his sinister
theme, punctuated with a resounding cymbal clash that echoes the very beginning of
the film [1:07:24–1:08:07]. In the next scene, when Marty and Ethan discover Look's
absence, her theme is transformed by being slowed down and played lower (on an oboe
rather than a flute), along with being made somewhat sinister, and thus subtly closer
to Scar's music through heavier percussion [1:08:15–1:08:34]. The musical variation
thus emphasizes the narrative point of Look returning to her tribe. The original and
the developed variation of Look's theme fuse when Marty and Ethan find her dead at
the Nawyecka Comanche village: her theme is returned to the flute, but much slower
than the original version, and developed through minor cadences [1:11:50–1:12:27].
Thus her theme is developed with more complexity and variance than we might expect,
giving her a certain degree of atypical, musically reinforced status. The pathos of finding Look is quickly displaced, however, by a sudden aural shift to a rousing rendition
of the "Gary Owen" jig led by high-pitched woodwind and supported by brass drones
[1:12:28–1:13:23].[43] The jig reinforces the briskly positive power of the white cavalrymen returning to the fort, even as Marty is shown tucking the doll Debbie once had into
his coat. (It is the same doll Debbie held when Scar's shadow first fell over her: Marty's

---

[43] In parallel to this musical point, Pye argues that the "sentimentalization of Look's death can also seem
a conventional way of evading the problems of her continued presence in the narrative" (2004, 227).
Prior to Look's death and with regard to Ethan's and Marty's misogynistic treatment of her character, he
reads the film as being "uncomfortably close" to the problematic attitudes of its central characters (227).

action therefore takes us back to the original scene of terror even while the music takes us elsewhere.) The upbeat tempo and colorful orchestration of "Gary Owen" as the cavalry return, observed by *silent* Indians, emphasizes that the film moves us quickly on from Look's death: thus, yet again, the musical score smoothes over a moment of most acute disturbance. Though we may determine that the music is deliberately disjunctive with what the film shows, such irony seems less embedded in the score than determined by the revisionist tendencies of Ford's film that are *not* reinforced by its music.

Such musical emphasis on disavowing that which is most disturbing is especially noticeable during the mass shooting across the river (about a quarter into the film). In this scene, the shooting of Indians is anticipated by the silliness of Mose Harper (Hank Worden), an eccentric who tags along with Marty and Ethan. Mose mockingly imitates an Indian rain dance while the Indians are singing a death song [32:46–33:06]. The contrast between Mose's parodic and clownish attempt at musical appropriation in contrast with the indigenous death song in anticipation of actual bloodshed, is repugnant in its extremity, and perhaps intentionally so.[44] Then, right before the extended shooting match, one in which Ethan shoots numerous Indians and in which the Indians show themselves to be woefully inept fighters (despite much historical evidence to the contrary),[45] Mose even offers a mock prayer: "For that which we are about to receive, we thank thee oh Lord." The sequence that follows is defined by contrasting extremes of sound [33:58–35:02]. The diegetic sound of Indians singing and whooping mixes with standard-sounding "chase music" for the shootout (built on repetitious short phrases rather than melody, rhythmically driven by regular accents, and defined by quick swells in loudness), but this transforms into low drones as the Indians are shown falling off their horses, and beginning to turn away.[46] The shift in musical emphasis from the chase to the dead parallels the contrasting behaviors of Mose and Marty: the former gleefully picks up the rifle when the latter, temporarily overcome with his own participation in the violence, buries his face and lets it fall (see Figure 1.13).

The moment of Marty's flinching despair is, however, quickly followed by his determinedly rejoining the fight with a pistol. Then there follows a cut to the Reverend/Captain Clayton (Ward Bond) shooting without hesitation, and crying "Hallelujah" after each "successful" shot. When Clayton quickly runs out of ammunition, harp glissandi comically punctuate Ethan throwing him a gun saying "watch it, it's loaded!"

---

[44] Though Marty is preparing to shoot Indians himself, he looks critically at Mose at this point.

[45] See Colonnese (2004, 337).

[46] For a fuller definition and discussion of chase music in the context of action scenes, see Buhler, Neumeyer, and Deemer (2010, 224).

FIGURE 1.13 Marty temporarily lets his gun fall while Mose keeps his ready to fire.

String-led chords also playfully punctuate when Clayton then throws his hat at Ethan in pantomimesque annoyance before resuming his shooting. Thus the music Mickey-mouses the comedy of a scene which makes Marty bury his face (at least for a few moments). In this sense, the music is the most "loaded" part of the scene. Such lighthearted aural punctuation serves to take precedence over, or at least to contain, the most ideologically disturbing aspects of what happens.

Kalinak argues that the sheer abundance of music associated with the Indians in *The Searchers* represents a challenge to the white-dominated frontier of *Stagecoach* (among other Ford westerns). She even argues that the power of the Indian music is in reminding us "that the land is theirs and white settlers are the encroachers" (2007, 173). Though she persuasively emphasizes that it is Indian music that opens the film, that the music associated with Indian characters is important even when they are not on-screen, and that Look's theme is atypically well developed beyond clichéd musical evocations of Indianness, her reading of Steiner's cues goes against the grain of the tight binary logic that his score establishes from the outset of the film and, for the most part, maintains (173–74). Though the Indian music is surely as powerful as Kalinak argues, that does not necessarily lead to the culturally progressive reading of, or the interrogative syntactic implications that she finds in, Steiner's scoring. It is telling that in his study of generic film music Scheurer argues that *The Searchers* affirms that "the only good Indian is a dead one" (2008, 166): though this claim is surely reductive with regard to the whole of the film, it is hardly surprising given Scheurer's focus on Steiner's music alone.

The final sequence of *The Searchers* represents the culmination of generically and ideologically loaded tensions within the film. Steiner's music insists upon the straightforwardness of resolution, but the overall film experience offers anything but this. Though several crucial semantic elements of narrative closure are there (the death of the barbaric Other, the beautiful damsel saved, the end of a cowboy's quest, and the return to family friends at the homestead), they are handled with syntactic complexity by the overall film. When Ethan discovers Scar already dead, it signifies an aborted moment of closure and triumph for the former. Moreover, the emptiness of Scar's death is emphasized—not only through the film not showing it to us, but also through the scalping we see Ethan about to do before a precisely timed cut. It is as though the film cannot deny Ethan that moment of satisfaction but it flinches, *and* protects us, from what that action means. The film does not present Ethan's capacity for barbarism fully, but his equivalency to the brutality associated with Scar is momentarily implied. Parallel to this, Marty's discovery of Debbie is the answer to several years of searching, but the reunion is soon followed by Ethan's galloping intent to kill her. His murderous intent is turned around in a moment of lifting her up off the ground, much as he did when she was still a child. Thus the moment of saving Debbie is also about belittling her. Martin Scorsese (among others) argues that Ethan's final decision fully redeems him (as he explains in *A Personal Journey*), though this is the work of *one moment* after years of Ethan's searching for her with murderous intent: whether Ethan's sudden turnaround is enough to answer all that has preceded it is surely debatable. And when Ethan turns away from the closing door at the end of the film, thus turning away from the place of home and family, it is a moment of iconic complexity: his wandering back into the wilderness relates to the film's opening with superficially simple circularity, but that he is incapable of crossing the threshold beyond searching reveals the vulnerability of the myth-making that he represents.

THE MUSIC OF FINALITY

Though the entire experience of *The Searchers* leaves troubling truths unresolved, the *music* of its final sequence places emphasis on the settling of disputes, the emphatic restatement of ideologically loaded binaries, and the musical elimination of the Other by the end. In other words, where the film develops its own syntactic complexity right through the final sequence, Steiner's score ultimately emphasizes its own neatness in terms of generic expectation. His cues often reinforce the directness of the visuals without problematizing them. In the final film sequence, a descending scale Mickey-mouses Marty being lowered from a rock (his safe landing punctuated by a harp chord)

[1:50:50–1:51:04], Scar's emergence from a tent is accompanied by the slow and sinister tom-tom music associated with him [1:51:31],[47] and strongly resounding chords with timpani rolls herald the entrance of young cavalrymen [1:51:33–1:51:43], just to name a few examples of musical parallelism. The soundtrack does suddenly change in tone when Ethan forcibly lifts Scar's head in preparation to scalp it—there is a sudden minor second figuration of shrill brass, typical of Classical scoring for the Indian [1:54:31–34]—but as quickly as the cutaway redirects attention, this music is superseded by a return to chase music (with strings imitating the galloping horses) and the bugles of the cavalrymen [1:54:35–1:55:06]. This music for the final shoot-out then merges with a minor key variation of the opening of "What Makes a Man to Wander?" [1:55:06–1:55:13], preparing us to see Ethan at his most frightening in the pursuit of Debbie. As soon as Ethan sees Debbie and begins galloping towards her, the music becomes frantic [1:55:19–1:55:53], dominated by furtive chromatic figures, descending slides on strings, and another low, minor-key variation on the first phrase of "What Makes a Man to Wander?" Much like the melody of "Lorena" gets "lost" in the scoring for Ethan's discovery of the massacre, here the musical message seems to be that Ethan himself might be lost. As Ethan bends down towards Debbie cowering from him on the ground, there is a sudden held note, a moment of suspension which suddenly leaps an octave above and leads into a resounding reprise of "Lorena" [1:55:53–1:56:14].[48] Thus, the most terrible moment neatly turns into its opposite. As Ethan says "let's go home Debbie" along with the music, there is strong aural sense of coming full circle. The moment of suspension being answered by the full theme echoes that moment early in the film when Ethan first lifted Debbie high up above the ground. The intensity of these juxtaposed opposing moments is thrown into relief by a brief scene of Clayton's bottom being treated for a bullet-wound. Thereafter, the film cuts back to the Jorgensen homestead. As we saw near the beginning of the film, a family gathers on a porch to greet the return of its heroes (see Figure 1.14). This final familiar scene is elevated by a swelling restatement of "Lorena," which then dovetails with a verse from "What Makes a Man to Wander?" sung by the *Sons of Pioneers* [1:57:01–1:58:39].

In the final scene, Laurie and Marty are soon visually reunited despite their previous meeting at her wedding having ended with a vicious argument (one in which Laurie reveals the full destructive extent of her racism, to which Marty represents the fullest

---

[47] We also hear the sound of a dog yelp off-screen when Scar throws a stone at it, aurally demonizing him along with the music.

[48] For a highly compressed version of some main arguments from this analysis of *The Searchers*, especially in relation to the cue for Ethan lifting up Debbie at the film's climax, see Walker's introduction to a pedagogically themed issue of *Music and the Moving Image* (2012, 3–5).

FIGURE 1.14 The final scene shows another family (the Jorgensens and Mose) greeting Ethan as he returns with Marty and Debbie: a strong visual parallel to the opening scene where Martha's family greets Ethan, as is reinforced by the final iterations of the film's main musical themes ("Lorena" and "What Makes a Man to Wander?").

vocal opposition).[49] As Laurie runs to Marty from the porch, "What Makes a Man to Wander?" returns:

> A man will search his heart and soul,
> Go searching way out there.
> His peace of mind, he knows he'll find,
> But where oh Lord, Lord where?
> Ride away, ride away, ride away.

The last "ride away" is extended for the closing of the door and "The End" appears on screen. In echoing the film's opening, *minus* the opening Indian theme, the music suggests not only neat closure, but also the elimination of the Other threat. Again, the

---

[49] After Marty and Ethan interrupt Laurie's wedding to Charlie, and Marty prepares to resume the search for Debbie, Laurie attempts to stop his leaving again. Though her romantic attachment to him provides some justification for her impulse, she provides a repulsive rationale that turns Debbie into a "thing" that is only worth killing. In response to Marty saying he must "fetch [Debbie] home," Laurie cries: "Fetch *what* home? The leavings of Comanche bucks sold time and again to the highest bidder with savage brats of her own? Do you know what Ethan'll do if he has a chance? He'll put a bullet in her brain. I tell you, Martha would want him to." "Only if I'm dead," responds Marty with grim determination. This extreme argument between the lead romantic couple of the film is clearly thrown aside when they reunite in the film's closing moments. The final music emphasizes only the sweet romance of their reunion.

FIGURE 1.15 The final shot of Ethan, a suddenly isolated figure without even a horse to "ride away."

logic of the music does not match the ultimate syntactic logic of Ford's overall film. The musical implication of triumph is particularly complicated by the final image of Ethan walking away: here, he does not represent the myth of a man with "peace of mind" but, in Mrs. Jorgensen's words, "a human man way out on a limb" (see Figure 1.15).

It is Ethan's isolated, ever-searching figure that audiences tend to remember more than the finality of a closing door.[50] So, even if the film's music reinforces a sense of closure, this belies the greater complexity of *The Searchers*. If the music communicates that which was always going to be resolved, the door closing on Ethan at the film's end raises as many questions as it blacks out.

---

[50] Nugent's revised final screenplay did have Ethan join everyone else in entering the house at the film's end, but Ford determined otherwise (Eckstein 1998, 15). Kent Anderson reads the moment of the door closing on Ethan as signifying the destabilization of genre to the extent that "it is John Ford who is being left to 'wander forever between the winds'" (2006, 19). Eckstein reads Ethan's exclusion as an example of punishing the character's "savage racism," making of him "an example sharply relevant in 1955–56 when the Supreme Court's Brown v. Board of Education decision had just brought race relations back to the forefront of American national consciousness" (1998, 15). Similarly, Susan Hayward argues that *The Searchers'* "reflects America's contemporary late 1950s' anxieties about the growth of the Civil Rights Movement's campaign activities" (2006, 46). In relation to this point, Kalinak summarizes her own response as follows: "If what *The Searchers* cannot express directly are the tensions of contemporaneous white-black relations, then music may be one of the telltale markers of both Ford's intentions to address race and racism and the ultimate impossibility of doing so within the genre of the western in 1950s America" (2007, 175).

 # DEAD MAN

PLOT SUMMARY

The first sequence of *Dead Man* shows the main character William Blake (Johnny Depp) on his way to the town of Machine, a place identified as "the end of the line" by the train fireman (Crispin Glover). Though Blake has been promised a position as accountant for Mr. Dickinson (Robert Mitchum), the owner of the Metalworks around which the town of Machine is built, the promise turns out to be as flimsy as the paper it was written on. Having lost his family, and with no immediate prospects before him, Blake pays for a (pathetically small) bottle of liquor at the town saloon, a place where the clichéd honky-tonk piano music (a version of the American folk tune "Billy Boy") provides the only traditional scoring in the film. Upon leaving the saloon Blake meets Thel (Mili Avital), a former "whore" who has since transformed herself into a maker of paper roses. Their brief love affair is, like other promising possibilities (such as those represented by the letter from Dickinson's company and Thel's flowers), easily destroyed when Thel's long-absent fiancé, Charlie (Gabriel Byrne), finds them in bed together. After Charlie shoots Thel dead, the bullet traveling through her body into Blake's chest, Blake clumsily shoots and kills Charlie in self-defense. The film soon reveals Charlie to have been the son of Mr. Dickinson who hires three inept killers—Cole Wilson (Lance Henriksen), Conway Twill (Michael Wincott), and Johnny "The Kid" Pickett (Eugene Byrd)—to catch Blake, dead or alive, for "more money than you've ever seen." Meanwhile, Blake is befriended by a Native American outcast named Nobody who, having been ostracized by his own people, guides Blake to the place where earthly realities will be "of no concern."[51] Nobody misidentifies

---

[51] Nobody explains to Blake that by being born of two tribes (half Blood and half Blackfoot) he has been doubly rejected for his hybrid identity. As Rosenbaum points out, Nobody's "foreign" role in *Dead Man* touches "on the scandal that Native Americans are treated in the United States as if they were foreigners" (2000, 19).

Blake as the nineteenth-century English visionary poet, the writer whose powerful words fuelled Nobody's strength in escaping the Englishmen who took him captive as a child.[52] Though therefore built on a fundamental misunderstanding, the friendship between Blake and Nobody represents the possibility of interracial goodwill. By the end of the film, they are ultimately united in death—Blake having been sent into the ocean by the canoe Nobody prepared to "deliver" him, and Nobody being shot by the most vicious bounty hunter, Cole Wilson, while Blake watches on helplessly. Along with their deaths, the film's end also points to an ironic new beginning of transcendence: Nobody kills Wilson at the same moment he is shot and the two men fall in a choreographed, almost-graceful moment of strange confluence; and Blake escapes the hostile shoot-or-be-shot terrain of the Wild West as his canoe is swept out to be enveloped by sea and sky.

A REVISIONIST WESTERN

Like *The Searchers, Dead Man* contains many obvious semantic elements of the western, including scenes on the "iron horse" (the train), in a saloon, in a small frontier town, as well as in the landscape of America in the late nineteenth century. The film incorporates much violence, another mainstay of the genre, though with considerable critical distance. The film also incorporates stock characters of the genre such as bounty hunters, marshals,[53] a (former) whore, and a white main character who becomes an outlaw. Such familiar semantic details aside, the revisionist significance of *Dead Man* is extreme in relation to *The Searchers*. Most important, the syntactic logic of *Dead Man* consistently invokes conventions in order to displace them, not least because the many familiar semantic elements of the film ironically offset those elements that are unexpected. Instead of the powerful and staunch cowboy we might expect, for instance, we meet Blake, a buttoned-down accountant with frail features and uncommon vulnerability, one who must "learn" how to speak with this gun as an unintentional outlaw. Depp's slight build makes him an especially ironic visual contrast with the imposing

---

[52] This aspect of the film's story is also based on historical accounts read by Jarmusch: he says, "I read accounts of Natives that were taken all the way to Europe and put on display in London and Paris, and paraded like animals. . . . I also read accounts of chiefs that were taken east and then murdered by their own tribes when they got back because of the stories they told about the white man—which became part of Nobody's story" (Rosenbaum 2000, 48).

[53] The two marshals are named Lee and Marvin in tribute to one of Jarmusch's favorite film actors (Rosenbaum 2000, 31). Lee Marvin is famous for playing an archetypal villain in *The Man Who Shot Liberty Valance*, another of Ford's most celebrated westerns, and a precedent for the black-and-white form as well as the revisionist power of *Dead Man*.

physique of John Wayne.[54] And instead of the barbaric Other or "noble savage" of an Indian (such as Scar or Look), we meet Nobody (Gary Farmer), a complex and compassionate Native American with a mighty presence, one who literally and figuratively dwarfs William Blake. The images in Figures 1.16 and 1.17 are representative of how much Farmer dominates the *mise-en-scène* of *Dead Man* in relation to Depp, even when the latter is in sharper focus.

Farmer/Nobody is a powerful visual "answer" to Ethan's/Wayne's towering presence in *The Searchers*. With reference to Sergio Leone's parodic western entitled *My Name Is Nobody* (1973), Gregg Rickman argues that Nobody's singled-out, larger-than-life, and often solitary presence in *Dead Man* defines *him* as the true protagonist.[55] Whether or not we define him as Rickman does, the physical and narrative centrality of Nobody is certainly representative of *Dead Man*'s revisionist stridency.

In addition to the atypical relative power of Nobody, his name being an ironic acknowledgment of the lack of power enjoyed by his people, the unconventionality of *Dead Man* is most strident in Neil Young's music for the film. Unlike Steiner's score for *The Searchers*, this music does not incorporate familiar songs, musical clichés, fanfares, or full orchestral sounds in the late Romantic style favored by mainstream Classical Hollywood, nor is it shaped in terms of predictable rhythms, melodies, and harmonies. Young's use of the solo guitar does semantically connect it with many other westerns, whether classical or revisionist: westerns as different as *The Searchers* and *Unforgiven* (1992) are united in using the folksy traditionalism evoked by an instrument that was especially popular in America during the mid-to-late nineteenth century, the time during which westerns are typically set. However, Young's exploitation of the *electric* guitar's capacities at distortion and reverberation defamiliarizes the musical experience, in keeping with Jim Jarmusch's overall directorial approach to combining the familiar with the eccentric.

There is a lack of consensus with regard to defining the classical western as opposed to the contemporary revisionist manifestation of that genre, not least because many westerns dating back to the second decade of the twentieth century demonstrate that "hyperconsciousness" of the genre emerged early on (Gallagher 2003, 265). In other words, as Tag Gallagher explains, the idea of a straightforward "evolutionary" process from naiveté towards self-reflexivity is an inaccurate assumption with regard to how

---

[54] It is also significant that Depp's grandfather was a Cherokee Native American, in tribute to whom he has a forearm tattoo of a Native American man in full head-dress. This detail is never seen in the film but is frequently mentioned by Depp's biographers (Rosenbaum 2000, 21).

[55] Rosenbaum provides the citation for Gregg Rickman with reference to a range of "solitary" Western heroes across history: from Ethan Edwards and Shane, to John MacCabe and the lone cowboys played by Clint Eastwood (2000, 55).

FIGURE 1.16 Nobody is the ironically named Native American who frequently dominates the *mise-en-scène* of *Dead Man.*

FIGURE 1.17 Here again, Nobody dominates the frame.

the western has developed (266–67). Even with the example of *Stagecoach*, Ford's first sound western, we witness what Gallagher calls:

> a virtual anthology of gags, motifs, conventions, scenes, situations, tricks, and characters drawn from past westerns, but each one pushed towards fresh

intensities of mythic extremism, thus consciously revisiting not only the old West but old westerns as well, and reinterpreting at the same time these elements for modern minds (268).

Thus Gallagher presents a cyclic rather than evolutionary model for the genre's lifespan.

In light of a cyclic approach to the western, it would be overly simplistic to set up *Dead Man* as a trailblazing example in contrast to *The Searchers*. *Both* films draw upon well-established histories within the genre. *The Searchers* draws its resonance from mythology that dates at least as far back as the dime novels of the 1860s which charted how the West was won and therein "elevated the cowboy to mythic status" (Hayward 2006, 498). The film knowingly engages with and *challenges* long-standing ritualistic functions of the western. The problematic aspects of Ethan Edwards may be read as a reaction against much that defines the genre—for in *The Searchers*, the dream of frontier progress seems reliant on a white man intent on barbaric revenge. Equally, *Dead Man* resonates with various self-conscious forms of the western since "the death of studio Western in the 1960s" in which (as Roger Bromley puts it) "the nineteenth-century frontier myth has come under sustained attack" (2001, 51). Examples of revisionist westerns include: Sergio Leone's parodical, spaghetti westerns of the 1960s that "poke fun" at the genre's iconography, make its baddies into ugly, dirty caricatures, and redefine the cultural frames of the western with references to Mexican and Hispanic history (as in, for example, *The Good, The Bad, and The Ugly* (1966)); the "demythologizing westerns" of Sam Peckinpah (including *The Wild Bunch* (1969), and *Pat Garrett and Billy the Kid* (1973); and various other forms of revisionist western, such as Robert Altman's *McCabe and Mrs. Miller* (1971), as well as John Ford's *The Man Who Shot Liberty Valance* (1962) and *Cheyenne Autumn* (1964).[56] *Dead Man* was released in the more immediate context of several other contemporary attempts to redress aspects of the history of the West, including: Sam Raimi's *The Quick and the Dead* (1995), a western that features an uncommonly strong female lead (played by Sharon Stone) in order to subvert the usual gender roles of the genre; Clint Eastwood's *Unforgiven*, a film that incorporates much violence in order to critique that mainstay of the genre;[57] and Kevin

---

[56] See Kollin on the cultural politics of Leone's westerns (2000, 127), Kupfer on "demythologizing" examples of the western (2008, 104), and Hayward on the history of various revisionist westerns (2006, 507–8).

[57] Though this was the well-publicized intention of *Unforgiven*, some critics have read the film as being disingenuous because the final sequence revels in the excessive violent revenge taken by its lead character, William Munny (Eastwood). See Ingrassia (1998) for a full analysis of the film's contrary statements on violence.

Costner's *Dances with Wolves* (1990), a key example of portraying Native Americans in an atypically sympathetic light (albeit problematically for some).[58] Taken together, these films include a rich range of scoring that reflects their generic diversity.[59]

SELF-CONSCIOUS INTERTEXTUALITY

With the understanding that *Dead Man* playfully and knowingly draws upon much that precedes it, the film also breaks new ground. Its ritualistic value is uniquely different from that of *The Searchers* because, as Jonathan Rosenbaum points out, it is "the first Western made by a white filmmaker that assumes as well as addresses Native American spectators" (2000, 18).[60] In *Celluloid Indians: Native Americans and Film*, a critical analysis of the many problematic cinematic representations of her people, Jacquelyn Kilpatrick acknowledges that "Jarmusch's film shows a significant effort to depict Native American existence stripped of the stereotypes of the last hundred years of filmmaking. It is a very good start" (1999, 176). Though Native American music is sparingly used in the film, the audiovisual prominence of Farmer in a leading role is especially significant. Farmer is a successful Native American actor of the stage and screen, a promoter of Native cultures, and a founder of the journal *Aboriginal Voices* (Suárez 2007, 106).[61] He joined Jarmusch in delivering the film to reservation video stores as well as planning a screening at the Makah reservation. The film was greeted by enthusiastic "whooping expressions of approval" from several Native American audiences (Rosenbaum 2000, 23). In relation to its intended ritualistic value, the film's *mise-en-scène* is made in terms of respecting indigenous culture. The Makah village shown towards the end of the film, for instance, was made to look as authentic as possible,

---

[58] Since each of these films has been a career-defining moment for its director (with the exception of Raimi), it is appropriate to mention them all by name here, although that is not the pattern throughout this book.

[59] For more details on various scores for liberal westerns, see Gorbman (2000).

[60] Similarly, for Jacquelyn Kilpatrick (a Native American critic), *Dead Man* is the "only western by a white director to assume Native American perspectives and to acknowledge Native Americans as a prospective audience" (cited by Suárez 2007, 105).

[61] Suárez cites Farmer's stage performance in *Tom Highway's Dry Lips Ought to Move to Kapuskasing* and on screen in *Powwow Highway* (1989) as being "most memorable" (2007, 106). We might also consider Farmer's role in *Smoke Signals* (1998), a loose form of the western and an adaptation of Sherman Alexie's short story collection entitled *The Lone Ranger and Tonto Fistfight in Heaven*. This film features several songs, including one entitled "John Wayne's Teeth" which characterizes a Native American community in terms of cultural mixing—the song is "what Alexie calls a blending of English lyrics and Western musical rhythms," along with Native American vocals and traditional drums (Cummings 2001). For a fuller exploration of cross-cultural connections between *Dead Man* and *Smoke Signals*, see Kollin (2000) as well as Cummings (2001).

being modeled on genuine old photographs and worked on by Makah artists. Jarmusch also hired a First Nations Cultural Advisor to "certify" the set as "appropriately "Native" (Rosenbaum 2000, 49).

In keeping with his focus on cultural fidelity, it is especially significant that Jarmusch has spoken out specifically against *The Searchers'* having "Comanche" Native Americans who speak Navajo: indirectly echoing Colonnese, Jarmusch says "it's kind of like saying, 'Yes I know they are supposed to be French people, but I could only get Germans, and no one will know the difference'" (Rosenbaum 2000, 47). *Dead Man*, by contrast, includes dialogue in *several* Native American languages (Blackfoot, Cree, and Makah). It is also significant that Jarmusch chose not to subtitle any of the Native American in *Dead Man* as "a little gift for those people who understand the language" (Rosenbaum 2000, 22–23). So, the lack of subtitling does not signify the lack of importance given to Native American speech that it does in *The Searchers*. We should also consider that, in the earlier film, anything spoken by a Native American is said to and/ or translated by Ethan Edwards, signifying his ultimate dominance over the language he misidentifies.[62]

Dead Man references *The Searchers* in other, more direct ways. Some specific details of its narrative and sound track further illuminate profound ideological differences between the two films. Early on, we witness the shooting of buffalo, an institutionally sanctioned action that reveals Ethan's increasing brutality in *The Searchers*. In *Dead Man*, the action is shown to be common practice, as it is enthusiastically enacted by several men in the first scene. In *The Searchers*, the thumping sound of buffalo running is louder than Ethan's gunfire, as if to emphasize that which the main character "runs away from" in refusing to accept Marty's protest. In *Dead Man*, there is *no shout of protest* as numerous men suddenly leap up from a train car to shoot buffalo through open windows. Their shooting is, moreover, punctuated by repeated, heavily reverberating, and exponentially amplified notes on electric guitar. In this aural context, the train fireman has to shout as he tells Blake that a million buffalo were slaughtered in the previous year alone. Even as the fireman shouts over the thunderous sound of gunfire, he still manages to look and sound casual while Blake watches on helplessly in barely concealed terror. Thus the film places unsettling aural emphasis on the carnage that is normalized, and that we do not see, but which we can imagine. The aggression of the

---

[62] In light of this overarching pattern, there is an especially ironic point at which Scar throws Ethan's own words back at him: after Ethan has told Scar he speaks "pretty good American, someone teach you?," Scar tells Ethan "you speak good Comanche, someone teach you?" (The further irony of Scar's words being in Navajo is, of course, buried in the film, but complicates what we may understand as Ethan's or Wayne's mastery of the Other language.)

FIGURE 1.18 Clinging to his suitcase (all that he has), Blake timidly witnesses white men shooting buffalo.

firing sounds places us in a position like that of Marty in *The Searchers*: we may want to protest as he did, but we are as helpless as Blake (or, an especially vulnerable-looking Johnny Depp), clinging to his suitcase in a passive, seated position (see Figure 1.18).

One of Nobody's scenes also alludes to a specific scene from *The Searchers*, one that features Look. In a comparatively light moment from the earlier film, we are introduced to Look while she is trying on a bowler hat, one of the items being sold or bartered by Martin and Ethan to her people. The comedy of her smilingly putting on an item of white man's clothing is gently underscored by Steiner's introduction of her theme: as mentioned before, this theme (in its original form) features the airy sweetness of a flute carrying the melody. In *Dead Man* there is a scene that harkens back to this particular scene from *The Searchers*, one in which we see Nobody playfully place Blake's tuxedo top hat on his head while the latter is barely awake (see Figure 1.19).

With this hat on his head, an ironic prop in contrast with his authentic Native American clothing, Nobody opens and closes his mouth in a pompously shuttering manner, as if to wordlessly imitate the English people who took him hostage when he was a child (as we later learn). Ironically, in response to being captured, the young Nobody "mimicked [the English], imitated their ways, hoping that they might lose interest in this young savage, but their interest only grew." Thus, his imitation here is a way of reclaiming the subversive freedom of parody that was previously misunderstood. Though we do not hear Nobody speak, his mouthing invites us to invent a voice *with* him: in that sense, the action creates the possibility of a kind of mutually

FIGURE 1.19 Nobody playfully tries on Blake's bowler hat, a visual echo of Look's first scene in *The Searchers*.

imagined subversive ventriloquism. So, the film here invites us to share a quiet but significant moment *with* Nobody creating comedy. Since this is not a scene about Nobody as a figure of fun, he is characterized very differently from Look. Nobody's wordless imitation of white men is also the inverse of countless moments in which Native Americans are seen and not heard in *The Searchers*. In this scene, then, the soundless speaking of Nobody is as eloquent as anything else we might actually hear. That Blake falls asleep while Nobody mouths his words only makes us more awake to the action. When Nobody then places the hat carefully back next to Blake, his action is punctuated by part of Young's main theme for *Dead Man* that carries over into the next episodic scene through extended reverberating notes, reinforcing a sense of its resonance [40:51–41:36].

It is clear that Jarmusch meant for *Dead Man* to prompt comparisons with Ford's best-known films: he even says, "Robby Müller, the director of photography, and I went scouting locations, and if we saw a landscape that looked so magnificent, like a calendar or a postcard, we would deliberately turn our backs. Instead of a John Ford-like vista, we would find a tree or a rock or something else interesting" (Susman 1996). *The Searchers* and *Dead Man* represent points of extreme stylistic contrast. Not only do the spectacular, Technicolor and Vistavision Monument Valley scenes of *The Searchers* become the black-and-white "anti-postcard" landscapes in *Dead Man*, the classical editing and careful pacing of long takes in *The Searchers* become erratic elliptical editing as well as abbreviated episodes in *Dead Man*, and the often "objective" or observational camerawork in *The Searchers* which foregrounds Ethan Edwards's stature becomes the frequent subjective camerawork which foregrounds the presence of Nobody in *Dead Man*. Moreover, Steiner's classical scoring, which utilizes a full orchestral range of sound along with the incorporation of traditional and popular songs in *The Searchers*, is "answered" by the unpredictable, improvisatory, and pared down scoring of Young's electric guitar music for *Dead Man*. Though Young uses other instruments including acoustic guitar, Native American drums and flutes, a pump organ, and a piano, the electric guitar dominates most cues and it is these cues we shall, therefore, dwell upon. Young's heavy dependence on this single instrument might have led to a relatively a limited range of expression; however, Young exploits the possibilities of playing even single notes differently as well as varying degrees of chordal complexity, along with changes in tone quality, pitch, dynamics, rhythm, reverberation, and distortion. The effect is to demand our attention to the smallest units of musical sound and to the minutiae of Young's score that, unlike much of Steiner's music, forbids our getting lost in a wash of sonorous details that might lull us away from the disconcerting visuals.

JIM JARMUSCH AND NEIL YOUNG: COLLABORATORS

Dead Man literally sounds different from any other western, and therein reflects the radical possibilities of independent cinema, as well as Jarmusch's filmmaking. Though the western and the period (rather than contemporary, urban) setting represents new ground for Jarmusch, *Dead Man* is connected with Jarmusch's other films in forcing our contemplation of details that are uncomfortable, strange, messy, ironic, and absurd, and Young's score frequently punctuates such details with particular emphasis.[63] It is important to acknowledge the importance of Jarmusch as an auteur here (just as we acknowledged the directorial control of Ford in *The Searchers*), not least because he retains atypical control over the final cuts of his films, including their sound tracks. Jarmusch is therefore known for retaining his independent credibility, even when his narrative features get mainstream exposure (Rosenbaum 2000, 15–16). His absolute insistence on keeping control has also cost him: in particular, he lost much promotional support from Miramax for *Dead Man*.[64] The lack of strong marketing for the film no

---

[63] *Dead Man* is also connected to Jarmusch's other films—especially *Ghost Dog: The Way of the Samurai* (1999)—in terms of its episodic and elliptical structure, its tonal complexity, and its meditative and poetic density. The meditative aspects of *Dead Man* and its playfulness with genre also resonate with *The Limits of Control* (2009), an atypically esoteric crime drama.

[64] Rosenbaum even reports that when an acquaintance wanted to include *Dead Man* in a film festival he was organizing, a Miramax representative flatly advised him against it as a "dog" of a film (2000, 16).

doubt partly accounts for its poor box office performance.[65] However, the very form of the film probably put automatic limits on its relative success: in its enigmatic and stylistically affronting form, *Dead Man* represents Jarmusch's most profound challenge to narrative expectations of linearity, causality, and closure. More specifically, the film challenges mainstream representations of the Wild West as the frontier of possibility, creation, and civilization. This is most obvious in *Dead Man*'s emphasis on a journey towards death (not progress) from the outset. The film does not represent the Western frontier in terms of the democratic energy that Frederick Jackson Turner conceptualized.[66] Instead, the film represents a world in which white American settlement is inextricably connected with death, decay, absurd violence, and inhumane individualism. In other words, the syntactic logic of the film is consistently revisionist. Jarmusch's revisioning of the western parallels Young's atypical use of the electric guitar—he plays upon the genre much like Young creates surprising sounds from the instrument.

The revisionism of *Dead Man* is consistently reinforced by Young's original score. This score, in turn, has immediate meaning in terms of Young's radical star persona. Despite having achieved widespread critical success as "one of rock's senior statesmen," and the "grandpappy of grunge," Young is also much associated with political and artistic activism (despite his brief support of Ronald Reagan during the 1980s).[67] Though his music has been canonized, Young's "deliberately unpolished style," and drug-fueled improvisations (in concert *and* in recordings) are repeatedly discussed in terms of countercultural integrity (Barker and Taylor 2007, 209). Hugh Barker and Yuval Taylor connect Young's star status with a quest for authenticity and realness that is consistently and uniquely his, even across different genres of music. From *On the Beach* (released in 1974), his album featuring "three long, slow, depressing stream-of-consciousness blues songs, to his freewheeling "drugged-out, driven, and death-soaked" album *Tonight's the Night* (1975), to his comparatively fierce hard rock album *Zuma* (1975), Young's defining work of the 1970s is consistently perceived as rebellious, immediate, and truthful (Barker and Taylor 2007, 206, 204). In addition, some of his most famous songs—including such examples as "Heart of Gold," "Old Man," and "Harvest Moon"—are defined by his "countryish" style of guitar-playing. The power of Young's

---

[65] According to Box Office Mojo (2007), *Dead Man* had gross domestic box office takings of approximately $1,037,847. (The film cost approximately nine million to make.)

[66] See Suárez 2007, 104.

[67] See Sorensen 2007, 113, 106. Sorensen's whole article is a full consideration of the political meaning of Young's music in relation to his 2003 film *Greendale*, a production of protest against "a security-obsessed state that cares little for the environment, peace, or human rights (114). More recently, Young became a "vociferous opponent of George W. Bush" (as emphasized in his protest album *Living With War* [2006]) (108).

using-and-redefining aspects of country music is inevitably associated with his work for *Dead Man*, not least because that musical genre is much associated with the western.

Barker and Taylor define Young's style in terms that are echoed by his work on *Dead Man*: from the release of his second solo album, *Everybody Knows This Is Nowhere* (1969), he developed music in terms of "simple, evocative songs; extremely basic rhythms; extended and suspended chords, but only a handful of them," "non-virtuosic yet intense guitar solos," and a "countryish twang; an unhurried intensity; and an emphasis on the darker side of life" (205). Young's music for *Dead Man* also echoes the more "filthy, distortion-heavy guitar playing" of *Rust Never Sleeps* (1979), an album in which he rejects melody with consistent aggression (224). Young also has a reputation for eschewing recording technology (preferring to record live and largely avoiding post-recording), which relates to the improvisatory process by which he composed music for *Dead Man*. Young speaks of how he records music in filmic terms: "Cinema verité? I got audio verité. The concept of capturing the moment on camera? I just translated that right into the recording studio" (214).

In relation to his collaboration with Jarmusch on *Dead Man*, Young said "the movie is my rhythm section and I will add a melody to that" (Rosenbaum 2000, 44).[68] In describing the film as the rhythm to his melody, Young implicitly inverted the typical hierarchical relationship between film images and music. Whether or not this was his ultimate intention, Young's music was crucial for Jarmusch's process: the director wrote the screenplay for *Dead Man* while "listening constantly to Neil Young and [his band] Crazy Horse" (Kubernik 2006, 220). In the context of analyzing *Dead Man* as a revisionist western that makes use of Young's radical star persona, it is also worth mentioning that Crazy Horse is named after an iconic Native American who fought against the U.S. Federal Government in the 1870s in order to protect the Lakota people and their territories.

As a strong indicator of their successful collaboration, Young later asked Jarmusch to make a documentary about Crazy Horse which became *The Year of the Horse* (1997). This film spans the band's twenty-eight-year history, including archival footage dating back to their tour in 1978. With this production, Jarmusch himself has spoken of inverting the typical hierarchy between filmic image and sound by using "the contradiction of Super-8 film on a big screen with music that is recorded in forty-track digital

---

[68] Young even made an album that Rosenbaum has called a "composer's cut" of his music for and inspired by the film (2000, 44). The album includes sounds of cars passing on a highway (emphasizing the passing of time, and alluding to the film's status as a contemporary reimagining of the past), as well as Depp reading some of Blake's poems that were never included in the film.

Dolby." This combination of high-tech sound with low-tech image is, for Jarmusch, a combination of aural "beauty and bigness" with visual "smallness" in order to emphasize the ultimate transcendence of the band's music (Kubernik 2006, 219). Though *The Year of the Horse* was made after *Dead Man*, its construction emphasizes the director's understanding of music's potential power. Therefore, Jarmusch's particular attachment to Young's music should prompt our special sensitivity to how it is used in *Dead Man*.

THE OPENING

The radicalism of *Dead Man* is emphasized from the beginning of the film, especially through its sound track. The opening is a series of elliptical glimpses of Blake's journey to Machine. These are interrupted by fade-outs to blackness and fade-ins from it. Parallel to the fragmented visual structure, Young's score begins with minimalist, intermittent, and disconnected cues that communicate anything but the Classical Hollywood establishment of identifiable musical themes [0:30–8:42]. Rosenbaum, whose book on the film is of decisive influence here, writes of the music as "anything but tuneful" and therein "closer to a rhythmic sound effect than to any sort of recognizable melody" (2000, 8). The very absence of what we might expect from the scoring of a Classical Hollywood exposition (such as a melody, clear-cut harmony, or definable form) establishes the expectations that are met throughout the film: in that sense, Young's music ironically prepares us like a more traditional score would.

The very first diegetic sounds of *Dead Man* are tinny and clanging sounds of a train. These are the sounds associated with the quotation by Henry Michaux that is provided before the title: "It is preferable not to travel with a Dead Man."[69] Thus, the film begins with aural emphasis on the "iron horse" that has traditionally represented progress in the settlement of the American frontier in the western. But the sounds of the train are initially separated from the source of the locomotive, being first attached to the idea of a *Dead Man* with whom the film assures us we would prefer not to travel. Then the film shows various parts of the locomotive in medium-close-ups, delaying a full establishing shot of its movement across the tracks until four minutes have passed. The concept of

---

[69] This line, as Suárez notes, comes from *Un certain Plume*, a collection of sketches focused upon a naïve man who repeatedly and absurdly finds himself in a series of compromised and disturbing situations: "in the first sketch of the series, he wakes up repeatedly during the night to confront a number of disasters and, unable to deal with them, he just falls asleep again" (Suárez 2007, 106). Suárez's description of this sketch neatly matches Blake's often semiconscious or sleeping state during the opening sequence of *Dead Man*. We *might* be lulled into a similarly passive position as his were it not for the intermittently accosting snippets of Young's music: from the beginning, it insists we stay "awake" to the form of the film.

industrial progress asserted and enacted by white men is thus audiovisually connected with fragmented forms and death. The first semantic element (the locomotive) is therefore revisionistically used from the outset.

The first character to speak in *Dead Man* is the fireman who warns William Blake (*the* "Dead Man") that in travelling to Machine he is on his way to "the end of the line." In keeping with this sardonically grim presentiment of death, Blake looks out the window to see a landscape that becomes more stark as the journey progresses: from dense forestry and snowy mountain ranges, to unimpressive table rocks and arid desert land. Equally, the journey begins in the familiar Midwest, but then moves into much wilder terrain "scarred by traces of the Indian wars of the 1870s," as indicated by the scorched tepees as well as an abandoned village (Suárez 2007, 112). Though violence against Native Americans is not foregrounded through the film, Denise K. Cummings points out that the abandoned village and tepees represent the residue of genocide (2001, 66). In addition to the history of white violence evoked by such images, the white characters first shown in Blake's company are critically represented. As the train carries him from the familiar Midwest into wilder terrain, other white passengers are repeatedly shown in his carriage but none of them appear to be travelling *with* him. All look at him with some form of distance, their expressions ranging from critical bemusement to hostility (thus matching the peculiar and inhospitable aspects of the landscapes outside the train).

Many aural aspects of the opening for *Dead Man* work interdependently with its unsettling visuals. First, there is no dialogue for several minutes, even though many characters are shown. In addition to the noticeable "lack" of anchored meaning in voices—and we should consider that the voice is the most traditionally emphasized aural component of cinema[70]—the sound track emphasizes extreme contrasts that further destabilize the position of the perceiver. Young's music cues are erratic in form and duration. Thus, rather than lending greater coherence to the episodic structure of the film's opening visuals, the music serves to reinforce the unnervingly irregular editing. The frequent cuts from outside to inside the train happen at an unpredictable rhythm. Moreover, each shift between shots of the exterior and interior train is marked by a change in aural emphasis: from the outer sounds of the train's mechanical power (wheels, steam, clanging metal, high-pitched whistling), to the quietness inside the train offset by a squeaky lantern swinging above Blake; from the heavy, grainy sound of coal being shoveled onto flames to power the train to the strange quiet of its passengers

---

[70] Throughout *The Voice in Cinema* (1999), Michel Chion assumes this widely accepted and historically weighted fact, at least when it comes to narrative films.

whose silence is thick with inscrutable meaning. In addition, throughout the film's opening, Young utilizes the extremities of the electric guitar in terms of pitch, reverberation, and relative density (from repeated individual notes with minimal reverberation to heavily reverberating, thick, *forte* chords). The heavy reverberation with some fragments of Young's music has the effect of extreme distortion, along with obscuring our impressions of clear cadential direction. Moreover, the music is broken up by many rests, and the content of each individual cue is far from predictable.

The rhythmic sound of the train sometimes lulls us into a false sense of security. Yet every time it lulls us into a state of relaxation (reinforced by our sometimes seeing Blake's own heavy eyelids), the editing and music "play against the rhythms of the westbound train," jolting us into a freshly unpredictable moment (Rosenbaum 2000, 42). This pattern reinforces our understanding of Blake's vulnerability, and perhaps our own. This is, in turn, reinforced by the weak sound of Blake's pocket watch ticking in comparison with the melee of other, irregular, and more forceful sounds. The marking of time through ordinary means is a weak defense, the film seems to say (indeed we do not see the watch again, signifying that its action becomes meaningless). The unpredictable marking of time in the film's opening is visually emphasized through there being no repeated length of time between a shot inside the train to a cut outside it: the time frames for these transitions range from eight seconds to fifty seconds, and there is no pattern in terms of progressive length or compression in the opening episodes. The irregularity of silence and noise, along with the brokenness of Young's music cues, serve to emphasize the destabilizing structure that defines *Dead Man* as a revisionist western.

As a genre film, *Dead Man* relies upon numerous film precedents (across genres) in order to make sense: understanding that the film plays upon and "revisions" the semantic and syntactic patterns established by (and expected from) other films helps us to make sense of an opening that repeatedly teeters on the edge of incomprehensibility. For instance, the absence of dialogue for several minutes makes the initial inscrutability of the film's characters, and the film's expository direction through them, extreme. Even when a character finally does speak, he makes little obvious sense. The very first line of the film, from the aforementioned fireman to Blake, is "look out the window." Given the several atypically unspectacular shots of landscape the film has already shown through the window, the film thus directs us to confront its unfamiliar terrain in a literal and figurative sense. The fireman then speaks to Blake in almost hallucinatory terms, of being "in the boat," of "looking up at the ceiling," and of "the water in your head [which] was not dissimilar from the landscape and you think to yourself 'why is it that the landscape is moving but the boat is still?' And also, where is it that you're from?" Thus the fireman speaks of physical, visual, and perceptual relativity. His words take on more concrete meaning at the end of the film when we see Blake in a canoe, straining to see other characters on land, and eventually becoming part of the sea. For the film's beginning, however, the words most immediately emphasize its self-aware, disorienting, and playful inscrutability. The delayed expository question ("where is that you are from?") is more than a non sequitur in this context; its blunt conventionality is patently out of place. The ensuing conversation in which Blake reveals his home (Cleveland), and his personal history defined by loss (the death of his parents and the end of his engagement) is suddenly interrupted by the shooting of buffalo. That the buffalo shooting interrupts the first exchange of relatively high narrative comprehensibility only serves to emphasize the moral *incomprehensibility* (or "indefensibility") of such brutal action all the more. It is this shooting that leads into the film title, the opening credits, and the first time we hear Young's main musical theme [8:43–9:30].

Young's main theme for *Dead Man* is in a lilting 6/8 time. The rough outline of this theme, one that is presented in many forms of subtle variation through the film, is first articulated as follows (see Figure 1.20):

The tune is squarely based in B minor. The simple accessibility of the rhythm and harmony, along with the identifiability of the main melody are, however, ironically complicated or obscured by Young's use of heavy reverberation. The contrary sound of the music,

FIGURE 1.20 Neil Young's main theme for *Dead Man*, first heard during the opening credits (transcribed directly from the DVD).

being both accessible and affronting, is matched by the extremes of its internal structure: it begins in an almost whimsical, folksy-sounding way at a relatively moderate pitch, but this is soon undercut by the more menacing sections at a lower pitch that "answer" the opening phrases. On the sustained reverberating note of the end, dovetailed with an abbreviated restatement of the theme, the film title "Dead Man" appears [9:31–9:35], each letter being imaged as bones which separate—it is a moment of audiovisual parity since the title falls apart while the strength of the note disintegrates

FIGURE 1.21 The title as it first appears.

FIGURE 1.22 Within a few moments, the title of *Dead Man* falls apart.

(see Figures 1.21 and 1.22). This detail is representative of the moment-to-moment subtlety of Young's score. Such subtlety is surprising given that most of the score was created out of improvisation.

AN OVERVIEW OF YOUNG'S SCORE

In a 2004 interview with Terry Gross, Young described himself creating music for and accompanying the images of *Dead Man* by imitating much scoring for silent cinema. He created his improvised score through playing along to the film as it was projected onto multiple screens in a circle around him. All his instruments (including electric guitar, piano, tack piano, portable pump organ, and Native American drums) were at hand within that circle, so he could simply move from one to another as the film played. He told Gross "I played all the way through live. [. . .] And, basically, it was all a real-time experience."

Jarmusch has said that Young played through the rough cut of the film (of two and a half hours' duration, thus thirty minutes longer than the final cut) three times over a two-day period, refusing to stop the film at any point. Even though Young was not therefore composing with the final cut, almost all of his music was retained. Young had been given a "kind of map" in the list of places for which Jarmusch had requested music, but Young's scoring process was more about recording his own immediate "emotional reaction to the movie" while it was playing (Rosenbaum 2000, 43). Young's description reveals the extent to which he composed directly for the film, and in an intuitive way, responding to the scene shifts with immediate changes in instrumentation.

In his interview with Gross, Young also mentions having had two primary "themes" in mind, one of which is associated with violence. Though he does not detail the use of these two themes, close attention to the full score of *Dead Man* reveals the subtleties in their being used like leitmotifs. As already mentioned, Young's music is unlike Classical Hollywood scoring in that it is pared down, often minimalist, and the cues frequently enter suddenly or seem cut off. Moreover, the raw experimental power of Young's electric guitar music for *Dead Man* is particularly emphasized, not least because it repeatedly punctuates numerous scenes and transitions in a way that calls attention to discontinuity. In addition, the cues usually enter at *mezzo forte* or *forte*. And rather than sneaking into scenes, or simply reinforcing the meaning of scenes for pleonastic accessibility, Young's music contributes its own internal logic as well as being a crucial component of the film's overwhelming sensory, hallucinatory, and expressionistic power.

The entire narrative of *Dead Man* seems saturated in subjective experience, not least because Jarmusch treats time and space as fluid concepts in *Dead Man*: lengths of time are difficult to gauge in a film where a pocket watch has no meaning; and many locations are filmed more than once (first traversed by Blake and Nobody, then by the killers that follow them). This visual patterning makes for a more circular than linear experience of time. This patterning is matched by Young's obsessive use of the two primary musical themes for the film. Because the themes are most often played as undeveloped fragments, the impact is rather different than that of a more conventional leitmotif system (such as Steiner's various ways of using "Lorena" or "What Makes a Man to Wander?" in *The Searchers*). Indeed, Young's repeated articulations of musical fragments communicate the evident impossibility of moving forward: this in itself contains an embedded critique of the concept of progress built into the western genre mythology. Instead of hearing themes articulated, then developed, and then restated with greater fullness than originally presented, Young's score circles around the same musical ideas over and over again. Indeed, sometimes his music is but a single note or chord repeated numerous times. The overall impression is one of suspension, of being consistently caught in the moment before any clear direction may be anticipated or any Steiner-style resolution may be reached. Young's music does not let us presume anything to come, but it does prompt us to make many ideologically loaded thematic connections. Moreover, though Young's music sounds like anything but Classical Hollywood scoring, his repetition of musical ideas does, like Steiner's scoring, establish important syntactic connections between concepts.

THE MAIN THEME

The main theme of *Dead Man*, played with the opening credits and most obviously attached to the titular character, is repeated as Blake enters the town of Machine shortly thereafter. Here, the theme is slowed down and sometimes falters, as if having lost confidence along with Blake [10:40–12:37]. The brokenness of the music parallels the images of death and decay that dominate the *mise-en-scène* of a white people's town: coffins, animal skulls, heaps of bones and fur, and a man with a huge rifle with animal skins hanging over the barrel. There are other, crude and uncomfortable physical sights and sounds of degradation: a horse pissing, a pig squealing in Blake's way, a baby sneezing, and the gagged grunts of a prostitute giving a roughneck oral sex while he holds a gun near her head. The sound of whistling wind subtly underscores the whole sequence: even in the midst of a settlement, albeit a crude and life-cancelling attempt at community, then, *Dead Man* uses the threatening sound of nothingness even more markedly than *The Searchers*.[71]

When Blake finally arrives at Dickinson's Metalworks, he has to shout his request for directions over the sounds of machines whirring, rattling, and "exhaling." His theme and voice are thus immediately displaced by the sound of industry in Machine. That his place is aurally undermined so quickly, especially after he is mostly silent during the film's opening, reinforces the impression of his vulnerability and his smaller-than-life status in relation to the protagonists of other westerns (Ethan Edwards and the authoritatively deep voice of John Wayne being the obvious contrasting example here). When Depp delivers Blake's first enquiry to see Mr. Dickinson to the Metalworks head clerk (John Hurt), he does so with such crisp, precise, and polite intonation that it is startling after the appalling sights of death and degradation shown in the previous sequence of shots. "Excuse me, how do you do sir?," he says, "I'm Bill Blake, your new accountant from Cleveland." This manner of speaking is as out of place as Depp's delicate features, or his character's plaid suit and bow tie. In response to the enquiry, the clerk pointedly gets Blake's name wrong, calling him "Black" more than once. The deliberate misidentification of his name, and the comparison between his plain (non-regional) American voice with Hurt's flat delivery in a regional and unpolished English voice, along with the subsequent deep, gravelly drawl of Mr. Dickinson speaking through his teeth clenched around a cigar (in addition to the unmistakable, ironic and iconic gravitas of its being Robert Mitchum, a star of westerns before Depp's time), further emphasize Blake's marginality.

That Blake himself comes from a place named Erie, as he mentions in his first conversation with the train fireman, also conveys his vulnerability by sonically invoking that which is "eerie," or ephemeral, immaterial, mysterious, and indeterminate. Such associations help define the character as the "blank slate" Jarmusch describes him as being: indeed, for Jarmusch, Blake may be made into practically anything by the other characters because he (and Depp, as an atypically versatile star) lacks determinate character (Rosenbaum 2000, 68). Where Wayne walked into *The Searchers* as a fully established icon of the western, Depp makes his first western appearance in *Dead Man*. His vulnerability in this context is further reinforced by his being present in most scenes of the film, but often shown lost,

---

[71] The aural motif of wind is also featured after the death of Thel, around the voices of the killers on their first trek to find Blake, and towards the end of the film when it merges with sounds of the sea as Blake tells Nobody "I feel very weak." Such subtle aural design is reflective of Jarmusch's sound mixer Drew Kunin, with whom Jarmusch has worked on every feature film he has made except *Permanent Vacation* (1980), as mentioned by Jarmusch himself (Rosenbaum 2000, 85).

sleeping, or quite literally following Nobody. In terms of the sound track, his comparatively passive, "blank slate" identity is aurally emphasized through the use of numerous short silences after he speaks. His comparative vulnerability and shifting identity is also revealed through the many repetitions of his musical theme in a fragmented form.

The first phrases of Young's main theme punctuate those frequent moments in which Blake is redefined: for instance, we hear it when he escapes from Thel's room on horseback, as he then gallops over paper roses in the mud after his first kill (Charlie), and as the film then fades again to black, signaling the start of his own journey toward death [27:29–28:04]. The theme opening also punctuates Blake's delivery of his unknowingly ironic line "I'm not dead" in response to Nobody asking whether he killed the white man that killed him, and then accompanies Nobody asking "what name were you given at birth, stupid white man?" [36:40–36:53].

Though the main "Blake" theme recurs many times in relation to (re)defining his character alone, the film also uses it to emphasize the ironic connections between Blake and Nobody. Thus, Young's music also reinforces the gradual evolution of the relationship between a white man and a Native American, one that is especially surprising in a generic context. Young uses variations on the main theme after Nobody first quotes the poetry of *the* William Blake to Depp's character [38:11–38:59],[72] and after Nobody places Blake's hat on his head and then first leads Blake on horseback [40:51–42:28]. In the latter example, a version of the theme trails off into an extended distorted reverberating note that matches the sense of unease in some handheld camerawork from Blake's woozy point of view, connecting the discontinuance of the melody's line with his faltering consciousness. In this same sequence, the first part of the theme resurfaces in a dramatically ironic way that reflects Nobody's understanding of Blake as a "dead man," just as Blake rides past a skull that is shown in the foreground at ground level (see Figure 1.23).

Soon thereafter, the music breaks off as Blake is shown coming to a halt because Nobody inexplicably stops. But the music picks up again after Nobody smilingly and cryptically says "The eagle never lost so much time, as when he submitted to learn of the crow," from Blake's *Proverbs of Hell* (1997, 39) [43:13–43:34]. This line is one of several from William Blake's poetry quoted by Nobody, including two lines from *Auguries of Innocence*—"Some are born to sweet delight/Some are born to endless night" (123–24)—that become his vocal refrain. The meaning of these quotations always eludes Depp's character. Since Nobody resumes riding without offering explanation for "The

---

[72] Here, Nobody himself tells Blake his own identity: "you are a poet, and a painter, and now you are a killer of white men."

FIGURE 1.23 Blake rides past the skull, a grimly obvious and ironically foreshadowing symbol of his journey towards death.

eagle. . ." quotation, despite Blake's blank incomprehension, the music seems playfully "with" him at this point too, therein further complicating our initial understanding of the music being attached to Blake alone.

As the film progresses, the main theme eventually becomes impossible to separate from Nobody's self-definition, as well as the Blake–Nobody connection. We hear a broken-up and extended version of the main theme as Nobody tells Blake the backstory of why he is not with his people, and of being forcibly taken to England and paraded "like a captured animal, an exhibit" [48:57–51:38]. It was in England, while he was in the white man's schools, that Nobody discovered the poetry of William Blake and the "powerful words" that spoke to him (see Figure 1.24).

The sight of a young and once-vulnerable Nobody looking manifestly inspired by *the* William Blake's poetry, is movingly and sweetly imaged as a nostalgic vignette while Nobody speaks. Nobody's backstory thus leads to a visual emphasis on his becoming connected to the poet from an early age (and thus, in his mind, the Blake standing before him). The relatively long music cue ends when Nobody finishes speaking his backstory. Thus, Young's music is closely connected with his voice as well as aurally uniting him with Depp's character. Also, in being presented as elliptical fragments, the visual episodes of Nobody's past are ironically portrayed in a rhythmically similar way to the introduction of Blake in the film's opening, further reinforcing the two characters' connectedness.

Nobody and Blake are also united by the main theme being reiterated in scenes where they each commit violence. For instance, a low variation of the main theme

FIGURE 1.24 A brief flashback shows the young Nobody discovering *the* William Blake's poetry, powerful words that spoke to him.

punctuates the moment when Nobody deliberately saves Blake's life by slitting the throat of a man intent upon shooting him (a moment that is also audiovisually punctuated by lightning), and accompanies his inadvertently killing another would-be assailant by accidently firing a rifle. The cue then tapers off as Nobody leaves the scene [59:28–1:00:35]. More variation on the main theme occurs in the scene where Blake kills two Marshals who are also intent upon killing him, after he has become an outlaw. In this scene, the first melodic note and chord of the theme punctuate the moment after one of two Marshals asks Depp's character "are you William Blake?," to which Blake responds "yes I am, do you know my poetry?" [1:15:40–1:15:44]. Blake then shoots both Marshals, the second of whom does not die right away. The theme re-enters as Blake shoots them and continues in an extended variation at a low pitch, featuring reverberating distortion and inverted intervals, as the second marshal lies writhing on the ground, grunting his way awkwardly and grotesquely to death until Blake finally shoots him dead [1:15:49–1:16:53]. Before he fires this last shot, Blake looks at his victim and echoes Nobody (and, in turn, *the* William Blake) in saying that "some are born to endless night." The theme trails off with the echoing sound of gunfire. Here, the sound track confronts loss and compromise with a degree of dark resignation.[73] The aural "messages" parallel the primary visual one here. Where Blake was shown wiping a

---

[73] Bird song then ironically takes precedence as the camera pans over the dead men, as if to imply the impassivity of the natural world.

little dirt off his hands with a pristine handkerchief in an early scene of the film, now his shirt and suit are torn and muddied, visually emphasizing that the character has learned he "must" participate in the mucky violence that defines the world of *Dead Man*. The distorted variation on the main theme reinforces the visual emphasis on how Blake has transformed himself and been transformed by circumstance. The sound of Blake's echoing gunfire combined with Young's reverberating music further emphasizes the killer he has become. This change is shown to be "necessary" in the shoot-or-be-shot Wild West as *Dead Man* presents it.[74]

Part of the main theme also recurs after Blake almost casually shoots another would-be killer dead leading up to the final sequence of the film [1:39:33–43]. Such pointed musical emphasis on so many deaths does not make for melodrama: rather, the obsessive repetition of the main theme places emphasis on the commonality of the violence and, thus, the unspectacular waste of life. The repetition of the main theme is used so much as to become a kind of cliché within the film itself: so much so that when Blake kills his last would-be killer in the film, an action punctuated by yet more of the same musical material, his casual weariness after the deed makes sense: he simply says "I'm tired." Nobody even responds to the fact of Blake having been himself shot again by the same would-be killer with a matter-of-factly obviously statement: "I see you have collected some more white man's metal."

REHEARING VIOLENCE *AND* POETRY

Most of the violence in *Dead Man* is "white man's metal" exchanged between white men rather than between white men and Native Americans. This is yet another aspect of the film that makes it a revisionist reframing of the "cowboys and Indians" violence associated with more traditional westerns. Nobody first self-consciously speaks of "white man's metal" when we meet him, in an early scene showing his attempt to extract the first bullet in Blake's chest (see Figure 1.25). At the start of the scene we hear Nobody's imprecise blade scraping against the bullet, and the squelching sound of Blake's flesh [28:06–28:36]. We also hear Nobody's grunty breaths of concentration and effort. The action is anchored in what Michel Chion calls "materializing sound indices (M.S.I.);

---

[74] By the end of the film Blake has not only killed Charlie Dickinson, but also two unnamed marshals (Jimmy Ray Weeks and Mark Bringelson), the minister at the trading post (Alfred Molina), a frontiersman named Salvatore "Sally" Jencko (Iggy Pop), and two other unidentifiable pioneers who try to shoot him, presumably for the reward offered by Mr. Dickinson. For DeAngelis, this violence is about "righting past wrongs," specifically the wrongs of white oppressors who have decimated the Native American population: for DeAngelis, Blake as a kind of scourge against white tyranny (2001, 291).

FIGURE 1.25 Nobody attempts to remove the bullet from Blake's chest, a visually messy and sonically uncomfortable representation of failed healing.

that is, the scene emphasizes details of sound that "pull the scene towards the material and concrete" (1994, 114).[75]

While the blood looks "de-realized"[76] and black in the monochrome *mise-en-scène*, seeping out around the bullet with a mesmerizing effect, the sound track is designed to make us flinch at the *reality* of Blake's wound along with the impossibility of extracting metal that is, as Nobody points out, "too deep inside." With the kind of poetic intonation associated with Native American mysticism (at least in white mainstream culture), Nobody points out that attempting to remove the bullet would "release the spirit from within." However, lest we become lost in the tangible nastiness of the wound or Nobody's somewhat clichéd observation, Nobody then mumbles "stupid fucking white man" under his breath.[77] This line, one which becomes another kind of refrain for Nobody (along with his quotations of the original Blake's poetry), not only invites a knowing acknowledgment of the absurdity of cowboy violence; it establishes his disarming ability to critique Blake as a white man even while he tries saving his life.

---

[75] The concept of M.S.I. is more fully defined and applied to the analysis of *The Piano* in the next part of this book.

[76] This is Bromley's term for the impact of the black-and-white palette (2001, 52).

[77] Gary Farmer repeats this line in his reappearance in Jarmusch's subsequent film, *Ghost Dog: Way of the Samurai*, reinforcing its resonance beyond the scope of one film. The two films are also, as Rosenbaum points out, alike in that they engage with "a deeply felt relationship between the present and the historical past" (2000, 11).

Far from romanticizing the Native American, then, *Dead Man* establishes him as the only character apparently able to perceive and voice the truth of what happens within the film. Nobody also understands the film's action in a broader context of failed civilization and colonial oppression. *Dead Man* is aligned with Nobody in making this context important. Nobody most forcefully communicates his wide-scale awareness of colonial destruction when he explains that the trading post is a place of deathly disease because of the contagion in the blankets that his people have been sold by the white men (a fact that is apparently news to Blake). As well as being the mouthpiece of history, Nobody is also, ironically, the only one who speaks poetry—and nothing less than the canonized works of Blake. This is another important element of the film's aural patterning that has potentially revisionist meaning, though not without complication. For Mary Katherine Hall, Nobody's use of Blake's poetry signifies that he "depends for authoritative expression on white discourse" and the film therefore undermines its progressive cultural politics (2001, 4). She connects this with her interpretation of Jarmusch's presumptuous conception of himself as a researcher and representer of the Native American (7). To reinforce her reading of the director's and the film's dubious appropriation of Native American culture, she also notes Depp's increasingly "Indianized appearance" after being dressed by Nobody which, given how the film ends, leads her to equate "becoming Indian" with death (8). Hall's reading is usefully provocative but nevertheless reductive. First, it is clear that being with Nobody extends Blake's life through the film. Second, as Susan Kollin puts it, Nobody's "facility with language and knowledge of culture are clearly superior to those of William Blake" (2000, 137). This second point is pressed home when he becomes infuriated by Nobody's "Indian malarkey" because the latter is quoting Blake's poetry: at this point, Blake misrecognizes "British, Romantic poetry, for the wise but cryptic words of a sage [Native American]," and therein he "unwittingly foregrounds the New Age fetish of Native cultures who mistake their own romantic mappings of [Native Americans] for the real thing" (Kollin 2000, 136). That Nobody knows Blake's enigmatic poetic language makes him a kind of intellectual answer to the authority of Ethan Edwards as one who presumes to speak the language of "Comanche."[78] As Cummings puts it, Nobody "holds the cultural capital."[79] He also adapts the original Blake's words to articulate his own rejection of colonial

---

[78] Bromley refers to Nobody as "an outcast, left to wander alone," ironically and indirectly therein providing another ironic connection with the character of Ethan Edwards (2001, 54).

[79] Because of such details as this, Cummings argues that Nobody is also an "interesting variant of the Hollywood buddy-movie 'sidekick': he steals the show" (2001, 69).

tyranny. In one especially memorable example of this, Nobody enters the trading post run by a missionary (Alfred Molina) who begins praying for protection from evil as a knee-jerk reaction to Nobody's presence. Nobody's self-possessed and self-empowering response is a quotation from Blake's *The Everlasting Gospel*: "The Vision of Christ that thou dost see/Is my Vision's Greatest Enemy" (1997, 1–2).

Along with being personally significant to Nobody, the poet Blake is a strong influence on the film, even though he lived about a century earlier than the plot unfolds. In addition to being an important poet, *the* Blake was an unusually outspoken visionary who was anti-slavery, pro-revolutionary, and "openly critical of the British monarchy in the wake of the American revolution" (DeAngelis 2001, 286). The film incorporates lines of poetry from various Blake texts in a self-consciously anachronistic way to reinforce Nobody's counter-hegemonic power. For Michael DeAngelis, the film brings "the promise of a new prophet" in Depp's character by the same name, because he is "one who might renew the transformative possibilities revealed to the land one hundred years earlier" (287). However, since *Nobody* is the one who actually speaks Blake's words, whereas Depp's character is ironically unfamiliar with them, DeAngelis's claim might well be reassigned to him.

Jarmusch himself repeatedly emphasizes the connections between Blake's poetry and Native American speech, especially in terms of its rhythms and logic. Indeed, some of the lines from Blake's poetry that Nobody speaks, such as "The eagle never lost so much time as when he submitted to learn of the crow" as well as "Drive your cart and your plow over the bones of the dead" (both from *Proverbs of Hell* (1997, 39, 2)), were chosen because they sounded like Native American sayings to Jarmusch, just as some of Nobody's pronouncements are meant to sound like Blake (Rosenbaum 2000, 74). Thus Nobody's ways of speaking—quoting Blake as well as speaking in the terms of his own people, using contemporary slang as well as speaking lines composed in the nineteenth century—bring past and present, white and Native American together. If Depp's Blake seems to be a character perpetually of the present, ill-equipped by his past, and uncertain of his future, Nobody stands for being more conscious of the historical *and* personal past, for being well equipped and self-sufficient in the present, along with being intent upon preparing his companion for the future that he knows is coming beyond his death. That Nobody's words often highlight his broad perspective in contradistinction to the narrow perceptions of Depp's Blake is part of defining *Dead Man*'s radicalism. Moreover, Farmer's voice is, quite literally, deeper and bigger than Depp's.

THE LEITMOTIF OF VIOLENCE

Despite his radical power, Nobody is eventually killed by the white man's metal. And Young's music places particular emphasis on the violence of *Dead Man* which ultimately unites all its characters in death. A secondary musical idea, subsidiary to the main theme, becomes a leitmotif in the film. This leitmotif, a phrase rather than a "theme" as Young claims, is established as especially important when it punctuates Mr. Dickinson's announcement that "the hunt is on!" (after he has contracted the killers to find Blake) [33:10–33:23] (see Figure 1.26).

This secondary musical idea is most associated with the killers, and the actions of the cruelest one, Cole Wilson, in particular: we hear it as the killers ride together on their quest to kill Blake [35:18–35:34]; after Wilson kills Johnny "The Kid" Pickett, when the comparatively heavy reverberation places emphasis on seeing the blood slowly pour from his head into a puddle [1:05:29–1:05:56]; and again after Wilson calls Pickett "a Navajo mud-toy" in response to Twill's critical observation that "he's just a kid" [1:05:59–1:06:11]. Other heavily reverberating, slower-tempo versions of the phrase are also included right after Wilson steps on a marshal's head and makes it crack open like a rotten watermelon [1:18:26–1:18:53], and yet again after Wilson is shown (*and*, all too realistically, *heard*) eating Twill's cooked, greasy hand after having shot him dead [1:19:33–1:20:03]. We hear the phrase several more times when Wilson is shown riding alone on the hunt for Blake. Obviously, in being just a few notes, this second musical idea is minimalist in the extreme. In addition, the reiterations of it include little variance other than greater use of reverberation or the elimination of a note or two. Yet every time the phrase is used, it does so in an aural close-up that demands attention. In so doing, the phrase calls attention to the violence that is non-normalized in *Dead Man*. As Rosenbaum points out, "every time someone fires a gun at someone else in this film, the gesture is awkward, unheroic, pathetic; it's an act that leaves a mess and is deprived of any pretence at existential purity, creating a sense of embarrassment and overall discomfort in the viewer" (2000, 37, 39). Rosenbaum's emphasis on the violence we see should be contextualized in terms of what we *hear*—for Young's score places emphasis on the very discomfort that Rosenbaum highlights, not least through its punctuation of Wilson's actions in particular. Because Young's music repeatedly emphasizes the most grotesque and horrific moments of the film, it is a kind of aural violence in itself.

FIGURE 1.26 Young's leitmotif for violence in *Dead Man* (transcribed directly from the DVD).

To summarize so far, then, we have dwelt on *Dead Man*'s use of particular semantic elements such as the white frontier town, the lone white hero, outlaw violence, and encounters between white men and Native Americans. Because the film incorporates so many semantic elements of the western it is readily identifiable as a contribution to that genre. Ironically, as we have explored, *Dead Man* handles every one of its semantic elements with extreme unconventionality: the white frontier town is an inhospitable place of death and dread (far from a place worth saving like the homesteads in *The Searchers*); the lone white hero is initially inept and driven by little beyond an effort to survive (unlike the revenge-bound Ethan Edwards); the violence we see is consistently nasty, confronting, and brutal (unlike the violence shot from a distance or shown in abbreviated form in *The Searchers*); and the Native American presence of Nobody is most memorably authoritative (in contrast with the Othering of numerous silent Native American extras or "nobodies" in *The Searchers*). Though *The Searchers* undoubtedly complicates a simple syntactic reading of its cultural politics, not least through its complication of the barbaric/civilized binary of the white/Indian, Steiner's music consistently pushes towards clear-cut binary distinctions. By contrast, Young's accosting, broken-up, and unpredictable score works with all other components of Jarmusch's film to aurally assert and emphasize the film's consistently revisionist syntax.

THE FINAL SCENE

Dead Man culminates in deconstructing generic expectations of a triumphant hero (or, at least a projected end to violence), a final showdown, and a sense of restoration. By the end of the film, Blake is in a small canoe, dressed in Native American clothing and surrounded by the cedar bows that Nobody added in preparation for his "journey" (see Figure 1.27).

The final images of the film emphasize the smallness of the canoe which finally becomes nothing more than a speck in the middle of the sea (see Figure 1.28). The white protagonist's fading presence in itself constitutes a radical revisioning of the genre and the final, knowing obliteration of convention.

As Blake finally sails out to sea, the canoe is initially clearly visible. But the canoe eventually all but disappears, even though it is centrally positioned in the last image of the film (see Figure 1.29).

The isolated Blake sailing off into the distance ironically alludes to the many lone cowboys that have preceded him. In relation to this point, Rosenbaum's analysis of the ending indirectly emphasizes the semantic and syntactic significance of the film in its "combining traditional elements with transgressive details" (2000, 61):

FIGURE 1.27 Blake begins his final journey to death.

FIGURE 1.28 Blake's canoe is dwarfed by the sea and sky.

[Blake] may be sailing off in a boat rather than riding away on horseback like Shane [...] and he may be bound for oblivion rather than adventure, but the epic sense of closure is satisfyingly complete (58–59).

Though *Dead Man* incorporates many familiar components of the western it also, as Rosenbaum points out, reveals a revisionist impulse that "insists on rethinking

FIGURE 1.29 Though centrally placed, Blake's canoe soon becomes "lost."

virtually all the basic props and images associated with the form" (59). So extreme are *Dead Man*'s strategies of revisionism that Rosenbaum concludes many Americans simply "weren't ready for it in 1996" (67).[80] In keeping with Jarmusch's potentially alienating approach, Young's music finally communicates a sense of futile circularity. After Nobody and Wilson shoot each other dead, the score features another variation on the main theme, then several repeated pulsating chords over the fade-out of Blake's canoe drifting away into darkness, and then a final full repetition of the main theme with the closing credits [1:55:58–2:01:12]. The neat musical repetitions which attempt to communicate restoration in *The Searchers* here communicate inconclusiveness as unending as the movements of the sea. Young's music at the end of *Dead Man* suggests our coming back to a beginning that we need to rehear.

SUMMARY

When it was released in 1956, *The Searchers* represented a profound departure from previous films directed by John Ford and starring John Wayne. With Altman's "semantic/syntactic" analysis of genre in mind, *The Searchers* interrogates many ritualistic desires and ideological lures associated with the Classical Hollywood western. This

---

[80] Similarly, drawing on Lyotard's reading of Orwell's *1984* as a text about writing "against language but necessarily with it," Bromley writes of how *Dead Man* uses the language of the western—containing many "verbal, iconic, and optical clichés of the genre"—in order to narrate against its ideology (2001, 55).

is especially clear in its damning emphasis on the protagonist's pathological racism. Despite Ford's interest in foregrounding the darker aspects of Ethan's characterization, Steiner's score tells a different story: it never complicates his status. The music also communicates an "omniscient" view, Mickey-mousing the action in many sequences which, in its obvious "rightness" for the film's images, has the effect of masking the interpretive work that it does.

Dead Man is self-consciously designed to look *and* sound different from *The Searchers*. Young's original score consistently works with other elements of the film to reinforce its atypical treatment of semantic elements and, in turn, its syntactic radicalism. Many short and accosting cues break up the film experience, enforcing our alertness to the film's revisionist construction. Young's music features an electric guitar played in unconventional ways, much as the film "plays" against the ritualistic and ideological associations of the Classical Hollywood western.

Susan Hayward argues that the sheer longevity of the western "points to America's fascination with the frontier as a site of hope for something new and better" (2006, 498). *Dead Man* does not offer the hopes of frontier progress, settlement, or white civilization that we might expect. But the film *does* represent hopeful surprises through its emphatic aural emphasis on Nobody's power, and on the connection between its two main characters that crosses ethnic lines. Where *The Searchers* ends with a closing door, *Dead Man* ends with the openness of the sea and sky.

WORKS CITED

Altman, Rick. (1984) 2012. "A Semantic/Syntactic Approach to Film Genre." In *Film Genre Reader IV*, edited by Barry Keith Grant, 27–41. Austin: University of Texas Press. Originally published in *Cinema Journal* 23 (3): 6–18.

Anderson, Kent. 2006. "John Ford: The Man Who Shot Liberty Valance." *The Journal of Popular Culture* 39 (1): 10–28.

Barker, Hugh and Yuval Taylor. 2007. *Faking It: The Quest for Authenticity in Popular Music.* New York: Norton.

Blake, William. 1997. *The Complete Poetry and Prose of William Blake.* Edited by David V. Erdman, Harold Bloom, and William Golding. New York: Anchor (Random House).

Box Office Mojo. 2011. "*Dead Man.*" Internet Movie Database. <http://boxofficemojo.com/movies/?id=deadman.htm>.

Bromley, Roger. 2001. "Dead Man Tells Tale: Tongues and Guns in Narrative of the West." *European Journal of American Culture* 20 (1): 50–64.

Buhler, James, David Neumeyer, and Rob Deemer. 2010. *Hearing the Movies: Music and Sound in Film History.* New York: Oxford University Press.

Cawelti, John. 1984. *The Six-Gun Mystique.* Bowling Green: Bowling Green State UP.

Chion, Michel. 1994. *Audio-Vision: Sound on Screen.* Edited and translated by Claudia Gorbman. New York: Columbia University Press. Originally published as *L'Audio-Vision* (Paris: Editions Nathan, 1990).

———. 1999. *The Voice in Cinema.* Edited and translated by Claudia Gorbman. New York: Columbia University Press. Originally published as *La Voix au cinéma* (Paris: *Cahiers du cinéma* (Editions de l'Etoile), 1982).

Colonnese, Tom Grayson. 2004. "Native American Reactions to *The Searchers*." In *The Searchers: Essays and Reflections on John Ford's Classic Western*, edited by Arthur M. Eckstein and Peter Lehman, 335–42. Detroit: Wayne State University Press.

Cummings, Denise K. 2001. "'Accessible Poetry'? Cultural Intersection and Exchange in Contemporary American Indian and American Independent Film." *Studies in American Indian Literature* 13 (1): 57–80.

Cumbow, Robert C. 2009. "'Somebody's Fiddle': Traditional Music in *The Searchers*." *Parallax View: Smart Words about Cinema*. Accessed April 10, 2014. <http://parallax-view.org/2009/12/13/somebody's-fiddle-traditional-music-in-the-searchers/>.

DeAngelis, Michael. 2001. "Gender and Other Transcendences: William Blake as Johnny Depp." In *Ladies and Gentlemen, Boys and Girls: Gender in Film at the End of the Twentieth Century*, edited by Murray Pomerance, 283–300. Albany: State University of New York Press.

Donnelly, K. J. 2005. *The Spectre of Sound: Music in Film and Television*. London: BFI Publishing.

Eckstein, Arthur M. 1998. "Darkening Ethan: John Ford's *The Searchers* (1956) from Novel to Screenplay to Screen." *Cinema Journal* 38 (1): 3–24.

Gallagher, Tag. 2003. "Shoot-Out at the Genre Corral: Problems in the 'Evolution' of the Western." In *Film Genre Reader III*, edited by Barry Keith Grant, 262–76. Austin: University of Texas Press.

Gorbman, Claudia. 2000. "Scoring the Indian: Music in the Liberal Western." In *Western Music and Its Others: Difference, Representation, and Appropriation in Music*, edited by Georgina Born and David Hesmondhalgh, 234–53. Berkeley, CA: University of California Press.

Hall, Mary Katherine. 2001. "Now You Are a Killer of White Men: Jim Jarmusch's *Dead Man* and Traditions of Revisionism in the Western." *Journal of Film and Video* 52 (4): 3–14.

Hayward, Susan. 2006. *Cinema Studies: The Key Concepts*. 3rd ed. London: Routledge.

Ingrassia, Catherine. 1998. "Writing the West: Iconic and Literal Truth in *Unforgiven*." *Literature/Film Quarterly* 26 (1): 53–59.

JanMohamed, Abdul R. (1985) 2006. "The Economy of Manichean Allegory." In *The Post-Colonial Studies Reader*, edited by Bill Ashcroft, Gareth Griffiths, and Helen Tiffin, 19–23. 2nd ed. London: Routledge. Extracted from "The Economy of Manichean Allegory: The Function of Racial Difference." *Critical Inquiry* 12 (1): 59–87.

Kalinak, Kathryn. 2007. *How the West Was Sung: Music in the Westerns of John Ford*. Berkeley: University of California Press.

———. 2012. "Introduction." In *Music in the Western: Notes from the Frontier*, edited by Kathryn Kalinak, 1–18. New York: Routledge.

Kilpatrick, Jacqueline. 1999. *Celluloid Indians: Native Americans and Film*. Lincoln: University of Nebraska Press.

Kitses, Jim. 1969. *Horizons West*. Bloomington: Indiana University Press.

Kollin, Susan. 2000. "Dead Man, Dead West." *Arizona Quarterly* 56 (3): 125–54.

Kozloff, Sarah. 2000. *Overhearing Film Dialogue*. Berkeley, CA: University of California Press.

Kubernik, Harvey. 2006. *Hollywood Shack Job: Rock Music in Film and on Your Screen*. Albuquerque: University of New Mexico Press.

Kupfer, Joseph H. 2008. "The Seductive and Subversive Meta-Narrative of *Unforgiven*." *Journal of Film and Video* 60 (3):103–14.

Luhr, William. 2004. "John Wayne and *The Searchers*." In *The Searchers: Essays and Reflections on John Ford's Classic Western*, edited by Arthur M. Eckstein and Peter Lehman, 75–92. Detroit: Wayne State University Press.

Neale, Steve. (1990) 2012. "Questions of Genre." In *Film Genre Reader IV*, edited by Barry Keith Grant, 178–202. Austin: University of Texas Press. Originally published in *Screen* 31 (1): 45–66.

Pye, Douglas. 1975. "The Western (Genre and Movies)." *Movie* 20:29–43. Reprinted in Barry Keith Grant, ed. 2003. *Film Genre Reader III*, 203–18. Austin: University of Texas Press.

———. 2004. "Double Vision: Miscegenation and Point of View in *The Searchers*." In *The Searchers: Essays and Reflections on John Ford's Classic Western*, edited by Arthur M. Eckstein and Peter Lehman, 223–38. Detroit: Wayne State University Press.

Redding, Arthur. 2007. "Frontier Mythographies: Savagery and Civilization in Frederick Jackson Turner and John Ford." *Literature Film Quarterly* 35 (4): 313–22.

Rickman, Gregg. 1999. "The Western under Erasure: *Dead Man.*" In *The Western Reader,* edited by Jim Kitses and Gregg Rickman, 381–404. New York: Proscenium Publishers.

Rosenbaum, Jonathan. 2000. *Dead Man.* London: BFI Publishing.

Scheurer, Timothy. 2008. *Music and Mythmaking in Film: Genre and the Role of the Composer.* Jefferson, NC: McFarland & Company, Inc.

Scorsese, Martin, perf. and screenplay. 1995. *A Personal Journey with Martin Scorsese Through American Movies.* DVD. Co-directed by Martin Scorsese and Michael Henry Wilson. Santa Monica, CA: BFI TV.

Shively, JoEllen. 1992. "Cowboys and Indians: Perceptions of Western Films among American Indians and Anglos." *American Sociological Review* 57 (6): 725–34.

Sorensen, Sue. 2007. "Rocker Auteurs: David Byrne and Neil Young as Film Directors." *Studies in Popular Culture* 30 (1): 104–23.

Stilwell, Robynn J. 2007. "The Fantastical Gap between Diegetic and Nondiegetic." In *Beyond the Soundtrack: Representing Music in Cinema,* edited by Daniel Goldmark, Lawrence Kramer, and Richards Leppert, 184–202. Berkeley, CA: University of California Press.

Suárez, Juan A. 2007. *Jim Jarmusch.* Urbana: University of Illinois Press.

Susman, Gary. 1996. "Dead Man Talking." *The Boston Phoenix,* May 9–16. <http://www.bostonphoenix.com/alt1/archive/movies/reviews/050996/DEAD_BAR.html>.

Vernet, Marc. 1976. *Lectures du film.* Paris: Albatros.

Walker, Elsie. 2012. "Introduction: Teaching Music and the Moving Image and the Value of Praxis." *Music and the Moving Image* 5 (2): 1–8.

Young, Neil. Interview with Terry Gross. *Fresh Air.* NPR. March 25, 2004.

Postcolonialism

4

INTRODUCTION

"Colonialism, Racism, and Representation: An Introduction" by Robert Stam and Louise Spence

Our analysis of the sound tracks of *The Searchers* and *Dead Man* entailed some consideration of racial politics. In particular, we considered how the Native American characters of both westerns are aurally defined in relation to the white characters. However, this was but a part of our overall approach to the semantic and syntactic elements of the sound tracks. Here, we will be much more squarely focused on racial politics from a postcolonial perspective. Our case studies are two contemporary films from Australia: *Rabbit-Proof Fence* (2002) and *Ten Canoes* (2006).

Postcolonial theory is a vast area of interdisciplinary study. It is an especially challenging theory to introduce because the fundamental concepts with which it is primarily concerned—colonial and postcolonial realities, race, ethnicity, nationhood, and culture—are all themselves sites of complex debate. Where it is possible to define particular concepts for other theoretical approaches relatively easily—such as the syntactic versus semantic approaches in genre studies—the concepts of postcolonial theory cannot be "fixed" the same way. To quote the title of Chinua Achebe's groundbreaking novel, *"Things Fall Apart"* (1992)[1] as soon as we attempt to whittle down postcolonial theory to any essential meanings. As Robert Stam points out, there is a most immediate problem with the term "postcolonial" in itself because it implies that "colonialism is over," thus "obscuring deformative traces of the colonial

---

[1] As W. B. Yeats writes in his poem "The Second Coming" (1996, from which Achebe took his title), "the center cannot hold"—this phrase communicates a sense of radical indeterminacy, one that is repeatedly applied within postcolonial studies to shifting perceptions of its fundamental concepts.

hangover in the present, while at the same time delegitimizing research into the pre-colonial past."[2] Similarly, Linda Hutcheon explains that "the prefix *post* is not only premature but also has the disadvantage of embodying the ideology of linear progress that underpinned empire, as well as continuing to orient analysis around the colonial center" (1995, 9). And yet Hutcheon also argues that the prefix can signify "resistance and opposition, the anticolonial" (10). Moreover, as Laura Marks points out, the term "postcolonial" does have advantages in that it "emphasizes the history of power relations between the entities it designates" (1999, 8).[3] We shall use the term to acknowledge the historical *and* lasting impact of colonial rule in the context of analyzing two film texts that are resistant to it.

As with the other parts of this book, our approach is grounded in but one foundational article: "Colonialism, Racism, and Representation: An Introduction" by Robert Stam and Louise Spence ([1983] 2004). This article in turn draws from other foundational works on colonialism and racism. It directly cites Franz Fanon's *The Wretched of the Earth* (*Les Damnés de la Terre*, 1961), an important book about the devastatingly dehumanizing impact of colonization. Fanon's study relates to a key film cited by Stam and Spence, *The Battle of Algiers* (1966), a groundbreaking example of using "the identificatory mechanisms of cinema on behalf of the colonized rather than the colonizer" (885–86).[4] Stam and Spence cite numerous other examples of scholarly work about racism and colonialism in cinema. They write with a view to broad applicability, speaking to "all situations. . . in which difference is transformed into 'other'-ness and exploited or penalized by and for [those in] power" (878). Their arguments about filmic representations of colonial prejudice resonate with manifestations of sexism, class subordination, and anti-Semitism. Equally, not all their illustrative examples pertain to specific postcolonial experiences. So, their article not only works as our foundational text for

---

[2] Stam makes this point, with reference to Ella Shohat's article "Notes on the Postcolonial" (1992, 295). In addition, as Hayward points out, there is debate about whether to spell the word with or without a hyphen. "Post-colonial" tends to refer "to the historical concept of the post-colonial state," whereas "postcolonial" tends to refer to "varying practices that in some way are influenced by or relate to the post-colonial moment." The latter is therefore used more in relation to cultural practices (such as applying theory). Some critics use the spellings interchangeably. Like Hayward, we shall favor "postcolonial" except when referring explicitly to the "historical moment of post-colonialism" (2006, 293).

[3] For more on the complexities of the term, see Mishra and Hodge (1991). For more on how films allow us to understand the concept of postcoloniality, with emphasis on their *visual* messages from a pedagogical standpoint, see Heffelfinger and Wright (2011).

[4] Two other foundational works cited by Stam and Spence are Fanon's *Black Skin, White Masks* (1967), a psychoanalytic study of the traumas of racism and colonialism, and Edward Saïd's *Orientalism* (1978), a study of the Eurocentric prejudice behind "crude, essentialized caricatures" of Arab and Moslem peoples that has made them "vulnerable to military aggression" (Saïd 1980).

postcolonial study; it also resonates with the parts of this book about feminism and queer theory through which we will explore various forms of gendered and sexual prejudice.

Stam and Spence's article not only responds to other postcolonial scholarship, but also supplies definitions of key terms within postcolonial studies, and proposes a methodology of concerns "addressable to specific texts" (878). First, they take to task pre-existing scholarly work focused upon social portrayal, plot, and character in relation to questions of "narrative plausibility and mimetic accuracy, negative stereotypes and positive images" (878). Stam and Spence argue that such focal points have led to an overarching emphasis on realism that "has often betrayed an exaggerated faith in the possibilities of verisimilitude in art in general and the cinema in particular, avoiding the fact that films are inevitably constructs, fabrications, representations" (878). In turn, we will knowingly analyze sound tracks as constructions that work with other cinematic constructions, and which have coercive impact largely in relation to the *impressions of reality* within a given film. Though we shall not suggest that any film can represent reality without fabrication, we shall consider how each sound track engages us with the historical and contemporary actualities of colonial and postcolonial experience.

Though some sound tracks do not call attention to their own construction, we must be aware that they are all designed to create affective impact—to pretend otherwise is to assume the possibility of neutrality or unmediated authenticity. When it comes to approaching film from a postcolonial point of view, this can in itself be an insidious form of threat. If we assume it is possible to neutrally and/or authentically represent the reality of any history, and its people in turn, we risk not only assuming too much about what we know, but also limiting the forms of identity that that same people may have. We also run the risk of failing to hear (let alone see) the full implications of a given cinematic representation. This, in turn, goes against the grain of much postcolonial theory that is resistant to essentialism. In terms of representing colonial or postcolonial subjects in particular, Stam and Spence point out that even positive images can be a kind of trap: " 'nice' images might at times be as pernicious as overtly degrading ones, providing a bourgeois façade for paternalism, a more pervasive racism" (878). With this in mind, we should consider the extent to which each sound track prompts nuanced as well as non-essentializing possibilities for understanding a film's characters.

In the next section of their article, Stam and Spence provide definitions of some crucial terms, including "colonialism" and "racism." First, "colonialism" is defined as the process by which "European powers (including the United States) reached a position of economic, military, political and cultural domination in much of Asia, Africa, and Latin America" (878–79). Dating colonialism at least as far back as to the "voyages of discovery," Stam and Spence explain that it "reached an apogee between 1900 and the end of World War I (at which point Europe had colonized roughly 85 percent of the earth) and began to be reversed only with the disintegration of the European colonial empires after World War II" (879). The use of the term "reversed" is surprising here, for it suggests the possibility of literally undoing colonial impact. This quibble aside, it is important to absorb Stam and Spence's emphasis on the long history and massive outreach of colonial forces. While we should be alert to the irreducible specificities of time and space represented in each of our case study films, we should also consider their potentially widescale resonance. Ultimately, both *Rabbit-Proof Fence* and *Ten Canoes* "speak to" global, rather than solely Australian, audiences.

Stam and Spence define "racism" as a term not solely resonant in colonial contexts ("anti-Semitism being a case in point"), though is it often read as a product *and* ally of the colonization process. Many victims of racism are "those whose identity was forged within the colonial process: blacks in the United States, Arab workers in France, all of whom share an oppressive situation and the status of second-class citizens" (879). We shall consider how both our sound tracks communicate and represent resistance to racial oppression, especially through privileging the aural presences of Aboriginal peoples. There is, as we shall explore, a long history of underrepresenting *and* demonizing Aborigines on screen that both our case study films attempt to "answer." *Rabbit-Proof Fence* focuses on the historically documented colonial effort to eradicate Aborigines through marrying "half-castes" to whites, reflecting an institutionalized belief in the superiority of white culture. *Ten Canoes* seeks to reanimate history by representing memories of Aboriginal life *before* colonization. The films are united in using sound tracks that privilege Aboriginal perspectives, challenging the Eurocentric bias of Australian cinema to date.

As Stam and Spence explain, the cinematic camera is often wielded as a colonial tool, oppressing, marginalizing, or Othering the racial minority. Cinema can also be a kind of "magic carpet" that "flies us around the globe and makes us, by virtue of our subject position, its audiovisual masters. It produces us as subjects, transforming us into armchair conquistadors, affirming our sense of power while making the inhabitants of the Third World objects of spectacle for the First World's voyeuristic gaze" (880). This argument can be applied to the racially marginalized peoples of all nations, especially when the camera objectifies them. Note that the racial power relations identified by Stam and Spence are introduced in primarily visual terms. We will of course redirect these towards the aural dimensions of cinema. We shall especially consider how the sound tracks position us to perceive the Aboriginal peoples of both *Rabbit-Proof Fence* and *Ten Canoes* as much more than the objects of our conquering look.

The earliest cinema was contemporary with "the height of European imperialism," and colonized peoples were first filmically represented in that context of ideological oppression. In particular, Spence and Stam allude to the "hundreds" of Hollywood westerns that inverted history by making Native Americans "appear to be intruders on what was originally their land" (881). Crucially, Stam and Spence also point to the *absent* representations of oppressed groups. *King of Jazz* (1930), for instance, is a film focused on the origins of jazz in relation to several diverse European groups while "completely bypassing both Africa and Afro-Americans" (881). Here, Stam and Spence also allude to *The Wrong Man* (1957), a film that includes scenes on the subways and in the prisons of New York City without showing any blacks. Such examples are referred to as "structured absences" by Stam and Spence to denote the intentional disregard or deliberate avoidance of marginalized peoples. In this context, we should remember that Aborigines are seldom the main characters within mainstream Australian cinema, let alone the audiovisual focal points that they are in *Rabbit-Proof Fence* and *Ten Canoes*. This will help us understand how much is at stake in our hearing both films fully.

Stam and Spence give an aural dimension to their discussion of "structured absences" by noting that "the absence of the language of the colonized is also symptomatic of colonialist attitudes" (882). In particular, "the languages spoken by Third World peoples are often reduced to an incomprehensible jumble of background murmurs, while major 'native' characters are consistently obliged to meet the colonizer on the colonizer's linguistic turn" (882). This point could be extended to representations of any non-English-speaking peoples in Western cinema. The dominance of English at the expense of other languages is alluded to in *The Searchers* when Scar throws back Ethan's condescending acknowledgement of his linguistic proficiency ("you pretty good American, someone teach you?") by saying "you speak good Comanche, someone *teach you?*" That said, the confrontational moment is complicated because the actor playing Scar is actually speaking Navajo. Our case study films for postcolonialism are much more explicitly concerned with incorporating Native speech. In *Rabbit-Proof Fence*, the frequent absence of Aboriginal language and the dominance of English is represented critically, and *Ten Canoes* may be heard entirely in Aboriginal languages (though there are alterative audio options that incorporate English on the DVD).

As Homi Bhabha has influentially argued, representations of "the [racial] other" tend to be "more defined by the colonist or settler's self-interested projections than actual indigeneity" (Crosbie 2007, 136).[5] Stam and Spence point out that many

---

oppressed peoples have attempted to challenge their being objectified within colonist histories of representation by attempting to represent reality "from within." Moreover, such groups have favored "progressive realism," a form of representation that gives the voices of those who are typically marginalized more primacy, thus inverting the ideological status quo. Both *Rabbit-Proof Fence* and *Ten Canoes* attempt to progressively privilege Aboriginal stories "from within." The sound tracks of both films are crucial in this process. As we shall hear, the more recent film is especially authoritative in this regard because its entire cast is Aboriginal actors who improvised their own lines in Aboriginal languages.

In relation to the progressive possibilities of cinema, Stam and Spence hasten to add that the concept "realism" itself is highly problematic when applied to any film. After all, we may debate the extent to which any "truth" can be immediately and fully captured by the camera. It is here that they make a crucial distinction between a Brechtian concept of realism that lays bare its own constructions and realism "as a style or constellation of strategies aimed at producing an illusionistic 'reality effect'" (883).[6] In terms of representing realism, *Rabbit-Proof Fence* is focused on creating an illusionistic, enveloping experience based on historical truths, although at times it deliberately foregrounds clashes between aural and visual messages that invite Brechtian comprehension. *Ten Canoes*, on the other hand, provides us with an aurally immersive experience of specific Australian terrain and its indigenous inhabitants, while at the same time consistently calling attention to its own sonically controlled processes of construction. It is, therefore, more consistently Brechtian. Again, however, the films are united through using sound to amplify progressive challenges to the dominant white cinema of Australia.

Along with exploring what is at stake in the structured absences as well as the forms of realism represented on film, Stam and Spence also zoom in on the relative value (and danger) of the racialized "positive image." They argue that while scholarly work on racism in cinema previously stressed the importance of positive images, such an approach is reductive and potentially dangerous. First, to insist on positive images of a minority people could translate into characters that are either implausible or made in the image of the white man: as examples, they cite the non-threatening role played by Sidney Poitier (a black man "on white terms") in *Guess Who's Coming to Dinner* (1967),

---

[6] The case study of *Rabbit-Proof Fence* includes a much fuller discussion defining Brechtian cinema. Though we must acknowledge that Brechtian theory is a Western avant-garde approach not necessarily commensurate with Aboriginal culture, both our case study films show the benefits of applying it. This analysis is by no means a presumption of how either film might resonate for the Aboriginal people of Australia.

along with the black heroes of *Shaft* (1971) who are simply substituted for roles usually played by white actors.[7] Here, Stam and Spence also resist the essentialism that comes with representing and understanding characters as only either "good" or "bad" (884).

In opening up more nuanced possibilities for exploring what characters embody, we must consider the exact filmic context in which they appear, or all the *"mediations which intervene between 'reality' and representation"* (884, original emphasis). Stam and Spence themselves consider generic frameworks: for example, satirical films tend to be more concerned with challenging stereotypical prejudices than with "constructing positive images" (885), as in the example of *Blazing Saddles* and how it "lampoons a whole range of ethnic prejudices" by having whites sing "Ole Man River" and blacks sing "I Get No Kick from Champagne" (885). Here is a key (albeit fleeting) example of Stam and Spence calling attention to the importance of sound in mediating reality. We shall develop this genre-based approach with regard to Peter Gabriel's scoring for *Rabbit-Proof Fence*. On the one hand, the score is generic in several ways: it is traditionally structured (featuring leitmotifs and memorable themes), it is easily classifiable as world music, and it works for the film as a road movie/historical drama. But Gabriel's music also expands the limitations of generic frameworks through its ultimately unconventional honoring of the three young Aboriginal protagonists. *Ten Canoes*, by contrast, does not fit within a Western generic narrative framework. In being the first feature film entirely in Aboriginal languages, it also literally sounds different from any other film before it.

Along with considering films within generic contexts, Stam and Spence consider the positioning of the spectator. They especially dwell on how and what the camera prompts the spectator to see. In watching a western, for instance, the viewer will often be positioned as if behind the barrel of a rifle aimed at Indians for whom sympathetic identification is disallowed.[8] Stam and Spence here mention *The Battle of Algiers* because it dignifies the representation of a colonized people with close-ups and camerawork from their perspectives (886). They also highlight the importance of point-of-view editing

---

[7] Stam and Spence make an important connection between such film roles and Roland Barthes's famous analysis of a *Paris Match* cover featuring a black soldier in French uniform as he looks up to and salutes what we presume to be the French flag. The image collapses difference in terms of the ideological statement that all citizens, "regardless of color, can serve law and order" ([1983] 2004, 883). Thus, by implication, it is an image of how to hegemonically maintain the status quo that oppresses the marginalized subject (Barthes 1972, 116).

[8] Here Stam and Spence draw on Tom Englehardt's work on filmic depictions of encounters between whites and Indians. This argument also resonates with JoEllen Shiveley's article about *The Searchers* (1992), which explores how even Native American audiences have found themselves siding with Ethan, largely due to the visual logic of the film.

and subjective aural techniques that foreground the perceptions of the colonized people in the film. In short, the film "exploits conventional identification mechanisms on behalf of a group traditionally denied them" (887). Though sound is again at the margins of Stam and Spence's analysis, we will bring it to the fore. Both *Rabbit-Proof Fence* and *Ten Canoes* use visual techniques to subversively focus our attention on Aboriginal characters, but in both cases the sound track goes even further in prompting us to understand who they are and why they matter.

In the context of considering film style, Stam and Spence refer to how a film "speaks" in a figurative sense: here they mention plot and character, as well as visual elements of style (composition, framing, scale), in addition to off- and on-screen sound and music. They also highlight the importance of hearing *as* characters do in terms of connecting us to them. For instance, *Black Girl* (1966) invokes sympathy for a Sengalese maid through showing her work assiduously while we hear her employers complain about her "laziness" off-screen. In addition, some close-ups during this scene make it clear that we hear as she does: we thus perceive the injustice against her through a strongly sympathetic perceptual alignment. Both our case study films resonate with this example, for *Rabbit-Proof Fence* and *Ten Canoes* repeatedly ask us to hear everything *with* their Aboriginal characters, and they both use visual techniques to reinforce this aural alignment.

Stam and Spence rightly argue that music can be crucial in terms of a film's postcolonial politics and its positioning of the spectator. Indigenous music may be used as a form of "Othering," as in the clichéd use of the tom-tom beat in the western to presage or accompany the presence of "barabaric" Natives. We have already considered the power of such loaded music in relation to *The Searchers*. That said, there are strong examples of using indigenous music differently: Stam and Spence specifically mention *Der Leone Have Sept Cabeças* (*The Lion Has Seven Heads*, 1970) for treating African polyrhythms "with respect" while it ironically associates "La Marseillaise" with "the puppets of colonialism" (889). We shall, in turn, pay particular attention to how the Aboriginal music of *Rabbit-Proof Fence* and *Ten Canoes* positions its audience. We shall open up the discussion further by considering how music works with other elements of film sound, especially with *Ten Canoes* since it uses music rather sparingly.

Towards the end of their article, Stam and Spence open up further broad considerations for analyzing film because single examples can seem to be *both* progressive and regressive (889). Similarly, we shall balance our attention to the progressive elements of the sound tracks for *Rabbit-Proof Fence* and *Ten Canoes* with some consideration of their ideological limitations. We shall explore how Peter Gabriel's music for *Rabbit-Proof Fence*, for example, favors globalizing and universalist aural implications, rather than rooting the Aboriginal protagonists' experiences in a specific time and place. Such music potentially detracts from the film's ability to represent a particular history from a uniquely Aboriginal perspective. Similarly, the dialogue of *Ten Canoes* was entirely improvised by its Aboriginal actors, yet their white director received screenplay credit, prompting us to acknowledge the enduring inequalities built into film production. Because Stam and Spence prompt us to allow for readings against the grain, we shall consider some unsettling possibilities within both films that pull away from what they manifestly represent.

Ultimately, Stam and Spence empower us with a series of possibilities for decoding and deconstructing racist images and sounds, *and* for perceiving progressive representations of race (891). Because their article is extremely broad-ranging in its application, it has been constructively applied in numerous scholarly works about diverse cinematic representations of race. A few representative examples include Gary Edgerton's (1994) study of "Hollywood Indians" and *The Last of the Mohicans* (1992), N. Finnegan's (1999) analysis of how *Like Water for Chocolate* (1992) positions the non-Mexican spectator as an "armchair conquistador," Ryan Trimm's (2007) discussion of the British film *Prospero's Books* (1991) in relation to postcolonial readings of its primary literary source *The Tempest*, and Catriona Moore and Stephen Muecke's (1984) survey of racist filmic representations of Australian Aborigines. Stam and Spence's article is often assigned in current tertiary courses on postcolonial theory and world cinema, and has also been repeatedly anthologized, as in the recent second edition of *The Post-Colonial Studies Reader*, edited by Bill Ashcroft, Gareth Griffths, and Helen Tiffin (2006).[9]

However, the article is not without its detractors. Lola Young, for instance, takes Stam and Spence to task for disavowing the importance of "realism" to many spectators in favor of a Brechtian approach: she writes that "the desire for 'authentic' representations of 'life as it really is' is not only strong but also encouraged by the continued use of those forms of realism which purport to be a 'window on the world'" (1996, 6). Young also argues that Stam and Spence tend to avoid necessary complexity in two ways: first by failing to place racially stereotypical representations in specific historical contexts and, second, by failing to account for different spectorial positions within specific cultural contexts (6–7). We shall therefore complement our application of Stam and Spence's fundamental arguments with some consideration of how the sound tracks for *Rabbit-Proof Fence* and *Ten Canoes* bolster the illusion of authentic access to history,

---

[9] This anthology is an excellent source for further reading, with a view to expanding the possibilities of analyzing the postcolonial meaning of sound tracks beyond the scope of this book.

resonate with historical trends of representing Aboriginal culture on screen, and invite different spectorial positions within specific interpretive contexts.

ABORIGINES ON SCREEN

Numerous filmic representations of Aboriginal culture resonate with those examples provided by Stam and Spence as further evidence of long-standing racism within mainstream cinema. Before we zoom in on our case study films, we should consider the historical cinematic trends that set their progressiveness apart. As Moore and Muecke observe, Aborigines played a "very minor part" in Australian narrative cinema prior to the 1970s. Those Aboriginal characters that were included were typically cast "as savages, as ferocious nuisances to colonial endeavor. Their roles, sometimes even their appearances, were indistinguishable from those of blacks in Tarzan-type movies" (1984, 38). Similarly, Sylvie Shaw writes that "representations of Aboriginal peoples in Australian film have historically been both informed by racist ideologies and conducive to the strengthening of those ideologies in mainstream Australian culture" (2009).[10] She also notes that the concept of Aboriginality has been largely informed by "the imagined representations of white Australia" rather than direct dialogue with Aboriginal people (1). Or, as Marcia Langton puts it, "Australians do not know and relate to Aboriginal people. They relate to stories told by former colonists" (2003, 33). Graeme Turner writes that most Aboriginal characters in Australian films are confused primitives, or people "constrained by their race (or their 'blood')," or members of a "disappearing, anachronistic species for whom we should accept responsibility and feel sympathy" (1988, 136).

In short, Aboriginal characters are not only marginally represented, but limited to certain "types" of Othered people. White actors played Aboriginals in blackface from 1907 (in *Robbery Under Arms*) to 1967 (in *Journey out of Darkness*). Since the early days, many Australian films focus on a white bush ranger being served by an Aborigine as "faithful companion" and "Noble Savage": for example, in *Assigned to His Wife* (1911) the "dramatic highlight" is an Aboriginal boy named Yacka diving 250 feet over a precipice into a river to save his white friend named Jack.[11] Even the notable exceptions, those films featuring more complex sympathetic Aboriginal characters, are controversial. One important such exception is *Walkabout* (1971). On the one hand, the film

---

[10] Here Shaw draws on Graeme Turner (1988, 135).

[11] The main historical points of this paragraph draw from Gillard (2009). Gillard's argument about *Assigned to His Wife* echoes Pike and Cooper's description (1998, 28).

fetishizes the iconic presence of a mostly silent black man in contrast with much more vocal white characters; on the other hand, the film prompts our keen interest in him as both heroic and tragic. The Aboriginal character is an adolescent (David Gulpilil) who meets a white teenage girl (Jenny Agutter) and her little brother (Luc Roeg) after they are abandoned by their father in the outback. He breaks the protocol of his own solitary "walkabout" (an important rite of passage in Aboriginal culture) to help the other children. After becoming attracted to the white girl, he eventually commits suicide, an action that is never explained but which is the climactic sadness of the film.

The aural patterns of *Walkabout* reflect the shifting racial politics of the 1970s.[12] White Australian culture is associated with negative sounds: oppressive voices, shouting, distorted noises, sounds of violence (a gunshot, a butcher's hacking, a radio chef's descriptions of killing and eating animals), and extracts from Karlheinz Stockhausen's *Hymnen* (an unsettling example of *musique concrète* that electronically transforms national anthems). These sounds contrast with the more positive potential power of Aboriginal singing and instruments (clapsticks and the didjeridu).[13] The most pleasing (Western) scoring in the film, by John Barry, is associated with scenes of the white main characters when they are in the Aboriginal adolescent's safe company. Though Barry's score romanticizes the Aboriginal lead in ways that might seem reductive, along with the many scenes that reduce him to an iconic embodiment of "nature," *Walkabout* was still subversive for its time. Because it aurally inverts the dominant pattern of Australian cinema as it typically sidelines or negatively represents Aboriginal presences, it is an important sonic precursor to both *Rabbit-Proof Fence* and *Ten Canoes*.[14]

Both our case studies feature Aboriginal characters who are aurally dominant. Their aural dominance defines the comparative radicalism of these films, especially in the context of Australian cinematic history. With this history in mind, and with regard to Stam and Spence's article, we shall apply the following questions to the sound tracks of *Rabbit-Proof Fence* and *Ten Canoes*. Considering the open-ended and ever-changing

---

[12] Particular legislative changes reflected new attitudes of the 1970s: the Aboriginal Embassy in Canberra was established in 1972, and a year later the National Aboriginal Conference was established with the goal of communicating "the wishes of the Aboriginal and Islander people to the Federal Government" (Moore and Muecke 1984, 39).

[13] For a much broader, musicological exploration of relationships between Western musics and non-Western musics, one that is much-influenced by postcolonial theoretical approaches to "race/class power," (8) "representations of difference" (46), and "forms of appropriation" (46), see the collection of essays edited by Born and Hesmondhalgh (2000).

[14] For more on *Walkabout* in relation to other cinematic representations of Australian Aboriginals (in *Bitter Springs* (1950), *Jedda* (1955), and *The Chant of Jimmie Blacksmith* (1978)), see Hickling-Hudson (1990).

expansion of postcolonial studies, these questions are but a beginning in relation to sound tracks:

- What forms of colonial and/or post-colonial reality does the sound track represent?
- Does the sound track attempt to reinforce an illusionist perspective, thereby suggesting an authoritative (or presumptuous) representation of a marginalized people? Or, does the sound track call attention to its own construction in a Brechtian manner, thereby foregrounding the film as self-conscious representation of a people?
- Does the sound track amplify the goodness or badness of colonized peoples? Or, does it offer the possibility of a more nuanced interpretation of colonized peoples?
- How does the sound track represent the historical fact of the colonizing process and its impact? Does the sound track, for instance, amplify the violence or exploitation of the colonial process?
- What, if anything, does the sound track do to undermine the self-flattering image or the power of the colonizer/oppressor?
- Does the sound track reveal, or conceal, any "structured absences"?
- How does the sound track position the perceiver in relation to the characters? In particular, whose perspectives are we encouraged to hear most strongly?

5

RABBIT-PROOF FENCE

PLOT SUMMARY

Rabbit-Proof Fence is based on a true story of three Aboriginal girls—Molly (Everlyn Sampi), Daisy (Tianna Sansbury), and Gracie (Laura Monaghan)—who ran away from an Australian colonial school in 1931 (see Figure 2.1).

Early on, the film shows the girls being captured from their home by a white official named Constable Riggs (Jason Clarke). Riggs drives them to the school at Moore River Native Settlement where they are forbidden to speak their own language and instructed on how to assimilate themselves within white culture. In taking the girls there, Riggs is following the instructions of the "Chief Protector of Aborigines," Mr. A. O. Neville

FIGURE 2.1 Daisy, Gracie, and Molly (from left to right): the protagonists of *Rabbit-Proof Fence.*

(Kenneth Branagh), who spearheads a governmentally authorized plan to phase out a rising population of "half-castes" in colonial Australia: first, by making sure they have white education; and second, by ensuring that they are married off to whites. Neville himself explains to his secretary that Daisy is of "particular concern" because she has been "promised to a full blood."

Neville's plans are critically represented in *Rabbit-Proof Fence,* and the school at Moore River is portrayed as a sickening and dangerous place in connection with him. Nina (Natasha Wanganeen), the head girl or "Dormitory Boss" of the school, tells Molly, Gracie, and Daisy that many others like them have attempted escape but have always been found and violently punished. The new girls even witness one such escapee being brought back by the Aboriginal tracker, Moodoo (David Gulpilil), and then violently punished during their short stay there. Undeterred, Molly initiates her escape with Daisy and Gracie. The girls then traverse over one thousand miles over a period of nine weeks.[15] Well into the journey, Gracie is recaptured after hearing a rumor spread by Neville about the location of her mother, and separating from the other girls to find her mother there. Molly and Daisy witness her recapture by Riggs from a safe distance and then find their way home after identifying the rabbit-proof fence that extends all the way back to their camp near Jigalong (Southwestern Australia). The film's climactic scene shows Daisy and Molly united with their mother Maude (Ningali Lawford) and their grandmother (Myarn Lawford).

The title of the film is historically important. Rabbit-proof fences were built in Australia by the white settlers as a strategy for keeping the rabbit plague in the east from spreading to the farming of the west. As Doris Pilkington,[16] the author of the book upon which the film is based (and Molly's real-life daughter), puts it:

[T]he fence was a typical response by white people to a problem of their own making. Building a fence to keep the rabbits out proved to be a futile attempt by the government of the day. For the three runaways, the fence was a symbol of love, home and security.

Rabbit-Proof Fence focuses upon how the girls make a symbol of colonial rule their salvation, and how they turn their own story of potential tragedy into one of

---

[15] The exact distance covered by the girls differs in various accounts of the film and in relation to Pilkington's memoir (2002).

[16] Pilkington's "traditional name is Nugi and kinship name is Garimara" (Emberley 2008, 152).

extraordinary endurance. Despite the film's emphasis on their victory, however, the film closes with several explanatory titles revealing that the practice of removing children from their families continued right up until 1970, thirty years after Neville retired. The film finally asks us to consider the ongoing legacy of this practice: the closing titles assert that "Today many of these Aboriginal people continue to suffer from this destruction of identity, family life, and culture. We call them the Stolen Generations."[17] The use of "we" and "them" here reflects that the film's storytelling is primarily from a white, or non-Aboriginal, point of view. That said, as we shall explore, the film also attempts to give us intimacy with the experiences of the Aboriginal girl protagonists, especially because its affecting sound track almost always amplifies what they perceive.

PHILLIP NOYCE: SUBVERSIVE DIRECTOR OR CINEMATIC CONQUISTADOR?

The director of *Rabbit-Proof Fence*, Phillip Noyce, first made his name through subversive Australian documentaries and fiction films. One of his short documentaries titled *God Know Why But It Works* (1975), for example, is designed to prompt frank discussion of racial politics in high schools. It features archival and reconstructed footage to represent the life's work of Dr. Archie Kalokarions, "a radical champion of the use of vitamin C to treat health problems of Aborigines in remote rural areas" (Villella 2002). One of his early "iconic" fiction films is *Backroads* (1977), a story focused on a white drifter and young Aborigine who steal a car, drive across the country, and pick up various people on the road. The car they drive is a microcosm of the nation, and is the means by which the lead characters are compelled to confront truths together within a confined space. In the context of surveying many stereotypical representations of Aborigines (especially as demonized Others, or as useless welfare-dependents), Marcia Langton points out that in *Backroads* "we are taken for the first time to an Aboriginal reserve where people are happy, not only because they are inebriated, but because they possess a radical sense of humor and sing in the laconic Aboriginal country and western style" (1983, 42). The film was released ten years after Australian Aborigines had been granted the right to vote ("and thus finally acknowledged as human beings") and it was "an obvious political statement about their plight" (Petzke 2007). Though the film was not a commercial success, it attracted strong interest in foreign film festivals and established Noyce's name "both at home and abroad" (Petzke 2007).

Having grown up "almost never hearing an Australian voice on the cinema screen," Noyce began his career with films that defined Australianness in strong,

---

[17] The concept of the "Stolen Generations" was coined by Peter Read in 1981 (Frieze 2011, 122).

countercultural, and sometimes anti-American ways (Petzke 2007).[18] During the 1990s, however, he moved to America to direct a series of mainstream action-thriller movies, including *Patriot Games* (1992), *Sliver* (1993), *The Saint* (1997), and *The Bone Collector* (1999). He eventually became disillusioned with the realities of working in Hollywood, and he abandoned a project with Harrison Ford (*The Sum of All Fears*, 2002) because the actor kept demanding changes to the script that became unworkable for him (Cordaiy 2002, 128). *Rabbit-Proof Fence* represented a return to Noyce's "roots of making controversial films very cheaply" (128). It also signified Noyce's renewed commitment to making cinema to promote progressive social change within Australia. Noyce himself "believes *Rabbit-Proof Fence* to be both his best film and the one closest to his heart" because "it portrays Aborigines in a positive way not seen before in Australia" (Petzke 2007). Noyce has been equally outspoken about Australia's history of "denying that Indigenous experience was valid to be recorded, commented on, and examined" (Cordaiy 2002, 127).

Despite Noyce's own progressive intentions, his directorial role in *Rabbit-Proof Fence* has met with some criticism. Two thousand children were interviewed for the lead roles, of which Noyce saw 800 in person, "touring outback settlements in a four-wheel drive truck and light plane" (Petzke 2007). He cast himself as a kind of lone ranger who sought out the children he needed, plucking them from obscurity to showcase their talent. The young girls of the film were eventually found in remote Aboriginal communities where traditional life still exists, and they left their homes for the first time to make the film under his control.

With such a backstory behind the film's making, it is perhaps unsurprising that Noyce's intentions have met with skepticism. Fiona Villella, for instance, argues that *Rabbit-Proof Fence* stops short of radicalism largely due to Noyce's exploitative control over its marketing campaign. She writes of Noyce's tactics for piquing interest in "Australian audiences reluctant to see a film about indigenous Australians and colonial history" by calling attention to the "side issues" of casting three young unknown leads, the challenges of working with non-professional actors, and the emotion of filming the scenes where the girls are forcibly taken from their home. She also reads the celebrity-status given to the young girls as a result of the film, especially as they appeared on magazine covers, as "tacky" (2002).[19]

---

[18] Hollywood films have dominated the Australian box office (at least up until 1991) "to a greater extent than in almost any other foreign market: between 70 and 80 percent, compared with, say, 50 percent in Germany in 1978 and 50 percent in France in 1989" (Crofts 1991, 2).

[19] Similarly, Kibby details how the film was aggressively marketed, with numerous tie-in products (from the album of Gabriel's music to school study guides) and which included multiple "premieres" for Aboriginal communities. In short, Noyce knew how "to sell an indigenous story into the mainstream" (149).

Though Villela is not alone in arguing that Noyce exploited his lead actors, Noyce himself speaks of how the film was designed in terms of honoring its Aboriginal leads. Despite having renowned cinematographer Christopher Doyle shoot the film, one who could have exerted his own controlling influence, Noyce insisted that "the camera had to be at the service of those kids, not the other way around" (129). He felt that too much predetermined, "formal" camerawork would be too much like imposing the hand of A. O. Neville on the girls' story (127).[20] He even had Doyle light scenes well enough so the young actors could move about unpredictably instead of having to hit exact predetermined marks (129). In an interview about his commitment to representing Aboriginal truth, Noyce mentions that he chose Peter Gabriel to compose the film score on the basis of his music for *The Last Temptation of Christ* (1988). The scores for the two films are united in being suggestive of deep, mythological proportions, and this is relayed through multicultural instrumentation, variable systems of tonality, and great ranges of pitch, texture, and dynamics. Though Noyce does not make a direct correlation between the Christ narrative and the girls' experience in *Rabbit-Proof Fence*, Gabriel's music implicitly connects them, and in so doing elevates the significance of the girls' story for a Western (primarily non-Aboriginal) audience.

IN THE BEGINNING

From the outset, *Rabbit-Proof Fence* positions us to compassionately perceive the oppression of Aborigines in a colonial context. The film begins with several explanatory title cards that establish the place and time of "Western Australia 1931," and which then provide some more specific historical information:

> For 100 years the Aboriginal peoples have resisted the invasion of their lands by white settlers. Now a special law, the Aborigines Act, controls their lives in every detail. Mr. A. O. Neville, the Chief Protector of Aborigines, is the legal guardian of every Aborigine in the State of Western Australia. He has the power "to remove any half-caste child" from their families from anywhere within the state.

The words immediately establish the film's position as viewing the Aborigines from outside, as is most obvious in the reference to "their" lands. Along with the explanatory cards, white words on a black background, the sound track features harmonized

---

[20] Noyce does however acknowledge one "formal" element of camerawork, the crane movements near the beginning (Cordaiy 2002, 129).

FIGURE 2.2 "Grandmother's theme" by Peter Gabriel (transcribed directly from the *Rabbit-Proof Fence* DVD).

Aboriginal voices slowly rising in volume. These voices are also clearly heard with the opening production credits (that is, before as well as during the explanatory cards). The opening therein subtly suggests the presence of Aboriginal peoples on Australian soil before white history was created there, as well as literally asking us to hear Aboriginal voices over white text. The first dominant Aboriginal vocal line is an undulating pattern of repeated phrases. The most repeated section is as follows (see Figure 2.2):

This music becomes a leitmotif through the film and, as we shall explore, it is directly connected with Molly's grandmother: later we see her singing it as a way of calling Molly, Gracie, and Daisy home. We shall therefore refer to it as "Grandmother's theme."

As soon as the explanatory cards finish, the film proper begins with a series of aerial tracking shots that traverse increasingly vast expanses of Australian desert, anticipating the girls' long walk through the harshest terrain. Along with these tracking shots, we hear the first speech of the film. An old, Aboriginal woman speaks her language in a subtitled voiceover as follows:

This is a true story—story of my sister Daisy and my cousin Gracie and me when we were little. Our people, the Jigalong mob, we were desert people then, walking all over our land.

We retrospectively understand that this voice belongs to Molly, the oldest of the three girls and their leader for the walk home (see Figure 2.3).

Therefore, just as we rehear the first music of the film when we understand that it belongs to the grandmother, we have to rehear the voice that belongs to the film's leading protagonist by later identifying it as such. This becomes part of a pattern whereby *Rabbit-Proof Fence* demands a high degree of aural alertness to the shifting representations of its main Aboriginal characters. Molly's opening voiceover is also deeply significant in that it claims the film's story in the first person, in contrast with the third-person title cards that do not belong to anyone in particular. Within the opening moments of the film, then, two contrasting perspectives are established: the white (or non-Aboriginal), outsider, third-person point of view; and the Aboriginal, insider, first-person point of view.

FIGURE 2.3 Molly, the leading protagonist of *Rabbit-Proof Fence*.

A BRIEF OVERVIEW

Throughout *Rabbit-Proof Fence*, the sound track amplifies the contrasts between white and Aboriginal perspectives. White Australians, especially Neville, are associated with hard, sterile, or mechanical noises. For example, there is the closely miked scratching of Neville's pen when he fills out forms with instructions regarding the "half-castes." The hard and sterile sound of Neville's pen [5:41–5:54] is a striking contrast with the grainier, organic sound of Moodoo drawing chalk lines on a rock as he waits for the girls, a moment suggestive of his writing a different (though unexplained) truth on the land [1:10:26–1:10:31]. Along with such specific contrasts between diegetic noises, there is an overarching pattern of contrast in the music for *Rabbit-Proof Fence*. Gabriel's score is almost always aligned with the Aboriginal girl protagonists, and it works in powerful opposition to music associated with the white colonial "ideal." We shall give particular attention to Gabriel's score in contrast with the critical representation of "white" songs sung by the pupils at Moore River: the minstrel song "The Swanee River," the British national anthem, and the Anglican hymn "All Things Bright and Beautiful."

Though Gabriel's score is primarily aligned with the perceptions of the girl protagonists, we should also consider that it is far from fully Aboriginal. Indeed, much of Gabriel's instrumentation suggests world music. The concept "world music" is elastic but generally refers to "music from cultures other than those of Western Europe and English speaking North America" (Jones 2006, 234). Gabriel's scoring features Aboriginal voices, drone effects that are historically associated with Aboriginal music, and instruments with ancient Aboriginal origins (especially the didjeridu and clapsticks). In addition, the score features common acoustic and non-acoustic Western instruments, including keyboards, synthesized drums and bass, electric and acoustic guitar, piano, and accordion. The score is multicultural through Gabriel's incorporation of several traditional instruments from around the world, including: dhol drums (primarily associated with the Indian subcontinent), surdu (a large Brazilian bass drum), berimbau (a Brazilian single-stringed percussion instrument), djembes (goatskin-covered African drums), and gong (a disc hit with a mallet, originating in East and Southeast Asia). The score also includes traditional folk instruments that have been used the world over, such as the hammered dulcimer, shaker, and bowed crotales (antique cymbals). All these instruments and their tonal qualities are combined to create a strong sonic experience of variety.

Gabriel's blend of instruments could be interpreted as a retrograde form of tokenism through sound. On the other hand, in the only other detailed scholarly discussion of his music for *Rabbit-Proof Fence* to date, Majorie D. Kibby argues that the "de-territorialised" music works with the sounds of the Australian landscape to communicate a concept of the country as ancient and spiritual (157). For Kibby, the music is used most coercively in the film to communicate an impression of the land speaking (157). However, Gabriel's music is more immediately affective in relation to communicating what the protagonists feel, and enlarging the scale of their story through its multicultural associations. The music frequently "speaks" for the girls who say comparatively little, making their experience more transparent to a broad—domestic *and* international—audience. Through musically signifying their perspectives with multicultural implications, the scoring makes one story representative, and one reality of colonial oppression cross-cultural. Gabriel's music also helps the film appeal to a global audience that might be alienated by too many subtitles (as Noyce feared),[21] but who are willing to be compassionately interested.

Along with foregrounding the girls' perspectives and appealing to a broad audience, Gabriel's world music also comforts us with the grandiose assurance of a macrocosmic, benevolent understanding of the girls' experience. Even one of the most distressing scenes in the film, the one in which Gracie is recaptured by government officials, is *both* intensified and mediated by the presence of Gabriel's music [1:08:29–1:10:23]. Gabriel's cue for this scene features a melodic line built on rising phrases. The music

---

[21] In the context of noting that "it is difficult to have commercial success with movies involving indigenous stories," Noyce explains he "did not want to marginalize the movie by using subtitles—I did not want it to become an art house movie. I also did not want the audience to have to read subtitles and thus escape the emotion of the movie" (Hoschka).

reaches its climax (with a thickening texture, including a strong percussive line) as we see Gracie run in slow-motion from her captors and then be caught, as witnessed from Molly and Daisy's helpless perspectives. Though the scene visually foregrounds the girls' panic and powerlessness, the music conveys a mixed message. Because the music is obviously "with" the girls, it provides the comfort of compassionate alignment, as well as giving the slow-motion of Gracie's running a strong aesthetic contour. The music also seems to grieve and protest on Gracie's behalf because its rising patterns fall to low descending notes after she is driven away. Later, when Molly is finally reunited with her Grandmother, and she laments Gracie's recapture ("I lost one.. . . I lost one"), the score features synthesized strings sliding down in pitch, as if "wailing" with her [1:22:29–1:22:34]. Because the music gives voice to the girls' pain, it reinforces the entire film's focus on representing specific historical experiences that have been all too often silenced or dismissed.

The resonance of *Rabbit-Proof Fence* is in speaking back to the "structured absences" of compassionate Aboriginal representation throughout *Australian* cinematic history. That the film was clearly made and marketed for a global audience does, however, place limits on its radicalism: consider, for instance, how differently the film would work upon us were it to feature entirely Aboriginal language and music. Steven Aoun critiques the film for not only providing us with "a cathartic sense of closure antithetical to the subject matter," but also circumventing the question of indigenous land ownership by its emphasis on universality rather than cultural specificity: he argues that "the narrative structure needn't even be built on the experience of an Aboriginal family—it just happens to be" (2003, 206). Perhaps Gabriel's world music supports this reading. That said, many critics have been quick to defend the film for bringing international attention to the "Stolen Generations," especially at the time of its release.

AN HISTORICAL CONTEXT

To understand the resonance of the *Rabbit-Proof Fence* sound track more fully, we must first consider its historical context in further detail. The film was released a decade after the Mabo land rights decision of 1992, "a crucial *caesura* in Australian film history" and after which "Australian films have increasingly engaged with issues of reconciliation and interracial history" (Haag 2010, 117). The Mabo case was a ten-year legal battle by the people of Murray Island in the Torres Strait against the Australian legal system. The case was led by Eddie Mabo, a Torres Strait Islander who argued that the British had wrongly claimed that Australia was *"terra nullius"* (that is, "empty land, or land belonging to nobody") when they colonized it. The British used this claim to authorize their seizing lands belonging to Aborigines and Torres Strait Islanders "without agreement or payment," even though the Native inhabitants had "occupied Australia for 40,000 to 60,000 years before the British came in 1788." The case ran for ten years until the High Court of Australia finally ruled that the principle of *terra nullius* had been wrongly applied to Australia. The High Court ruling in favor of the native inhabitants of Australia "acknowledged their unique connection [and claim] to the land," and led to the Native Title Act (1993) which, in turn, led to renegotiating the indigenous use of one million square kilometers of land ("about 15 per cent of Australia").[22] Simpson explains that the term "post-Mabo" is widely used to denote "the cultural shift" brought about by this landmark decision, especially the acknowledgment of the Aboriginal presence when the British arrived in Australia, whereas "[t]here had been no mention of this in Australian laws or the Constitution" (2010, 93).

Rabbit-Proof Fence is an important post-Mabo film. It was also released at a time "when sensitivity to, and awareness of, Australia's colonial history and how Australia defines itself as a nation [were] greater than ever" (Villella 2002). Most significantly, it came several years after the well-known *Bringing Them Home* Report by the Human Rights and Equal Opportunity Commission (1997), "the first national history of the forced removal of Aboriginal children from their families" (Kevin 2010, 146). *Bringing Them Home* was the result of a "landmark National inquiry into the policies, practices and effects of removing children of mixed Aboriginal and Caucasian descent from their families and communities" (Kennedy 2008, 163). The inquiry involved nationwide interviews with Aboriginal people, many of whom described "being callously removed from their families, and later discovering in their files letters from their grief-stricken mothers, whom they had been told were dead or had abandoned them" (163). The report claims that Aboriginal child-removal polices of the 1930s to 1970s were a form of "genocide" (Windshuttle 2003, 12), and therefore included a recommendation for an official apology to the victims of the Stolen Generations, one that the white Australian Prime Minister John Howard refused to give. For almost a decade after the report was published, Howard maintained this position, basing his refusal "on arguments against intergenerational responsibility and the collective guilt that he believed an apology would imply" (Kevin 2010, 154). Although he was widely supported in this, "his refusal did not reflect the journey that was taken by many Australians in the wake of *Bringing Them Home*" (154). The report "reinvigorated" a

---

[22] These historical points about the Mabo case come from an online publication by Reconciliation Australia (n.d.), an independent and nonprofit organization focused on creating harmonious connections among Australian peoples.

national conversation about the past and how to address it—thousands of Australians signed Sorry Books all over the country, and thousands more participated in reconciliation marches in December 2000 (154).

Kibby argues that *Rabbit-Proof Fence* contributed to this national conversation (147). After the film was released, political figures directly discussed the film's significance in the wake of Howard's intransigence. The former leader of the Australian Liberal Party, John Hewson, even argued that "John Howard and his ministry should, as a matter of compulsion, take the first opportunity to see and discuss the movie *Rabbit-Proof Fence*. . . they should immediately say 'Sorry!' along with, and on behalf of, the rest of us" (82).

The National Apology to the Stolen Generations finally came from the new Prime Minister, Kevin Rudd, in 2008. His speech has been critiqued as "both compassionate and conservative," both reconciliatory and tokenistically connected to projected neo-assimilationist measures, but it still represented a "long overdue release of national emotion" (Kevin 2010, 154). *Rabbit-Proof Fence* has been frequently credited with contributing towards this historical event by providing "a sober accurate account of the racial fantasies and phobias, as well as the frankly genocidal thoughts that masqueraded as policies for the welfare of Aborigines in Australia's interwar years" (Manne, 2003a).[23] Such a reading supports Noyce's own belief that his domestic audiences *wanted* "to look at themselves in the mirror" (Cordaiy 2002, 130), rather than seeing a representation of the past from which they could dissociate themselves.[24]

Another testimony to the deep progressive significance of *Rabbit-Proof Fence* is the vitriolic response it received from the notoriously Conservative historian, writer, and former ABC (Australian Broadcasting Corporation) executive, Keith Windshuttle. Windshuttle is well known for arguing that the story of the Stolen Generations is a "myth" in his book *The Fabrication of Aboriginal History, Volume Three: The Stolen Generations 1881-2008* (2009). Windshuttle makes this claim despite the existence of numerous historical documents that incorporate references to the systematic and forced removal of Aboriginal children from their homes to white settlements.[25]

---

[23] Corinn Columpar, among others, argues that the film "helped, in some way, to prepare the ground for" this apology (2010, 181). For further discussion of the film as it represents genocide in urgent terms for a contemporary audience, see Frieze (2011).

[24] Ironically, Haag claims that *Rabbit-Proof Fence* "is not a mainstream film that appeals to broad audiences as do romance and adventure films" and "its strong focus on Australian history, particularly that on Western Australia, attracted, not unsurprisingly, only a small number of overseas viewers" (2010, 119).

[25] For fuller counterarguments, see Robert Manne's direct rebuttal of Windshuttle's work in the anthology he edited: *Whitewash: On Keith Windschuttle's Fabrication of Aboriginal History* (2003b).

Along with accusing the film of being "anti-Australian," and dismissively mentioning the Pilkington source as "fictionalized," Windshuttle argues that the *Bringing Them Home* report is an inaccurate and biased representation of history. The report claims that child-removal policies "caused from ten to thirty per cent of all Australian Aborigines to be forcibly removed from their families" from the 1930s to 1970s. By contrast, Windshuttle claims that "a number of influential critics" (none of whom he directly cites) have argued that Aboriginal children were only taken from their families in situations of serious parental neglect or abuse. He therefore argues that the film irresponsibly presents Molly's situation as typical even though it was a rarity: of the 1,067 children at Moore River, he claims that only sixty-four "could possibly have been removals from their mothers" (2003, 13). Windshuttle also claims that the *Bringing Them Home* report is unduly biased since it solely grew out of "claims made by Aborigines themselves" rather than "testing" their claims with the (white) officials who "allegedly removed them" (13). Ironically, Windshuttle then reveals his own bias by using the film to justify his dubious claim that white Australian settlers have been too often misrepresented as inhumane. His reactionary criticism certainly seems unduly heavy-handed, though it makes more sense if we analyze the coercively affective power of *Rabbit-Proof Fence*. The strength of his criticism is at least a tacit acknowledgement of this. Our analysis of the film's power is based on what the sound track prompts us to perceive and experience: a distressing *and* factually based narrative of white oppression and Aboriginal strength.

ADAPTING PILKINGTON'S BOOK

The factual basis of *Rabbit-Proof Fence* is Pilkington's book. Though the memoir is primarily based on Daisy's personal account, it also cites no fewer than thirteen official historical documents by white officials who were directly involved in trying to recapture Molly, Gracie, and Daisy.[26] The book was republished by Miramax Books in anticipation of the film's release, prompting us to understand them in relation to each other. Julie Emberley describes Pilkington's writing it as "an invitation extended to the reader, a potential foreigner, sister, settler, refugee, and even mother, to *listen* to a story about the history of colonization, to listen to a different way of storying history" (2008, 168, my emphasis). She also argues that the text invites the reader "to *listen* and learn" (168).

---

[26] For a fuller consideration of these archival documents within an historical, post- colonial context, see Brewster.

Though Emberley writes of listening in a more figurative than literal sense, the memoir itself emphasizes the culturally loaded power of sound, especially since startling sounds are frequently mentioned in connection with the colonial presence. Early on, Pilkington describes the Nyungar people being startled from their "peace and tranquility" by the "loud boom" of "an eighteen-pounder cannon by the [white] soldiers as they raised the British flag, the Union Jack, for the first time on the shores of Western Australia" (2002, 5). Though the military post that is then established (at Albany) does not pose a threat, Pilkington writes of the native forest echoing with "the anguished cries and the ceaseless weeping" of thousands of [other Aboriginal] people as they were driven off their land (2). She later writes of Nyangur men who hear but cannot understand one Captain Fremantle who arrives on the English gunboat HMS Challenger and who "announced in a loud voice, 'I name this land Western Australia' " before saluting a British flag. Colonial threat is also associated with the sounds of dogs "barking wildly" (28), the barking of a "terrorizing fox," and "the bleating of lambs" (104). Later still, Pilkington recounts the "agonized" cries of mothers and women, and the "deep sobs" of "grandfathers, uncles, and cousins" that "filled the air" when Riggs took Molly and Gracie away from them (44–45). After Gracie is also stolen (from a separate camp) she writes that:

> In their grief the women asked why their children should be taken from them. Their anguished cries echoed across the flats, carried by the wind. But no one listened to them, no one heard them.

Here, the emphasis is on a deep pain that is *not heard*. Though *Rabbit-Proof Fence* portrays the pain of grieving, it also prompts us to hear the Aboriginal women and children most strongly. Ultimately, the film inverts the pattern of Pilkington's book in which the sounds of colonial threat are loudest.

OVERARCHING AURAL PATTERNS

The whole sound track of *Rabbit-Proof Fence* (the sound effects and dialogue, as well as the music) is primarily used to reinforce our alignment with the Aboriginal protagonists, and therein lies the film's subversively affective power. That the film aurally privileges the girls' perspectives is especially clear when Riggs first comes to capture them. This scene [7:01–12:01] begins with emphasis on the sounds of colonial presence: the metal of the Jigalong storehouse creaking, a dog barking, a bell rung by the white Jigalong depot manager (Andrew S. Gilbert), and paper rustling. Against this texture of "white" sounds are the indistinct voices of Aboriginal children and wind. The

FIGURE 2.4 Maude, the girls' mother, desperately attempts to protect her children from Riggs.

sound track thus emphasizes the children being drowned out by the colonial presence. When Riggs approaches, dogs growl loudly, a camel brays, the sounds of his car engine are amplified along with the sounds of the girls' panicked breathing as they run, and Gabriel's scoring features intense percussion that builds as Riggs pulls them to a stop with his car [9:05–9:56] (see Figure 2.4).

In response to Maude's screams of protest, Riggs shouts "It's the law Maude, you've got no say in it," and he points to several paper documents in his hand as he runs towards the girls (see Figure 2.5). His handful of documents is a visual synecdoche for the assimilationist polices of the Australian government, and the Empire by extension. That said, the image of this paper flapping in Riggs's moving hand represents the absurdly flimsy justification of his actions (from a moral, if not institutional, standpoint), especially when contextualized by a loud and multilayered sound track of terror.[27]

---

[27] In foregrounding Maud's grief when Riggs takes the children away, *Rabbit-Proof Fence* talks back to all those who enforced the removal of half-caste children. Robert Manne cites one "most enthusiastic enforcer," James Isdall ("travelling protector for the north"), who did not believe that "the Aboriginal mother felt the loss of her child any more deeply than did the bitch of a lost pup." In 1909, Isdall himself wrote, "I would not hesitate to separate any half-caste from its aboriginal mother, no matter how frantic momentary grief might be. They soon forget their offspring" (2003a). For more on the forced removal of Aboriginal children, see Manne's "In Denial: The Stolen Generations and the Right" (2001).

FIGURE 2.5 Constable Riggs claims his right to steal the girls away by pointing to some governmental documents.

Gabriel's music frequently amplifies the physical movements and emotional responses of the girls so as to further foreground their experiences. Sometimes the score obviously Mickey-mouses the girls' actions, such as when two alternating notes become slower in parallel to the girls' own footsteps slowing as they become exhausted [1:10:36–1:12:09]. Sometimes the sound track more expressionistically matches the girls' physical and interior experience. When Moodoo is tracking the girls on horseback, splashing along all-too-closely after them through a stream, the deep didjeridu music associated with him is combined with percussive notes in a non-accent/accent pattern like a heartbeat, suggestive of the girls' fear of capture [36:51–37:56]. Then, after Molly says "shhh," the sonic texture is stripped down to nothing but the girls' breathing and a few low drum beats for a few moments. Each girl is shown in close-up turning their heads around to survey the land around them [36:51–38:08]. It is as if the whole film stops to fall quiet on Molly's instruction.

Given that the sound track repeatedly prompts us to align ourselves with the girls, it is surprising that Frieze argues that the film's "effects expose the girls' very Otherness; indeed, there is never a sense that the audience can know the girls" (2011, 127). Similarly, Matthew Dillon argues that "we travel several thousand . . . [miles] with the girls without coming to know them much better than we did at the start" (2002, 35). Agreeing with Dillon, Frieze also argues that if the film allowed us to know the girls it would be "tantamount to the violations of the Chief Protector, who claimed exhaustive knowledge of his captives" (2011, 127). On the other hand, we might conclude that the film's allowing us access to the girls is a crucially subversive intervention. Like *The Battle of Algiers*, the form of *Rabbit-Proof Fence* inverts the colonized/colonizer hierarchy, and its sound track demands our emotional investment in this action.

GRANDMOTHER'S THEME

Perhaps the most memorable musical idea is Grandmother's theme. The part of this theme transcribed in Figure 2.2 recurs in various forms during the film, becoming its most subtly significant leitmotif. After being first stated, the theme recurs in quieter, often submerged or abbreviated forms, especially during pivotal moments in the girls' journey. For instance, it resurfaces after the girls receive food and clothing from a brusque but kind white housewife who provides directions to the fence. As the girls continue walking, and Molly assures Gracie and Daisy "[if we] find that rabbit fence, we go home"; Daisy simply responds, "then we see our Mum." Molly then continues walking with renewed determination, and the theme rises to the surface, reflecting her optimism [45:43–52]. The theme also reinforces our sense of the girls' resilience. In a later music cue [46:45–48:02], just after Nina reads a newspaper account of the runaways to the other Moore River children who delight in their escape, the theme recurs as Molly finds the fence. The cue begins with the women's singing somewhat submerged, but it is then mixed with a higher-pitched motif that suggests rising hope, especially when combined with the sound of Molly whistling to the other girls upon seeing the fence. The film then crosscuts between Grandmother and Maude holding the fence, and the girls grabbing and pulling the fence. Only later do we, along with Molly, learn that they were actually holding different fences at this point. Here, the music sutures the crosscutting and thus provides a sense of transcending space and time, binding the girls with their female elders.[28] The music is ultimately about something bigger than what can be seen, especially since we later learn the characters were not actually connected by the fence. Though not literally connected through the tangible object, the girls and women are nevertheless connected by the power of faith now attached to the music.

---

[28] "Suturing" music carries over cuts, providing sonic continuity that aids a smooth narrative flow. Such practice allows audiences to perceive coherence in the cinematic construction, while also being so conventionalized as to become almost imperceptible. "Suturing" is a loaded concept in psychoanalytic approaches to the coerceive power of cinema. For more on the term, see Hayward (2006, 404–10).

The determination and faith associated with Grandmother's theme is complicated when it recurs as Gracie hears that her mother is at Wiluna and resolves to separate from Molly and Daisy. The girls hear this rumor from a hegemonic figure, an unnamed Aboriginal man (David Nagoombujara) who, dressed in colonial clothing, passes on the word spread by Neville to trap the girls. Here, Grandmother's theme is merged with the wind as he speaks, and it is barely perceptible under the sounds of footsteps and dialogue [1:03:51–1:04:24]. It fades out as Molly urges Gracie to stay with her. The music works on a subtle, perhaps subconscious level here. It gently reinforces the pull that Wiluna now has for Gracie, but its association with her home is sadly ironic.

Even if Grandmother's theme is associated with Gracie's tragic defeat, however, it nevertheless returns to reaffirm Molly and Daisy's triumph. It briefly resurfaces when Riggs gives up on waiting for Molly and Daisy, after several weeks at his assigned post with Moodoo [1:10:53–59]. In this scene he describes the girls as being like "a needle in a haystack," and tells Moodoo "pack your stuff, we're getting out of here." In response, Moodoo allows himself a silent and discrete smile. Here, the theme anticipates the girls' escape as well as punctuating Moodoo's quiet admiration for them. Several sequences later still, Grandmother's theme resurfaces again most strongly, and at the precise point when it seems all hope is lost. En route home, Molly and Daisy must move deep into the treacherous dessert, a part of the country that Neville will not even send men to track them. Here the music works with the increasingly hazy and abstract images to signify the girls' faltering strength [1:13:04–1:14:12] (see Figure 2.6).

Molly and Daisy's steps are underscored by long and unearthly sounding drones in a deep minor key. As their bodies are shown distorted and ghostly though a haze of heat, the music itself has disintegrated from melody, becoming a series of musical howls and extended notes that match their slowing down. The girls' heavy breathing dominates the music right before they fall unconscious onto the ground. Suddenly, Grandmother's theme accompanies a cut to show Maude in close-up, followed by Grandmother in close-up as she finally sings the theme on-screen [1:14:13–1:14:39]: it is a crucial moment of attaching the voice to the body (see Figure 2.7).

Michel Chion has influentially emphasized the power of an acousmêtric presence on film. He defines it as a sound, especially a voice, that is not located within the image (1994, 129–30). He explains that a moment of audiovisual restoration, the point at which the voice is visually attached to its enunciator (or, as Chion puts it, "de-acousmatized"), typically reduces the power of such a presence (130). Consider the quintessential example of the Wizard of Oz: after his artificially amplified voice is identified as such in relation to his small body, the illusion of his larger-than-life sound is undone. In this scene from *Rabbit-Proof Fence*, however, the effect of locating the musical theme within

FIGURE 2.6 In the hazy heat of the desert, Molly and Daisy's strength falters, and their bodies become less distinct.

FIGURE 2.7 Grandmother sings her theme.

Grandmother's body has a different impact. The music has gathered abstract, conceptual associations (determination, hope, resilience, faith, transcendence) up to this point, and these are made suddenly more concrete through being attached to her body. In addition, there is power in the surprise of Grandmother's theme being attached to her body on-screen. We always know that the Wizard of Oz's voice comes from within the diegesis, but the diegetic representation of Grandmother's theme being sung cannot be anticipated: in this way, her music has been ahead of us from the beginning.

THE RETURN HOME

The climactic iteration of Grandmother's theme comes with Molly and Daisy's return home. The music works with sound effects to create a strong impression of their ability to transcend white control, especially as it is embodied by Riggs. As Molly and Daisy approach home, Riggs is shown looking out towards the bush from where the women of the Jigalong camp sing.[29] Riggs is alert to their sounds but he cannot see them: the camera pans across the bush from right to left, just as his eyes are then shown moving accordingly. His voice is unnerved (rather than "full of authority and purpose," as Pilkington wrote it (2002, 44)), and he asks the storehouse keeper "what's all that about?" The storehouse keeper dismissively replies "just some women's business. . . been going on all day." This moment is about doubly Othering the singing (as both Aboriginal and female), but it still compels Riggs's attention: "they're up to something," he says, before announcing his intention to "take a look." The film then cuts to show Grandmother and the other women of her camp singing her theme strongly, and in close-ups. Ironically, then, Riggs's idea of having a "look" at them is immediately followed by the film's emphasis on their audiovisual presences, reinforcing our impression that they cannot be subjected to his power.[30]

The closest thing we get to a narrative cliché is the moment where Riggs then confronts Maude and Grandmother with his rifle. It is reminiscent of a climactic showdown, but it revisionistically appropriates the semantics of the western in that the white man loses. By the time Riggs sees the women, the singing has become submerged within the overall aural texture. Here, diegetic noises are predominant: Riggs's rustling movements, the sounds of Molly and Daisy walking and then coming to a stop

---

[29] The singing is dimly perceptible at first, but a cut to Molly carrying Daisy shows that they can perceive it from some distance. For about two minutes, it is the dominant melodic material until Gabriel's instrumental score becomes more prominent [1:17:45–1:19:13].

[30] At this point, Gabriel's scoring only includes low drones accompanying the singing, reinforcing its power. Only when Riggs approaches the women do Gabriel's synthesized extended notes rise to prominence.

in hiding, and Riggs's walking towards Maude and Grandmother with a rifle in hand [1:19:50–1:21:13]. Riggs's nervous breathing is also amplified, in ironic contrast with the amplification of only Molly and Daisy's stronger breathing for much more of the film, especially as they run across rugged terrain. The film thus emphasizes that *he* is now vulnerable in terms of feeling the limits of his body. Maude silently and slowly raises her spear at Riggs, by which point Grandmother's theme can be clearly heard under the thick texture of diegetic natural sounds (animal screeches, crickets, birds). As the sound track thus reaches a climactic *forte*, there is an uncomfortably tight close-up of Riggs's face. This suggests that the sounds are now amplified in terms of his fear and vulnerability: this is, again, an exception to the film's much more consistent aural emphasis on the protagonists' experiences. Riggs soon runs clumsily away from Maude and Grandmother, and the film quickly redirects attention to the perceptions of its Aboriginal leads. Moments later we hear (and then see) a "spirit bird" in the sky whose call Molly imitates, in response to which Maude responds with a parallel imitation [1:21:16–1:21:42]. The bird looks exactly like the hawk (and may be the same one) that Maude and Molly admire together in a scene near the beginning of the film. Mother and daughter are now reunited through the bird's sound before they see each other. And the sound connects them across some distance, before they can even touch.

Once Molly and Daisy have finally made it back to their camp, there is another emphasis on a variation of Grandmother's theme. This time it is diegetically sung in combination with Gabriel's non-diegetic scoring [1:22:52–1:23:59]. The two forms of music combine to create an impression of harmonious fullness. Along with the music, we can make out dim images of the girls' smiling, and the women of their camp circling them, especially Maude and Grandmother as they touch the children's faces. This reunion scene dovetails with the final reentrance of Neville's voice [1:23:39].

We cannot but feel the contrast between the sonic fullness of the reunion scene and the thin hollow sounds of Neville's voice. We hear him before he visually reappears: in other words, we return to him with a sound advance. Delaying the cut to Neville as we view the happily reunited family places emphasis on the incongruence of his final words with how the film has shown them to us. His last words begin with a letter dictated to his secretary as follows:

To Constable Riggs, police station, Nullagine—at present we lack funds the funds to pursue the missing half-caste girls—Molly and Daisy. I would ask to be kept informed of their whereabouts so that at some future date they may indeed be. . . recovered. [*The letter completed, Neville sits down, as if in defeat before he continues speaking.*]

We face an uphill battle with these people, especially the bush natives who have to be protected against themselves. If they would only understand what we are trying to do for them.

As Neville dictates his letter, we hear the scratching of his secretary's pen across her note paper, another example of the film referring to documented history. Despite the power of men like Neville in making and recording history, however, *Rabbit-Proof Fence* ends by dwelling on his limitations. Where Neville's words are about what "these people" fail to understand, the film is about what he *cannot* understand. Our last sight of Neville shows him looking out his office window, failing to look directly at a new group of Aborigines lined up outside to appeal for his help. The musical score changes as Neville speaks, becoming lower and less prominent, but never petering out. Since Gabriel's score is almost entirely devoted to the perceptions of the girl protagonists throughout the film, its continuance here further emphasizes that, even when Neville's voice dominates, their presences always "speak" loudest through the film. And even if Neville has the last words of diegetic dialogue, the final speech is a voiceover by Molly, after which the final credits are accompanied by music that features Aboriginal voices. This last music ends with Grandmother's *a cappella* singing voice. Both visually and aurally, then, the film refuses to end with him.

WHITE SINGING AND SPEAKING ENGLISH

The historical significance of Molly and Daisy's struggle and victory is always sonically reinforced. This contrasts with the more fleeting, smaller, and critically represented sounds of colonialism that are attached to confined spaces within the film. There is, for example, nothing more sonically rich in Neville's office than the sound of pen scratchings. We are repeatedly made to dwell on the power represented by Neville's (and sometimes his secretary's) pen, especially as his hand is shown in close-ups while filling in forms regarding the half-castes' future. But the sound of the pen itself is banal, just as other sounds associated with colonial rule are thinner and less commanding than those elements of sound attached to the protagonists.

During the several scenes dealing with the girls' brief life at Moore River, colonial sounds temporarily dominate, though their primacy is undermined by their being critically represented. The first breakfast at Moore River is a strong example of attaching colonial sound to oppression. Here, the head nun (Celine O'Leary) commands all the children to bow their heads to pray "with eyes closed." Though the instruction is standard for a prayer, this moment has a deeper ideological resonance. "With eyes closed" the children speak as one monotonous collective, and they speak familiar words that are entirely incommensurate with the hopeless representation of the school: "Thank you for the food we eat, thank you for the world so sweet, thank you for the birds that sing, thank you, God, for everything" [18:56–19:05]. "There will be no talking" the nun then says as the children begin eating, thus equating the girls' speech with insubordination.

The very next scene includes yet another form of aural control. Here we see the head nun roughly scrubbing Molly down in an outside bath. She demands that Molly respond to her question "doesn't that feel much better?" with "yes Miss Jessop, thank you Miss Jessop." Molly flatly repeats the phrases in muted obedience. After her bathing, the film cuts to an image of several Moore River girls working at sewing machines. For a few seconds, the sound track is dominated by the sounds of these machines. A girl's foot pressing down a pedal to create stitches is shown in close-up, foregrounding the already-amplified sound it makes (see Figure 2.8).

The sounds of the sewing machine suggest the importance of conformity, and the need for compliance within the "machine" of colonial rule. Just as the girls are all dressed the same way in plain off-white mission clothing, there are many machines making the same sounds for the same stitches. This is a strong aural parallel to the girls' speaking in unison at breakfast [20:02–20:33]. Miss Jessop hands new mission clothing to the protagonists, so that they can dress like every other girl there. Though Gracie happily

FIGURE 2.8 A young Aboriginal girl's foot powers the sewing machine, a hegemonic symbol of colonial control (reliant upon her physical obedience).

accepts the clothing, and thus seems readily compliant, she inadvertently breaks protocol with her speech: "look, new clothes!" she excitedly exclaims in her own language. The Nun leans down in condescension to say "this is your new home. We don't use that jabber here. You speak English." The Moore River scenes thus emphasize the oppressive consistency with which Aboriginal language is forbidden.

The most memorable scene featuring colonial music also takes place at Moore River. Standing up in two straight lines at an outdoor assembly between the school buildings, the children sing "Old Folks at Home," also known as "Swanee River" [20:35–21:06]. This is a minstrel song, one associated with the practice of white performers wearing blackface.[31] The song lyrics are for a black slave who longs for "de old plantation" and thus romanticizes his own oppression. Stephen Foster wrote the song specifically for *Christy's Minstrels*, a successful blackface troupe from Buffalo, New York, that was formed in 1844.[32] Such was their success that the name "Christy's Minstrels" became "synonymous with the performance tradition of blackface minstrelsy" (Bewley, n.d.). "Swanee River" became the official state song of Florida in 1935. The immediate familiarity of the song, along with its disturbing history, makes it a doubly powerful choice for Moore River scene. The recognizability of the song is a way of sonically connecting the past of the film to the present day. It subtly disallows us the luxury of dismissing the action of the film as something of the past. That the song is specifically connected with minstrelsy also relates to the transnational resonance of *Rabbit-Proof Fence*.

After we hear the girls sing some of the song at *mezzo forte* ("... way down upon the Swanee River. Far, far away. There's where my heart is turning ever, that's where the old folks stay"), it continues more quietly upon a cut to Molly whispering to Nina. That the song is quieter here makes sense in terms of the cinematic convention of privileging dialogue, but the dipped-down volume takes on greater resonance when Molly simply asks Nina "What are they doing?" For Molly, the singing is itself an *act* of compliance and hegemony, whether intentional or not.[33] The subtext of Molly's question might be "why are they singing the language and music of this white place?" Nina responds by deliberately distorting Neville's name, a form of aural rebellion in itself: "[they're] singing Mr. Devil's favorite song."

---

[31] The song was composed before the practice of black people wearing blackface rose up after the Civil War.

[32] For more information, see the Center for American Music website (2008) devoted to the song.

[33] The film also dwells on the power of speech to force action, as when Neville spreads the rumor that Gracie's mother will be in Wiluna: "I want the word spread," he says, "let's see what that *does*" [1:02:32–34, my emphasis].

When we learn that "Swanee River" is "his favorite," the film foregrounds Neville's attachment to the cross-cultural racism associated with it. That the girls' sing it for Neville collectively, even if weakly, is clearly meant to impress him. Ironically, he does not give it his entire attention, murmuring to an official person affiliated with the settlement as the girls sing. This suggests his attachment to the song is superficial, and that he is thus incapable of fully hearing what it means. But the film clearly expects *us* to perceive the song's resonance, beyond his attention *and* his comprehension.

A few minutes later, we hear another important example of colonial music: part of the British national anthem, "God Save the Queen" [26:31–26:42]. We hear it directly after the sound of babies crying at Moore River, a significant juxtaposition that suggests widespread grief in association with the Empire. Molly directly comments on the crying by asking Nina where the babies' mothers are. "They've got no mothers," says Nina. "Nobody here got any mothers," she adds sadly, her words now underscored by the other settlement girls singing the anthem off-screen. "Happy and glorious, long to reign over us, God save our queen" are the lyrics we hear, ironic in their celebratory anticipation of the Queen's longevity. "I've got mother" says Molly, directly after the song ends. Her answer is more than a response to Nina's claim that the babies have no mothers. It also signifies a rejection of the "Mother country," England, and of the assumption of parental authority taken on by those at Moore River, as well as Neville by extension. Nina looks down without responding. What Molly has declared is too big for an answer from Nina: as dormitory boss, she has taken on a hegemonically controlling role, parallel to Moodoo's role as the Tracker, even though she sometimes vocally resists it. Given that she is the lead protagonist, Molly says comparatively little throughout the film. But this is one of several moments where her few words resonate deeply.

Neville speaks much more than Molly in his scenes, but there is nothing around his words to affirm their power: more often than not, his words are answered by almost nothing, such as the quiet sounds of his secretary taking down his dictation or the near-silence of an audience of white women to whom he presents his plan for eradicating Aboriginal blackness (a scene discussed more fully below). By contrast, the significance of Molly's words is consistently reinforced by the sounds around them: here, the babies' crying, the English national anthem, and even Nina's silence, all makes us understand the significance of her saying "I've got mother." She represents resistance to the grief suffered by all the children at Moore River, by all the Stolen Generations, and by all Aboriginal people oppressed by colonial rule by extension. *Rabbit-Proof Fence* is a knowing fantasy of retrospectively empowering Molly by making her representative on such a macrocosmic scale: along with Gabriel's world music, the Anglo-American colonial music (especially "God Save the Queen"), and sound effects like the chorus of babies' crying also open out the resonance of her story beyond its deep Australian significance.

The last colonial music that we hear is when Molly begins her escape with Gracie and Molly: the film crosscuts between their first fleeing the settlement and the other girls at church singing "All Things Bright and Beautiful," accompanied by a thin-sounding piano. It is an Anglican hymn, and thus immediately alludes to the British Empire asserting itself on Australia. This time, however, the colonial music is preceded by the crashes of thunder before the rainstorm that covers the girls' tracks, as well as over- lapping with some stirring non-diegetic music suggestive of Molly's rising heroism [29:48–32:09]. While the girls are singing, the film cuts to show Moodoo among them, and the (non-diegetic) low didjeridu sounds associated with him briefly re-enter with their voices. Perhaps this suggests Moodoo's comprehension that something is amiss, or perhaps it represents another aural challenge to the colonial music. Where "Swanee River" is only briefly interrupted by Molly's questioning, this later song is bookended by the stronger underscoring for Molly's escape. We might conclude that this last exam- ple of colonial music is put in its place by the non-diegetic scoring aligned with Molly. Certainly, the music aligned with her has a much richer texture of sound: along with that, its affective impact is clearly greater.

ILLUSIONIST OR BRECHTIAN?

Rabbit-Proof Fence provides an illusion of relatively close access to all its characters, both Aboriginal and white—from the relatively inscrutable Moodoo, to the transpar- ently limited Neville. The sound track is a crucial part of its overseeing approach. In particular, the music communicates an omniscient perspective as it binds together con- centrated montages of narrative development. For example, Gabriel's scoring almost ceaselessly underscores the last fifteen minutes of the film, from the time Molly and Daisy collapse in the desert to their making it home and the final credits. This musically saturated section of the film not only provides strong sonic cohesion, but also creates the aural impression of an all-encompassing point of view.

Because much of the music does not entirely come from the indigenous charac- ters, the scoring implicitly suggests that the film's dominant vantage point cannot be entirely Aboriginal. At the same time, the film foregrounds its authority to tell the truth of its Aboriginal characters through several techniques associated with the documen- tary: the opening explanatory title cards that provide some historical background for the film's action, the archival footage of Molly and Daisy at the end, and the use of Molly's voiceover at the beginning and end. The first of the final credits is for the film being based on the "book by Molly's Daughter, Doris Pilkington Garimara," which further reinforces the film's claim to represent Aboriginal truth. Overall, then, the film foregrounds its own based-on-a-true-story authority as well as its ability to reveal the true interior lives of the indigenous people.

However, though *Rabbit-Proof Fence* claims its own authority to represent the perspectives of its Aboriginal characters, and in such a way that has universal appeal, the film avoids being straightforwardly illusionist. Though it does not *require* our self-consciousness about perceiving its mediation of reality (and thus, as we shall explore, differs from *Ten Canoes*), there are moments where it aurally foregrounds its own construction in a Brechtian manner. Stam and Spence are broadly concerned with the techniques through which cinema non-neutrally represents, or challenges, the dominant order. They more specifically mention Brechtian film strategies as important for critically scrutinizing the ideology of colonial and postcolonial situations. We should therefore consider *Rabbit-Proof Fence* accordingly.

A Brechtian film incorporates at least some of the following: characters who are of their own historical moment, rather than being transcultural or transhistorical and fable-like; narratives through which historical and social substructures are made manifest, rather than artificially presenting the individual in isolation; representations of reality that are multifaceted rather than simplistic, since no one perception of the truth can encompass all; and constructions of representation that are revealed as such, on the understanding that no construction is ideologically neutral. In short, the Brechtian text self-consciously presents us with constructions within specific socio-historical contexts. The Brechtian text is driven by a Marxist imperative to represent the truths of power dynamics within its social contexts, the complexity of which must be approached from multiple angles and perspectives. The Brechtian text resists well-worn formulas and generic approaches in the process of demanding that audiences actively perceive its meaning without losing themselves in the overfamiliar experience. Ultimately, Brecht "wished to provoke audiences into active responses that would be a prelude to intervention in politics beyond the theatre" (Lapsley and Westlake 164).[34]

Stam and Spence themselves provide a Brechtian reading of *The Battle of Algiers*, a film that self-consciously presents a multifaceted approach to the colonial history of France and Algeria, and one that subversively foregrounds the perspectives of native Algerians who are oppressed. *Rabbit-Proof Fence* similarly attempts to invert the usual pattern of marginalizing colonized people on screen. But *Rabbit-Proof Fence* also runs

---

[34] Lapseley and Westlake provide a useful summary of that which defines the Brechtian film (162–65).

the risk of enacting a cinematic form of appropriation: consider that it is the work of a white director, that it purports to fully represent the truth of indigenous characters, and that it is produced in accordance with Western principles of filmmaking. While the film is an adaptation of Pilkington's book, an Aboriginal text, its very form also works like a generic road movie: the journey matters more than the destination, the plot "goes from A to B in a finite and chronological time," and the girls largely define themselves by moving through "wild open spaces" (Hayward 2006, 336).[35] Moreover, Gabriel's score interprets the action for us through a combination of indigenous and non-indigenous sounds, bridging the gap between cultures, rather than requiring that we become enveloped within a fully Aboriginal experience. Because the score follows the narratively and emotively structured "rules" of Classical scoring (especially through leitmotifs), it does not obviously prompt a Western audience's particular attention to its construction any more than the road-movie structure of the narrative. Despite all this, there are many moments within the overall structure of the sound track (including sound effects and dialogue, as well as music) that allow for the possibility of our perceiving their ideological weight *and* their anti-illusionist construction in a thoroughly Brechtian manner.

BREAKING THE AUDIOVISUAL ILLUSION

Rabbit-Proof Fence frequently, and self-consciously, breaks a conventional expectation that what we see and hear will complement each other. Chion refers to this as a "phenomenon of *audiovisual illusion*" whereby the "sound enriches the given image so as to create the definite impression," one in which the sound "is already contained in the image itself" (1994, 5). For instance, in the very opening voiceover, Molly speaks of what she and her people were given on "ration day" at the Jigalong storehouse (clothes, flour, tobacco, tea). At this point the camera has tracked and tilted upward to reveal a vast expanse of the desert against the distant horizon [1:44]. The concept of "rationing" goes against the grain of the expansive image, one that is suggestive of the land and its indigenous people (represented by Molly's voice) being bigger than what can be contained or given out from the storehouse. When Molly reaches the end of this same voiceover, she says "they were building a long fence" [1:52]. By this point, the sky has filled the screen: the notion of setting a limit (the fence) clashes with the image of expansion farther than the eye can see. Instead of simply illustrating what Molly says, then, the film shows us ironically incommensurate images. The first shot of Molly is a

---

[35] That said, as Hayward also points out (2006, 336), road movies historically tend to focus on male travelers, allowing us to perceive *Rabbit-Proof Fence* as subversive from a feminist point of view.

FIGURE 2.9 The first shot of Molly.

medium close-up [2:18] that clearly establishes her as the protagonist, though somewhat disempowered by a high-angled perspective (see Figure 2.9).

In a voiceover she explains, "My dad was a white man working on that fence. The white people called me half-caste." So, the voiceover is about how she was vocally reduced even though her voice dominates the sound track. Again, the audiovisual messages are mixed.

The first diegetic words of the film are in English, and they are spoken to Riggs, the man who captures the girls. The camera introduces Riggs by tracking up his weathered boots and the shaft of his gunholder as he sits astride a horse. The camera's movement up his body is slightly shaky and from a low angle, emphasizing his visual power (see Figure 2.10).

However, our first sight of Riggs is complicated by the non-diegetic sound of the didjeridu. The sonic emphasis on the didjeridu complicates our focus on him, due to its ancient association with Aboriginal life as well as its first being heard in *Rabbit-Proof Fence* to accompany Aboriginal singing [4:23]. After we have been visually introduced to Riggs, as well as Molly with her family, we hear a white man's voice say, off-screen, "that's them." The off-screen voice then identifies who the three girls are, and the three girls are shown as he names them: Molly (who he identifies as "the big one"), Daisy ("the little one"), and Gracie ("the middle one"). Finally, we see the speaker, the Jigalong depot manager, imaged as an archetypal Aussie settler [4:50]. On the one hand, the

FIGURE 2.10 The first low-angle shot of Riggs.

emphasis on Molly and her family as objects of Riggs's and the manager's gaze, as well as the initial absence of the person attached to the first white voice, suggests white power beyond the limits of the frame. That said, there is a marked contrast between how the camera singles out and/or moves with Molly and her family, even when it simply serves to illustrate what the storehouse keeper says, and how it scrutinizes the white faces of the scene. The camera is subjectively aligned with the Aboriginal characters, whereas the white men are more like the objects of its gaze: put simply, the white men are "*them*" to the camera. Moreover, where we see the faces of Molly and her family almost immediately, the camera delays showing us the white faces of the scene, thus further objectifying the colonial presence. Thus, yet again, the verbal and visual messages are far from straightforwardly aligned.

Our sight of the most powerful white face in the film is delayed: the first glimpse we have of Neville is his hand writing the name "Molly," scratching his ink pen on the letterheaded paper of his office [5:46]. We then see the "Chief Protector's" face from a low angle, a shot that parallels our low-angled introduction to Riggs (see Figure 2.11). The camera's position indicates his power as well, but this is ironized over the course of the film as Molly outwits him and his men. That the sound of Neville's writing Molly's name dominates the sound track right before we see his face subtly anticipates this.

Perhaps the most striking element of our introduction to Neville is his *visible* whiteness. As Richard Dyer has written, white power is often secured by it being

FIGURE 2.11 The first low-angle shot of A. O. Neville.

"especially difficult for white people and their media, to 'see' whiteness" ([1988] 2000, 735). Indeed, white power partly "secures its dominance by not seeming to be anything in particular" (733), or as appearing as the "norm" against which alternatives are identified as such: for instance, film scholars rarely identify white characters as such, unless in relation to ethnic minorities, whereas the ethnic identity of non-whites is almost always mentioned. The common scholarly practice of looking at "non-dominant groups" (such as women, ethnic minorities, lesbians and gay men) "has [often] had the effect of reproducing the sense of oddness, differentness, exceptionality of these groups, the feeling that they are departures from the norm.[36] Meanwhile the norm has carried on as if it is the natural, inevitable, ordinary way of being human" (733). In contrast with such patterns of cinematic and critical practice, *Rabbit-Proof Fence* not only highlights Neville's whiteness, but also makes him appear abnormally pale in contrast with everyone else in the film. In making whiteness visible, the norm is revealed as "constructed" rather than a given (733). In parallel to this, the sound track sets Neville apart by never working *with and for* him. As we have already discussed, even when his favorite song "Swanee River" is sung for him within the film, it is critically presented and his failure to fully listen is highlighted by the camera.

---

[36] Even though Dyer made these claims decades ago ([1988] 2000), they remain widely applicable.

In contrast with the roughly tanned skin of Riggs and the depot manager, Branagh's pale pallor is strongly illuminated to the extent that it is a visual shock. He is also shot from an unflattering low angle, one that slightly distorts his features, and which encourages us to view him critically: the self-flattering image of the colonizer is thus absent from the beginning. Along with our perceiving Neville's whiter-than-white face, the sonic elements of his first scene subtly undermine his power. Neville is visually placed in a well-equipped office full of neat filing boxes and immaculate lines: the *mise-en-scène*, along with the first low-angle shot of him, establish his institutional power. At the same time, we can also perceive the sudden sterility of the noises that define Neville's space: the thin texture of his scratching pen, the shrill sound of an office phone ringing, and the hard sounds of his secretary knocking before she enters the room. Neville's secretary enters to provide details on the "next batch" of Aborigines appealing for his help, including Mary Wilson who is "applying for permission to visit her child at Moore River." "She's quite agitated," Neville's secretary flatly states, but as she says this we see Mary through the office window, wiping tears from her eyes as a car honks on the street next to her (see Figure 2.12).

The honking sound [6:18] is a slight stinger that swiftly communicates the coldness of a white world rushing past Mary, as well as punctuating the image of her in distress. Yet again, image and sound clash with each other. The failure of image and sound to

FIGURE 2.12 The aggrieved Mary Wilson bows her head in distress. She waits with many other Aborigines who must appeal to Neville for help.

"cohere" has deep significance here, for it suggests the breakability of the world that Neville inhabits and, by extension, the ideological fault lines within it.

After hearing of Mary, and offering no response, Neville's secretary lists another item: "Gladys Phillips has written for permission to buy some new shoes." Neville immediately responds "she had a new pair a year ago," and then thuds his stamp into an inkpad and onto his official paper. This is the moment where Neville sonically punctuates his own authority. Where the non-diegetic music of *Rabbit-Proof Fence* often punctuates the actions *for* the Aboriginal characters, Neville gets no more than the sound of his own stamp. The next part of the scene is Neville briefing his secretary on "the three little half-caste girls" (Molly, Gracie, and Daisy) and his "authorizing their removal." Though Neville's words emphasize his particular governmental authority, and Branagh delivers his lines with unwavering assuredness, by the time he mentions their "removal" he is shot with a canted angle. The visual movement off balance undermines the solidity of what he says [6:40–50].

Branagh further undermines Neville's words by flattening the emotional capacities of his voice. Branagh has been celebrated for the vocal range in his performances of major Shakespearean characters on film (including Benedick, Iago, Berowne, Hamlet, Henry V, Richard III). More recently, Branagh played Laurence Olivier in *My Week with Marilyn* (2011), imitating Olivier's vocal virtuosity and dynamic range. In the role of Neville, however, Branagh voice is relatively unchanging: he consistently avoids dramatic shifts in the volume, pitch, or fullness of his speech. He is the best-known white actor of the film, and his image was featured on many promotional materials for the film. However, in the experience of *Rabbit-Proof Fence* itself, Branagh's character is not only the least visually appealing, he is the least *sonically* compelling. The film refuses to let him hold sway, except insofar as Branagh's performance might impress us with its surprising flatness when compared with his other performances.

On one level, *Rabbit-Proof Fence* might seem far from Brechtian because it presents a fable-like story in which the Aboriginal girls represent righteous native strength and Neville (the "Devil") represents white evil. Noyce did not want Neville to be a "clear-cut baddie" because he "killed thousands of Aborigines with kindness, or what he perceived to be kindness" (Cordaiy 2002, 130). He also did not want to give an easy answer to how the stolen generations happened by vilifying Neville (131). Such intentions aside, the film clearly establishes him as the villain. But the film *is* Brechtian insofar as it self-consciously interrogates Neville's assumption of power. This is most aurally obvious in the banal, overfamiliar colonial tunes associated with him, as well as the flatness of Branagh's vocal delivery. Moreover, the film overwhelmingly inverts the reality of colonial power through consistently honoring the perspectives of its Aboriginal characters—the music associated with them throughout the film is texturally much fuller, louder, more complex, and bigger in scale than the music associated with colonial rule.

Rabbit-Proof Fence falls in line with the long history of representing Aborigines in crisis. However, the film also places at least as much emphasis on Molly's strength. And the sound track, in turn, consistently amplifies what we see the Aboriginal characters experience, in hardship as well as triumph. Though the film portrays the violent impact of colonial rule, especially through the scene where the girls are caught, it also amplifies what these experiences are to the girls: they are *always* the primary focus, just as Branagh is pushed to the margins of the film. This is, in itself, a subversive inversion of the historical reality explored by the film.

One other particular scene strongly resonates from a Brechtian perspective. This is the scene in which Neville presents a slideshow to "the Perth Women's Service Guild about the 'problem' of 'half-caste' Aboriginal children" (Frieze 2011, 124–25). Here, Neville presents the Australian government's plan for "biological absorption," showing how "a policy of apparent benevolence of the law [was] transformed into genocide" (123).[37] This scene is immediately preceded by Maude and Grandmother wailing in agony, and Grandmother repeatedly hitting her own head with a rock, after the girls have been captured by Riggs. The audiovisual emphasis on their grief dovetails with the re-entrance of Neville's voice, a sound advance into his slideshow that begins "as you know, every Aborigine born in this state comes under my control." The film thus makes a tight aural connection between the women's misery and Neville's control.[38] This connection undermines the authority Neville then assumes over his female audience.

The film cuts to show Branagh at the front of a room, standing next to strongly projected images that reinforce his speech. The most significant slide shows three people: the "progression" from obviously Aboriginal "half-blood grandmother," to "quadroom daughter," to "octoroon grandson" (see Figure 2.13).

Neville explains that by repeatedly ensuring that Aborigines marry whites, "the continuing infiltration of white blood finally stamps out the black color." By such means he proposes to eliminate "an unwanted third race" of "half-caste" people. The film visually emphasizes Neville himself inserting the image for projection within an old projector, an action that resonates with a long history of white control over the cinematic

---

[37] Frieze explains that Article 2 (e) of the "Convention on the Prevention and Punishment of the Crime of Genocide" (CPPCG) states that the forcible transference "of children from one group to another, with the intention to destroy a particular group in whole or part, constitutes genocide" (2011, 123). *Rabbit-Proof Fence* invites comparisons between the eradication of the Aborigines and Nazi Germany's attempt to eradicate Jews. For more on this subject, see Rosanne Kennedy's discussion of the Stolen Generations and Holocaust memoirs (2008).

[38] Frieze makes the same connection (2011, 124).

FIGURE 2.13 The crucial image from Neville's slideshow, showing a generational "progression" from Aboriginal to white skin.

image. Neville's voice alone dominates, aside from the sounds of his clicking of the slide into place. Yet again, the thin texture and sterility of the sound track is a marked contrast with those scenes focused on Aboriginal characters. There are no musical sounds accompanying or reinforcing Neville's speech, and his on-screen audience is silent. As he points to the final person on his image, the grandson whose face shows no trace of Aboriginality, he pronounces "the Aboriginal has simply been bred out." Branagh uses extra pausing through this statement: "the Aboriginal [*pause*] has simply been [*pause*] bred out" [13:10–13:16]. Ironically, while he says this with assured emphasis, the film shows him literally merge with the slide behind him [13:16]. At the precise point when he speaks of Aborigines being absorbed into the white population, he is thus himself absorbed within the image (see Figure 2.14).

Neville closes his speech by explaining that hundreds of half-caste children have been gathered up to become domestic servants and farm laborers and to enjoy everything "our culture has to offer," for "in spite of himself, the native *must* be helped."[39] Yet again, his words are ironically undermined, this time with a cut to the train carrying the girls further from their home, with its whistling as a stinger that jolts us back to their experience [14:00]. We soon see all three girls in a cage aboard the train, so Neville's claim that "the native must be helped" is therein immediately undercut. That his words

---

[39] This is the emphasis in Branagh's delivery.

FIGURE 2.14 Neville's body ironically merges with his slideshow image of mixed-race generations.

are frequently undermined, in contrast with the sound track's consistent reinforcement of what the Aboriginal characters experience, should "speak" to us most strongly.

HOW IT ENDS

In contrast with the undermined voice of Neville, *Rabbit-Proof Fence* ends with the uncontested voice of Molly speaking her own language. In voiceover, Molly explains to us how she and her family hid in the desert after she made it home with Daisy. Then she surveys the rest of her life:

> Got married. I had two baby girls. Then they took me and my kids back to that place, Moore River. And I walked all the way back to Jigalong again, carrying Annabelle, the little one. When she was three, that Mr. Neville took her away. I've never seen her again. Gracie is dead now. She never made it back to Jigalong. Daisy and me, we're here living in our country, Jigalong. We're never going back to that place.

In under a minute, Molly speaks of how her entire nine-week walk was undone. But right after she mentions "that Mr. Neville" taking away Annabelle, the film cuts to show Molly and Daisy in old age [1:25:19]. They are identified by on-screen captions (see Figure 2.15).

FIGURE 2.15 The real Molly and Daisy in old age.

The shot appears to be actual archival footage, and the picture quality is substantively different from the rest of the film. The shot rests on the women for a few seconds. We see they are talking but hear only non-diegetic music after Molly's voiceover ends [1:25:48–1:26:04]. In another film context, the absence of their voices might negate the film's progressive objectives. Indeed, our not hearing them speak could seem like a literalization of Gayatri Spivak's famous axiom "The subaltern cannot speak." But Spivak herself claims this has often been misunderstood, because "the question 'Who should speak?' is less crucial than 'Who will listen?'" (1990, 59). With reference to this, Corinn Columpar concludes that "the subaltern cannot speak insofar as he or she *cannot be heard*" (2010, 79, my emphasis). Because *Rabbit-Proof* prompts us to "question received versions of reality and history," it makes us "capable of hearing a counterhegemonic perspective," even despite the absence of speech in this final glimpse of the women (77).

This final glimpse comes as a shock, even though the film began with an emphasis on its own status as historical representation. All at once, the mythological properties of the film are grounded in the appearance of the bodies that actually made the journey we have seen adapted to film. They are not timeless characters: they are real people now aged. Because we cannot hear their voices in this final image of them, the film invites us to imagine what they might be saying, to make our own contribution to the film's dialogue.

 # TEN CANOES

PLOT SUMMARY

Ten Canoes is focused on several generations of Aborigines, and therein distinguishes itself from two dominant practices within Australian cinema: undermining the power of main Aboriginal characters by showing them from white perspectives, and the more frequent practice of only featuring Aborigines in minor roles. *Ten Canoes* is also widely acknowledged as the first Australian feature film in entirely indigenous languages, a point that in itself represents a radical break from that which precedes it. The action takes place in Ramingining, "a town of about 800 Yolgnu people in the northern part of central Arnhem Land," near the Arafura Swamp region, thus giving us access to an especially remote area where traditional Aboriginal life is still lived (Palace Films 2006).[40] This setting is an important "character" within the narrative, especially as it is enlivened by diegetic sound.

Ten Canoes presents a story-within-a-story: an unseen narrator tells the story of his ancestors, one of whom is an old man named Minygululu (Peter Minygululu) who in turn tells a story to his younger brother named Dayindi (Jamie Gulpilil).[41] While Minygululu tells his story, the brothers are engaged in two main activities with the other men of their camp: building canoes and hunting magpie geese eggs. Dayindi is infatuated with one of his brother's wives, in response to which Minygululu's story works as a cautionary tale. His story first focuses on how their ancestors were disturbed

---

[40] As is also explained in the press kit for *Ten Canoes*, "Yolgnu" translates simply as "the people" but is now also used to refer to Aborigines "originating from central and eastern Arnhem Land in Australia's Northern territory" (Palace Films 2006).

[41] Jamie Gulpilil is the son of Aboriginal screen icon David Gulpilil. He also stars in de Heer's *The Tracker* (2001), a film that is explicitly focused upon the dangerous power of racism in twentieth-century Australia.

by the sudden presence of a stranger near their camp. When Nowalingu (Frances Djulibing), the second wife of one of these ancestors suddenly disappeared, her husband Ridjimiraril (Crusoe Kurddal) believed she had been kidnapped by the stranger. Along with another member of his camp, the "Honey Ant Man" named Birrinbirrin (Richard Birrinbirrin), Ridjimiraril hunted the stranger down and speared him, only to discover he had killed the wrong man (the stranger's brother). Though Ridjimiraril and Birrinbirrin hid the body, their crime was discovered and they were soon confronted by the stranger and other angry warriors from his camp. In accordance with the law of his people, Ridjimiraril agreed to a payback ceremony (a *makaratta*) during which he danced to dodge the spears of stranger's people until there was bloodshed. Without this ceremony, there would have been a war between the two tribes. Ridjimiraril's brother, Yeeralparil (also played by Jamie Gulpilil) joined him during the ceremony to help deflect the spears, but Ridjimiraril was fatally hit. When The Sorcerer (Richard Gudthaykudthay) could not heal him, he eventually performed his own dance of death. Once the mourning for Ridjimiraril was ritually completed after his death, Yeeralparil took over as the husband to all three of his wives: even though Nowalingu was indeed abducted, she escaped and made it home over a treacherous distance only to find her husband gone. Like Dayindi, Yeeralparil desired one of his brother's three wives, the youngest one named Munandjarra (Cassandra Malangarri Baker), and he believed Ridjimiraril's death was his long-awaited chance to simply be with her. However, Yeeralparil soon realized that he must answer the needs of all three wives when they began haggling for his attention almost immediately. Thus, Minygululu's story is a warning to Dayindi who may similarly long for that which is all-too-quickly complicated. Though Minygululu's story is from the past, it is represented within the film in its entirety: thus the diegesis is driven by a consistent fusion between the past and present.

THE GENESIS OF THE FILM

Ten Canoes was co-directed by the Dutch/Australian auteur Rolf de Heer and the Aboriginal artist Peter Dijigirr, and it immediately averted the accusations of appropriation leveled at Philip Noyce for *Rabbit-Proof Fence*. Though the extent of Dijigirr's control is difficult to gauge, the film is widely written about as the result of de Heer's "true partnership"[42] with the Yolgnu people of Ramingining (Shaw 2009). De Heer himself self-consciously describes the process of fusing what the Yolgnu people wanted

---

[42] This is as de Heer himself describes it in his "Personal Reflections" (2007).

the film to be in terms of perspective and truth with traditions of Western cinematic storytelling: he says, "it's authentic to them but it [also] works for us" (Walsh, 2006, 17).

Columpar refers to *Ten Canoes* as an important example of "fourth world cinema"—that is, cinema which "derives its potency from" ancient cultures that "persist within, yet separate from, modern nation-states and thus offers up an outlook that is markedly distinct from that which informs the institutions that typically lend it financial and/or infrastructural support" (2010, xi). Fourth world cinema is "an elusive ideal," but Columpar singles out *Ten Canoes* because it foregrounds "the perspectives, experiences, storytelling traditions, and thus 'core values' of the Indigenous characters" (xi–xii). Though the film cannot be defined as "fully [i]ndigenous" (xii)—and indeed it is "nearly impossible" to find a film "that is shaped by [i]ndigenous protocols or personnel on all relevant counts, from content to aesthetics, funding to cast and crew, mode of production to means of distribution" (xiii)—if viewed on a continuum with "indigenous" and "non-indigenous" on opposite poles, *Ten Canoes* is certainly closer to fourth-world cinema than *Rabbit-Proof Fence*.[43]

The film was originally conceived through conversations between de Heer and David Gulpilil, the most celebrated Aboriginal actor. Gulpilil later became the film's narrator. Having collaborated with de Heer on his "subversive western" *The Tracker*,[44] he wanted to work with him on a film set in Ramingining, the traditional lands where his family lives. Their initial plan was to create a film about Aboriginal characters that would end with their being massacred by white invaders (Davis 2006). As the film built towards a climax "everyone [would be] wiped out. You [would] never find out the end of the story" (Davis 2007, 14). But one day Gulpilil overturned this plan by telling de Heer they would need ten canoes and then, when de Heer failed to immediately understand, he showed him a photograph. It was a black-and-white image of ten Yolgnu men poling canoes in the Arafura swamp, taken by the anthropologist Donald Thomson in the 1930s (Davis 2007, 14).

As de Heer explains in many promotional materials about the film, Thomson was an important inspiration beyond this individual photograph.[45] He was sent by the government to the Arnham lands from 1935–37 to "make peace" because there had been some violence against white intruders ("some Japanese pearlers had been speared and

---

[43] This continuum approach is adopted by Columpar (2010), who in turn draws on Houston Wood's approach throughout *Native Features* (2008).

[44] Starrs refers to the film as such (2009, 173).

[45] Exhibitions of Thomson's photographs accompanied the premiere screenings of *Ten Canoes* at the Adelaide Arts Festival (Davis 2007, 12).

a policeman had been killed"). Though Thomson was sent as an institutionally sponsored investigator and recorder, he wound up also becoming a "community advocate and mediator between the Aborigines and the government" (Bell 2007, 35). Thomson gained the community's trust to the extent that he was able to take about 4000 photographs of them.[46] Here are just two representative examples of Thomson's photographs (on the left) and stills from *Ten Canoes* that imitate them (on the right) (see Figures 2.16 and 2.17):[47]

Though Thomson first took his photographs with the aim of "preserving" a dying culture, "they have since been *re-appropriated* by the Yolgnu people as a new form of cultural memory."[48] In other words, Thomson eventually played a dual role as "colonial explicator of indigeneity, *and* preserver of local traditions" (Crosbie 2007, 143, my emphasis). His photographs show the ancient activities of making bark canoes and goose egg hunting, both of which are central actions within *Ten Canoes*. The photographs are also "[c]herished for their evocation of lost, rarely seen moments of non-settler-influenced culture" (140). *Ten Canoes* represents an attempt to breathe moving life into the memories that Thomson recorded and which are historically and spiritually significant to the Yolgnu people.[49]

Thomson's photographs have come to stand for an atypical, forward-thinking capacity to challenge the ideology of white Australia. *Ten Canoes* represents a similar subversiveness for its own generation, not least because it visually "quotes" many of his photographs in its black-and-white sequences. The photographs themselves also inspired casting decisions: Yolgnu community members identified all the people from the photographs as "someone's grandfather or uncle and so on" (Bell 2007, 36). Those members most closely related to those photographed were cast accordingly. De Heer explains that the process was "more subtle than [actors] playing their ancestors," because a man who was to be cast would say "He is my ancestor, therefore I am him" (36). That the Yolgnu participants thus determined the cast in terms of their actual kinships obviously goes against typical processes of casting for Western films: although

---

[46] Thomson also shot 20,000 feet of film that was destroyed by fire in 1946. His photographs, now known as "the Thomson Collection," are held at Museum Victoria (Davis 2006). For more on the nuances of Thomson's photography as ethnography, see Rutherford (2012).

[47] These images are frame captures from a DVD extra (on disc two) for *Ten Canoes* titled "Thomson Time." The photographs were included in "Thomson Time" courtesy of the Thomson family and Museum Victoria.

[48] Davis explains de Heer's own understanding of the photographs as such, with this emphasis (2006).

[49] In addition to his photography, Thomson set up several expeditions to study Aboriginal peoples and campaigned for justice for them, although his recommendations were not acted upon until shortly before his death in 1970 (Bell 2007, 35).

 Two photographs by Donald Thomson (on the left of each frame) and their counterparts in *Ten Canoes* (on the right of each frame).

films often have personnel in charge of casting, the director usually has the ultimate say in who is chosen based on talent and appearance (Davis 2006).

Along with deferring to the Yolgnu people for casting the film, de Heer explains how the script ultimately took shape in terms of Yolgnu culture. First, he explains critical differences in language that affected the script: "[Aboriginal] stories are structured quite differently to [white Western peoples' stories]. That's reflected in their language: for instance, they have no pronouns for 'I,' 'you,' 'he,' or 'they' but they have sixteen different words for 'we.' They could say 'we' and just describe you and me, or describe your family and my family and so on" (Bell 2007, 36). De Heer also explains that rehearsing did not work because "there was no understanding of the repetition." The elders felt "ashamed" when they were asked to repeat their performances "as though they weren't doing it right" (36). Early on, de Heer realized that the filmmakers had to therefore capture the actors' performances as they happened organically, without expecting second chances. In this context, he made the decision that all the dialogue would be improvised "and the parameters were very broad" (36). Thus, we might reasonably argue that everything said in *Ten Canoes* is at least coauthored by the actors. Though the genesis of the film was visual, in homage to Thomson's photographs, the entire production took shape from sounds *belonging* to the Aboriginal cast. And once the film was made, the Yolgnu people literally claimed the story as their own. De Heer explains that "they have no notion of fiction, so stories by their very nature have to be true, at least in perception" (Bell 2007, 36). The story of *Ten Canoes* has "been subsumed into their culture as a story that has always existed" (36).[50]

TEN CANOES AS A NEW EXPERIENCE

The story of *Ten Canoes* features three time frames: the unspecified present of the narrator, the past of his immediate ancestors, and the ancient or more "mythical past," also known as Dreamtime (Clothier and Dudek 2009, 85–86).[51] Though Dreamtime is an especially difficult concept to translate for Western audiences, especially since it has nothing to do with sleeping, Hodge and Mishra simply define it as "a time in the past whose values are still active in the present" ([1991] 2006,

---

[50] For more on the collaboration between de Heer and the people of Ramingining, see the documentary *Balanda and the Bark Canoes* (Molly Reynolds, Tania Nehme, Rolf de Heer, 2006). The film includes de Heer's explanation of the *Ten Canoes* agreement, a "detailed legal contract struck between the film's producers and the Yolgnu people of Ramingining." The contract "recognizes the Ramingining community's property rights for all artifacts and sets made for and used in the film," unlike most films which give producers the rights of ownership for all materials used (Davis 2007, 6–7).

[51] Henderson notes that the temporal structure of the film is even more elaborate than this, for there are depictions of "the conditional immediate past in the historical present of the ancient past (the imagining by Dayindi's ancestors of events that would explain a mysterious disappearance), and a conditional future in the ancient past (the imagination and projection of possible actions by Dayindi's ancestor)" (2009, 60).

361).[52] Distinctions between time periods are visually marked within the film through contrasts of black and white, color, and washed-out color. The sound track, however, provides *consistent* emphases on diegetic sounds as well as the narrator's voiceover, uniting the disparate times. It is an aural challenge to what Henderson refers to as "habitual Western divisions of time" (2009, 60).

All time periods within the film take place before the arrival of *Balanda* (white people). What Stam and Spence refer to as the "structured absence" of marginalized peoples within cinema is knowingly inverted here. The unprecedented emphasis on exclusively native language, along with the absence of white Australians, means that not only are the film's characters not obliged to "meet the colonizer on the colonizer's linguistic turn" (Stam and Spence [1983] 2004, 882) but the colonizer has no say in the matter. That the film does not deal with the colonial era directly may be read as a new form of "structured absence." The film avoids being trapped by the "ubiquitous racist framework" through reaching back further into the past than the era of colonialism.[53] That the film focuses on Aboriginal lives dating back to ancient times reminds us that the native people of Australia lived there thousands of years before colonial rule, and for much longer than colonial rule has lasted. The film offers a fantasy of direct access to ancient Aboriginal life, but not in such a way to position us as "armchair conquistadors." Instead, *Ten Canoes* demands that we immerse ourselves in an experience that it does not expect us to understand right away. It presents us with a way of life that we *cannot* already know. From the outset, the sound track plays a crucial role in reinforcing this progressive unpredictability.

In the context of her doctoral thesis on oral storytelling traditions, Caroline Josephs writes about the Yolgnu belief in "an experiential approach to knowing" (Caldwell 2009, 106). In parallel to this, de Heer himself emphasizes the value of filmmaking as an experience and of perceiving a film in order to have "an experience that I don't already have" (Walsh, 2006, 17). The immersive sensory experience of *Ten Canoes* requires our attention at least as much as the story which is, by the narrator's own admission, designed to frustrate us. First, the story's nonlinearity is repeatedly used by the narrator to avoid or interrupt a course of action. Second, the narrator repeatedly compares the story to a huge tree with branches ever-spreading and taking new shapes, thus prompting us to

---

[52] Sacha Clelland-Stokes cites a character from another Australian film, *The Last Wave* (1977), in which a character named Dr. Whitburn explains Dreamtime as follows: "Aborigines believe in two forms of time, two parallel streams of activity: one is the daily, objective activity to which you and I are confined, and the other is an infinite spiritual cycle called the Dreamtime—more real than reality itself. Whatever happens in the Dreamtime establishes the values, symbols, and laws of Aboriginality" (2007, 125).

[53] Moore and Muecke refer to Australian cinema in this way (1984).

perceive its growing and reaching far beyond what we can grasp.[54] The film also avoids predictable patterns of cause and effect, in connection with which we might consider de Heer's observation that the word "because" does not exist in Aboriginal language. The narrative unfamiliarity of *Ten Canoes* makes the sound track all the more important for anchoring us in the film experience.

In one representative sequence of nonlinear storytelling, the narrator's voice ties together many pieces of film [12:49–15:57]. The sequence crosscuts from a black-and-white scene of Dayindi and Minygululu engaged in canoe-building after the latter has begun his story, and the narrator's own introductions to the main characters of that same story-within-the-story, each of whom is shown in frontal close-ups. After the narrator introduces Ridjimiraril as a main character in Minygululu's story, he then says the storytelling "must stop for a while" to show the men preparing bark for the canoes. Soon he announces that the story can continue, and then introduces another character, Ridjimiraril's "good" wife Banalandju, only to return to the canoe-building because the bark that has been soaked and warmed with fire must be bent. "But we better keep this story going," he says, redirecting our attention yet again to introduce another new character: Ridjimiraril's second, "jealous" wife, Nowalingu. The two storylines merge when the film shifts back to Dayindi still engaged in making the canoe, but also asking Minygululu about the youngest wife (Munandjarra), who is then shown as the narrator introduces her. Finally, when the narrator then introduces Ridjimiraril's younger brother, Yeeralparil, we see he is by played by same actor as Dayindi (see Figure 2.18). Along with the shifts between color and black and white, the narrator's voice anchors us through such sequences of numerous temporal and stylistic shifts, and the potential confusion of the Yeeralparil/Dayindi casting.

OVERARCHING AURAL PATTERNS

Before zooming in on the scenes of *Ten Canoes* any further, we should consider more of its overarching aural patterns. Several elements of the *Ten Canoes* sound track are immediately foregrounded in the first scene, and consistently maintained thereafter: the use of Aboriginal language, the emphasis on diegetic sounds designed to immerse us within

---

[54] After having introduced the film's main characters, the narrator says "Now this story is growing like a young tree that is flowering for the first time" [32:45–32:46]. Dayindi himself says to Minygululu "This story is a proper tall tree now" [38:30]. Well into the development, the narrator says "This story is growing like a large tree now, with branches spreading everywhere. All the parts of the story have to be told for proper understanding" [54:01–54:12].

FIGURE 2.18 Jamie Gulpilil, the actor playing both Yeeralparil and Dayindi in *Ten Canoes*.

a specific landscape, and the privileging of the narrator's voiceover. The voiceover not only holds together the many shifts back and forth from the distant to the ancient past; it also reflects the deep oral traditions of Aboriginal cultures that predate recorded history. As Langton explains, oral traditions are profoundly important for Aborigines in terms of cultural longevity, artistic expression, social and individual identities, art and spirituality, and pedagogical purposes (2003, 109). Moreover, the film foregrounds the power of Aboriginal speech by repeatedly implying that the narrator's voice can *control* its reality. The narrator's power to actualize the story through speaking is implied by the fact that those scenes from the more distant mythical past are shown in color, whereas those scenes in the more recent past are in black and white. That the scenes from a greater temporal distance are ironically given greater visual vitality, the reversal of what we might expect, is attributable to the narrator's power to make something "be" through speaking. Equally, the more mobile camerawork for the mythical scenes matches the energy of the narrative commentary (Davis, 2007, 13).

Many images of the film illustrate the narrator's words, such as when the frontal, close-up introductions of its main characters are timed with the voiceover. Moreover, the characters themselves seem to respond to the narrator's descriptions of them, as if "on cue." For instance, after the narrator introduces Birrinbirrin and tells us his favorite thing was "honey," we see him smilingly lick his lips [18:48], and when the narrator claims he would even steal honey, Birrinbirrin laughs as if in response [18:54–18:58] (see Figure 2.19).

FIGURE 2.19 Birrinbirrin laughs, as if in response to the voiceover narrator.

Such moments break down the diegetic/non-diegetic divide and reaffirm the narrator's guiding power. The narrator also assumes our compliance with his controlling voice, as he repeatedly tells us to "look," listen," "watch carefully," and "see" numerous details of the film.[55]

That images so often follow or illustrate words in *Ten Canoes* "highlights the vibrancy of a continuing linguistic heritage," one that is crucial for the endurance of Aboriginal culture (Clothier and Dudek 2009, 87). This is another reversal of expectations in that Aboriginal culture is far more often represented as dying or under threat in Australian cinema, as we have already explored through the example of *Rabbit-Proof Fence*. As Mike Walsh writes, "the overwhelming theme of Australian feature films dealing with Aboriginal people has been the unhappy fate they have suffered at the hands of the European colonizer" (11). *Ten Canoes*, by contrast, represents Aboriginal culture as alive as well as ancient, especially through its emphasis on Aboriginal voices

---

[55] Now and then, some on-screen characters also exert controlling influence over the image. For instance, in one sequence after Nowalingu has disappeared, several characters suggest what happened to her and their words are visually supported: one man says he wonders whether a crocodile ate her, for instance, and the film cuts from his face to a crocodile moving slowly through the swamp; Birrinbirrin suggests she ran away and we then see her doing so; and Ridjimiraril claims the stranger took her and we then see that happen too [35:06–08, 35:30–43, 36:02–07]. This pattern of images actualizing the possibilities of words emphasizes a theme of relative truth as well as further reinforcing the power of sound to make reality appear.

and languages. Bruno Starrs refers to de Heer's insistence that the film be entirely in Aboriginal language as a "subtle statement" (2006, 18). Yet in terms of Australian cinematic and postcolonialist history, this is an understatement. Where Noyce feared using Aboriginal language in *Rabbit-Proof Fence* because did not believe mainstream audiences would pay to see it subtitled, de Heer insisted that *Ten Canoes* be entirely in Aboriginal languages.[56] Though there are international versions of the film with the narration spoken in English by Gulpilil, de Heer and his seven co-producers did not allow much dubbing in deference to "the importance of language" for the film's "form and meaning."[57] As Davis writes, it is unlikely that few people beyond the Ramingining area will understand the language spoken, but "the film leaves us with a strong sense that what we were hearing is a language that is very much alive" (2006). In addition, because all dialogue of the film is filtered through subtitles we are constantly reminded that the culture must be *translated* for us; the story is never offered up to us as something to which we can have direct access. In this way, *Ten Canoes* avoids positioning us like armchair conquistadors more markedly than *Rabbit-Proof Fence*.[58]

ROLF DE HEER AS AURAL AUTEUR

That the sound design of *Ten Canoes* prominently and self-consciously focuses attention on its characters' perspectives connects with other films directed by de Heer. Starrs argues that the "fundamental goal" of de Heer's films is to provide "an amplified voice for the unheard, the marginalized, the Other" (2006, 20).[59] He also mentions a pattern within de Heer's work of foregrounding aural manipulations in the service of

---

[56] As is explained in the press kit for *Ten Canoes*, the Ramingining town was formed in the 1970s by Aboriginal people from several different areas, and there are "about eight different language groups." In *Ten Canoes*, Ganalbingu, the language of one of the local Arafura Swamp clans, is dominant. However, some characters speak other languages and still understand each other "perfectly well": Minygululu speaks Mandalpingu, for instance, and Ridjimiraril speaks yet another language from Maningrida (Palace Films 2006).

[57] Since foreign films are routinely dubbed in Italy, de Heer took particular care to explain to the Italian distributor how much would be lost in that process. Eventually, de Heer saw the need for compromise: he sought out an Italian whose voice would at least approximate the storytellers' accent and intonation because an entirely subtitled version would have automatically "marginalized" the film by its being then only released in small Italian arthouses (Starrs 2007a).

[58] Recall that *Rabbit-Proof Fence* only subtitles a few Aboriginal lines, and that the dominant language is always English (even if the dominance of English over Aboriginal languages is critically represented within the scenes set at Moore Settlement).

[59] Though de Heer's own approach is "deliberately not intellectualized" in terms of intentionally creating such a pattern, he agrees to this having unconsciously happened in an interview with Starrs (Starrs 2007b, 20). The term "aural auteur" is borrowed from the title of Starrs's PhD thesis (2009).

amplifying such voices. Similarly, Cat Hope draws a parallel between de Heer's consistent emphasis on needing to understand disempowered characters and sound itself as a marginalized but essential ingredient in our visual culture" (2004). Sound is a consistently crucial element of de Heer's films, especially in terms of binding us to their characters and thematically emphasizing transformational possibilities: the protagonist of *Bad Boy Bubby* (1993) connects to the world by vocally mimicking others;[60] a little girl in *The Quiet Room* (1996) protests her parents' feuding by making herself mute; the central female character of *Dance Me to My Song* (1998) is disabled with cerebral palsy to the extent that she relies upon a computerized voice box; and the alienated wife of *Alexandra's Project* (2003) "finds her voice via her video recorder" (Starrs 2006, 20).[61]

Hope provides a useful summary of sound as a "defining creative tool" in the making of de Heer's films, especially *The Tracker*, a film that features songs composed by Graham Tardiff with lyrics by de Heer himself. For de Heer, it was crucial to have an indigenous performer, Archie Roach, perform the songs that comment on the action of *The Tracker* (Hope 2004). The songs in themselves constitute an important challenge to white domination within the film. Roach later performed live as the film was screened at the 2002 Adelaide Arts Festival, literally amplifying the power of the songs in relation to the film. For *The Tracker*, de Heer's longtime sound designer John Currie also recorded about eight hours of different sounds from Arkaroola (South Australia), a catalog of sonic ways to represent "the truth in location" (Starrs, n.d.). The film's emphasis on providing a full soundscape to relay localized authenticity is another strong precedent for *Ten Canoes*.

In order to create a parallel illusion of being *with* his characters on location for *Ten Canoes*, de Heer worked with Dr. Matthew Sorrell, Research Director of the Convergent Communications Research Group at Adelaide University to create a custom device for dialogue recording: the MSI Megastick 256. The device runs on a single AAA alkaline battery and has enough memory for nine hours of recording, enabling comparative freedom with filming without need to interrupt it for changing batteries. Sorrell himself explains that each actor in *Ten Canoes* was given such a microphone that was then hidden in their hair or hung from their neck in a traditional pouch. Simultaneous recordings with these microphones amounted to about a hundred hours of sound recording per day of shooting, over a seven-week period, thus generating a particularly full aural archive of the environment in which filming took place (Starrs, n.d.).[62] The recording

---

[60] For more on *Bad Boy Bubby* as it reflects de Heer's consistent focus on aural strategies of characterization and audience manipulation, see Anna C. Hickey-Moody Melissa Iocca (2004).

[61] See Hope (2004) for another fuller discussion of de Heer's use of sound leading up to *Ten Canoes*.

[62] For all this behind-the-scenes information, Starrs cites Oster (2005, 45).

technology enabled minimal interruptions, meaning that the film could easily capture numerous moments of instantaneous creation that were not authored by de Heer. This was especially important given that (as noted above), the actors were invited to create dialogue related to the scenarios he envisaged.

The MSI Megastick 256 enabled de Heer to capture the on-location voices (and sounds) for *Ten Canoes* that are consistently privileged within his work, with the aim of avoiding the contrivances of post-synchronization dialogue dubbing. Currie explains that post-synchronization dubbing was "out of the question" for the film, and not just due to financial considerations: the reality of filmmaking an Aboriginal group of actors in a remote area for whom "the art of make-believe was natural" but for whom film-making practices were new meant that post-synchronized dubbing would have introduced an unworkable level of artifice. In addition, post-synchronization would have been complicated due to the unscripted nature of the dialogue. Even though de Heer is credited at the end of the film for its screenplay and the Australian Film Institute gave de Heer the prize for best original screenplay in 2006 (Hiatt 2007, 72),[63] de Heer himself claims that "all [his] decisions" were tempered by what the local Yolgnu community wanted and they "had a strong sense that we [the film crew] were the means by which they were telling their story" (Davis, 2007, 16). The sound technology that de Heer and his collaborators used to record the unscripted words of the actors led to a comparatively direct representation of *their* storytelling over his.

THE FILM'S BEGINNING

Right from the start, the sound track of *Ten Canoes* resonates in terms of the fundamental arguments within Stam and Spence's article: it emphasizes the perspective of indigenous people who are all too consistently marginalized in the dominant (Australian) cinema; it makes demands of us rather than allowing us to be distanced and presumptuous "armchair conquistadors"; it makes us perceive the structured absence of white Australians; it features native language and therein rejects the "colonist attitudes" all-too-often indicated by the lack of it in other Australian films; it presents Aboriginal realities as if "from within," thus inverting the more typical cinematic representations of Aboriginal culture as viewed from white perspectives; and it invites our comprehension

---

[63] The screenplay credit reads as follows: "written by Rolf de Heer in consultation with the people of Ramingining." There are five translators acknowledged in the final credits as well, and they surely have some claim on the final script. Hiatt also emphasizes that Gulpilil was undoubtedly a decisive influence on the screenplay, and perhaps a significant collaborator, despite being uncredited as such (2007, 73).

of its processes in a Brechtian manner, especially through its self-consciously unconventional sound track.

The film begins with several long, tracking, aerial views of Arafura swamp as we hear the sounds of its teething with life: birds, insects, wind, and stirring water. Visually, the opening works as a relatively standard series of establishing shots that convey an omniscient or overseeing perspective. The sound of the film, however, immediately works more unconventionally. First, there is the musical impact of the landscape sounds in place of more familiar opening credit scoring: Clothier and Dudek write of the aerial shot being "underscored by native bird calls," instead of music, for instance (2009, 82). The sounds of native birds anticipate an aural motif of birds "answering" or punctuating characters' experiences throughout the film, emphasizing the inextricability of nature and the native people, yet not in a clichéd sense.

Many other times through *Ten Canoes*, the sound track similarly emphasizes that the Aboriginal characters are inseparable from the life of the landscape. This is an important departure from the more familiar filmic emphasis on the presence of white men on Australian soil. As the main characters of the story-within-the-story are introduced in frontal close-ups, their presences are not only explained by the narrator but also reinforced by sounds of nature, especially birds and insects. Later, the narrator tells us to listen to the men "honking like geese" [26:14], and to the women also "chattering like magpie geese" [28:06]. When the stranger is imaged stealing Nowalingu away, an off-screen bird screeches as if it were her voice [36:06]. Similarly, the screech of a bird punctuates the scene of Ridjimiraril and Birrinbirrin finding the man they have speared [53:09]. The narrator says Dayindi thinks of Yeeralparil and Munandjarra's "destinies... like butterflies in the air... they could go here, they could go there" [45:05–45:14]. And one diegetic song sung by Dayindi as he strips bark for his canoe-building [45:16–46:23] is mixed with the familiar sounds of the swamp—birds, water, insects, slight wind—emphasizing that his life is inseparable from other forms of life there. The environment not only underscores his song, but merges with it. The inextricability of the characters and nature is also in the narrator's describing Dayindi's experience of going with Minygululu to "learn the swamp and hear more story" [32:42].

The overall impact of insisting on the characters being interconnected with all forms of nature is *not* a clichéd representation of Aboriginal life as natural in a primitive, primal sense, as from the perspective of the colonizer.[64] Instead, the film represents

---

[64] For much more on clichéd patterns of associating "the natives" with nature, see Terry Goldie's important study of the limited range of roles played by indigenous characters in Canadian, Australian, and New Zealand literature, and especially the chapter titled "The Natural" (1989, 19–40).

FIGURE 2.20 Ridjimiraril returns home with the wallaby he slaughtered.

the lives of the native inhabitants as simply inseparable from their immediate natural surroundings, including all those forms of life that surround and sustain them. Instead of presenting their lives in nature with condescension, then, the film creates the impression of a never-ending conversation between nature and the Aboriginal characters, and one that often involves so many layers of landscape sounds and overlapping dialogue that we perceive the impossibility of taking it all in. The film also avoids the trap of sentimentally representing its characters in harmony with nature.[65] Even the film's only wallaby, that most iconically sweet symbol of Australian nationalism, is shown slaughtered by Ridjimiraril and gleefully eaten by his people (see Figure 2.20). Ridjimiraril's second wife delightedly greets him after he approaches her with the animal slung over his shoulder (see Figure 2.21).

That the film emphasizes the place of the Aborigines *in* nature, as unsentimentally and emphatically part of it, is also made explicit in the narrator's first voiceover: almost casually, he speaks of himself as having "looked like a fish" before he was a child that was willed into his mother by his father. Later, he also tells us "When I die, I will go back to my waterhole. . . waiting to be born again."

---

[65] The film also avoids easy sentimentality in some scenes that use physical humor, such as when characters tease each other about farting, or when Dayindi teases Minygululu by implying he has a "limp dick" because he is an older man.

FIGURE 2.21 Ridjimiraril's wife delightedly greets him, anticipating their wallaby feast.

As noted in the above references to Kibby's work on *Rabbit-Proof Fence,* it was possible to hear the landscape in that film "speaking" like a separate entity from the characters. By contrast, *Ten Canoes* sonically represents the landscape and its people as more obviously inseparable: this is clearest in the many points at which bird cries, insect buzzes, and human conversations overlap. But it is also firmly established from the outset, by the film's first aural emphasis on the sounds of the landscape that precede the human voice and that become a form of underscoring for it. The film's immediate emphasis on a sonic sense of authentic place (foregrounding the sounds of *native* birds and insects), and on meeting characters only after that place is aurally emphasized, also makes it clear that the film is much more interested in representing a specific people within a particular context than in presenting a transnational myth designed for a global audience. Therein, *Ten Canoes* again differs from the myth-making tendencies of *Rabbit-Proof Fence.* And although *Ten Canoes* clearly speaks to a primarily non-Aboriginal and potentially non-Australian audience, it does not impose the language of the colonizer on its characters at any time.[66] This is another crucial difference from *Rabbit-Proof Fence.*

---

[66] There are different audio options on the Australian DVD release of *Ten Canoes*: the entire film in Aboriginal language without subtitles, the entire film in Aboriginal languages with subtitles in English, or a "theatrical version" of the entire film in English with dubbed dialogue. (All quotations from *Ten Canoes* in this analysis are from the English subtitles.)

The very first voiceover of *Ten Canoes* begins after the sounds of rumbling thunder and rain overlap with a return to the very first sounds of the film: birds, insects, wind, and stirring water [0:44–0:59]. In under a minute, the sound track suggests cycles of nature that pertain to the inter-related stories of three generations through the film as well as dramatically leading up to the narrator's voiceover. That his voice takes precedence after the implied beginning of a storm suggests the film's assuredness as a response to the "storm" of that which precedes it through colonial and post-colonial history (including representations of Aboriginal life on film). The opening minute of the film sonically communicates a kind of natural purging, one that paves the way for a new voice to assert itself. The voice of the narrator has particular authority in that it belongs to David Gulpilil: it is also instantly recognizable as an archetypically Aboriginal Australian voice.[67]

The narrator begins his first speech in a familiar way—"Once upon a time, in a land far, far away..." [1:07–1:08]—only to stop as he laughs and restarts, "No, not like that, I'm only joking." As Clothier and Dudek point out, this beginning alludes to Western traditions of orality, and Western fairytales, as well as the beginning of *Star Wars* in particular: "A long time ago in a galaxy far, far away" (2009, 82). The narrator's laughter may be at our expense, or may be more about preparing us to receive "a very different kind of story" (Henderson 2009, 54).[68] This is a story that the narrator then explicitly claims as his own: "It's not your story, it's my story. . . . a story like you've never seen before. But you want a proper story, eh? Then I must tell you some things of my people, and my land. Then you can see this story, and know it." This section of the voiceover assumes that the audience will not regard the narrator's story as "proper" and this immediately suggests that the narrator must make allowances for his non-Aboriginal audience. However, this does not entail compromising his intentions, as the narrator also anticipates that his telling the story will mean our being able to see it. (This connects with those other moments where the narrator's words seem to summon the film's images "on cue.") His anticipation of what we will see through hearing him immediately challenges the broad assumption of film as a visual-over-aural medium, or the more familiar filmic emphasis on that which is seen "speaking for itself." Here, instead, the story will be told so that we may *then* see it. The word "see" surely has figurative as well as literal meaning here. The narrator's act of speaking, as well as our act of hearing,

---

[67] This would at least be obvious to most Australian audiences (Starrs 2009, 173).

[68] Henderson also writes of how the film positions the audience from the outset, with emphasis on the knowing self-referentiality of the narrator's first voiceover as it deliberately alludes to *Star Wars* (2009, 54).

will lead to the picture not only being literally perceivable, but also understandable. This is not, however, an invitation for us to presume insider's knowledge, for the narrator restates his intention to tell a story of "my people, and my land."

Lest I seem to presume too much here, I must myself make a brief break with the convention of this book and its publisher to make my own subject position explicit. As Dyer writes, it is important to acknowledge "the place of the writer in relation to what s/he is writing about" ([1988] 2000, 733). Equally, Stuart Hall emphasizes that the "I" who writes must be understood as writing from "a particular place and time": what we say is always "'in context,' *positioned*" ([1989] 2000, 704, original emphasis). I identify myself as a white New Zealander with limited experience of white Australian, and even less exposure to Aboriginal Australian, culture. In my analysis, I make no claim to understand Aboriginal culture except as the film prompts me to do so. *Ten Canoes* assumes my outsider position: when the narrator says "It's not your story, it's my story," he makes it clear that I cannot own what he says.[69] This analysis is far from an attempt to fix the meaning of the film or claim my full understanding of anything in its sound track. Rather, I am humbly focused on opening up new possibilities for understanding the film's aural significance.

That the narrator says "It's not your story, it's my story" and then never appears to us on-screen establishes and preserves his power. He is separate from and authoritative over us, even as he is our primary guide and sonically "nearest" to us in terms of the consistently, closely miked sound of his voice. That he never appears on-screen may again remind us of Chion's writing about the acousmêtre. The narrator has the authority of being positioned outside the diegetic space because his body is not ever seen as he speaks, nor does his voice come from a straightforward off-screen place, "in an imaginary 'wing'" (1994, 129). The narrator's power is well reflected by Chion's description of the acousmêtre's unearthly possibilities: "the character who has [. . .] a voice but no body, is taken as more or less all-seeing, all-knowing, often even all-powerful" (1999, 100). With the opening of *Ten Canoes*, there is an immediate sense that the narrator/acousmêtre might intervene and redirect the film at will, that his voice might change the visual direction of the film at any point without our being able to anticipate it. But he is never reducible to an image himself.

After the opening aerial shots that set the scene and the opening voiceover that establishes the narrator's voice of irreducible authority, the narrator himself begins

---

[69] In the second voiceover, after having introduced the two main characters, he makes a similar point: "it is my story for you now. It is a good story. Maybe this story will help you live the proper way, eh?" [9:10–9:22]. After these lines he laughs gently, playfully underlining that he assumes nothing about our ability to apply the story to our own lives.

the film a third way: "This land began in the beginning. Yurlunggur, the Great water Goanna, he travelled here. Yurlungger made all this land then" [1:50–2:05]. Yurlungger is subsequently identified as the spiritual being who transformed the land by making the swamp and the water that brings life to it, including the waterhole where the narrator came from before he asked his father to be born. In response to his son's request, the narrator says his father chose "one of his wives" and dreamed of the baby inside her. That baby became the narrator himself. Now the narrator anticipates that he will return to the waterhole when he dies: he will then be "waiting, like a little fish. . . to be born again." After explaining all this to us, the narrator simply asks us "You didn't know all that, did you? But it's a true thing. It's always like that for my people." Next, he informs us "we have to find where this story is, this story I'm going to tell you," thus assuming our complicity in his process of educating us. "We have to go back longtime, back to the time of my ancestors." The narrator thus challenges us again with what we do not know, with his awareness of our difference from him, and then directly tells us what we must do.[70]

The narrator's aural presence consistently controls what the film shows us. Over the course of this entire first voiceover, tracking shots take us further and further into the swamp land, immersing us further and further within his world. As the narrator anticipates going "back to the time of my ancestors" the image slowly and subtly shifts from color to black and white, seemingly at his will [4:04–4:24]. The process happens gradually, in a ponderous rhythm with the narrator's speech. The subtle slowness of the visual shift emphasizes the interconnectedness of the generations (the color seems to "flow" into black and white), as well as the controlling power of the narrator's voice as it presides over the change. With the first change to black and white, the film title "Ten Canoes" appears, punctuating the visual change that he seemed to bring about. Then, after a cut to a different landscape view of bushland around the swamp, the narrator says "shhh. . . I can hear them coming. . . my ancestors" [4:41] who then slowly enter from a medium distance, reminding us of his control as well as obliging us to listen before we can see any of the film's characters. The simple fact that the characters are first shown from some distance while the narrator's voice is always closely miked in itself places our aural connection with him over the image of on-screen characters, even when he lowers his voice.

---

[70] The educational authority of the film, including its narrator, is supported by a school study guide by Robert Lewis (2006). The existence of this study guide (designed for all students from middle school upwards) indicates the film has been intended as a pedagogical tool, in keeping with the explicit approach of the film's narrator.

A BRECHTIAN REALITY

Despite how *Ten Canoes* immerses us within its location shooting, a tendency that might have led to an overwhelming illusionist impact, the film repeatedly demands that we perceive its structure and our participation in it. In light of Stam and Spence's article, it matters that the film does not claim to represent the full truth or reality with window-on-the-world authority, nor does it allow us to lose ourselves in the fictional experience. From the first voiceover, the narrator repeatedly addresses the audience as "you"—a pattern that creates an impression of intimacy, but which also prompts our active, self-conscious engagement with his storytelling. That the sound track repeatedly prompts such engagement is especially clear in the numerous times that the narrator literally tells us how to perceive the image, as in Ridjimiraril's death scene when he instructs us on what we should see *and* hear: "see how Ridjimiraril makes one very big effort," "look at him get up while he still has the strength," "hear the clapsticks start," "see how he keeps dancing," and "hear now. They are starting to sing."[71] The repeated use of imperatives again connects speaking with making reality, much as the opening voiceover takes controlling precedence over the images it accompanies.

As Moore and Muecke write, in the context of their critical summary of racist representations of Aborigines on film, "it cannot be assumed that a just and 'true' Aboriginal expression can be unleashed through a supposedly neutral medium. If, as we have assumed, the filmmaking medium regularly activates racist representations, then the first job might be to expose *their* operation" (1984, 46).[72] The self-consciousness with which the sound track, and the narration of *Ten Canoes* in particular, asserts its control over us, positions us to learn. It therefore represents a strong challenge to the racist representations of Aborigines that precede it, and which allow us to presume too much.

PATTERNS OF MUSIC AND "SCORED" SOUND EFFECTS

The narrator's voice is the most consistently powerful sound of *Ten Canoes*. Music is used much more economically within the film and it does not bathe us in affect like

---

[71] Clothier and Dudek also call particular attention to this speech as it interpolates a non-Yolngu viewer to follow the narrator's "commands and questions" (2009, 90).

[72] Moore and Muecke cite several films that represent resistance to dominant representations of Aborigines using conventional filming techniques, one of which is *Two Laws* (1982), a documentary focused on the Borroloola Aboriginal community facing issues of land rights and welfare. The film features the community's own voices in the process, although it was directed by two non-Aboriginals, Carolyn Strachan and Alessandro Cavadini (1984, 46).

Gabriel's scoring for *Rabbit-Proof Fence*. Instead, the film seems designed to avoid being explicitly emotive—it is focused on providing us with an immersive experience within the localized landscape of its characters, rather than on enveloping us within transcendent sound. About half of the music of *Ten Canoes* originates from within its diegesis, in contrast with the dominant non-diegetic music of *Rabbit-Proof Fence*. Even the music which comes from an off-screen source in *Ten Canoes* sounds as though it could be created by the characters because it features indigenous instruments, especially that instrument most internationally identified with Aboriginal culture: the didjeridu.[73] The didjeridu was developed by Aborigines about 1500 years ago and *Ten Canoes* immediately reminds us of its ancient power: we first hear it early on, when the narrator speaks of all his ancestors as "little fish in their waterholes," before they were even born [9:50–9:55].

The music of *Ten Canoes*, including several of the didjeridu-dominated non-diegetic cues, all seems to come from the same place as its characters, whether or not we see it emanate from within their bodies or by their physical performances.[74] This pattern in itself serves several functions: first, the music in itself reflects the film's concern with cultural authenticity; second, the music does not reflect an outsider's perspective on the action and is instead aligned with the characters, from whom the primary audience is assumed to be separate (at least by the narrator); third, the use of indigenous instruments as well as voices reinforces a particular and localized sense of place without the sweeping possibilities of transcendence and globalized outreach that are implied by Gabriel's transnational and synthesized sounds for *Rabbit-Proof Fence*; fourth, that much of the music is diegetically controlled by the Aboriginal characters or non-diegetically associated with ancient Aboriginal history amplifies the film's focus on the indigenous "from within," rather than on reacting to them as from an outsider's point of view. In short, the music of *Ten Canoes* is a deep contrast to Gabriel's score from *Rabbit-Proof Fence*. Even though the latter soundtrack communicates a strong alignment with the Aboriginal

---

[73] The emphasis on Aboriginal characters making their own music in *Ten Canoes* makes for a fascinating comparison with *The Sapphires* (2012), a film based on a true story about an all-female Aboriginal singing group who perform for American troops in Vietnam in 1968. The women are managed by a white man who tutors them on singing American soul music: though *The Sapphires* privileges the voices of its Aboriginal characters, they do not perform much music they can reasonably call their own. The racial politics of the film are consistently confusing: while the main female characters overcome prejudice in a postcolonial context, they do so by performing for troops who are fighting for what can be perceived as "the cause" of colonial oppression against the Vietnamese.

[74] All of the music in *Ten Canoes* is performed by Aborigines, including the non-diegetic, incidental music, as well as the more prominent diegetic music. Since there is no composer credit, we might conclude that the performers co-created the music under the leadership of sound designer James Currie and co-designer Tom Heuzenroeder, as well as director Rolf de Heer.

protagonists, we may nevertheless readily perceive that much of it comes from a different place than they do.

Lest this comparison seem too critical of Gabriel's music, we can hardly doubt the humane and progressive objectives of his scoring for *Rabbit-Proof Fence* in that it is clearly designed to foster our emotional engagement with the young girl protagonists. That said, we might also consider how that music sometimes softens the truths of what the girls must endure to some extent, and that his separates us from what they actually experienced. Gabriel's score represents a comforting liberal capacity to empathize with the girls, and it invokes that capacity in us. It also mediates the impact of several scenes that might be almost unbearable without it, such as those showing the girls struggling across vast expanses of formidable (though beautifully shot) desert landscapes that are inhospitable to most forms of life. The transcendent implications of Gabriel's particular form of world music repeatedly reassures us of a benign understanding of the girls, one that comes from somewhere beyond what they themselves can perceive, and one that represents a perspective that can see historically beyond the vicissitudes of living under the colonial rule of the twentieth century. The music itself also suggests an all-seeing or omniscient perspective, one that aurally anticipates the completion of the girls' goal. Finally, Gabriel's music frequently sutures scenes and sequences together, without necessarily calling attention to its own purpose as such. *Ten Canoes*, by contrast, does not use music to soften the film's action, or to communicate a benign sense of predetermination from an outsider's point of view, or to provide a sutured sense of coherent film form. Instead, the music of the film punctuates how the characters themselves perceive action or give shape to it in their own right. The non-diegetic "incidental" music of the film most often punctuates moments of danger, such as when the mysterious stranger appears (discussed more fully below). But both diegetic and non-diegetic sounds frequently change *on* the cut to a change of scene. This reinforces the film's focus on representing truths from an insider's perspective while also making us aware of the necessary construction involved in this process. In addition, the film does not appeal to its assumed non-Aboriginal audience through using Western music more familiar to them. Instead, it confronts us with an aural experience that literally differs from any other.

NON-DIEGETIC MUSIC, AND "MUSICAL" DIEGETIC SOUND

The non-diegetic music of *Ten Canoes* is occasionally startling as it punctuates some narrative shifts, and amplifies the impact of climactic scenes. For instance, a low and ominous non-diegetic didjeridu cue marks the entrance of the stranger who has not "signaled he was coming" and amplifies the threat of his presence, even when he is shown from a visual distance [19:40–20:23]. The narrator tells us "he had the smell of someone very dangerous," and the sound track self-consciously alerts us to that which the characters similarly perceive beyond what they (or we with them) can literally see from a distance. Here, the subjectivity of sound is also emphasized in that the stranger's words are not translated after the narrator explains that the other ancestors do not understand his language well. When the stranger makes a later, sudden reappearance, his arrival is punctuated by his shouting loudly enough that all other sounds of the characters and their landscape suddenly stop [54:33]. In moments like this, diegetic sound is most obviously "orchestrated" with as much care as music: the sudden interruption to diegetic sound is as impactful as a blaring instrumental cue.

The distinction between musical and non-musical sound often breaks down within *Ten Canoes*, especially since both forms of aural material frequently work together. The sound track when Ridjimiraril dances for the payback ceremony provides another representative example. This scene is aurally anticipated by the narrator saying that "it's time for the makaratta spears to starts flying" [1:03:43]. At this point, he speaks over a scene of his immediate ancestors (Dayindi and the other goose egg hunters gathered to eat). But immediately after the word "flying," the film cuts to the scene of the payback ceremony in the mythical past—yet again, the very form of the film is shaped by his voice. The scene that follows [1:03:44–1:04:54] features a combination of plausible and obviously manipulated diegetic sounds with musical and other non-diegetic sounds. The sounds of spears are foregrounded, along with an aural motif of wind that dominates the film at times of sudden narrative change, until the didjeridu makes a sudden *forte* entrance [1:03:56]. Here Ridjimiraril and Yeeralparil begin their "dance," moving like "ghosts" in slight slow-motion, just as the narrator describes them (see Figure 2.22).

The sonic texture of spears, wind, and didjeridu builds to a peak until there is the sound (before the sight) of Ridjimiraril being hit [1:04:41]. His fall to the ground is punctuated with a rise in the sounds of wind that build to approximate the sound of muffled and airy voices [1:04:41–1:04:55], as if evoking the collective witnessing of the fatal blow or the spirits who the sorcerer later tells Ridjimiraril are waiting for him. Ridjimiraril himself hardly makes a sound. But the sound track makes the far-reaching importance of the fatal blow explicit in terms of the earthbound and the unearthly, the present and the mythical, the real and the imagined, the felt and the witnessed. Here, the merging of diegetic and non-diegetic, musical and non-musical sound surely suggests the interconnectedness of these different forms of reality. The scene therefore reflects a challenge to Western forms of filmmaking that tend to keep such distinctions more intact.

FIGURE 2.22 Ridjimiraril and Yeeralparil begin their "dance," moving like "ghosts" in the pay-back ceremony.

Though this is the climax of the narrative action, and it represents closure in that the narrator tells us "justice has been done," he also assures us there is more of the story to tell. Soon thereafter is the most memorable and extended use of diegetic music [1:11:16–1:13:45]. Even as we see Ridjimiraril's body wounded, weak, and near death after the failed efforts of his wives and their sorcerer to heal him, the narrator instructs us to see him making one last great effort to stand. Sounds of earth (especially insects), fire, and wind "underscore" his slow, painful rise from lying down, giving it a combined elemental power. Then, positioning himself near the fire so that "everyone can see," Ridjimiraril begins his own death dance [1:10:59]. The narrator vocally anticipates the music (others' singing, clapsticks, and didgeridu) that will "soon join him," helping him "begin to make connections with his ancestors in the spirit world" (Palace Films 2006). Though Ridjimiraril's body loses strength through the dance, the music becomes progressively stronger. As the sound track builds to a *forte* peak within a couple of minutes, the narrator urges us to see him dancing until all his strength is gone. After this he must lie down, and the other warriors finish the dance for him. The warriors' dancing includes several leaps up and down on the earth that are punctuated by non-diegetic low drum beats rather than the actual sounds of feet landing. When the dance suddenly ends [1:13:45], there is a return to the sight of Ridjimiraril's body lying down, with the quiet sounds of fire and insects accompanying it. This scene is representative of the film in that it combines textures of diegetic noises with music: again, there is no hard distinction between sound effects and musical structures. This reinforces the power of *Ten Canoes* in making us hear a filmic reality that challenges some familiar sonic classifications.

The sound track also connects directly with the beliefs of the characters. Most obviously, it communicates the spiritual strength within Ridjimiraril that is greater than his body. In addition, the music communicates the importance of a collective and ritualized experience of his death. The narrator explains to us that following his death dance Ridjimiraril waits for his people to sing the death song "so that all his fathers will know that he is dying." "Hear now," commands the narrator when Ridjimiraril's people begin singing for him. Though he seems dead, the narrator assures us "he is only waiting for this singing." "See? See?," asks the narrator as we see Ridjimiraril's hand and foot move in medium close-ups: the movement means he is listening. That the act of listening is here emphasized in a corporeal way further emphasizes the power of sound in a tangible sense. Ridjimiraril's physical indication of his own listening is his last action before death. The film thus communicates that listening is in itself an extremely significant activity, and one that keeps people connected to each other, even in the face of death. Even after Ridjimiraril has died, the narrator also explains that he wants his people to keep singing "to help him find his ancestors." His heart still beats with this purpose after he has died, as the narrator urges us to perceive, though a tight close-up of his chest shows only minute movement: we thus rely on the narrator to explain the image and to make its movement manifest. Here, yet again, the power of sound to shape reality is paramount.

When Ridjimiraril's people sing for him, their words are not subtitled or translated by the narrator. This is unusual, especially since most of the dialogue is subtitled throughout the film. At this point, however, "the songs belong only to the community within the film and to select audiences who have been initiated into their sacred sacrifice" (Clothier and Dudek 2009, 91). So it is that the dramatic peak of the film is not decoded for a non-Aboriginal audience. Since almost everything else spoken or sung in the film is subtitled, this allows us to re-perceive that which we cannot presume to know at the precise point when the action is potentially most all-consuming. The film invites us (as non-Aborigines) to be part of its structure, to perhaps register its sounds with our bodies in parallel with Ridjimiraril, while at the same reasserting that we come from a different place from its characters and we cannot completely understand their language. Thomas Caldwell argues for the film's appeal in its representing "universal" lessons and "values that resonate with white audiences" (2009, 109). Similarly, Paul Byrnes argues that the film's meanings "are accessible, even universal," (2006) and Scott Foundas favorably reviews the film as testimony to "the power of stories to transcend all barriers of space, time, and language" (2007). Yet the climactic scene of *Ten Canoes* is designed to offer something more complex than the illusion of a universal experience. Our being privy to a private ritual is enough. We cannot assume access to all the meaning in it.

In the scene following Ridjimiraril's death, the men and women of his camp continue singing while they paint an image of the waterhole to which his spirit will return onto his body [1:17:13–1:17:48] (see Figure 2.23). The image itself is abstract to a culturally uninitiated audience but the narrator explains what it represents. After this process is complete, the didjeridu soon becomes prominent again, overlapping with the clapsticks, and the singing that fades away [1:18:10–1:18:34]. The music suggests that ancient truths (signified by the didjeridu) are taking over, especially as it accompanies tracking aerial shots over the swamp that suddenly dip down close to the water, implying the flight of Ridjimiraril's soul back to its waterhole home. This implication is paralleled by a cut back to Dayindi and his people as they return to their home camp. Such visual and narrative parallels not only provide a sense of cohesion, but also push towards the end of the film in a satisfying way. That said, the ending of the film is not meant to offer neat closure. Certainly, as the narrator tells us in his final voiceover, the end of Minygululu's story is not what Dayindi "expected." The narrator's last words also anticipate our own frustrated expectations: "And they all lived happily ever after. No, I don't know what happened,"

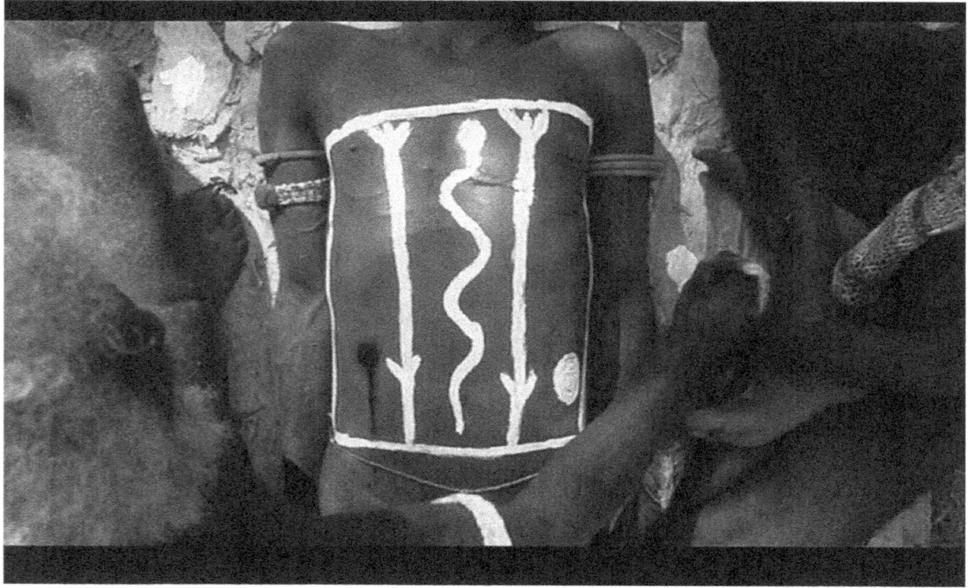

FIGURE 2.23 The symbol of a waterhole, which Ridjimiraril's people paint on his torso.

he says, then giving his deepest laugh before finishing the film. The last lines are as follows:

> Maybe that Dayindi found a wife. Maybe he didn't. It was like that for my people. But now you've seen my story. It's a good story. Not like your story, but a good story all the same.

These last words are followed by one more example of aural unconventionality: the final credits are accompanied by the sounds of the Arafura swamp, much like those that were foregrounded at the beginning. This ultimately reinforces the sounds of that specific place which frequently take precedence during the film. Though the narrator's voiceover is always in aural close-up (that is, closely miked, and clearly separated from the sounds around it), the dialogue within the diegesis is often subdued in relation to diegetic sounds of the swamp. The film thus never lets us forget that its people come from a particular place, and cannot be separated from it.

CRITICAL RECEPTION

Ten Canoes has been widely recognized as a landmark in Australian cinematic history, especially as it breaks with patterns of representing Aboriginal peoples as subordinate to the story (see Zachariah 2009), as it asserts a living indigenous heritage (see Martin 2007), as it represents complex Aboriginal characters in a self-consciously progressive way (see Fuchs 2007, and Kuipers 2006), and as it "gives voice to the silenced past" (Crosbie 2007, 139). Paul Byrnes argues that Australian films about Aboriginal life are "always about the 'problem' of black Australia, rather than the more basic questions of who people are. Aborigines can never really just 'be' in our (white) films. They're always a threat, an accusation, a regret or an ideal." In this context he dubs *Ten Canoes* "the first film to deal with Aborigines as other than an 'issue'" (2006).

In reviews and articles about the film, its aural properties are much more often acknowledged than is standard, signaling a relatively widespread comprehension of the sound track's power. De Heer himself has repeatedly stated that he believes that sound accounts for sixty per cent of a film's emotional content (Starrs 2007b, 20). Currie goes even further by arguing that "cinema overall is 70% sound. Because your ears are far more developed than your eyes. You cannot stop yourself hearing, even if you put your finger in your ears, you still hear. Because it goes through the cheek bones and everything. But eyes are... you can shut your eyes and that's it" (Starrs, n.d.).

Even when critics do not mention the sound track, the film is celebrated in a figuratively sonic sense because it "gives voice to Australians who don't usually have one."[75] Similarly, Shaw argues that the film gives the "Aboriginal people a voice to speak loudly for themselves" (2009). This notion of "giving a voice" has also extended far beyond the film itself in the form of numerous interviews and international attention to the film's significance. It was the winner of the Un Certain Regard award at the Cannes Film Festival in 2006 and won the Best Film Prize from the Australian Film Institute. It was also featured in the 2009 Australian Film Festival in Mauritius.[76]

The Aboriginal actors and crew working on *Ten Canoes* have also been vocal about its significance to them. In particular, Michael Dawu, who plays one of the canoeists, has repeatedly thanked de Heer for the experience. His words below have been cited by several of those who applaud the film:

> *Ten Canoes* [. . .] brings me my memory back and my energy. You wake me up. I have to thank you [Rolf] for it, because you was like this [. . .] "Hey, come on, get up, you'll have to bring your memory." But memory gone. "Here, you'll have to follow like that then, like the old people, and you can make this one film and bring that memory back!" (Davis 2007, 12; Shaw 2009).[77]

Given the film's radicalism, some of the unwittingly reactionary reviews of it are surprising. Stephen Holden of *The New York Times*, for instance, refers to the people of *Ten Canoes* as "primitive" (2007).[78] Stanley Kauffmann also uses the word "primitive" twice with regard to the people represented in *Ten Canoes* and concludes his brief review for *The New Republic* by saying that the film has "the interest of a good travelogue." For him, "[t]he film's rewards are in the enactment of these people's lives: the hunting, the eating, the polygamy, the role of the sorcerer, the intricate face and body painting, the music, and especially the making of a canoe" (2007, 34).[79] Kauffmann

---

[75] Sandy George makes this point in an article for *The Australian* (dated March 21, 2006, titled "Storybook charm avoids guilt buttons"). The online version of this article, as cited by Starrs, is no longer available (2007a).

[76] The Australian High Commissioner to Mauritus, Catherine Johnstone, refers to this festival as a "cultural diplomacy program," devoted to "deepening other communities' awareness of [. . .] Australian multicultural society, going beyond beaches, kangaroos, and koalas" (Aboukhater 2009, 140).

[77] The quotation comes from the press kit for *Ten Canoes* by Palace Films (2006).

[78] This is in the context of Holden raising important questions about how the Aboriginal people "should" be filmed and about how to avoid filming "the noble savage" with condescension or sentimentality. So, his use of the term "primitive" is unintentionally offensive.

[79] Ironically, Kuipers makes the exactly opposite point, pronouncing that *Ten Canoes* distinguishes itself "without any hint of travelogue" (2006, 70).

thus reduces the film to touristic observations, and he Others rather than engages with its people. Appalling though his response may be in its failure to meet the film on its own terms, it surely reminds us that not only do we need *Ten Canoes*, we need many more films like it.

SUMMARY

Both *Rabbit-Proof Fence* and *Ten Canoes* are important cinematic landmarks, especially as they consciously address the structured absences of Aborigines in Australian cinema. The sound tracks of both films affectively draw us into the worlds of their Aboriginal protagonists: Gabriel's world music for *Rabbit-Proof Fence* amplifies the interior lives of the runaway girls on a macrocosmic scale, whereas the diegetic sounds of *Ten Canoes* immerse us within the localized life of its characters.

Rabbit-Proof Fence has been rightly celebrated for prompting worldwide attention to the Stolen Generations. The film uses numerous aural strategies to ensure our consistent sympathetic interest in the Aboriginal characters, especially in contrast with Neville. *Ten Canoes* is more radical through focusing *entirely* on a range of Aboriginal characters without the need for contrast with their white oppressors. Aboriginal voices preceded white voices on Australian soil by 60,000 years, but *Ten Canoes* is the first feature film to demand a complete sonic return to what the nation might have sounded like before it was colonized. In having this status, the film invites us to consider how Australian cinema can more fully explore and represent Aboriginal lives.

With both films, we may question the extent to which empowerment can happen when Aboriginals are given a voice by a white director with a white cameraman. Indeed, Noyce was repeatedly critiqued for his control over the young female actors in *Rabbit-Proof Fence*. Though de Heer's collaboration with the Yolgnu people in *Ten Canoes* has been more positively perceived, he is described like a modern-day conquistador in many promotional materials for the film: specifically, he speaks of standing in a swamp up to his waist for six or seven hours a day, with leeches, mosquitoes, and crocodiles in close proximity (Starrs 2007a). That said, we might equally dwell on de Heer's determination to overcome logistical difficulties to film a specific place so as to create the experience of being immersed within it. Moreover, though de Heer had most control over the final film product, the film itself foregrounds the narrating voice that is not his, and an explicitly Aboriginal voice speaking from "within" native culture rather than perceiving it from the outside. Where Gabriel's music often has to speak for the Aboriginal characters of *Rabbit-Proof Fence*, the strongest guiding sound in *Ten Canoes* is the Aboriginal narrator's voice, especially as it "directs" us to understand what we see. Where *Rabbit-Proof Fence* primarily uses music to affectively align us with its protagonists and to appeal to our compassion, *Ten Canoes* foregrounds the power of David Gulpilil's aural presence. "Shhhh… listen now," he tells us in voiceover, demanding our receptiveness from the beginning: it is not a request or a plaintive appeal to our emotions; it is an instruction.

WORKS CITED

Aboukhater, Jacinta Le Plastrier. 2009. "Taking a Canoe to Mauritius: The Embassy Film Roadshow." *Metro Magazine* 162:138–41.

Achebe, Chinua. 1992. *Things Fall Apart*. New York: Alfred A. Knopf

Aoun, Steven. 2003. "*Rabbit-Proof Fence*." *Metro Magazine* 136:205–6.

Ashcroft, Bill, Gareth Griffiths, and Helen Truffin, eds. 2006. *The Post-Colonial Studies Reader*. 2nd ed. London: Routledge.

Bandt, Ros. 2001. "Hearing Australian Identity: Sites as Acoustic Spaces, an Audible Polyphony." *Australian Sound Design Project*. The University of Melbourne. June 28. Accessed October 8, 2013. <http://www.sounddesign.unimelb.edu.au/site/NationPaper/NationPaper.html>.

Barthes, Roland. 1972. *Mythologies*. Translated by Annette Lavers. New York: Hill and Wang.

Bell, James. 2007. "The Way It Was." *Sight and Sound* 17 (6): 34–37.

Bewley, John. n.d. "Philadelphia Composers: Edwin Pearce Christy (1815–1862)." Penn Library (Department of Special Collections). Accessed November 16, 2013. <http://www.library.upenn.edu/collections/rbm/keffer/christy.html>.

Bhabha, Homi K. 1985. "Sly Civility." *October* 34:71–80.

Born, Georgina, and David Hesmondhalgh, eds. 2000. *Western Music and Its Others: Difference, Representation, and Appropriation in Music*. Berkeley, CA: University of California Press.

Branagh, Kenneth. 2011. "Mark Kermode and Simon Mayo's Film Reviews (Interview with Kenneth Branagh on *My Week With Marilyn*)." *BBC Radio: 5 Live*. Podcast. November 18. Accessed October 17, 2013. <http://www.bbc.co.uk/podcasts/series/kermode/all>.

Brewster, Anne. 2002. "Aboriginal Life Writing and Globalization: Doris Pilkington's *Follow the Rabbit-Proof Fence*." *Southerly: A Review of Australian Literature* 62 (2): 153–61.

Byrnes, Paul. 2006. "*Ten Canoes*." *The Sydney Morning Herald*. July 1. Accessed December 10, 2012. <http://www.smh.com.au/news/film-reviews/tencanoes/2006/06/30/1151174381066.html>.

Caldwell, Thomas. 2009. "Yolgnu Storytelling in *Ten Canoes*." *Screen Education* 54:105–9.

Center for American Music (Stephen Foster Memorial). 2008. University of Pittsburgh. Accessed November 13, 2013. <http://web.archive.org/web/20090111125756/http://www.pitt.edu/~amerimus/ofah.htm>.

Chion, Michel. 1994. *Audio-Vision: Sound on Screen*. Edited and translated by Claudia Gorbman. New York: Columbia University Press. Originally published as *L'Audio-Vision* (Paris: Editions Nathan, 1990).

———. 1999. *The Voice in Cinema*. Edited and translated by Claudia Gorbman. New York: Columbia University Press. Originally published as *La Voix au cinéma* (Paris: Cahiers du cinéma (Editions de l'Etoile), 1982).

Clelland-Stokes, Sacha. 2007. *Representing Aboriginality: A Post-Colonial Analysis of the Key Trends of Representing Aboriginality in South African, Australian and Aotearoa/New Zealand Film*. Højbjerg, Denmark: Intervention Press.

Clothier, Kim, and Debra Dudek. 2009. "Opening the Body: Reading *Ten Canoes* with Critical Intimacy." *Kunapipi Journal of Postcolonial Writing & Culture* 31 (2): 82–93.

Columpar, Corinn. 2010. *Unsettling Sights: The Fourth World on Film*. Carbondale, IL: Southern Illinois University Press.

Cordaiy, Hunter. 2002. "The Truth of the Matter: An Interview with Phillip Noyce." *Metro Magazine* 131–32:126–32.

Crofts, Stephen. 1991. "Shifting Paradigms in the Australian Historical Film." *East-West Film Journal* 5 (2): 1–15.

Crosbie, Thomas. 2007. "Critical Historiography in *Atanarjuat The Fast Runner and Ten Canoes.*" *Journal of New Zealand Literature* 24 (2): 135–52.

D'aeth, Tony Hughes. 2002. "Which *Rabbit-Proof Fence?*: Empathy, Assimilation, Hollywood." *Australian Humanities Review* 27. Accessed October 20, 2013. <http://www.australianhumanitiesreview.org/archive/Issue-September-2002/hughesdaeth.html>.

Davis, Therese. 2006. "Working Together: Two Cultures, One Film, Many Canoes." *Senses of Cinema* 41. Accessed October 8, 2013. <http://sensesofcinema.com/2006/feature-articles/ten-canoes/>.

———. 2007. "Remembering Our Ancestors: Cross-Cultural Collaboration and the Mediation of Aboriginal Culture and History in *Ten Canoes* (Rolf de Heer, 2006)." *Studies in Australasian Cinema* 1 (1): 5–14.

de Heer, Rolf. 2007. "Personal Reflections on Whiteness and Three Film Projects." *Australian Humanities Review* 42. Accessed September 15, 2013. <http://www.australianhumanitiesreview.org/archive/Issue-August-September%202007/Deheer.html>.

Dillon, Matthew. 2002. "Summertime Blues." *Metro Magazine* 133:30–35.

Dyer, Richard. (1988) 2000. "White." In *Film and Theory: An Anthology*, edited by Robert Stam and Toby Miller, 733–51. Malden, MA: Blackwell Publishers Inc. Originally published in *Screen* 29 (4): 44–65.

Edgerton, Gary. 1994. "'A Breed Apart': Hollywood, Racial Stereotyping, and the Promise of Revisionism in *The Last of the Mohicans.*" *Journal of American Culture* 17 (2): 1–20.

Emberley, Julia. 2008. "Epistemic Encounters: Indigenous Cosmopolitan Hospitality, Marxist Anthropology, Deconstruction, and Doris Pilkington's *Rabbit-Proof Fence.*" *English Studies in Canada* 34 (4): 147–70.

Engelhardt, Tom. (1971) 1987. "Ambush at Kamikazi Pass." In *American Media and Mass Culture: Left Perspectives*, edited by Donald Alazere, 480–98. Berkeley: University of California Press. Originally published in *Bulletin of Concerned Asian Scholars* 3 (1): n.p.

Fanon, Frantz. 1967. *Black Skin, White Masks.* Translated by Charles Lam Markmann. New York: Grove Press.

———. 1968. *The Wretched of the Earth.* Translated by Constance Farrington. New York: Grove Press.

Finnegan, N. 1999. "At Boiling Point: *Like Water for Chocolate* and the Boundaries of Mexican Identity." *Bulletin of Latin American Research* 18 (3): 311–26.

Foundas, Scott. 2007. *"Ten Canoes."* *The Village Voice*, May 22. Accessed December 12, 2012. <http://www.villagevoice.com/2007-05-22/film/ten-canoes/full/>.

Frieze, Donna-Lee. 2011. "The Other in Genocide: Responsibility and Benevolence in *Rabbit-Proof Fence.*" In *Film and Genocide*, edited by Kristi M. Wilson and Tomàs F. Crowder-Taraborrelli, 122–32. Madison, WI: University of Wisconsin Press.

Fuchs, Cynthia. 2007. "Ten Canoes." PopMatters, 5 September. Accessed 15 April 2014. <http://www.popmatters.com/review/ten-canoes/>.

Gillard, Gary. 2009. "Indigenous Issues in Australian Cinema." *Australasian Cinema*, June 12. Accessed September 24, 2013. <http://ozcin.net/indig.html>.

Goldie, Terry. 1989. *Fear and Temptation: The Image of the Indigene in Canadian, Australian, and New Zealand Literatures.* Montreal: McGill-Queen's University Press.

Haag, Oliver. 2010. "Tasteless, Romantic and Full of History: The German Reception of Australia and *Rabbit-Proof Fence.*" *Studies in Australasian Cinema* 4 (2): 115–29.

Hall, Stuart. (1989) 2000. "Cultural Identity and Cinematic Representation." In *Film and Theory: An Anthology*, edited by Robert Stam and Toby Miller, 704–14. Malden, Ma: Blackwell Publishers Inc. Originally published in *Framework* 36:68–81.

Hayward, Susan. 2006. *Cinema Studies: The Key Concepts.* 3rd ed. London: Routledge.

Heffelfinger, Elizabeth, and Laura Wright. 2011. *Visual Difference: Postcolonial Studies and Intercultural Cinema*. New York: Peter Lang.

Henderson, Ian. 2009. "Stranger Danger: Approaching Home and *Ten Canoes*." *South Atlantic Quarterly* 108 (1): 53–70.

Hewson, J. 2002. "A Moving Picture of Hope." *Australian Financial Review* 12 (4): 82.

Hiatt, L. R. 2007. "Who Wrote *Ten Canoes*?" *Quadrant Magazine* 51 (11): 70–75.

Hickey-Moody, Anna C., and Melissa Iocca. 2004. "Sonic Affect(s): Binaural Technologies and the Construction of Auratorship in Rolf de Heer's *Bad Boy Bubby*." *Metro Magazine* 140:78.

Hickling-Hudson, Anne. 1990. "White Construction of Black Identity in Australian Films about Aborigines." *Literature/Film Quarterly* 18 (4): 263–74.

Hodge, Bob, and Vijay Mishra. (1991) 2006. "Aboriginal Place." In *The Post-Colonial Studies Reader*, edited by Bill Ashcroft, Gareth Griffiths, and Helen Tiffin, 359–63. 2nd ed. London: Routledge,. Originally published in *The Dark Side of the Dream* (London: Alllen and Unwin).

Holden, Stephen. 2007. "Ancient Aboriginal Tales, Parallel Across Epochs." *The New York Times*, June 1. Accessed December 12, 2012. <http://movies.nytimes.com/2007/06/01/movies/01cano.html?_r=0>.

Hope, Cat. 2004. "Hearing the Story: Sound Design in the Films of Rolf de Heer." *Senses of Cinema* 31. Accessed December 11, 2012. <http://sensesofcinema.com/2004/31/sound_design_rolf_de_heer/>.

Hoschka, Philipp. n.d. "Phillip Noyce Press Conference on *Rabbit-Proof Fence* at the 2002 Taormina BNL FilmFest." Film Scouts Interviews. Accessed September 23, 2013. <http://www.filmscouts.com/scripts/interview.cfm?File=2972>.

Hutcheon, Linda. 1995. "Colonialism and the Postcolonial Condition: Complexities Abounding." *PMLA* 110 (1): 7–16.

Jones, Andrew. 2006. *Dictionary of Globalization*. Cambridge, UK: Polity Press.

Kauffmann, Stanley. 2007. "Stanley Kauffman on Films instead of Stories." *The New Republic*, June 18, 33–34.

Kennedy, Roseanne. 2008. "Vulnerable Children, Disposable Mothers: Holocaust and Stolen Generations Memoirs of Childhood." *Life Writing* 5 (2): 161–84.

Kevin, Catherine. 2010. "Solving the 'Problem' of the Motherless Indigenous Child in Jedda and Australia: White Maternal Desire in the Australian Epic before and after *Bringing Them Home*." *Studies in Australasian Cinema* 4 (2):145–57.

Kibby, Marjorie D., 2005. "Sounds of Australia in *Rabbit-Proof Fence*." Reel Tracks: Australian Feature Film Music and Cultural Identities, edited by Rebeccca Coyle, 147–57. Bloomington: Indiana University Press.

Kuipers, Richard. 2006. "*Ten Canoes*." *Variety*, April 3, 70.

Langton, Marcia. 1983. "Well, I Heard It on the Radio and I Saw it on the Television: An Essay for the Australian Film Commission on the Politics and Aesthetics of Filmmaking by and about Aboriginal People and Things." Sydney: Australian Film Commission. Accessed September 26, 2013. <http://afcarchive.screenaustralia.gov.au/profile/pubs/default.aspx>.

———. 2003. "Aboriginal Art and Film: The Politics of Representation." In *Blacklines: Contemporary Critical Writing by Indigenous Australians*, edited by M. Grossman, 109–24. Melbourne, Victoria: Melbourne University Press.

Lapseley, Robert, and Michael Westlake. 2006. *Film Theory: An Introduction*. 2nd ed. Manchester: Manchester University Press.

Lewis, Robert. 2006. "*Making Ten Canoes: A Study Guide*." *Metro Magazine*, FFC Australia (Film Finance Corporation), Australian Teachers of Media Inc. *Screen Education* series.Accessed November 5, 2013. <http://svc068.wic021v.serverweb.com/tencanoes/makingtencanoes.pdf>.

Manne, Robert. 2001. "In Denial: The Stolen Generations and the Right." *Australian Quarterly Essay* 1:1–113.

———. 2002. "The Color of Prejudice." *Sydney Morning Herald*, February 23. Accessed October 13, 2013. <http://www.storage.canalblog.com/27/55/486154/31404396.doc>.

———. 2003a. "A Long Trek to the Truth." *The Washington Post*, February 13. Accessed August 20, 2013. <http://www.recordnet.com/apps/pbcs.dll/article?AID=/20030215/A_LIFE/302159992>.

———. 2003b. *Whitewash: On Keith Windschuttle's Fabrication of Aboriginal History.* Melbourne: Black Inc.

Martin, Adrian. 2007. "Ten Canoes." Sight and Sound 17 (6): 77–78.

Mishra, Vijay, and Bob Hodge. 1991. "What is Post(-)Colonialism?" *Textual Practice* 5 (3): 399–414.

Molloy, Bruce. 1993. "The Breaking of the Drought: Australian Feature Films, 1946-1974." *Literature/Film Quarterly* 21 (2): 83–89.

Moore, Catriona, and Stephen Muecke. 1984. "Racism and the Representation of Aborigines on Film." *Australian Journal of Cultural Studies* 2 (1): 36–53.

Oster, Sam. 2005. "Walkie Talkie." *Inside Film* 80:45.

Palace Films. 2006. "*Ten Canoes*: Press Kit." Sydney: Palace Films. Accessed October 1, 2013. <http://www.festival-cannes.com/assets/Image/Direct/016942.pdf>.

Petzke, Ingo. 2007. "*Rabbit-Proof Fence*: Phillip Noyce, Australia, 2002." In *The Cinema of Australia and New Zealand*, edited by Geoff Mayer and Keith Beattie, 233–39. London, England: Wallflower.

Pike, Andrew, and Ross Cooper. 1998. *Australian Film 1900-1977: A Guide to Feature Film Production.* Rev. ed. Melbourne: Oxford University Press.

Pilkington, Doris (Nugi Garimara). 2002. *Rabbit-Proof Fence.* New York: Hyperion.

Read, Peter. 1996. *The Stolen Generations: The Removal of Aboriginal Children in New South Wales 1883 to 1969.* Sydney: NSW Department of Aboriginal Affairs.

Reconciliation Australia. n.d. "3 June: A Significant Date, The Mabo Decision." <http://oldsite.reconciliation.org.au/getfile?id=1515&file=The+Mabo+decision.pdf>.

Rutherford, Anne. 2012. "*Ten Canoes* and the Ethnographic Photographs of Donald Thomson: *Animate Thought and The Light of the World*." *Cultural Studies Review* 18 (1): 107–37.

Saïd, Edward W. 1980. "Islam Through Western Eyes." *The Nation*, April 26. Accessed December 13, 2010. <http://www.thenation.com/article/islam-through-western-eyes#>.

———. 1978. *Orientalism.* New York: Random House.

Shaw, Sylvie. 2009. "Cross-Cultural Collaboration and Representation in 'Indigenous' Film: An Analysis of Collaborative Outcomes in *Ten Canoes*." University of Queensland: Religion and Spirituality Studies (Course Blog), November 5. Accessed February 15, 2013. <http://religionandmediacourse.blogspot.com/2009/11/cross-cultural-collaboration-and.html>.

Shively, JoEllen. 1992. "Cowboys and Indians: Perceptions of Western Films among American Indians and Anglos." *American Sociological Review* 57 (6): 725–34.

Shohat, Ella. 1992. "Notes on the Postcolonial." *Social Text* 31 (2): 99–113.

Simpson, Catherine. 2010. "Shifting from Landscape to Country in Australia, after Mabo." *Metro Magazine* 165:89–93.

Spivak, Gayarti Chakravorty. (1999) 2006. "Can the Subaltern Speak?" In *The Post-Colonial Studies Reader*, edited by Bill Ashcroft, Gareth Griffiths, and Helen Tiffin, 359–63. 2nd ed. London: Routledge. Originally published in *Toward a History of the Vanishing Present* (Cambridge, MA: Harvard University Press).

———. 1990. "'Questions of Multiculturalism': Interview by Sneja Gunew (August 30, 1986)." In *The Post-Colonial Critic: Interviews, Strategies, Dialogues*, edited by Sarah Harasym, 59–66. New York: Routledge.

Stam, Robert, and Louise Spence. (1983) 2004. "Colonialism, Racism, and Representation: An Introduction." In *Film Theory and Criticism*, edited by Leo Braudy and Marshall Cohen, 877–91. New York: Oxford University Press. Originally published in *Screen* 24:2.

Stam, Robert. 2000. *Film Theory: An Introduction.* Malden, MA: Blackwell Publishers Inc.

Starrs, Bruno. 2006. "The Audience as Aurator Again?: Sound and Rolf de Heer's *Ten Canoes*." *Metro Magazine* 149:18–20.

Starrs, Bruno. 2007a. "The Authentic Aboriginal Voice in Rolf de Heer's *Ten Canoes* (2006)." *Reconstruction* 7 (3). Accessed September 1, 2013. <http://reconstruction.eserver.org/073/starrs.shtml>.

———. 2007b. "Sounds of Silence: An Interview with Rolf de Heer." *Metro Magazine* 152:18–21.

———. 2009. "Aural Auteur: Sound in the Films of Rolf de Heer." PhD diss., Queensland University of Technology. Accessed October 1, 2013. <http://eprints.qut.edu.au/29302/>.

———. n.d. "An Interview with James Currie, Sound Designer for Rolf de Heer." Edited by Sven E. Carlsson. *FilmSound.org: Learning Space Dedicated to the Art and Analyses of Film Sound Design*. Accessed December 10, 2012. <http://filmsound.org/theory/JamesCurrie.htm>.

Trimm, Ryan. 2007. "Moving Pictures, Still Lives: Staging National Tableaux and Text in *Prospero's Books*." *Cinema Journal* 46 (3): 26–53.

Turner, Graeme. 1988. "Breaking the Frame: The Representation of Aborigines in Australian Film." In *Aboriginal Culture Today*, edited by A. Rutherford, 135–45. Copenhagen: Dangaroo Press.

USF Libraries. 2012. "History of Minstrelsy." Accessed January 14, 2014. <"http://exhibits.lib.usf.edu/exhibits/show/minstrelsy/jimcrow-to-jolson/christy-and-foster>.

Villella, Fiona. 2002. "Long Road Home: Phillip Noyce's *Rabbit-Proof Fence*." *Senses of Cinema* 19. Accessed August 1, 2013. <http://sensesofcinema.com/2002/19/rabbit/>.

Walsh, Mike. 2006. "Interview with Rolf de Heer." Metro 149: 10-17.

Windshuttle, Keith. 2009. *The Stolen Generations 1881-2008*. Vol. 3 of *The Fabrication of Aboriginal History*. Sydney, Australia: Macleay Press.

———. 2003. "*Rabbit-Proof Fence*: 'A True Story'?" *New Criterion* 21 (7): 12–16.

Wood, Houston. 2008. *Native Features: Indigenous Films from Around the World*. New York: Continuum.

Yeats, W. B. 1996. *The Collected Poems of W.B. Yeats*. 2nd Rev. ed. Edited by Richard Rinneran. New York: Scribner.

Young, Lola. 1996. *Fear of the Dark: "Race," Gender and Sexuality in the Cinema*. London: Routledge.

Zachariah, Lee. "Ten Canoes: No Microphones." 2009. *Inside Film: If.* 121 (49). Accessed 18 July 2014. <http://search.informit.com.au/documentSummary;dn=808385178594377;res=IELAPA>.

Feminism

 # INTRODUCTION

"Visual Pleasure and Narrative Cinema" by Laura Mulvey

Postcolonial theory is much concerned with how and why marginal voices are suppressed, just as it focuses on enabling those same voices to be heard. Similarly, feminism is much concerned with the ways that women are disempowered in relation to men and considers ways to redress the balance, whether by exposing the mechanisms of patriarchy or by subversively reading its effects. Here, we begin by drawing upon Laura Mulvey's groundbreaking article "Visual Pleasure and Narrative Cinema."[1] Mulvey's article was written in 1975 but it remains one of the influential pieces of film theory. Her analysis of the processes by which films reinforce patriarchal power has been anthologized many times because the fundamentals of her approach have enduring resonance. In short, though many films after (*and* before) 1975 represent challenges to patriarchy, and many feminist critics have offered ways of seeing films that challenge Mulvey's generalizing approach, the patterns identified by Mulvey run deep and recur.[2]

The purpose of using Mulvey's article in the context of this book is to analyze sound tracks with close reference to her most influential feminist arguments. This

---

[1] Mulvey's article is but one seminal feminist text. For a brief survey of some other key works in feminist film criticism by Claire Johnston, Molly Haskell, Mary Ann Doane, Teresa de Lauretis, E. Ann Kaplan, and others, see Hayward (2006, 137–48).

[2] One of the most critical summaries of Mulvey's article is in an introduction to a recent collection of contemporary feminist essays, edited by Corinn Columpar and Sophie Mayer: "With its hermetic logic, its immaterial spectator, and its tight-lipped refusal of pleasure, [Mulvey's article] is utterly out of step with our current cultural climate" (2009, 6). Nevertheless, Columpar and Mayer note that Mulvey's article is "still offered up in many contexts as the summation (and the summit?) of feminist film theory" (6).

analysis is also about engaging with the visual bias of Mulvey's article by applying her ideas to aural aspects of cinema. To this end, we will explore two films in detail: first, an example of Classical Hollywood cinema, *To Have and Have Not* (1944); second, a more contemporary, revisionist film, *The Piano* (1993). The sound tracks of these films play with, and also play out, what Mulvey has described as being typical in mainstream cinema. Before creating a feminist analysis of each sound track, we should establish the fundamental principles of Mulvey's article. In the close analyses themselves, we will contextualize the films with regard to a range of more contemporary feminist criticism.

Mulvey argues that the dominant perspective of mainstream Hollywood cinema—the one with which we are encouraged to identify and take pleasure in—is a male, patriarchal point of view that represses female power. Her approach to spectatorship is shaped by several fundamental concepts of psychoanalysis, including: scopophilia, ego libido, castration threat, voyeurism, subjectivity, and the gaze. However, as Robynn J. Stilwell puts it: "one need not even buy the psychoanalytic trappings of such an [approach] to recognize the camera as an extension of male directors and male cinematographers working for an audience in which the male audience is not just presumed but assumed to be the norm" (2005, 50). Even when female characters are empowered through their own beauty and talents, their potential ability to take control and to thus potentially "castrate" the admiring male is contained within particular conventions of looking. Mulvey argues that the potentially threatening power of the female presence is held in check by specific visual techniques. First, camerawork indulges the scopophilic instinct, gratifying the pleasure of looking at women as erotic objects and, therein, exerting control over them.[3] Moreover, camerawork flatters the audience's ego libido through primarily showing women from the dominant male perspective. Conventionalized and "invisible" editing practices, especially shot-reverse-shot cuts between characters, also emphasize the female's "to be looked-at-ness" (Mulvey [1975] 2004, 841). Editing often breaks up the female body into parts and thereby emphasizes that she may be iconically dissected, this being especially important in those sequences when a female character "freeze[s] the flow of action" by performing for the protagonist *and*, by proxy, us (841). In addition, Mulvey writes of the illusionist tendencies of narrative films which prompt spectators to lose themselves in patriarchal stories without their necessarily being aware of the cinematic strategies that (often imperceptibly) harness the power of women. Mulvey is thus known for deconstructing stylistic elements of

---

[3] Here, Mulvey is drawing upon Freud's concept of scopophilia, the pleasure in looking that he associates with actively "taking other people as objects," especially through voyeurism ([1975] 2004, 839).

mainstream cinema that represent the unconscious of patriarchal society. Mulvey does not directly address sound tracks (few critics did in 1975), but her claims for the visual tendencies of cinema are often reinforced by film music that, in Claudia Gorbman's terms, manipulates the audience into consuming what they see without question and without calling attention to itself (1987, 57).[4]

In relation to cinematic processes of female subjugation, Mulvey is very much concerned with how films position their spectators. More specifically, she focuses on illuminating how dominant film practices involve spectators in establishing women as "Others" and as objects of the male gaze. The male gaze is active where the female look is passive, and male characters make meaning while female characters bear meaning (Mulvey [1975] 2004, 841). Along with exposing such patterns whereby the patriarchal subjectivity of cinema represses female power, Mulvey uncovers the buried reasons for such practice. Drawing upon some fundamental principles of psychoanalysis, Mulvey asserts that the (often rigid) containment of female power points to an anxiety that is constantly being allayed through cinematic practice: for the male protagonist (and the viewer who typically shares his perspective) the woman embodies sexual difference which must be contained or else she represents the threat of castration. So, as Toby Miller writes (in summarizing Mulvey's work), women on screen are repeatedly used as "sights for sore male eyes, icons of pleasure that confirm for men their sex and their sexuality" (2000, 481).

Since mainstream film does not tend to call attention to its own processes of disempowering women, Mulvey argues that the viewer (like it or not) enters into complicity with a patriarchal way of seeing the world, along with the dominant male character/s. We may wonder whether identification with the active hero necessarily entails an acceptance of the "masculinization" of spectatorship as Mulvey describes it. That said, it is important to acknowledge that Mulvey brings to light that which had previously been all-too-easily ignored.[5]

Mulvey's feminist psychoanalysis of film brings the unconscious, the repressed, and the unspoken to light. This process may thus seem inherently contradictory, or even counterintuitive because it often requires reading against the grain of a film

---

[4] Gorbman writes of the particular coercive power of film music to make audiences unquestioning consumers, even when it is not necessarily designed to be consciously "heard" any more than the easy-listening music in elevators or other public spheres (1987, 56–59).

[5] In her later work ("Afterthoughts on 'Visual Pleasure and Narrative Cinema'"), Mulvey modified her approach to allow for different viewing possibilities for the heterosexual female spectator: first, a masochistic identification with the female who is subjected to the male gaze; or, second, a "transsexual identification" with the active male viewer (Erens 1990, xxi).

that actively discourages such analysis. For instance, a film that showcases a female character's desirability, thus potentially objectifying her, may discourage a critical response through seducing its audience with an apparent celebration of her power. For a specific example, consider the scene where Nicole Kidman (Satine) makes her first entrance in *Moulin Rouge!* (2001). The film shows her swinging above a crowd of men in her shimmering slip of a dress, singing "Diamonds Are a Girl's Best Friend" in a breathy rendition that evokes nostalgia for Marilyn Monroe's performance in *Gentlemen Prefer Blondes* (1953). Here, the *mise-en-scène* foregrounds the woman's elevated position over men, thus emphasizing her sexual power while she is literally shown above them. The scene does not invite criticism of its conservatism as a throwback homage. On a superficial level, the visual display even empowers Satine because we see numerous shots from her point of view, including many long shots of the men gazing up at her in collective adoration. We also see closer shots of Satine's individual admirers, especially of the sympathetic hero Christian (Ewan McGregor), which emphasize her awareness of her own spectacular impact on men. Satine has a visual presence, *and* a voice, that enthralls her male audience. Satine's subsequent vocal expression of great frustration at her own imprisonment by courtesan life may be thus read as disingenuous in a film that encourages us to revel in the set pieces devoted to her being on audiovisual display.

Satine's appeal is a paradoxical mixture of innocence and sultriness communicated through contrasting visual and aural messages: the clear sweetness of her voice, and her wide-eyed pantomimesque facial expressions communicate youthful innocence while her elaborately seductive costumes emphasize her sexuality. Thus we have a film that ostensibly emphasizes its female character's hope for escaping her subjugation to men but which, perhaps unconsciously, encourages our scopophilic admiration of her as *naively* subject to the (male) gaze. Satine tells Christian, "I make men believe what they want to believe" in a moment of apparently savvy and self-conscious awareness of her primary role as a character of fantasy. Yet even when Satine sings "One Day I'll Fly Away" to herself, thus voicing a fantasy of escape, the film holds the dream of fantasy-defying power in check through making her into an iconic image: her body is showcased through a figure-hugging red dress, and the interior truth of her song is offset by the spectacle of her singing atop an elaborately adorned elephant. Further, this particular private "performance" is witnessed by Christian and we are invited to admire her *with him*. This scene is thus representative of the film's emphasis on her to-be-looked-at-ness. Moreover, in the entire film there are very few point-of-view shots of Satine that are from a female character's perspective: we primarily see and understand her through male characters' perspectives (the numerous male audience members at the Moulin Rouge, Christian, the Duke [Richard Roxburgh], and Satine's boss/pimp Harold Zidler [Jim Broadbent]). Thus, even in an example of comparatively recent and highly self-conscious cinema, we find an echoing of those patterns Mulvey identified as dominant within Classical Hollywood.

Mulvey pays particular attention to films directed by auteurs who worked within the studio system of Classical Hollywood. She notes, for instance, a pattern of encouraging scopophilic enjoyment of women from a male, voyeuristic position in the work of Alfred Hitchcock. This pattern is perhaps most obvious in *Rear Window* (1954), a film focused upon a wheelchair-bound man (James Stewart) who repeatedly watches his female neighbors through binoculars. Mulvey also cites *To Have and Have Not* as a representative example, due to its emphasis on the seductive appeal of Lauren Bacall. Mulvey is, like the psychoanalytic theoreticians who preceded her, primarily (and often solely) focused on the power of the *image* and its impact on the hypothetical *spectator*. What follows here is an analysis of sound track for *To Have and Have Not* with Mulvey's foundational ideas in mind.

Before beginning our first feminist close analysis, it is important that we consider some fundamental questions about sound tracks in relation to "Visual Pleasure and Narrative Cinema." The following questions adapt and develop Mulvey's primary feminist concerns to consider aural aspects of cinema.

- Is the sound track aligned with one or more male or female characters? If so, does the sound track ostensibly support or challenge the gendered ideology associated with one or more characters?
- Does the film's sound track support or work against the strong actions or feelings of a female character? Does the sound track thus empower that character or fix her within a hegemonic structure? (or perhaps a paradoxical combination of the two?)
- Does the sound track appear to support or challenge feminist (or anti-feminist) messages of the film? Drawing on Mulvey's work, we can arrive at answers to this question by considering visual elements in relation to aural ones.
- How does the sound track enforce a particular understanding of each female character's relative power?
- How does the sound track encourage us to view the identity formation, representation, bodily presence, and/or star power of each female character?

As Anahid Kassabian writes, a close study of Mulvey's article may give the impression of disallowing "differences in identification processes," whether among men or women or "along lines other than gender or sexual difference" (2001, 64). Further, as Sharon Willis argues, "identification is not a state, but a process" that is "likely to be mobile and intermittent rather than consistent" (1997, 102). Therefore, the following analyses of *To Have and Have Not* and *The Piano* are explorations of possibility rather than essentialist summaries of what the films do.

/// 8 /// TO HAVE AND HAVE NOT

PLOT SUMMARY

To Have and Have Not revolves around Harry Morgan (Humphrey Bogart), a professional fisherman who, along with his alcoholic sidekick Eddie (Walter Brennan), mans a boat for hire on the island of Martinique during the Second World War. After one of their customers fails to make a large payment, Harry accepts payment for transporting an important French Resistance fighter named Paul de Bursac (Walter Szurovy) and his wife Hellene (Dolores Moran) who are running away from the island under Vichy rule. Harry is thus politically active, though he professes neutrality in the exposition. By the end of the film, Harry has not only transported the de Bursacs, but also saved Monsieur de Bursac from a near-fatal bullet wound, killed a Gestapo officer, and ensured the de Bursacs' safe carriage from Martinique by outwitting and beating up a Gestapo official named Captain Renard (Dan Seymour). Through most of the film, Harry is also involved with a woman named Marie "Slim" Browning (Lauren Bacall) who stays in the hotel of the club where Morgan lives. Slim first attracts Harry's attention by her looks and quick wit, but their relationship develops further through her assisting in his political actions. She also gives several seductive singing performances which culminate in their joyful, musically accompanied exit together at the close of the film.

AN OVERVIEW

The music of *To Have and Have Not* begins with a big-scale fanfare over the Warner Bros. logo, a flourish typical of Classical Hollywood cinema [0:01–0:07]. The opening music then establishes the coexistence of the leading ("masculine") and related, but subsidiary, ("feminine") action [0:08–0:33]. The first main melodic idea is introduced with the appearance of Humphrey Bogart's name. It is conflict-connoting music, featuring heavy brass, drums, timpani and cymbals, harp glissandi, and stately, march-like figurations. Along with the directorial credit to Howard Hawks, the main musical idea is fully established and quickly transitions into a slower and more sonorous, romantic and abbreviated variation of itself that is led by strings.[6] This musical variation accompanies the credits for the supporting cast for Bogart (including, of course, Bacall). After the introduction of these two, related and hierarchically organized musical ideas, the orchestration becomes rhythmically quicker and more complex. The next main musical section begins with a low strings pizzicato ostinato that is offset by fragments of melody, featuring high-pitched woodwind [0:49–1:36]. This section of the score also includes several especially shrill, and slightly discordant, woodwind *sforzando* trills that, along with some fully orchestrated sliding notes, establish a loose musical impression of "Otherness" in parallel relation to the visual emphasis on a map of the Caribbean. The pizzicato ostinato combined with the rhythmic urgency of the accented trills also establishes intrigue as the camera closes in on a map of the Caribbean, then Martinique, and then the Fort de France before transitioning into the film's first scene. The three main parts of this opening musical score thus establish the main narrative components of the film: war, love, and politicized suspense. Thereafter, the music of *To Have and Have Not* oscillates between non-diegetic cues that are most intermittently prominent in action sequences focused upon Harry, and diegetic music featuring live singing by the hotel piano-man named Cricket (Hoagy Carmichael) and, more memorably, Slim. Thus, the soundtrack shifts between being aligned with Harry and being literally "led" by another voice, Slim's singing being the strongest musical presence in the film. The main musical themes of the film opening are not much elaborated upon or fully developed as in other examples of Classical Hollywood, such as those themes of Max Steiner's scores for *Casablanca* (1942) or *Gone with the Wind* (1939). So, in *To Have and Have Not*, the set pieces in which accessible songs are performed have atypical importance.

Except in those scenes focused on singing performances, dialogue dominates the rest of the sound track for *To Have and Have Not*: the sound design is therein mostly "monophonic."[7] Non-diegetic music only becomes prominent when dialogue is suspended. Also, there is a minimum of ambient sounds. These patterns keep dialogue

---

[6] For a useful summary and analysis of how gender distinctions and power relations are often communicated through film music, see Kassabian (2001, 27–89).

[7] The term "monophonic" is used this way by Buhler, Neumeyer, and Deemer (2010, 48). Such sound design is about maintaining a Classical emphasis on narrative clarity, as is fully explored in their work with reference to the technical possibilities during that era. In particular, see their chapter titled "Music and the Sound Track in the Classical Studio Era" (308–35).

consistently in the "foreground" (again, except during the performances). This is typical of the Classical Hollywood era, before sound technology had developed to the extent that numerous aural elements could be incorporated, and during which time "sound effects were carefully marshaled and sparingly used" (Buhler, Neumeyer, and Deemer 2010, 14, 16). Excepting the sounds of Harry's boat and of gunshots, few sound effects call attention to themselves. As is also representative of films of the Classical Hollywood era, non-diegetic music primarily underscores scenes of high tension and culmination. The music has little status without close reference to the film's visuals.

The original non-diegetic music for *To Have and Have Not* was composed by William Lava and Franz Waxman, and orchestrated by Leonid Raab, but they are uncredited. (As is again representative of the era, only the music director, Leo F. Forbstein, is credited.) As already indicated, the film also features an early film appearance by Hoagy Carmichael performing three of his songs: "Hong Kong Blues" (which Carmichael cowrote with Stanley Adams), and two others with lyrics by Johnny Mercer titled "How Little We Know" and "The Rhumba Jumps." Within the diegesis, Cricket is shown composing "How Little We Know" and then "spontaneously" receiving help from Slim as co-composer. A final song called "Am I Blue?," composed by Harry Akst with lyrics by Grant Clarke, is co-performed by Cricket and Slim as their fictional co-creation. "Hong Kong Blues" most particularly showcases Carmichael's comic flair, while "Am I Blue?" and "How Little We Know" draw particular attention to the sight *and* sound of Lauren Bacall as a show-stopping (or "film-stopping") icon. It is important to note that Bacall actually performed, rather than lip-synched these songs, despite some controversial claims that she was "a ventriloquized siren" with another's voice dubbed in for hers (Parker, 1947,).[8]

The contrast between Carmichael's and Bacall's styles serves to reinforce her comparative musical power. Cricket's lyrics are sometimes tangential to the main plot of *To Have and Have Not*—"Hong Kong Blues" and its "semi-surrealistic lyrics," for instance, are about a "very unfortunate colored man" who played in a dive in Hong Kong and yearned for a return to San Francisco (Hewitt 1983, 46). Slim's singing, however, places direct emphasis on the development of the love story that is at the heart of the film. Carmichael's "off-center" star status is partly defined by his jazz background and

---

[8] Wagner usefully summarizes the controversy on her fan site (2007). The singer Andy Williams recorded Bacall's numbers, in accordance with Warner Bros.' initial plan for post-synchronized dubbing (a relatively common practice that is parodied most famously in *Singin' in the Rain* (1952)). That it was a male singer who was to dub Bacall's voice is atypical, however, and points again to the unusual vocal power that Hawks wanted his new female star to embody. In the end, as Wagner explains, it was Hawks who insisted that Bacall's own singing voice be used.

his "nasalized singing style" in imitation "of the slurred rhythmic way that black men sang the blues."[9] His voice is a sharp contrast with Bacall's deep, richer voice. Indeed, the timbre of Bacall's voice establishes her as a musical presence of relative authority. Ironically, Carmichael brought his status as an established musician into the film while Bacall was relatively unknown, making her screen debut in *To Have and Have Not*.

MALE AND FEMALE MUSICAL PRESENCES: HARRY VERSUS SLIM

The music of *To Have and Have Not* clearly establishes the dominant male and female presences in contradistinction to each other. While the diegetic music of the film most memorably features Slim, the soundtrack uses non-diegetic music most often in accordance with *Harry*'s actions. The non-diegetic music of *To Have and Have Not* reinforces the narrative with pleonastic directness, while the diegetic songs of the film "interrupt" and change the film's rhythm several times. Where the non-diegetic music is mostly aligned with Harry in driving the action forward, Slim's performances represent points at which the narrative flow slows down. So, the film puts Slim in a clear subsidiary relation to Harry. Moreover, since Harry is played by one of the most famous Hollywood stars when the film was released, and the one given top billing in the opening credits— Humphrey Bogart—his centrality is undeniable. The film's soundtrack non-diegetically reinforces our understanding of Harry/Bogart being in the driver's seat.

The non-diegetic music of *To Have and Have Not* follows specific patterns associated with Classical Hollywood scoring as defined by Kathryn Kalinak, including selective use of cues that correspond to and are synchronous with particular action, and Mickey-mousing effects that enhance the action without demanding attention to the soundtrack in its own right (1992, 113).[10] Further, the tight, classical coherence between

---

[9] Hewitt explains that the melodic and harmonic structures of Carmichael's songs often echo the blues feel of traditional black songs in a minor key, such as "Go Down Moses" or "St. James's Infirmary Blues" (1983, 40). (In parallel to this point, Sudhalter argues that the African American actor, Arthur "Dooley" Wilson, most famous for being the piano player named Sam in *Casablanca* (and therein accompanying Bogart's most successful romantic lead role before *To Have and Have Not*) "set the stage for Hoagy Carmichael" (2002, 233).) Carmichael's music also reflects the popularity of the so-called "latune" ("a tune with a Latin beat and an English-language lyric") that was first fashionable in America in the 1930s (Firmat 2008, 180). The Cuban rhythms of latunes are "domesticated" by the English lyrics, thus "muting" their "foreignness" (184). Despite his achieving mainstream success (well before *To Have and Have Not* was made), Carmichael's complex musical identity, as a white man drawing on the blues as well as Latin American songs, is worth more attention, as is the fact that Bacall joins him in the performances of such music.

[10] As Kalinak writes, Mickey-mousing music is particularly useful for creating "certain effects on a semi-conscious level without disrupting narrative credibility on a conscious level" (1992, 115–16).

visual and aural messages sets firm boundaries on interpretation.[11] This coherence also encourages perceivers to focus uncritically on what takes place and to absorb its meaning on a purely literal level. Thus, the (non-diegetic) music that is primarily associated with the lead male character is grounded in conventions that were well established by 1944. In other words, the music associated with Harry is weighted in the sort of tradition that buttresses his superior standing and his controlling agency within the film, even if only on a subconscious level for the audience.

The sequence in which Harry travels to pick up and transport the de Bursacs, his first perilous and politically pivotal action, is a good representative example of non-diegetic scoring in *To Have and Have Not* [54:09–1:00:32]. Here, the orchestral underscoring places particular emphasis on the sequence's meaning for a contemporary audience living through the Second World War, reinforcing every key action and shift in direction: when Harry flashes his light three times to the shore, for instance, his signal is punctuated by high-pitched strings and woodwind; and when there is shooting between an unseen party and Harry's boat, suddenly shrill trills on woodwind emphasize the danger. The scoring for this sequence is often shaped by furtive, chromatic, and non-melodic lines for strings and/or woodwind, accented brass phrases, and sporadic use of percussion. The music is further characterized by frequent shifts in harmonic direction (enforced by frequent semitones and sliding notes), occasional but marked dissonances, and extremes in dynamics and pitches, as well as contrasts of timbre. The sequence also features some fragmented, somber, slowed-down, minor-key variations of the film's opening "masculine" theme that are not fully developed. The overall effect of the music is to communicate melodic and harmonic indeterminacy—this emphasis, along with frequent rhythmic shifts, reinforces the impact of the action as suspenseful, turbulent, and dangerous. Thus, the sequence features many well-worn musical devices that cumulatively communicate easily decoded meanings, even for the half-listening perceiver. To again quote Gorbman's influential work on the conventions of narrative film scoring, the music "guides the spectator's vision both literally and figuratively" (1987, 11). In other words, the music serves to emphasize the power of what we see, in both senses. It rises and falls in rhythm with the ebb and flow of action during the sequence, rather than being prominent in its own right.

This non-diegetic music also guides us in terms of several narrative functions as defined by Johnny Wingstedt: the *Emotive* function (communicating emotive qualities belonging to characters and/or audience members); the *Informative* function

---

[11] See Kassabian (2001, 77), who makes a similar point in relation to how even a youth-in-expressive-revolt film like *Dirty Dancing* (1987) uses the conventions of Classical Hollywood scoring.

(communicating what is to come, clarifying the events we see); the *Descriptive* function (communicating what happens in programmatic terms, in relation to the physical setting); the *Guiding* function (communicating how we should direct our attention); and the *Temporal* function (providing continuity as well as giving an easily decodable structure to the entire sequence) (2010, 194–95).[12] The Emotive function not only binds us to the tension experienced by Harry in particular, it also encourages us to admire Harry's cool-headed ability to handle the situation. The Descriptive function is most obvious in the Mickey-mousing that directly matches what takes place. This function is relatively important given that the sequence features shots through fog and at night-time: the music mediates some visual ambiguities and obscurities. The Guiding function of the music anticipates and foreshadows action, along with punctuating the high points of conflict, such as the moment when de Bursac is shot. The Temporal function is especially important through the sequence as one that features relatively unpredictable editing and multiple shifts in the line of action: even though the scoring is intermittent, the music provides some continuity across cuts, bringing coherence to a sequence that, without music, would be much more disorienting. Even if the characters are at sea, then, the music has a decisive anchoring and orienting impact. And even if the music communicates disturbance, the tight *synchresis* of visual and auditory elements contains the sense of threat.[13]

Where the non-diegetic music of *To Have and Have Not* is clearly dictated by action, and designed for those aspects of the film already made without music (in postproduction), Slim's music has its own logic within the diegetic space. Thus, it seems obvious that camerawork and editing were at least partly determined in relation to the rhythm of the music as well as Bacall's physical movements. The power of Slim's performances and her music is thus offset by what surrounds her in the film's construction. Also, by contrast with the music associated with the war and political action, Slim is primarily associated with full melodies that are both memorable and hummable. The exact synchronicity of audiovisual detail during her songs, and the clear primary focus upon her

---

[12] Wingstedt also mentions the Rhetorical function, in which music contributes a meta-commentary on the action, perhaps through contrast with images and/or being music that is already well known. Though this function is the only one that he mentions which is not immediately applicable to this sequence from *To Have and Have Not*, we should remember that the music nevertheless draws upon many precedents of musical form and signification (even if it does not do this self-consciously or encourage our meta-comprehension of that) (2010, 194).

[13] The term "synchresis" is defined by Chion as "the spontaneous and irresistible weld produced between a particular auditory phenomenon and visual phenomenon when they occur at the same time" (1994, 63). This kind of visual "weld" to the musical material ensures that, even when the latter comes from a non-diegetic place, the two inextricably work together.

during her performances allows for us to adopt a comparatively relaxed position. Her audiences within the film also cue our responses, making the experience even more relaxed as well as engaging. Slim's performances are "rest-points" in the film, signifying that she represents "safe harbor" for Harry and, by extension, us.

Right after the aforementioned sequence in which Harry and Eddie transport the de Bursacs, the film further emphasizes musical and narrative contrast with a scene featuring Slim singing "with a smile" (to quote one of her lyrics). The non-diegetic and non-melodic music accompanying the scene of Harry transporting the de Bursacs even dovetails with the piano accompaniment to Slim's melody, bringing aural relief [1:00:32]. The new scene initially reinforces Slim's power over Harry (and us), but eventually displaces her. The scene is therein representative of the film's striking establishment of Bacall as a show-stopping star as well as its keeping her power in check according to the "rules" of Classical Hollywood. Moments into the scene we hear Slim singing *before* we see her [1:00:41–1:00:50].[14] We see the happy look of wonderment on Harry's face in response to seeing her while we hear Bacall's low mellifluous voice from off-screen. What we see on-screen is, for a few moments, all about her presence out of the frame, as if her voice exceeds that which may be contained by it. This is a memorable example of a sound advance, a moment in which we hear the source of a sound before seeing its associated image (Buhler, Neumeyer, and Deemer 2010, 93). A cut then shows Slim leaning over the piano at the hotel bar, accompanied by Cricket's playing, and four other men humming in harmony [1:00:50]. The men who musically support Slim also form a visual circle with her (see Figure 3.1). Thus they complement her audiovisual presence as she apparently extemporizes a song about "a lady indeed beyond compare," a phrase easily applied to Slim/Bacall as character and star-in-the-making.

Slim's centrality is subtly emphasized by the *mise-en-scène*: her tailored outfit of black-and-white stripes sets her apart from the light-colored shirts and jackets around her. Notwithstanding Harry's show of objection to her having stayed despite his having given her a ticket to leave Martinique, his pleasure in her musical presence is obvious and is meant to gratify the film audience. After the performance is cut short soon after Harry's entrance [1:01:14], Slim announces her plan to continue working in the bar because "Frenchy" (Marcel Dalio), the hotel/bar manager and political activist, "thinks I can sing." Harry's response is one of calculated nonchalance: "well, it's his place," he says, walking away. Before Slim can fully object ("sometimes you make me so mad I could—")

---

[14] The moment is echoed in James Kaplan's opening for an interview with Bacall: "Lauren Bacall's voice precedes her into Coco Pazzo, its deep husk cutting a swath through the eager-to-please young staff" (1994, 58).

FIGURE 3.1 Slim sings of a "lady beyond compare," lyrics that resonate with how *To Have and Have Not* presents her to us.

she is interrupted by Frenchy's entrance and his plea to Harry for help with de Bursac's bullet wounds. While Slim and Harry talk, Cricket resumes playing and the men who were accompanying Slim continue humming and whistling the tune Slim was singing, eventually singing it low so that it becomes underscoring as Harry involves Slim by asking her to fetch a medical kit and hot water [1:01:28–1:03:37]. Thus, the diegetic music of this scene subtly reinforces the love and political plots fusing together, which becomes a pattern for the remainder of the film. The sequence also emphasizes the following: Slim's performance power and Harry's knowing ability to undercut that power; the importance of Slim's performances as "relief" from the more action-filled scenes but the greater importance of Harry's political involvement; Slim's iconic power as a singer and Harry's enjoyment of her as an image despite his easy dismissal of her voice; the film's self-conscious establishment of Slim as one to be adored ("a lady beyond compare" with an enthralled male audience accompanying her), along with its pattern of pushing her to the margins (aurally *as well as* visually) when serious political matters take precedence.

Much of the film's remainder is focused upon the treatment and safe carriage of a wounded Monsieur de Bursac, the key representative of the French Resistance in the film. Along with this emphasis, the film becomes quieter: the silence around de Bursac's sickbed (signifying the most grave fear), makes the moment when Harry removes a bullet from his arm more tense, and the "clink" of Harry's dropping that bullet into a basin more chilling.[15] Talking too much or too loudly is emphasized as being dangerous in *To Have and Have Not*, as is most obvious in a subsequent scene where Captain Renard interrogates Eddie while the latter is drunk and prone to monologue. In their conversations with Harry, both the de Bursacs talk more than he does, and they echo each other in talking of fear and weakness, as well as in terms of politicized conjecture and explanation. Monsieur de Bursac humbly tells Harry, "I wish I could borrow your inner nature" because "the word failure does not even exist for you." Harry, meanwhile, speaks more to instruct than to explain, to tell rather than to ask, and to make statements about what *will* happen rather than what *might*. The kind of certainty that he embodies is an ideal of masculine Americanness, as is humorously emphasized near the start of the film when his straight-talking request for a fishing pass is treated with officious incivility by a thickly accented Frenchman. Harry's focused, undoubting, and unwavering certainty about the correct course of action is reinforced by the music that accompanies what he does, as well as by Bogart's quick-fire way of speaking in a "general American" accent.[16]

The intermittent non-diegetic music of *To Have and Have Not* might be said to support Harry's patriarchal control of the narrative. Furthermore, during many scenes of the film Slim is comparatively quiet or silent, notably in those scenes about Harry's involvement with a political mission. The visual elements of *To Have and Have Not* also work in accordance with Mulvey's description of dominant Hollywood cinema. Bacall is repeatedly set up as an icon, fetishized, and made the object of Bogart's look. She is not present in a scene without Bogart being there from the beginning or entering it, usually early on (by contrast, he is in many scenes without her): it is as if she cannot exist as a character without him as a reference point. In addition, the editing establishes a strong but easily missed pattern whereby almost every point-of-view shot from her perspective is followed by a point-of-view shot from his perspective or from over his shoulder: thus, her look is consistently supplanted by his. In addition, the *mise-en-scène* consistently emphasizes her to-be-looked-at-ness, not least through her plaid and striped outfits that are especially striking in the black-and-white film, but also through

---

[15] There is also extreme quiet around the longest conversation between de Bursac's wife and Harry during which she explains the importance of her being with her husband so as not to be questioned by the Germans back in France.

[16] Bogart's voice signifies all-American plain-speaking in contradistinction to the so-called "Transatlantic accent" (also called the "Mid-Atlantic accent") favored by many of his contemporaries, a way of speaking that communicates the "pedigree" or prestige of some Britishness. The Transatlantic accent was naturally spoken by the English-born Cary Grant but deliberately cultivated by Katherine Hepburn.

FIGURE 3.2 Slim ignites Harry's cigarette, an obvious phallic symbol.

a pattern of her being often "framed" by doorways, or black-suited men (when she is lightly dressed), or lightly dressed audiences (when she is dressed in black). In one particular scene, Slim's primary purpose is apparently to light Harry's cigarette, punctuating the end of his confrontation with an unpaying customer by offering him a flame: at this moment, Bacall becomes the most glamorous and ostentatious prop, as well as symbolically igniting the phallic symbol in Harry's hand (see Figure 3.2).[17]

MIXED AURAL MESSAGES

Though the visual details of *To Have and Have Not* are a match for Mulvey's paradigmatic descriptions, the sound track of the film contains more mixed messages about Bacall's character. On a superficial level, the dialogue emphasizes her character's lack

---

[17] Slim steals a wallet from the customer named Johnson (Walter Sande) who is intent on leaving Martinique without paying a substantial debt to Harry. Harry discovers this truth after seeing the contents of the stolen wallet: tickets for leaving Martinique, along with the money that Johnson has withheld from him. Slim punctuates the triumphant culmination of Harry's confrontation with, and dressing down of, Johnson by lighting his cigarette.

of identity, which in turn throws yet more emphasis on her visual appearance. Slim reveals few personal specifics of herself beyond homesickness for America, and thirty minutes of the film elapse before we even hear her proper name (Marie Browning).[18] Harry *guesses* at her history without her verbal response: for instance, he interprets her unflinching reaction to being slapped by a police officer as evidence of her having been previously abused. It is especially revealing that Bacall's character is seldom mentioned by her proper name in the film, being primarily referred to by *Harry*'s nickname for her: Slim.[19] Thus, she is literally identified in terms of her physicality, not so subtly reinforcing the film's preoccupation with her visual presence.

In another influential feminist article (and one that complements Mulvey's work), "The Fallen Woman and the Virtuous Wife" (1982),[20] Kalinak writes of how female characters are traditionally defined in terms of one of two extremes and in relation to male narrative agents. Slim, however, may be ironically defined in terms of *both* extremes: she is a woman with a shady past, demonstrably accomplished at manipulating men, but she is also finally partnered with Harry (presumably to be his wife) at the film's end (see Figure 3.3).

In addition to winning the hero despite her somewhat shady past, Slim's voice—in dialogue *as well as* singing—makes her more than the easily categorized woman. It is significant that Harry hears Slim's voice for the first time in the film just *before he sees her*—"anybody got a match" she asks, leaning against the doorframe of his hotel room, laconically requesting he ignite the cigarette that is already in her mouth (see Figure 3.4). Note here how the lines of the *mise-en-scène*, along with Harry's determining presence in the foreground looking towards Slim, encourage us to view her as he does. This is the moment at which Harry first sees Slim, and it defines how we might potentially see her throughout the film. As if the sexual innuendo were not clear enough in Slim's request for a match, the camera next shows Harry literally look down and up her body. Thus, the image of Bacall "upstages" the sound of her in their first meeting. This point aside, Bacall's voice is still unusually controlled, deep, and assured. Her habit of slurring words, along with her sonorous control, and languid tempo, establishes her as a vocal contrast to (and challenge for) Harry/Bogart: her warm mellow voice stands out in comparison with his metallic and staccato style of speaking. Bacall's slower voice

---

[18] A police officer is the first to say Marie's full name, upon inspecting her passport.

[19] Buhler, Neumeyer, and Deemer wrongly claim that Marie is "known only as Slim"—however, this is an easy mistake to make because Harry's nickname for her is repeated much more often than her real name (2010, 182).

[20] Kassabian also references this article, which signifies its enduring resonance (2001, 69).

FIGURE 3.3 The final partnership of Slim and Harry.

offsets Bogart's, and she literally brings a different rhythm to the film. Her speech, as well as her music, thus exists in strong opposition to his.[21]

Harry does, however, put Slim "in her place," at least to some extent: for instance, he makes it clear to her that he will maintain his unfettered lifestyle, literally instructing her to walk around his body so that she can observe the absence of figurative strings. Settling down with a woman is presented, in this and other films directed by Hawks, as a potentially perilous choice. As Dolores Burdick argues in her article about "the Hawksian woman" (tellingly titled "Danger of Death"), the women of his films often carry the threat of imprisonment and "tied-down-ness" to the home: once "unleashed, [each one is] capable of binding, injuring, or capturing the male in her turn" (1981, 40).[22] With this danger

---

[21] After the great success of *To Have and Have Not* in making Bacall an overnight star, one of her guiding "father figures," the agent Charles Feldman, wrote her that "your voice, its timbre, its low register, its rare quality, is ideally suited for Bogart roles" (Bacall 2005, 129).

[22] Burdick traces such patterns in several of Hawks's films including *Only Angels Have Wings* (1939), *Ball of Fire* (1941), *Bringing Up Baby* (1938), *El Dorado* (1966), *The Big Sleep* (1946), and *The Thing* (1951), as well as *To Have and Have Not*. She also pays particular attention to the end of *His Girl Friday* (1940) in which Hildy (Rosalind Russell) breaks down—not because she is ready to unleash the anger we know is due Walter (Cary Grant) for his unrelenting manipulation of her throughout the film, but because she fears he will let her marry Bruce (Ralph Bellamy). Burdick writes that, in accordance with Mulvey's

FIGURE 3.4 "Anybody got a match," Slim seductively asks Harry, not-so-subtly suggesting her willingness to be sexually ignited by him.

in mind, *To Have and Have Not* has been described as "the most fully realized view of his intuitive version of how a man should behave in the world" (McCarthy 1997, 391).

Ironically, Hawks is credited with having "created" Bacall as a powerful star and icon, largely through his directorial *control of her voice*. Hawks "discovered" Bacall after his wife, Nancy Hawks, saw her modeling on the cover of *Harper's Bazaar*.[23] Though he was therefore first inspired by the look of her (and her partial resemblance to his wife, the

---

claims for the hegemonic sway of mainstream cinema, "the female viewer finds herself participating in the celebration of a defeat for the heroine, who opened the film by striding into Grant's office to announce her marriage plans and whose tearful joy at abandoning those plans proves what the film must have been implying all along: that women don't know their own minds" (1981, 38). Such is the extremity of such narrative patterns in the director's work that Burdick expresses "the difficulty of loving Hawks and being a woman at the same time" (40).

[23] It was a Louise Dahl-Wolfe picture showing Bacall in a blue suit before a window with "American Red Cross Blood Donor Service" lettered on it. Thompson writes that the picture foregrounds "her 'lethal' look in leaning against the window" and that "the low lighting, and her wide mouth suggest vampiric power, along with vocations and urges above and beyond the war effort" (1999, 25). Bacall herself also mentions that Nancy Hawks saw the *Harper's Bazaar* magazine including this image and showed it to her husband (2005, 95). Nancy also "discovered" Joanne Dru and Ella Raines, other women who bore some physical resemblance to her slender self (Thompson 1999, 18).

original Slim), Hawks became particularly intent upon helping Bacall develop her voice so that she might become "another Dietrich" (Thomson 1999, 18).[24] He spent months training Bacall, changing her look, voice, and even her name (from Betty Bacal). When he discovered that Bacall's own voice was "high and pinched," he advised her to practice speaking in a low voice on the Hollywood hills (26). While he was readying Bacall for her debut, Hawks told Bogart he wanted to "make a girl as insolent as you are." When Bogart replied "Fat chance," Hawks said "I've got a better than fat chance . . . In every scene you play with her, she's going to walk out and leave you with egg on your face" (18). Hawks thus lauded her in terms of achieving vocal assertion and dominance over Bogart.[25] We might say Hawks was therefore using Bacall for (playful) one-upmanship over another man. Not only that, but Hawks's personal investment in Bacall's character was reinforced by his using his wife's own words. Nancy "Slim" Hawks said,

> Once he hired Betty, he suddenly became very interested in everything I had to say. Now he listened to me as if I were speaking lines created by the screenwriters Jules Furthman and William Faulkner. In his eagerness, Howard would sometimes show his cards and directly ask me what I'd say in a certain situation. Dutifully, I'd answer the question. The next thing I knew, Furthman and Faulkner were running it through their typewriter (Thomson 1997 21).

So, Hawks "stole" lines from his wife and used Bacall to ventriloquize the composite ideal he imagined: an American Dietrich modeled on Nancy.

Bacall herself writes memorably of Hawks's decisive and controlling role in making her a star with *To Have and Have Not*. It is easy to be beguiled by her story as the eighteen-year-old girl plucked out of obscurity, bidding a tearful farewell to her mother, and leaving a very modest home for a "lucky break" in Hollywood after Hawks sent for her (in 1943). Bacall writes of being "mesmerized" by Hawks and his industry stories ("he always came out on top"), of touring the Warner's studio and trying to absorb everything ("my head was on a swivel"), as well as becoming the "first girl" Hawks "signed personally" (2005, 87, 88, 91). She writes of Hawks in various terms of power in relation to her: as "a Svengali" (93), as a Doctor Frankenstein creating a "monster" (101), as one keeping her "in a cocoon" (105), and as one inventing the realization of a

---

[24] Thompson notes that Hawks and his wife often referred to each other as "Slim" and "Steve" (1999, 21).
[25] Ironically, for all his control over her physical being in addition to her performance, Hawks complained that Bacall did not live in terms of the film enough. He also reportedly stopped talking to both her and Bogart after they fell in love during the making of the film (McCarthy 1997, 391–94).

dream that would feature herself "emerging perfectly out of his mold after the proper baking time of all the right ingredients" (103). She writes, in particular, of how Hawks explained that she must maintain composure and attractiveness through her voice: he told her, "If you notice, Betty, when a woman gets excited or emotional she tends to raise her voice. Now, there is nothing more unattractive than screeching. I want you to train your voice in such a way that even if you have a scene like that your voice will remain low" (95). Though Hawks was interested in making Bacall into a force for Bogart to reckon with, he was also clearly shaping his own ideal of a woman.

In several respects, then, *To Have and Have Not* represents extremes of patriarchal control over Bacall as well as the character of Slim: the musical overture clearly establishes "feminine" music as subsidiary to the music of greater, "masculine" importance; and the non-diegetic score reinforces Harry's controlling importance, as well as his decisive agency in contradistinction to Slim's more laconic "going nowhere" presence. Even when Bacall's talent is being showcased, the importance of Harry's actions takes precedence, a pattern reinforced by the fact of the film being Bacall's debut whereas Bogart was an established star before it was released. The visual components of the film match Mulvey's descriptions of mainstream cinema, privileging the male desiring gaze and objectifying Bacall's appearance. Bacall's appearance, as well as her voice, was forcefully controlled by the male director, an auteur known for films that feature strident women who "must" be held in check. However, if we delve deeper into analyzing Slim's aural presence, aspects of her singing performances *and* dialogue, as well as the film's ending, she is much more than a straightforwardly submissive character. *To Have and Have Not* is, like any film, a product of its time and it would be anachronistic to call it "feminist." That said, Bacall as Slim sometimes pushes the boundaries of what we might expect from a woman of her time *or* her time's cinema.

SLIM'S TRANSGRESSIVE AGENCY

Late in the film, the loveable alcoholic Eddie seems unusually perceptive when he tells Slim that she talks like Harry. She does indeed literally echo Harry's words, most notably when Eddie tells her he has been stung by "a hundred" dead bees and she responds "why don't you bite them back?" Eddie then points out that Harry has said the same thing, and this automatically leads Eddie to believe "you're alright lady." That Slim echoes Harry's words here might emphasize her own lack of words. By the same token, her echoing of Harry also playfully suggests her ability to claim his words for herself as well as her own ability to "sting" back. Early on in the film, Harry fails at catching a swordfish which he refers to as "him." A few scenes later, Slim says that picking up men is "like shooting fish in a barrel." Without necessarily being conscious of it, Slim thus states her ability to outwit Harry (and men in general). Because Bacall delivers such lines with a voice that is comparatively deep for a woman, her power is further emphasized. Her voice has a sultry, seductively and softly undulating control that seems relaxed in relation to Bogart's characteristically fast talking. Kaja Silverman even argues that the "lowness and huskiness" of her voice connotes "masculinity rather than femininity, so that the voice seems to exceed the gender of the body from which it proceeds. That excess confers upon it a privileged status vis-à-vis both language and sexuality" (1988, 61).[26] Slim is an important counter-example to the far more dominant trend of Hollywood cinema that diegetically contains the female voice: Silverman has most influentially explored how female characters' voices are repeatedly subordinated to their gendered bodies, especially when male characters speak for them.

Bacall speaks slowly in comparison with Bogart: as already noted, he is the active center of the film, driving its rhythm, while she is often a form of accompaniment, offsetting his pace. However, the *interdependence* of their characters and performances should also be acknowledged. Furthermore, there are points at which Bacall seems to knowingly "freeze the flow of action" through her speaking or singing voice. Pauline Kael famously argued that the film was obviously "tailored to the personalities of Bogart *and* Bacall" (1963, 16, my emphasis). In other words, Kael acknowledged the importance of Bogart and Bacall as a *double-act*.

With the double-act in mind, some of the most memorable parts of the film are those where Slim alone takes control. She kisses Harry before he kisses her (telling him "it's even better when you help"), for instance, and she has the temerity to stay in Martinique after he has given her a plane ticket to leave. She thus grants the audience's desire for their romantic union—a desire cultivated by the film's narrative structure. In addition, Bacall decisively takes control of several scenes through singing, suggesting a counter-hegemonic awareness of her own power. These scenes are striking enough that Mulvey cites them as notable examples of a woman on display, and of a female "spectacle" subjected to the male gaze, but she does not consider these musical performances in detail ([1975] 2004, 841–42). There is, as already noted, other diegetic music played in the film by Carmichael's character, Cricket (nicknamed as such by Harry but, unlike Slim, given no other "real" name). Despite Carmichael's wry charisma and professional status as a musician, however, he is not a spectacle

---

[26] Silverman makes the same argument for the voices of Mae West and Marlene Dietrich (1988, 61). By contrast, Jacob Smith argues that "Bacall's deep, husky voice helps make her a spectacle" (2008, 70), implying that whatever vocal power she has is in the service of her becoming a visual icon.

like Bacall within the film world—instead, he provides comic relief, and moments of hiatus for music to establish a social atmosphere and narrative rest. Though amusing, Cricket's seated position at the piano reinforces his subsidiary status. Bacall, by contrast, both stands *and* stands out for her singing performances for the following reasons: the already-mentioned assuredness of her deep, mellow singing; her evident enjoyment in being looked at; her ability to self-consciously establish her star quality within (and beyond) the world of the film through her confidence; and her "spur-of-the-moment" ability to take the stage.

Slim's first performance in the film is "unrehearsed." To borrow terminology from Jane Feur, she thus reinforces a "myth of spontaneity" that encourages us to marvel at and participate in her greatness by being an attentive audience.[27] That her performance is presented as an impromptu one makes her confidence all the more impressive. Before she sings, she already bounces out of the *mise-en-scène* in a tailored plaid suit, another outfit that is especially striking in black and white. Soon after Cricket begins performing the song "Am I Blue?" at the piano, Slim notices Harry looking at her from across the room, and then rises from her seat to stand above Cricket at the piano [14:42–15:39]. Soon after she makes eye contact with Cricket, he literally tells her to "take over" his singing. The song, "Am I Blue?," is about bemoaning the absence of a beloved man. Ironically, Harry is very much present, and Slim knowingly performs the show of being forlorn with lighthearted nonchalance [15:49–16:16]: "I speak these lyrics of a woman forsaken," she seems to say, "but we both know that that can never happen to me." When the first words of singing escape her lips, Cricket smiles up at her with surprised admiration (see Figure 3.5). His admiration surely reinforces ours, though Slim is hardly reliant upon it. More than once, she turns around to observe the object of her performance, Harry, listening and admiring her as she duets with another man (see Figure 3.6).

With the object of her performance clearly identified, she does not falter in holding the melody, even when Cricket harmonizes with her in the final phrases of the last chorus. Though the melody is quite simple, and its standard thirty-two-bar structure (AABA) is surely predictable, Bacall's decisive assuredness communicates the authority of a grander feat. The myth of her spontaneous ability to perform is not only musically answered but also enthusiastically applauded by the on-screen audience as

---

[27] Feuer has authoritatively written of such myth-making in Classical Hollywood musicals where such "spontaneous" performances (like Slim's) are routinely expected ([1977] 2012, 545–49).

FIGURE 3.5 Cricket is manifestly impressed by Slim's impromptu ability to take over his song.

FIGURE 3.6 Slim looks across the room to check that Harry is listening to, and admiring, her performance.

FIGURE 3.7 Following Slim's playful instruction, Harry quietly wolf whistles after her exit: an unguarded moment of admiring her.

stand-ins for us.[28] When Slim has finished singing, the band continues making music without Cricket singing: hers is no act to follow.

Along with being a commanding performer, Slim clearly enjoys her own status as a woman to be admired. In one of the most famous scenes of the film, she reminds Harry (whom *she* nicknames "Steve") how to whistle: "You just put your lips together and blow." With this reminder, she leaves Harry's room. The sound of her closing the door is followed by Harry's quiet wolf whistle to himself: thus, the sound of her assertion of a barrier between them is followed by the sound of his unguarded moment of reverie about her (see Figure 3.7). The wolf whistle is usually a sound of admiration from a man looking at a woman: the sound indicates the admiring male gaze, along with suggesting his objectifying power over her. Here, however, there is a stronger

---

[28] Thus, the performance also plays out what Feuer calls "the myth of integration" ([1977] 2012, 549–51) and "the myth of the audience" (551–54). We are united with the on-screen audience in wanting to applaud the performance ("the myth of the audience"), and we are also invited by the film to believe that our presence as an audience is a necessary part of the whole show ("the myth of integration").

sense of Slim's agency: she has playfully *reminded* him how to whistle. She is inviting his admiring gaze.[29]

In Slim's final performance, she again repeatedly looks off-screen to see Harry looking at her. We are therefore continually aware of his watching presence even though we are not viewing her from his perspective. Her sexuality, bodily presence, and iconic beauty are especially emphasized by her stunning black gown (one that makes Harry say "you won't have to sing much in *that* outfit"). Harry also playfully suggests that the dress alone is enough to inspire romantic and sexual attachment regardless of the body within it: as he leaves the scene to check on the safety of the de Bursacs, Slim quips "give her my love" with reference to Madame de Bursac's flirtation with him, and Harry's quick response is "I'd give her my own if she had *that* on." Slim accepts the joke without any indication of believing herself to be interchangeable.

Soon thereafter, Slim gives her final performance with the song called "How Little We Know" [1:29:00–1:33:37], one that was written by Mercer/Carmichael specifically for the film. In keeping with their conversational playfulness, the song is a disingenuous message of noncommittal, questioning delight:

> Who knows why love comes along, casting a spell?
> Will it sing you a song?
> Will it say a farewell?
> Who can tell?

As Slim sings of such noncommittal love "as changeable as the weather" she is, ironically, visually defined as completely set apart from everyone else: her black dress is offset by pale suits, showcasing her physical presence as the opposite of interchangeable (see Figure 3.8). This image is a great example of what became the signature Bacall "look," here directed back at Bogart watching her perform. Ironically, this look evolved from Bacall's nerves. On her first day of being filmed for *To Have and Have Not*, Bacall was uncontrollably shaky for her "anybody got a match?" scene. After a few takes, she learned that "one way to control my trembling head still was to keep it down, chin low, almost to my chest, and eyes up at Bogart. It worked, and turned

---

[29] Several months before the film was made, Bacall was herself learning to enjoy the gaze of others. She writes of attending a big party at the Hawks' home, an occasion that was attended by many big-name stars and entertainers. At one point she found herself "near the piano, dancing by myself—in my own world, but aware of Hawks and others at the far end of the room watching me out of the corner of their eyes. There is strength in being a new young face thrust into a group of people too used to one another. I guess I used that" (2005, 98). Bacall's account reveals her slow appreciation of her own power, even under the pressure of extreme scrutiny.

FIGURE 3.8 Slim's final performance, with Bacall giving her trademark "look."

out to be the beginning of 'The Look'" (2005, 105). Ironically, then, Bacall's way of visually "answering" the male gaze began as a defense for concealing her fear of being filmed or consumed.

Ironically, in the immediate film context, Slim communicates unwavering awareness of her own power, and not least when she sings

> Maybe you're meant to be mine,
> Maybe I'm only supposed to stay in your arms a while,
> *As others have done.*

She not only directs this part of the song to Harry but literally *speaks* the last phrase to him with a pointed, wry smile (see Figure 3.9). Then, when she finishes the song with the following lines

> Is this what I've waited for, am I the one?
> Oh I hope in my heart that it's so, in spite of how little we know.

FIGURE 3.9 Slim wears an irresistible smile while she playfully delivers a critical lyric of her last song to Harry.

she gratifies our expectation for their final union, and the answer to her last question.

In all her performances, Slim communicates her assertion of and enjoyment in her own power.[30] Where Cricket's voice is sometimes relegated to the background, Slim's never is. The aural primacy of her performances, the soft low pitch and rich timbre of her voice, the predictable harmonic and melodic structures of her tunes, the humor and simplicity of her lyrics (especially those "directly" addressing Harry), and the harmonious repetitions of her hummable songs all make for accessible and pleasing experiences. So, Slim exerts considerable sway through the film, even if her power is tempered by the more consistent focus on Harry's authority. Her voice alone establishes her as much more than the kind of woman (say, Madame de Bursac) who is easily rebuffed by the protagonist and dismissed by the plot.[31]

---

[30] It is surprising that Buhler, Neumeyer, and Deemer downplay Slim's musical performances, even to the extent that they mention music is "never associated" with Bacall's character apart from her performance of "Am I Blue?" and "one other performance" (2010, 200). So, in focusing upon Slim's presence and her music, this analysis is deliberately "against the grain" of what others have found in the film before.

[31] Bacall explains that Dolores Moran (Madame de Bursac) was originally meant to have a bigger part in terms of becoming romantically involved with Bogart's character (and not least because she was established in Hollywood before the film was made). However, Hawks and Bogart made a decision to scale

In relation to musical theatre, Bradley Rogers has written about how a diva might gain power beyond that of being made into spectacle. More specifically, in relation to the work of an especially "famous belter," Vivienne Segal, he writes:

> [She] was more than merely a part of the plot: she was also a performing body, a body able to escape her position as narrative object and able instead to present herself as a defiant musical subject, one with whom [composer Lorenz] Hart could identify and sing along. This is indeed the beauty of the musical diva, whose body and voice can enact a utopian mobility, thwarting and transcending attempts at musical integration (2008, 97).

Though she does not necessarily "transcend" her place within the film narrative driven by male agency and patriarchal perspective, Slim *is* capable of defiance. She does not leave when Harry tells her to. She stays to not only assert her power as a performer but to make good on the living she is promised for her talent. And she not only ends the film with the man she wants, she leaves with the hotel band playing exit music developed from a song she has sung ("How Little We Know"). She playfully and irrepressibly wiggles her hips to this music before it segues into the final "The End" fanfare, also derived from the same song [1:39:22–1:39:54]. The film thus ends with a triumphant emphasis on her visual *and* aural presence (see Figure 3.10).[32]

At the 1993 Troia International Film Festival, Nadine Brozan reported the following as a "high point" in *The New York Times*:

> Lauren Bacall, sleek in black silk pants and pearls, unveiled a rose marble plaque in her honor on Saturday. Silence. Then with characteristic candor, she said in a booming voice: "It's too small. I can't see my name." Ms. Bacall pointed out that plaques honoring such male stars as Kirk Douglas, Robert Mitchum, Ben Gazzara and Mickey Rooney were considerably larger than those made for her and for Jane Russell (1993, 6).

---

back Moran's part after seeing several of Bacall's scenes and her chemistry with "Bogie" in particular (2005, 116).

[32] Slim's aural power resonates with Sjogren's challenge to understandings of Hollywood cinema "as invariably and monolithically 'male-centered,' as catering to the phallocentric gaze alone, as occluding the feminine, and as containing the woman and her desire, within not only images that objectify her, but inside narrative structures that constrict and oppress her subjectivity and point of view" (2006, 1). Though Sjogren does not focus on Bacall, *To Have and Have Not* complements her study of female characters that speak and are heard in other films of the 1940s.

FIGURE 3.10 After her final performance, Slim triumphantly exits the last scene of *To Have and Have Not.*

This account suggests that, even if it *was* sculpted by Hawks, the power of Bacall's voice has endured. Certainly, at this honorary event, Bacall's voice was much bigger than the visual tribute. In the end, what mattered to Brozan most was not the *visual* tribute to the star's legacy but the unmistakable strength of Bacall's giving voice to the endurance of gendered inequality.

 # THE PIANO

PLOT SUMMARY

The Piano revolves around Ada McGrath (Holly Hunter), a woman shipped off from
Scotland to New Zealand as a mail-order bride by arrangement of her father. Her
husband, Alasdair Stewart (Sam Neill) is an English colonist recently settled in New
Zealand. Ada's forced journey along with her daughter Flora (Anna Paquin) is representative of the limited control women had over their own lives in Ada's time: the
1850s. Ada is mute, evidently by her own choice, and she primarily expresses herself
through her own piano playing. Because her boat trip to New Zealand necessarily
entails that she will not play her piano for several weeks, the film quickly establishes
that her primary means of self-expression is cut off by patriarchal control. The point
is reinforced when, upon Ada's arrival in New Zealand, Stewart refuses to have her
piano transported to their home. Stewart's incapacity to appreciate the significance
of Ada's piano turns to cruel indifference when he trades the instrument for land
with a subordinate, George Baines (Harvey Keitel). Baines offers it back to Ada,
key by key, in exchange for escalating physical intimacies with her. Their bargaining
develops into a romantic and sexual affair and is inadvertently discovered by Ada's
daughter. Flora, threatened and displaced by her mother's intimacy with Baines,
reveals the secret to Stewart who attacks Ada with his axe, chopping off one of her
fingers and threatening to remove more of them if the affair continues. In response
to Ada's subsequent compliance, Stewart makes a surprising decision to free her
from their marriage. The final scene of the film shows Ada having made a final journey to settle down in Nelson with Baines and Flora, enjoying her new family life,
and relearning to speak.

A BRIEF OVERVIEW

The Piano was directed by Jane Campion, all of whose films reward feminist analyses, not least because she is an unusually successful auteur, but also because her films are united in focusing upon female experiences beyond "proscribed gender and sexual roles" (Rueschmann 2007, 289).[33] Campion works within various genres: from a coming-of-age story about a young woman (*Sweetie*, 1989), to an adaptation of Henry James's work (*The Portrait of a Lady*, 1996), to a woman-centered neo-*noir* (*In the Cut*, 2003). However, Campion's female characters are united in undergoing profound internal transformations, several of which are expressed through artistic expression: from writing, as in the biopic of the writer Janet Frame, *An Angel at My Table* (1990); to clothing design, as in the historical representation of Fanny Brawne in *Bright Star* (2009). In *The Piano*, the most affecting possibilities of female expressivity are explored through Ada's music.

We shall begin this second, feminist analysis by exploring how *The Piano* immediately establishes the unconventional strength of its heroine, especially as she uses music to deliberately define herself against patriarchy. With Campion's standing as an unusually successful female auteur in mind, we shall also consider Michael Nyman's unconventional musical scoring practices, Holly Hunter's authoritative performance of the pieces Nyman wrote for her, and the sound track's counter-hegemonic status in relation to comparable examples of aural female representation. After having analyzed Ada's music as a strong expression of female empowerment in all these contexts, we shall consider contrary responses to the film which foreground its mixed messages from feminist perspectives. Once we have explored the connotative power of, and complex reactions to, Ada's piano-playing, we shall consider the precise impact of the whole film's sound track with regard to a scene in which her music is notably absent. Thereafter, we shall pay particular attention to the film's final sequence, one which does not resolve the film's contradictions but which reinforces the unending fascination of Ada's musical agency.

---

[33] Campion first made her name during the era of Second Wave feminism in Australia. During the 1970s "the role of women in media was a national concern," and when Campion had begun filmmaking in the 1980s at the Australian Film, Television, and Radio School (AFTRS) her talent was immediately recognized and fostered. In other words, Campion "appeared at a moment when hard battles had been won" (Radner 2009, 14) and there was fertile ground for her to develop a cinematic voice. For more on Campion's background and her oeuvres, see the anthology entitled *Cinema, Nation, Identity: Jane Campion* (2009).

ADA'S SONIC POWER

From the beginning, *The Piano* privileges Ada's perspective and primes us to hear the music that will define her. In her opening voiceover, along with announcing her muteness, Ada tells us that she primarily communicates through the music she plays on her piano: "the voice you hear is not my speaking voice, but my *mind's* voice," she says. This paradoxical statement is an aural parallel to the first inscrutable image of the film: an image of abstract dark strips offset by light which is revealed to be an extreme point-of-view close-up of Ada peering through her own fingers. That the first shot of the film is from Ada's point of view and places emphasis on the concealment of her face not only establishes her perspective as dominant: it challenges the traditional expectation of woman-as-bearer-of-the-look (to use Mulvey's terminology). Because the image through her fingers is first slightly out-of-focus and inscrutable, the voiceover requires that we (in Britta Sjogren's words) "lay down the gaze to 'see' through our hearing."[34] That Ada initially blocks our vision of her face with the fingers that make her self-defining music also emphasizes that access to her is a matter of *her* choice and our privilege. Visually *and* aurally, then, the film makes it clear that we will not be able to "pluck out the heart of [Ada's] mystery" too easily.[35]

In the same opening voiceover, Ada prepares us to expect the music that will primarily define her in nonverbal (but none the less "articulate") ways: she says "the strange thing is I don't think myself silent. That is because of my piano." Ada only speaks (in the literal sense of words) in the two voiceovers that bookend *The Piano*. Drawing on Chion, we can speak meaningfully of these voiceovers as "sound close-ups" which not only draw us into Ada's consciousness but also encourage us to internalize her voice as our own (1999, 79–80). The close miking of Hunter's voice creates intimacy with her, giving it the aural definition that Chion associates with the "I-voice," an aural presence in the "foreground" without any reverb or distortion (51, 54). That the film begins and

---

[34] Sjogren discusses many parallel moments focused on female subjectivities, especially in films from the Classical Hollywood period such as *Letter from an Unknown Woman* (1948), *Secret Beyond the Door* (1948), *A Letter to Three Wives* (1949), and *All About Eve* (1950). Ada's voiceovers are examples of what Sjogren terms the "voice-off." She defines the "voice-off" as any vocal presence that is non-synchronous with the image and is irreducibly powerful in itself, being much more than a mere accompaniment to the image (2006, 6).

[35] This quotation comes from *Hamlet*, after the protagonist realizes that his friends (Rosencrantz and Guildenstern) have betrayed him by agreeing to observe his behavior on behalf of King Claudius. Upon discovering that his friends are more focused on the surveillance of him than joining him in the grief of his mother, Hamlet accuses Rosencrantz and Guildenstern of "playing upon" him like a pipe, and presuming to "pluck out the heart of my mystery" (Shakespeare 1988, III.ii.353–54) by treating him like an easily controlled instrument.

ends with aural emphasis on Ada's non-diegetic voice (one that only *we* can hear), not only emphasizes the primacy of her story but also the film's expectation that we will actively listen to her presence throughout. Even between her voiceovers, Ada's non-speaking, musical "voice" is almost always much louder than that of her husband, the colonist who is frequently heard (as well as shown) from a greater distance.

Music is unusually important in *The Piano* for binding us to its central character: it defines and reveals Ada more than any images (perhaps even those of her undressed) and, excepting the two short voiceovers and a few inarticulate sounds from Ada in the diegetic space, the music is her dominating "voice." This voice, moreover, frequently transcends the diegetic space when phrases from three of Ada's pieces ("Big My Secret," "The Heart Asks Pleasure First," and "Bed of Ferns") are reiterated non-diegetically. That Ada's music is used diegetically *and* non-diegetically not only suggests the Utopian possibility of her transcendence but also reinforces the power of her subjectivity, especially her resistance to objectification. Therein, the soundtrack encourages the audience to think beyond "the hegemonic structure of subject-object [or, male-female] that dominates film practice" (McGlothlin 2004, 26). In other words, the manner in which Ada is musically defined represents opposition to the dominant practices of patriarchal filmmaking as identified by Mulvey.

The non-diegetic scoring of Ada's music is typically in sync with her reactions and the rhythm of her movements, further reinforcing her atypical power over us, even when she is victimized. For instance, there is the climactic scene where Stewart cuts off her finger. Here, the non-diegetic musical cue ("The Heart Asks Pleasure First") begins quietly after Flora has revealed her mother's affair to Stewart, and he begins to seek Ada with his axe [1:36:12]. The music becomes louder as he charges towards her through rain. After he bursts in on Ada at their home and physically assaults her, his shouts are louder than the music: "Why? I trusted you! I trusted you, I trusted you!" he screams, as if trying to trump her music while he physically takes control of her body. He axes her piano (a symbolic extension of her body), the reverberations of which dissonantly blend with the non-diegetic music. But even though Stewart here competes with Ada's music, it takes precedence again after his act of violence. The music becomes most frantic right before Stewart cuts off Ada's finger, paralleling Ada's physical resistance to him. The music suddenly stops after the blow is struck [1:38:38]. For a few moments there is nothing but the diegetic sounds of Flora screaming, rain, and mud squelching as Ada rises up and away from Stewart. When her music then non-diegetically re-enters, along with her regaining some physical control, it is quiet and at a slower tempo than before [1:38:18]. The music reinforces the visual emphasis on her shock and her stumbling effort to walk until she slumps into the mud [1:39:11] (see Figure 3.11). Now, nothing competes with her musical voice.

FIGURE 3.11 As Ada slumps into the mud, Nyman's music wordlessly communicates her pain.

The interrupted cue of "The Heart Asks Pleasure First," followed by its subdued return (underscoring this image), wordlessly conveys the impression of a heart suddenly about to give up and then mustering strength in the pain of a horrific instant. Ada's music is without lyrics, but it forcefully communicates the impression of a voice trusting us to hear it. Its nonverbality further reinforces her atypical power, for it demonstrates that her capacity for emotional expression transcends the Word of the Father. That Ada's music plays non-diegetically even after Stewart has attempted to "castrate" her power by chopping off the finger also emphasizes her uncanny strength.[36]

Ironically, "The Heart Asks Pleasure First" is also featured during one of Ada's most joyful scenes. When Baines reunites Ada with her piano earlier on in the film,

---

[36] Caroline Bainbridge reads Stewart's violent action in terms of "symbolic castration" (2008, 157). Her analysis of Ada's silence in *The Piano* is as follows: she is a "woman trapped by a symbolic order that depends upon the exchange for women to maintain its sexual/economic/symbolic authority and law, [and] woman is unable to articulate her own desire, to exist on her own terms and in her own right" (156). Noting that Ada's having an illegitimate child further "reduces her status as an exchangeable object" (156), and the importance of Flora as a vocal extension of her mother who symbolizes "those aspects of Ada's character that are effaced as a result of the fact that Ada cannot/will not speak" (173), Bainbridge gives surprisingly short shrift to the significance of Ada's music. That said, her reading of the film might be used to develop a fuller psychoanalytic reading of the sound track.

the decorative sixteenth-note figurations on the "inside" of the tune emphasize Ada's delight, and her giddy enjoyment of the music as Flora literally dances around her [24:32–26:40]. In the scene of violence, the *same* figurations match the terrifying momentum of Stewart chasing Ada, and the energy of his violent intent, as well as her quickening heart. In her article "Music in *The Piano*" Gorbman emphasizes that the "stable meaning" of Ada's music "evaporates" through such varied use, and that the score therein offers something different from standard leitmotif repetitions or variations (2000, 52–53). In particular, the different uses of the same recording highlight the malleability of Nyman's composition as it represents Ada's feelings.

The Piano is a fantasy about the possibilities of music to enable the unconventional expressive freedom of a woman despite that which literally and figuratively surrounds her: a wild landscape that is physically threatening to her, and an historical context of unbending and extreme patriarchal power. In addition to privileging and luxuriating in her musical voice, the film also prompts us to dwell upon *every* wordless sound she makes: the slap of her hands signing when she is angry, for instance, or her stamping foot (especially when Stewart trades her piano for land with Baines), or her ripping off the fake wedding dress that she is made to wear in a photograph with Stewart. Indeed, the sonic details that characterize Ada register hugely enough that Stewart's first response to her petite *appearance*—"you're small, I never thought you'd be *small*"[37]—seems ironically reductive to the point of absurdity.

Ada's being forcibly taken from her homeland to New Zealand to be married off to Stewart is representative of an historically common occurrence. That Ada is nevertheless empowered by the film's emphasis on her aural presence makes it feminist *and* revisionist. Because the film is set at a time during which many American westerns are set, along with being located in an unsettled and often wild terrain, it invites analysis as a feminine reframing of the genre: instead of the lone cowboy picture on a desert wasteland, we see Ada forcibly carried through the sea and wading through mud alone.[38]

A montage early on in the film shows Ada's journey from Scotland to New Zealand, then her being carried by Maoris to shore. The image of her silhouetted figure, with bonneted head and billowing skirts, shakily brought to shore amidst vigorous waves, has become an iconic representation of a woman carried into a life in the New World that she would not choose for herself (see Figure 3.12).

---

[37] The italics indicate the Sam Neill's emphasis in his original delivery of the line in the film.
[38] The power of the western as a malleable genre is much more fully defined and explored in Part I of this book.

FIGURE 3.12 The iconic image of Ada being carried onto the New Zealand shore.

The film visually foregrounds the massivity of the landscape around Ada as well as its treacherous power. Several times, for instance, Ada's little boots are shown being swallowed in the sticky sludginess of the unsettled Antipodean mud, the point being emphasized by an aural motif of revolting squelchy sounds.

Ironically, in terms of representing Campion's work as well as foregrounding the creativity (as well as the oppression) of its protagonist, *The Piano* has been widely understood as a celebration of transcendent female expressivity. It was the first film by a woman director to win the Palme D'Or at Cannes (a fact that was much-publicized by Miramax, the film's American distributor). Holly Hunter's performance has also been widely celebrated, especially for its unconventionality. With her hair severely pinned back and *greasy* (a detail of historical authenticity that mattered to Campion), and with her severely tight Victorian black dresses that paradoxically hide her body, Hunter certainly *looks* different from a pretty archetypal heroine of a period movie.[39] Such is the relative severity of Hunter's appearance in the film that when she undresses with Baines,

---

[39] As Campion says (in some notes accompanying the screenplay of *The Piano*), "one of the clichés of romance is that the heroines are classic beauties, but I wanted there to be a reality to our actors that counters pure romanticism" (1992, 139). (Also, for a full analysis of the costumes in the film, see Bruzzi 1995.)

revealing the soft curves of her womanly body, it is a visual surprise. Thus, for much of *The Piano*, Campion avoids the kind of objectification that Mulvey wrote about. The sheer expressivity of Ada's music is also a surprising contrast with her corset-controlled body and self-imposed speechlessness. Moreover, the beauty of Ada's music encourages us to understand and luxuriate in the surprise of who she is rather than dwelling upon how she looks.

MICHAEL NYMAN

To create the interior life of her heroine through music, Campion chose the English composer Michael Nyman. Nyman's score for *The Piano* is true to his other film composing in that it is far from unobtrusive. Though he has written many concert works, Nyman has achieved most success as a film composer whose strident, lean style seems most obviously indebted to Bernard Herrmann. By the time Campion approached Nyman to compose music for *The Piano*, he had had a long collaboration with director Peter Greenaway (from 1976 to 1991).[40] With Greenaway, Nyman established his practice of composing *while* the director shot and edited the film, rather than the usual method of composing music for the film in postproduction. "So," asserts Nyman, "the music created an editing rhythm. The traditional Hollywood way is to do a final edit, list the cues then ask for the music. But this way round it meant I wasn't just a dummy who slotted in" (Russell and Young 2000, 97). By the time he worked with Campion, Nyman had thus thoroughly established himself as a composer whose work was integral to the development of films. Nyman's collaborative creative agency is perhaps most fully realized in *The Piano*, a point that amplifies the heroine's power at the center of the film.

Before becoming a composer, Nyman studied musicology and became a music critic for the British periodical *The Spectator*: he is, therefore, a composer well versed in theoretical approaches to classical music (in the loose sense), as well as being an expert in experimentalism. [41] His book about minimalist and experimental music details how John Cage treated the (musical) past as a collection of raw resources to be plundered and reshaped at will. Nyman himself uses a similarly eclectic and irreverent approach

---

[40] Nyman wrote scores for the following Greenaway films: *1-100* (1978), *The Draughtsman's Contract* (1982), *A Zed & Two Noughts* (1985), *Drowning by Numbers* (1988), *The Cook, The Thief, His Wife and Her Lover* (1989), and *Prospero's Books* (1991). It is well known that after Nyman was dismayed at how much of his music for *Prospero's Books* was edited and/or distorted in Greenaway's final cut, they discontinued working together.

[41] Nyman is even credited with coining the term "minimalism" as a description of music in 1978 (Russell and Young 2000, 95).

to canonized musical forms: his music for Greenaway's *Drowning by Numbers*, for instance, adapts the slow movement of Mozart's Sinfonia Concertante for violin and viola (K. 364); and his music for *The Draughtsman's Contract* adapts ground basses and lesser-known chaconnes by Purcell. (Purcell's use of closed harmonic systems provided Nyman with repeatable and layerable harmonic structures similar to those which often shape his own music.)[42] The music in both films is recognizably that of Nyman, even though he used material from other, canonized compositions.

Nyman is well known for such examples of playfully adaptive, "arthouse" unconventionality in his film scorings. He also writes idiosyncratic music outside familiar predictable musical paradigms for specific film genres. With his score for the science-fiction film *Gattaca* (1997), for instance, he made a point of telling director Andrew Niccol "I don't do futuristic sci-fi music, I don't do bleeps and blobs" (Russell and Young 2000, 105). Niccol's response was to tell Nyman that he should use Henryk Górecki's *Third Symphony*, an extraordinarily beautiful but unusually "modular" (in the sense of being built on small units of repeated sound) orchestral work as the basis for his score (97). This instruction suited Nyman's interest in building pieces out of modules and matrices, a process that relates to serial music techniques but which, as Annette Morreau writes, is combined with "his recognizable chords, chord progressions, condensed structures, and melodic fragments [and] his use of driving repetitions that make the result very different from serialism, with an energy and exuberance more associated with pop. . . music" (1995).[43] His music for *Prospero's Books*, the feature-film score that he wrote immediately before *The Piano*, represents another typically Nyman, anachronistic blend of Cageian aesthetics, popular music elements, and English experimental music, along with elements of Baroque, Classical, and Romantic music.[44] Overall, Nyman's music is stylistically eclectic, playful, unpredictable, and much more "audible" than most film scores.

Nyman's music for Ada challenges expectation in more ways than one. First, it is music unlike that which a typical bourgeois white woman of her time would have been encouraged to learn, or that which might be used in a more "authentic" period film. It

---

[42] See Morreau (1995) for further discussion of this point.

[43] Serialism is based in the twelve-tone row technique created by Arnold Schoenberg. As noted later with reference to Schoenberg's influence on David Raksin, twelve-tone row compositions are based on scales created out of the twelve chromatic notes within an octave. The row forms the basis of the piece's entire structure, including its melody and harmony. Serialism stretches beyond the conventional boundaries of most Western music because it has an inherently unfamiliar sound. Other, looser forms of serialism are grounded in sets of notes or patterns. In his book *Experimental Music: Cage and Beyond*, Nyman writes that his minimal processes of composition originate in serialism (1974, 119).

[44] For a fuller discussion of Nyman's music for *Prospero's Books*, see Walker (2000).

is also notably different from Nyman's music for Greenaway's films. In an interview on the music of *The Piano*,[45] Nyman speaks of writing music for Greenaway that was always meant to emphasize relationships between things, ideas, and structures, but never people. When writing for *The Draughtsman's Contract*, for instance, Nyman created late seventeenth-century pastiche in response to the thirteen architectural drawings provided by Greenaway. In this score, the "hard" sound of the harpsichord (an instrument that does not produce dynamics), strident brass, and woodwind meet the alienating harshness of Greenaway's storytelling: though the subject matter of the film is distressing (a daughter coolly observes the possibility and then the reality of her father's murder), the film seems to disallow an emotional response, not least because the characters are often viewed through square grids like those found on a draughtsman's drawing paper. By contrast, when Campion first approached Nyman about *The Piano*, she expected him to fill the "emotional chasm" of Ada with music that would say everything Ada might say if she were to speak. In response to this challenge, Nyman made a conscious choice to avoid any form of pastiche, and decided that Ada would not be one to play music from the established canon of nineteenth-century music.[46] Crucially, he also imagined Ada as a composer in her own right. Nyman transcribed the tunes from a volume of Scottish popular songs from the nineteenth century, music of the sort that Ada might have heard on the streets, or at dances, or in salons. When he found that all of the tunes from this volume had been harmonized like hymn tunes, Nyman stripped away all the heavy, staid chordal accompaniments, and "liberated" the tunes to create the work of an "eccentric amateur composer" with an anachronistic propensity for experimentation. For one of his pieces for Ada ("The Heart Asks Pleasure First") which is based on the traditional Scottish tune "Gloomy Winter's Noo Awa," for instance, Nyman created slowly changing harmonies that are complicated by sixteenth-note figurations in the style of mid-nineteenth-century music. Mendelssohn's "Songs without Words" were in his mind as particular influences over this process of adaptive creation. In Nyman's final scoring, however, the delicate undulations and figurations that imitate Mendelssohn's work are answered by relentless and restless repetitions that are designed to reflect Ada's "wild, eccentric, quixotic" character. What Ada plays is also representative of Nyman's repetitive experimental music that is very much of the twentieth century. In being an anachronistic, transnational blend of quaint and

---

[45] This is a special feature on the ten-year commemorative (UK) DVD release of *The Piano* (2005).

[46] In the DVD interview with Nyman (2005, from which all the key points of this paragraph come), he says that Ada "wouldn't be playing Mendelssohn and she wouldn't be playing Schumann or whatever. . . I had to create the work of a composer."

classic Scottish folk tunes, and indebtedness to European Romanticism, combined with structural harmonic patterns and sequencing of semi-experimental twentieth-century music, Ada's music is no more predictable than her character. Thus, Nyman literally gave Ada a musical voice beyond the limitations of her own time and place.

When Campion presented Nyman with the challenge of creating Ada's musical voice for *The Piano,* she was asking a composer who works against the unobtrusive or "unheard melodies" of many film scores to create music for her equally convention-defying work.[47] She was also asking the already-unconventional film composer to create something beyond even his well-established musical perimeters. The resulting score is therefore doubly unpredictable in terms of film music conventions, making it an unusually important indicator of the challenge that Ada represents to the mainstream. Because Nyman's music was crucial for the structure and development of Ada's character, as well as the shape of many scenes from *The Piano,* it had a strong influence on the filmmakers from the *preproduction* stage. Hunter herself learned Nyman's pieces in preproduction and performed all the pieces in the film during shooting. And lest we might question the degree to which the music composed by a man might truly "speak for" a woman, it is instructive that Nyman himself deferred to Hunter's performances of what he wrote (Nyman 2005).[48]

Even when Ada's music is cut off, as happens several times during the film, it maintains aural prominence. Moreover, sometimes Ada's discontinuing a performance has its own eloquence. The first two tunes that she plays, among the most important in terms of being repeatedly reused ("Big My Secret" and "The Heart Asks Pleasure First"), are interrupted in the first few minutes of the film. During the first sequence of the film, Ada suddenly stops playing "Big My Secret" when a maid suddenly enters her room, presumably in anticipation of the journey to New Zealand [4:10]. During the next sequence, Ada must stop playing "The Heart Asks Pleasure First" on a New Zealand beach because the inrushing tide forces her up the dry shore, away from the piano transported with her [8:12]. The film's exposition thus delays the full articulation of any of Ada's compositions, allowing her to hold the power of some mystery for some time. Interestingly, Campion originally asked Nyman to compose music for the entire

---

[47] The phrase "Unheard Melodies" refers to the title of Gorbman's important book on common practices of film scoring (1987, as first mentioned in the General Introduction).

[48] The fact that Ada is represented as a composer during the 1850s is all the more remarkable given that it was not until the era when Campion herself was coming of age (the 1970s and early 1980s) when "scholars began extensive excavation of women composers and musicians of the past" (Fuller 1996, 71). Up until that point, as Sophie Fuller points out, the music of women (at least in the Western world) was often ignored or forgotten.

opening ten minutes of the film, and he did indeed compose a cue that began with the first shots of Ada and led up to her first playing with Flora on the New Zealand beach.[49] Though this music was recorded, however, Campion chose not to incorporate so much music right away. The effect is to place more emphasis on the snatches of music that we first hear Ada play. And even though the cues are short, they immediately indicate a level of emotional and lyrical directness, technical range, and elements of uncontainable Romanticism (especially through chromatic ornamentation and melodic complexity) which belie Ada's muteness. The cues, in other words, make us want to know more of what defines and propels a character we cannot presume to know by simply looking at her.

"HIGH -PROFILE," AND UNPREDICTABLE, MUSIC

Nyman's music of *The Piano*, with its emotional directness, frequent *forte* entrances, driving rhythms, and heavy accents is "unusually high profile." The cues are anything but "inaudible" because their entrances are seldom sneaked into the soundtrack.[50] In addition, what Chion calls the "superfield," the contextualizing space created by other ambient sounds in the film (made possible by multitrack recording), often fades into nothing when Ada plays (1994, 150). The film's superfield incorporates many sounds that foreground the specific New Zealand context. Lee Smith's sound design features the aural motifs of native bird songs, squelching mud, and crashing waves, all of which also contribute to the representation of Ada as someone "out of place." The "substantial number of tracks" made possible with Dolby allows particular scope for such a range of textured sound effects.[51] The film also uses the great range of pitches and rich textures enabled by Dolby technology to create the sense of a tangible place that encroaches upon Ada. This atmospheric aural context makes Ada's claim for transcending her circumstances through music all the more poignant. The specific oppression of the *colonial* context is also emphasized through the English accents of several

---

[49] In his DVD interview (2005), Nyman explains that he wrote ten minutes of music for the opening of the film, following every development from Ada's boat journey to New Zealand, to the representation of the Maori welcomers on shore, to the establishment of Ada and Flora's tender relationship and their creation of a makeshift (petticoat) tent on the beach. The music was recorded but Campion felt that dialogue and sound effects were sufficient and that the music introduced too much too quickly: certainly, when Ada's music is first fully heard in the film it is more powerful than it would be if Nyman's music had already dominated the sound track without her playing.

[50] Kassabian makes a parallel argument in relation to the "unusually high profile" compilation soundtrack for *Thelma and Louise* (2001, 79), a film released just two years before *The Piano* and usefully compared with it in terms of featuring music to emphasize female agency.

[51] Chion writes of Dolby in these terms, though not with specific reference to this film (1994, 147).

prominent characters (notably Stewart and his Aunt Morag (Kerry Walker)), as well as the traditional songs that Ada's daughter Flora sings that are associated with the Empire (notably "The Grand Old Duke of York" and "The Ballad of Barbara Allen").[52] It is Ada's music in *The Piano*, however, that is most consistently emphasized and returned to throughout the film. In other words, the film not only insists upon the coercively emotional power of her music, it also aurally communicates that nothing else matters as much.

Nyman's works for Ada are not only different from many of his other scores, but are also very different from the music that is more traditionally associated with leading or "good" women on film. His score emphasizes Ada's power partly because it represents a decisive challenge to the "directional classical harmonies and legato phrasing" which Kalinak (among others) associates with representations of "the virtuous wife."[53] Without wanting to overgeneralize about the significatory possibilities of music, critics often identify the built-in associations of film music styles in terms of gender. Gorbman, for instance, has written that if a film of the forties is airing (that is, from the Classical Hollywood era in which *To Have and Have Not* was made), "you are likely to find that a certain kind of music will cue you in correctly to the presence of [a good] Woman on screen. It is as if the emotional excess of this presence must find its outlet in the euphony of a string orchestra" (1987, 80).[54] With reference to a wide range of Classical Hollywood and contemporary movies, Buhler, Neumeyer, and Deemer also rightly emphasize the long-standing tradition of love themes being primarily associated with female characters who are therein defined in terms of their relationship to a hero (and Erich Korngold's music for Arabella in *Captain Blood* (1935) is one of the key examples they provide of this well-known pattern (2010, 198)). Though Ada's music is often lyrical and euphonious, it does not evoke sentimentality of the sort we might typically associate with a female lead, nor is it necessarily defined its relation to another (male) character's music. Ada's music also differs

---

[52] The latter song may have originated in England *or* Scotland: either way, in the context of *The Piano* it represents the weight of the "Old World" and all the patriarchal traditionalism associated with it in the *New* Zealand. Similarly, though Stewart and his Aunt Morag presumably come from the same place (literally and metaphysically speaking), she speaks with a Scottish accent whereas he speaks with an English one.

[53] See Kalinak (1982) whose findings are described this way by Kassabian (2001, 32).

[54] Here, Gorbman refers to good, romantic, virtuous women, not old or humorous or chatty women, and not femmes fatales who are defined by different music. In her article on music in *The Piano*, Gorbman also provides a further intertextual analysis of Ada's subversive and unconventional stature in relation to classic films centered on musicians (like *Deception* [1946] and more contemporary examples (like *Shine* [1996]). As Gorbman points out, such films tend to define the "serious musician" as "a *man* who expresses the depth of his soul through consummate knowledge, skill, and passion" (2000, 44, my emphasis).

from that which is associated with contemporary so-called "woman's films."[55] We might, for instance, make useful comparisons between Ada's pieces and Georges Delerue's music for the near-contemporary *Steel Magnolias* (1989): the whimsicality, light textures, and delicate timbres of the Delerue's score seem innocuous and clichéd in comparison with the exuberant energy and stridency in Ada's music as performed by Hunter.

Every formal element of Nyman's music for Ada communicates her unusual strength of character, her artistic inventiveness, her emotionally expansive capabilities, her uncontainable expressivity, and her dynamic directionality. As already indicated, many of her melodies are built on Scottish folk tunes (in keeping with her background), but they are developed with extremes of pitch and ambitious ornamentations that belie their traditional origins. Moreover, the different structural elements of Ada's music work for consistently strident, and cumulatively arresting, impact: her harmonies frequently fluctuate between different tonalities;[56] her playing incorporates stylistic features such as sudden *szforzando* notes or accented chords that are surprising; her tempo is often unpredictable or uneven ("The Heart Asks Pleasure First," for instance, shifts from 12/8 to 9/8 to 6/8 as the melody becomes more florid); and her musical rhythms are made even more unpredictable through her frequent use of *rubato* and syncopation. The rhythmic unpredictability of Ada's music, and the confidence with which she manipulates rhythm, is an especially sharp contrast with the sound (and sight) of Stewart pedantically and awkwardly slamming his hand on the piano to force the "right" tempo when Flora plays and sings the Scottish folk tune "The Flowers of the Forrest." The power of his controlling, beating hand is emphasized in the foreground of the image (see Figure 3.13).

In contrast with Stewart's dogmatic emphasis on keeping the staid rhythm of Flora's music [1:10:39–1:10:52], Ada's music frequently communicates a sense of unendingly unpredictable motion.[57] The power-in-motion that defines Ada's music is, moreover,

---

[55] The "woman's film" is major cinematic form of melodrama "in which female desire must be accommodated within a system of patriarchy" (Man 1993, 43). Glenn Man provides such Classical examples of the genre as *Now Voyager* (1942), in which the woman is given "permission" for expressing agency as a professional psychiatrist (43), and *Mildred Pierce* (1945), in which the comparatively independent female lead is developed but finally "subverted and reincorporated into patriarchy" (44). He cites these examples, along with films directed by Douglas Sirk, as important precedents for the greater challenge to patriarchy represented by *Thelma and Louise* as a revisionist form of western, road movie, feminist gangster movie, *and* woman's film. Equally, in terms of genre, *The Piano* may be regarded as a trailblazing adaptation of the traditionally male-dominated western, costume drama, and music biopic, as well as being an important contemporary woman's film.

[56] Major and minor keys are often alternated in Ada's music, and one of her pieces entitled "The Mood That Passes through You" is almost unnervingly atonal (see Thompson 1999, 72).

[57] Similarly, Thompson points out the correlations between the movements of Ada's music, the movements of the camera, and the movements of the actors—especially in the scene where Ada is first joyfully reunited with her piano on the beach (1999, 69).

FIGURE 3.13 Stewart pedantically insists that Flora keep the correct beat by slamming his hand on the piano as she plays, becoming the awkward embodiment of a metronome.

matched by Stuart Dryburgh's cinematography for *The Piano*. Dryburgh uses many tracking shots, pans, crane shots, and swirling camera movements in 180-degree semicircles. Thus, the sense of dynamic agency built into Ada's music seems to extend into how the very *mise-en-scène* is framed. That the style of the film is apparently inspired (or even determined) by Ada's music is especially resonant when we consider that more mainstream Classical Hollywood cinema tends to associate women with music that is subsidiary to the main themes.[58] Ada's music also emphasizes the importance of that kind of movement that she *can* control, especially as opposed to the forced journey to New Zealand or the sequence in which Stewart literally traps her by boarding up their house

---

[58] Such a broad cinematic pattern is paralleled by musicological studies of sonata form in terms of gender: as Fuller explains, "for many years, musicologists and analysts labeled the first, often assertive tonic theme of sonata form as 'masculine' and the second, usually more lyrical them which introduces a different key as 'feminine.'" In this context, Fuller quotes the work of a "pioneering feminist critic" named Susan McClary who writes of how the masculine, tonic theme is "predestined to triumph" whereas the feminine, subsidiary theme is meant to be "grounded" or "resolved" (1996, 76). It is beyond the scope of this book to provide a full introduction to analyses of concert music as gendered: suffice to say, the standard practice of using women's themes as subsidiary to dominant themes is one that that *The Piano* knowingly plays against.

from the outside. Furthermore, Ada's music seems especially "colorful" in comparison with all that surrounds her: the cinematography and art design of the film were inspired by "a nineteenth-century color stills process called autochrome," the result being a representation of the New Zealand landscapes as murky and cold, as if under water (Thompson 1999, 69). Not only does the look of the film anticipate Ada's near-drowning, it expressionistically represents the oppressions of her life that she challenges through her music.

The power of Ada's "colorful" music in contradistinction to her literal surroundings—in other words, the power of her interior life over her exterior one—might be usefully summarized by analyzing some of her music next to representative images from the film (see Figure 3.14).

FIGURE 3.14 The opening of "Big My Secret" by Michael Nyman (transcribed directly from *The Piano* DVD).

This representative example, Nyman's opening for "Big My Secret," emphasizes Ada's emotional expressivity through its relatively extreme pitch range. The music also emphasizes her unpredictable energy through its *rubato* rhythm, marked accents, the sudden arpeggio in m. 10, and the progressively elaborate ornamentative developments (see especially mm. 10–13). In addition, the music represents Ada's complexity as one who embodies self-containment (as signified by the relative stillness of some sections for the left-hand part) but one who also embodies a restless and vibrant will (as signified by the rapid development of the comparatively ambitious right-hand part).

The second extract from Nyman's score, the opening for "The Heart Asks Pleasure First," is much simpler structurally but no less emotionally arresting (see Figure 3.15). Here, the driving rhythm and repetitions that are characteristic of Nyman's work serve to communicate a sense of urgency and relentless energy that also define Ada's counter-hegemonic status. The sudden shift in dynamics (from *mezzo piano* to *mezzo forte*) place emphasis on Ada as an unpredictable force whose aural power rises when we might not even be prepared for it. It also matters that Ada plays these pieces within

FIGURE 3.15 The opening for "The Heart Asks Pleasure First" by Michael Nyman (transcribed directly from *The Piano* DVD).

the film with "utmost confidence."[59] In Hunter's performance, each note of the main melody is accented. The assertion and cumulative force that is communicated by so many upper-note accents signifies the consistent strength of Ada's will.

Both the above musical extracts might be meaningfully compared with the limited palette of many images in the film. Though the film certainly uses color and lighting contrasts, and establishes some sequences of relative visual warmth, the overall impression is of a limited or "cold" range. Consider the comparative austerity of these juxtaposed images in relation to the "vibrancy" of Ada's music. These images come from a relatively early scene in the film, when Ada is lamenting her own separation from the piano left on the shore. Note the subdued palette of both images: Figure 3.16 emphasizes Ada's pale face obscured by rain and glass; Figure 3.17 shows the piano housed in a pale-brown box and left vulnerable to the elements. Such stark and haunting images as these serve to offset the "colorfulness" of Ada's music and its emotional sway therein. The images present a dampened-down world as Ada so often sees it, in contradistinction to the world of emotive possibility that she accesses through her own playing.

HOLLY HUNTER'S/ADA'S AGENCY

Both aurally and visually, then, *The Piano* represents a profound challenge to what Mulvey identified as being the dominant practice of objectifying women on film. In this context, it is significant that Campion's casting of Hunter was inspired by visual *and* aural imperatives. Hunter is an accomplished piano player and submitted a tape of "remarkable" recordings which Nyman then used as the basis for what he could expect her to perform. In other words, the music was written with Hunter's being able to perform it always in mind: the film thus avoided those distracting cutaways or the use of stand-ins that are so often necessary in cinematic representations of music-making. This is in itself worth attention for it reinforces the sense of authentic personhood (and our access to it) through Ada's music. In addition to Hunter being able to play Ada's music herself, Campion was also especially impressed by the power, believability, and humanity of Hunter's *eyes*.[60] The power of Hunter's/Ada's eyes was crucial for Campion

---

[59] Chion makes this point, contrasting Ada's playing with that of the protagonist in *The Pianist* (2002). In the latter film, Adrian Brody plays Wladyslaw Szpilman, a Polish-Jewish concert pianist who is forced to play before the German Nazi officer who discovers him in hiding during the Second World War. Szpilman performs Chopin's Ballade for Piano in G Minor with comparative hesitancy, and without being able to claim ownership of the piano he plays (2007, 94).

[60] Campion makes this point in her DVD interview (2005), along with remarking on Hunter's unique ability to communicate "hopes, aspirations, sadnesses, and pain" through her eyes alone.

FIGURE 3.16 Ada's pale face is obscured by rain and glass—the color seems literally "washed" from the image.

FIGURE 3.17 Another pale image shows Ada's piano contained within a box: the instrument that she uses to create music of great "colors" is enclosed within a brown box set against the light blue sea and white foam.

because "you've got to be *with* them" (as she says in her DVD interview) as well as swept up in the music. Certainly, the power of Hunter's/Ada's eyes is imperative in a film that demands she "speak" to us, and the other characters, without words: the power of her look alone seems to stop Stewart raping her in a pivotal scene near the end of the film, as well as communicating her pain to us most forcefully when she is separated from her beloved piano.

The literal and figurative emphasis on Ada's perspective is, as already indicated, emphasized in both visual and musical terms. Moreover, even those shots within *The Piano* that dwell upon Ada's to-be-looked-at-ness are undermined. The film does show Ada through several obviously voyeuristic points of view, including: the perspective of a photographer squinting through a camera at Ada in her fake wedding dress, Flora peering through the floorboards at Baines and her mother making love, and Stewart witnessing Baines seducing Ada under her petticoat skirts through a crack in the wall. However, all such moments are thrown into critical and ironic relief so as to destabilize their voyeuristic power: more specifically, the film places emphasis on Ada's rebellious anger in the bridal moment, on our anticipation of Flora's Freudian shock, and on the presence of a dog licking Stewart's hand while he sees Baines moving under Ada's garments. In other words, Ada is not disempowered by voyeurism in the way that Mulvey conceptualizes it in relation to other film examples. Even when Ada and Flora first arrive on New Zealand soil, and the film shows them as objects of "an otherly gaze" (to apply Bainbridge's phrase in relation to how Stewart, Baines, and the local Maoris see them),[61] the film is shaped so much in terms of honoring their experience as strangers in a foreign land that the effect is not to disempower so much as to invoke empathy *with* them.

Just as *The Piano* self-consciously challenges the visual conventions that Mulvey wrote about, it also demands that we make a make a more-than-usually conscious decision to understand its music, not least because that music means access to its central character. It also assumes our complicity in the counter-hegemonic power of her music. In relation to this, the film makes Stewart's Aunt Morag a particularly parodic figure of fun through her being irrationally unnerved by and critical of the nontraditionalism of Ada's music. When Morag speaks of this music "like a mood that passes into you," she unwittingly hits upon the saturating power of what Nyman composed, even though she is herself *resistant* to it. Morag stands for the kind of Victorian traditionalism that would deem it appropriate for a woman to learn the piano primarily as an accomplishment for

---

[61] The quotation is Bainbridge's phrase (2008, 156).

the purpose of selling herself: as Thompson puts it, "Victorian femininity positioned women as cultural trophies whose education was carefully delimited within a framework in which women functioned as cultural accessories within a bourgeois patriarchy" (1999, 72). Morag likes to hear her young niece Nessie (Genevieve Lemon) play the piano because Nessie's approach is as predictable as the world they live in, albeit an oppressive one. She explicitly contrasts Nessie's music with what she perceives to be the threat of Ada's music: "Your playing," she tells Nessie, "is plain and true and *that* is what I like. To have a sound creep inside you is not at all pleasant." Morag implies that which is sinister as well as that which is sexual in her description of what Ada's music does. That we see and *hear* Morag urinating in the bush as she says this (squatting behind by the falling blankets weakly held up by Nessie and two Maori mission girls) signifies a risible and weak effort to defile what Ada expresses. Equally, Ada's playing may in itself be understood as a form of *action* against hegemonic expectations of womanhood.

EMPOWERING OR CONSERVATIVE, OR BOTH?

So far, we have established the feminist power of music in *The Piano* in relation to Campion's auteur status, Nyman's atypical scoring practices, Hunter's coercive performances, as well as the audiovisual patterns and emphases of the whole film. Even with all this said, *some* responses to *The Piano* highlight its possibly conservative undertones. Such responses are partly attributable to the transformations in Ada's *appearance*, especially when she is playing the piano. Timothy Scheurer is a representative example when he waxes lyrical about the softening of Ada that comes about with her music. He writes that as Ada begins to play, "the hard edge of the stare gives way to a contemplative and loving expression and to supple, sensuous, and flowing movement throughout her body" (236).[62] In keeping with his aesthetically driven approach to the character, Scheurer also writes (with unintentional condescension) that Ada's music is a blend of "Romanticism and folk-like simplicity"

---

[62] Scheurer's Romantic reading of the emotional and bodily transcendence in Ada's music is paralleled by Peter N. Chumo's response to the scene where Baines reunites Ada with her piano on the beach and we hear Ada playing for almost two minutes [24:32–26:40]. Chumo responds to the scene as one that echoes the myth-making possibilities of the Classical Hollywood musical: "Ada plays her piano from the depths of her soul in what seems like a magic outpouring of music; she is enraptured by the moment and smiles joyfully for the first time as Flora dances and cartwheels along the beach. Ada's art, then, brings out the best in her daughter, who is able to perform spontaneously to the music. Like the singers and dancers of a traditional movie musical who could turn any setting into a site of musical expression, Ada and Flora can turn a natural setting into a personal concert space for themselves and create art in the most unlikely of settings" (1997, 173–74).

(236). Schuerer does rightly note the Romantic aspects of Ada's music that are most obvious in the main theme "The Heart Asks Pleasure First." For Scheurer, rather than evoking Mendelssohn, the piece features an accompaniment pattern "reminiscent of Schubert's lieder and his famous 'Impromptu in G-flat major' (op. 90, no. 3) especially" (236). Given the indebtedness to recognizable elements of canonized Romantic music, the soundtrack is manifestly designed to prompt an emotive response that circumvents defenses and which does therein make a critical analysis relatively difficult. The Romantic structural components of the music also "feminize" it and thus resonate with traditions of sentimentalizing cinematic female presences with masculinist biases. Such musical signification makes comments like Scheurer's understandable, *despite* claims by Campion (and others) for the unconventional passion and agency of Ada. In other words, Scheurer's reading of the film is (perhaps unintentionally) ideologically loaded in such a way as to potentially undermine the feminist work of the film.[63] This concession aside, and as already mentioned, Nyman's music is an eclectic mix of extremely different styles and structural influences. The traditional Scottish folk tunes and Romantic elements of Ada's music resist easy sentimentalization (*à la* Scheurer) due to the unconventional and unpredictable manner in which they are used.

The contrary impact of Nyman's music—Romantic and unromantic, sentimentalizing and complex, accessible and accosting—is even more certainly paralleled by Ada's ambivalent relationship with her piano. On the one hand, the piano represents freedom of expression that becomes inextricably connected to the sexual freedom that Ada finds with Baines. Over the course of her six piano lessons for Baines, it matters that Ada determines the music which defines the development of their relationship—from the rigidity of scales she plays in the first lesson, to her slow revelation of herself through her own compositions; from her interrupting a slowly intoxicating nocturne with a "loud and mechanical rendition of a Chopin waltz" when Baines touches her [50:19],[64] to her eventually touching him *instead of* the piano. That the piano is representative of her body is made obvious near the start of the film when it shows the piano in a box buffeted by waves, shortly after the corseted Ada has herself endured the same elemental ferocity. That the piano also represents the workings of her heart and her sexuality is made manifest by numerous

---

[63] For a full discussion of the heterosexist and masculinist biases of much film music in the late Romantic style, see Kassabian (2001, 35).

[64] Gorbman describes Ada's playing here as such, in the context of discussing the music's crucial conveyance of the "character's imperative to express" (2000, 43).

details of the film, not the least of which is her giving one of its keys to Baines as an ultimate sign of love.[65] Her carving the words "Dear George you have my heart Ada McGrath" into the key is tantamount to tattooing her own body. Her deliberate removal of the key to make the carving prefigures the horror of Stewart axing one of her fingers after Flora shows it to him (rather than delivering it to Baines). Thus the piano is not only connected with Ada's fulfillment and freedom in love, but also with the terrible and debilitating violence she suffers. Near the end of the film, Ada decides to drown herself with the piano before then rising out of the water while the piano is sacrificed to the sea: the instrument first associated with her uncontainable spirit is also a kind of coffin (indeed, one of the unnamed Maori canoers refers to it as such).

Just as Ada's music and her relationship with the piano might be read in contrary ways, many feminist readings of the film dwell upon how to view the complex bargaining between Ada and Baines. One the one hand, it enables the liberation of female desire, and on the other, it might be viewed as glossed-over prostitution or even romanticized rape.[66] Carolyn Gage goes so far as to read *The Piano* as "a gorgeously shot, utterly repellent film about a woman trapped between *two* rapists: a sleazy, black-mailing rapist [Baines] and a violent possessive rapist [Stewart]" (1994, 21). The collection of essays *Piano Lessons: Approaches to "The Piano"* (1999) reflects the film's being Campion's most controversial work. The various authors of this collection debate how to understand Ada's relationship with Baines, and how to understand Ada's automutism: some interpret it as symbolic of female oppression, while others interpret it as ironic self-empowerment through rejection of patriarchal language.[67] Overall, where

---

[65] We might also consider the scene in which Baines is shown looking lovingly at the piano after one of the lessons and then standing naked next to the instrument while he gently wipes it down with his shirt. (The moment is echoed by Ada caressing the piano after Baines has returned it to her, the instrument then becoming a stand-in for *his* body.) Shortly thereafter, Baines lies at Ada's feet while she plays for him and eventually touches a hole in her stocking. As his finger circles the hole in an obviously sexual gesture, Ada suddenly makes more use of the damper pedal, the effect of which is to make the notes run together, to create a sound of "melting." The close-ups of Ada's foot call attention to the change in sound effected by her use of the pedal, a change that signifies her softening towards Baines. All this aside, in her interview for the special edition DVD (2005), Campion also emphasizes that while the piano is a stand-in for Ada, Baines also realizes the importance of "the pianist, the person *making* the music."

[66] Lisa Sarmas, for instance, reads the bargaining between Baines and Ada as problematic in the extreme sense of "promulgating rape" (as quoted by Bainbridge 2008, 181). Sue Gillet provides a direct critique of this position in her article (1995).

[67] The film is also repeatedly referred to as Campion's most controversial in Rueschmann's summary of Campion's work and artistic standing. Though it is beyond the scope of this analysis, Rueschmann also notes the problematic representation of race in the film, especially in its privileging of white characters in contradistinction to several comical and "uncivilized" Maori figures of fun (2007, 295). For some further postcolonial analysis of *The Piano*, see Corinn Columpar (2010, 67–75): Columpar summarizes her findings by saying that "Campion's critique of imperialism is limited in ways that her critique of patriarchy is not" (75).

some scholars find the film feminist (even "too feminist"), others have "reviled it as misogynistic or, at the very least, anti-feminist."[68] Even though the film's style repeatedly emphasizes Ada's importance, the mixed reception of *The Piano* raises troubling questions about what it means when a mute heroine is almost unanimously celebrated for representing female empowerment. It is also surely significant that many of the film's first reviewers repeatedly emphasized Hunter's beauty *in* silence—*much* was made of the absence of Hunter's indelicate real-life southern drawl.[69]

Campion, however, insists that the decision to have Ada mute is a "strong feminist comment" because Ada's choice to not speak signifies her contemptuousness for the "lack of listening for women in general."[70] Campion also asserts that Ada's muteness signifies her refusal to be "in dialogue" with those who oppress her—including those who would condemn her for having an illegitimate daughter or who would (like Stewart) see her as a possession rather than an expressive being in her own right. Along these lines, Kirsten Moana Thompson writes of Ada's "withdrawal into music" as "an alternate mode of nonverbal expressivity," thus emphasizing that which Ada *does* "say" through it (1999, 66). Similarly, Mary M. Dalton and Kirsten James Fatzinger stress that Ada uses silence "as a tool of empowerment and self-assertion rather than a manifestation of oppression" (2003, 34). Although Dalton and Fatzinger point out that "breaking through silence has been a prevailing empowerment metaphor for women" (especially in late twentieth-century feminist analyses), and although "power exists in naming and claiming one's experience" (36), they argue that Ada's *choice* to be silent represents "an act of defiance and resistance" (34). Because Ada can have no voice in "dominant culture, particularly in the public sphere," they argue that she *must* "adopt silence to exhibit some control over [her] situation." In other words, Ada "elects not to speak rather than to speak and not be heard" (36). Dalton and Fatzinger do, of course, also acknowledge the power of Ada's communication through the piano, though they give little in-depth attention to her

---

[68] See Dalton and Fatzinger (2003, 35). The debate over whether to understand *The Piano* as feminist or anti-feminist is also usefully summarized by Erin McGlothlin who herself sees the film as hovering between extremes in such a way as to resist closure and therein ultimately resist conventionality (2004, 23, 30).

[69] In a representative example, an article written *ten years* after *The Piano* was released, MacKenzie comments on Hunter's southern drawl on the phone in the context of having noted the power of her silence in the film (2003).

[70] Campion makes this point in the DVD interview (2005), and she expands on Ada's muteness as follows: "it doesn't matter if she speaks or not, she doesn't want to be in dialogue with them [her oppressors]. As far as she's concerned she's not seen or heard anyway and also to have had a child illegitimately would really put her out of line with the culture. In my mind the choice to not speak [is] to do with a human who has a very unbending, inflexible view of right and wrong. This is her rebellion. . . . And all her communication and all her feeling goes into the piano and [in]to the piano playing and that's her big relationship."

music. Ironically, we shall find that Ada's music is even more powerful than speech would probably be for her, *even when we cannot hear it.*

IN THE ABSENCE OF ADA'S MUSIC

In order to further understand Ada's music in the full context of the film's whole sound track, it is worth our taking a close look at another, easily missed sequence, one that Campion herself talks *through* (rather than *about*) in her feature-length commentary.[71] It is one of the few sequences without Ada, and one that emphasizes the narrative action taking place within a specific historical, colonial context. Though aspects of Ada's music and characterization might tempt us to regard her story as one of heady sentimentality (as Scheurer does), the following sequence helps the film become much more than a transcendent or delocalized fantasy.

The sequence in question follows Stewart's witnessing Ada thumping out an imaginary accompaniment to Flora's singing on the kitchen table [27:09–27:40]. Her "playing" is a response to his refusal to bring her piano up from the beach (see Figure 3.18). Ada's imaginary playing for Flora displays a sensory and sensual memory of music that cannot be understood by Stewart. (Ironically, Stewart is the only character in the film who eventually presumes to "hear her," and this prompts him to allow her to leave with Baines.)[72] Her action also represents her ability to bring music into their shared space, even if only virtually so. And this remembered music is part of Ada that Stewart clearly cannot control. When he interrupts Ada's "playing," she leaps away from the table. Then, a close-up shows Stewart's fingertips touching the keys Ada has carved into the table, emphasizing his uncomprehending touch (see Figure 3.19).

The film soon cuts to the sequence for our close analysis [28:14–30:10], one that revolves around Stewart's anxiety over Ada. Here, he expresses particular disturbance about Ada's kitchen-table playing to his Aunt Morag. He begins by asking her what she

---

[71] Instead of discussing the scene itself, Campion talks *through* it with a description of Keitel's powerful methods of improvisation. Thompson's work is noteworthy in its atypical and reasonably thorough analysis of this scene, especially as she links it to Jane Austen's exposure of ideologically loaded realities through the use of calculated irony and wit (1999, 73–74).

[72] Stewart tells Baines that he "heard" Ada as follows: "I heard a voice, here in my mind. I watched the lips. They didn't make the words but the harder I listened, the clearer I heard her." Baines leaps in with saying that the affair was his fault and that Stewart punished her wrongly. Stewart, however, continues as if Baines had said nothing: "She said, I am afraid of my will, of what it might do, it is so strange and strong. She said, I have to go, let me go, with Baines, take me away. Let him try and save me. I wish her gone. I wish you gone. I want to wake up and find that this is all a dream. That's what I want." By the end of the film, then, Stewart claims power by putting words in Ada's mouth.

FIGURE 3.18 Without her beloved piano, Ada "plays" the kitchen table instead.

FIGURE 3.19 Bewildered by Ada's imaginary playing, Stewart touches the keys she carved.

would think "if someone were to play a kitchen table like it were a *piano*".[73] the notion of animating the inanimate is not only uncanny, it also signifies Ada's power to transform an object that is central to traditional domestic life.[74] "Strange isn't it. I mean, it's not a piano," Stewart says, apparently stating the obvious, "it doesn't make any sound." Ironically, Ada *does* make the table make a sound, and her thumping on the keys she carved is also full of musical *implication*.

Morag twice interrupts Stewart's story to bark "tea!," and then "biscuits!," at Nessie: she relishes the oddness of what Ada has done and her consumption of the tea and biscuits is a suitable accompaniment to her willing absorption of the story. The timbre of her voice, like Stewart's, is as hard and brittle as the biscuits she orders. Morag enjoys the story of Ada's playing on the table as a piece of salacious gossip. The camera slowly tracks past her face to emphasize her overblown reaction in a risible way. At the same time, perhaps Morag's reaction is not so overblown: for Ada's music not only signifies more than someone like Morag could ever willingly understand, it also signifies a profound challenge to her own limited expressivity.

Stewart's storytelling is diegetically underscored by the two Maori mission girls who, as indicated earlier, attend upon Aunt Morag. These girls (Mere (Mahina Tunui) and Heni (Carla Rupuha)) sit sewing and quietly singing "God Save the Queen." Their quiet and flat delivery of the tune emphasizes its staid, turgid, and hymn-like cadences. (By ironic contrast, recall that Nyman liberated Scottish tunes from their hymn-like settings for Ada). Here, we thus have an obvious musical emphasis on hegemonic order. It is also important that the Maori girls are literally cut off, significantly shooshed by Morag on the word "victorious" (in the lyric "send her victorious"). In their disempowerment and being silenced, these girls are stand-ins for the absent Ada. Or, they at least occupy a similar position to that of the mail-order wife in the colonialist society of the film. But the absent sound of Ada's music, compositions that have already crept inside us as well as the other characters, is "louder" than what these girls sing.

After repeating Stewart's point about a table making "no sound at all," Morag notes that Ada "was very violent with [her] wedding gown. She tore off a chunk of lace." Morag then says, "If I hadn't been there to see it, I'd have sworn she'd have used her teeth and

---

[73] The italics here indicate the original point of emphasis in Neill's delivery of the line.

[74] For a thorough analysis of Ada's uncannily shifting identity, see Maureen Molloy who writes of the piano as "almost an automaton, completing Ada by serving as one of her voices while at the same time being an inanimate object that functions as a character in its own right" (1999, 162). Drawing on Freud's definition of the uncanny power built into shifting definitions of words, Molloy writes that "the lack of clear boundaries between what is human and what is mechanical is encapsulated by Ada's relationship to her piano" (163).

wiped her feet on it." Here, Nessie chimes in with the phrase "wiped her feet on it," thus signaling this has been a repeated statement of judgment. In his book about *Eyes Wide Shut* (1999), Chion emphasizes the significance of echoing in dialogue which, in Stanley Kubrick's film, is connected with the self-imposed entrapment of the central character (2002, 72–78). In *The Piano*, the repeated echoing among Stewart, Morag, and Nessie signifies an unwittingly conspiratorial intransigence within the hegemony of colonization, and it emphasizes the limited language of a conservative Empire in the context of the New (unruly) Zealand. Such unselfconscious echoing is in itself a way of defining hegemony. After all, buying into the dominant ideology often requires only that.[75]

After this example of such loaded echoing, there is a revealing cut to a long shot showing Stewart, Morag, and Nessie having tea (a practice of quintessential British leisure), with the Maori girls literally at their feet at the bottom of the frame. We also now see Baines listening behind a panel in a dimly lit third of the frame (see Figure 3.20). This long shot allows us a crucial critical distance, as does the revelation of Baines's listening. We see Baines turned toward the main scene, but he also turns away from it, absorbing its meaning from the critical distance that we are likewise encouraged to adopt (see Figure 3.21).

Listening is an important action in *The Piano*—choosing when to hear, what to hear, and how to hear it is repeatedly shown to have decisive importance in relation to power structures, judgments, and changing relationships. Stewart is troubled because he has heard something he did not want to—and it was not even the full articulation of Ada's music, it was the *implication* of it on the kitchen table.

The scene soon cuts to a close-up of Morag's frenetically fluttering fan, the amplified sound of which signifies her self-indulgent agitation. Then the scene cuts to show Stewart's hand stirring his tea, along with the chink of his teaspoon against Morag's pretty china. Morag assures him, with risible seriousness, "there's nothing so easy to like as a pet and they're quite silent." This is followed by a new scene featuring the sound of Stewart's axe, Flora singing "The Grand Old Duke of York," and Baines making a verbal offer for the piano to Stewart [30:10–30:47].[76] In this short sequence, *The Piano* thus reinforces and contextualizes all the key conflicts within its drama through aural

---

[75] Nessie also echoes Morag with other lines that emphasize the reality of a patriarchal, colonial status quo. For instance, when Morag complains that the Maoris have become too powerful in Baines's life and that "they sit on his floor like Kings" without a "shred of manners," the latter phrase is echoed by Nessie in a way that reinforces the sense of "rehearsed" and unthinking compliance with the dominant ideology.

[76] Flora is also singing "The Grand Old Duke of York" when she runs to Stewart with the piano key that Ada carved for Baines. The music of the Old Empire is thus connected with Flora's betrayal of Ada and thus, by implication, Stewart's violent assault on Ada. Therefore, the song in this scene, as well as the sound of Stewart's axe, grimly anticipates the climactic violence of the film.

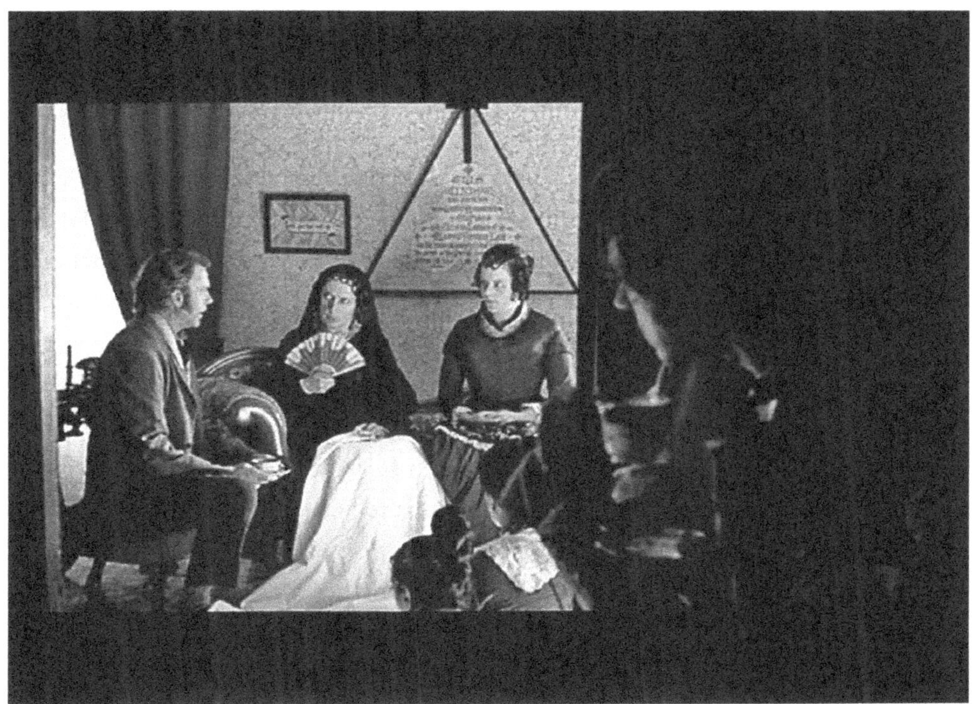

FIGURE 3.20 In the dim foreground, Baines silently listens to Stewart, Morag, and Nessie's judgmental talk of Ada.

FIGURE 3.21 Baines turns his head away from the conversation, a silently critical reaction.

cues and references. We hear the sounds of hegemony and Empire (British voices, a fan, a teaspoon, the English national anthem, verbal echoing, and Flora singing a traditional English nursery rhyme), *and* the suppressed or absent sounds of those who are disempowered (the Maori girls being shooshed, the absence of Ada's music as it is discussed, and Stewart's vocally recalling his memory of Ada's music on the kitchen table). We also hear the sounds of two men who embody completely opposing possibilities for Ada. Ada's possible end is anticipated (in the sound of Stewart's axe, the weapon of the colonist), but so too is her potential new beginning (in Baines's confident offer for the piano). Thus we may perceive how, with the arresting economy of cumulatively powerful aural details, *The Piano* defines a specific colonial, hegemonic structure and the importance of Ada's survival in that context. Ironically, then, the close analysis of a sequence *without* Ada's music emphasizes a context to help us more fully appreciate its significance in the rest of the film. This analysis also helps us appreciate the complexity of how different elements of the sound track work together.

THE FINAL SEQUENCE

The Piano ends with a sequence no less complex in terms of its sound track's cumulative connotations. The scene of Ada being rescued from drowning with her piano (after Stewart has allowed her to leave with Baines) cuts to this final sequence, starting with the image of her hand with a metal-tipped finger, and her beginning one final performance (for us, at least) on a new piano (see Figure 3.22).

The piece, titled "Silver-fingered Fling," is an old Scottish tune [1:54:20–1:55:48]. It is Nyman's resetting of "Flowers of the Forrest," the ancient Scottish tune that Flora sang while Ada accompanied her on the table, and which Flora played after Ada refused to perform for Stewart. Ada herself also played the tune in one of Baines's lessons, but at a hurried (*Allegro*) pace whereas the pacing is now sedate (*Andante*).[77] Ada's new playing of the tune suggests that she is more fully in control of her own music and, by implication, she is more at peace with her self as well as her circumstances. In keeping with this emphasis on her self-possession, Nyman's undulating harmonies for this version of the piece evoke the sea from which Ada chooses to rise in the preceding scene. However, even as Ada here plays with controlled and calm fluidity, the impression is aurally broken up by the sound of her new metal finger tip tapping against every few keys. The scene is a subtly startling example of using what Chion defines as "materializing sound indices (M.S.I.)" (1994, 114–17). In recorded music, as Chion explains, the objective is

---

[77] The points at which this tune is featured are also noted by Gorbman (2000, 50).

FIGURE 3.22 Ada's last on-screen performance in *The Piano*. Though Ada refers to the metal "fingertip" George made her, the attentive viewer will notice that two full joints of her finger are now metal, further complicating any sense we might have of her having fully healed by the end of the film.

often to remove M.S.I.s, the noises that are created by the effort to make an instrument or voice work. The M.S.I.s for a musical instrument typically include "the attack of a note, unevenness, friction, breaths, and fingernails on piano keys" (115). In Ada's final performance within *The Piano*, each note is precisely played without attack, friction, breaths, or the sound of a fingernail: the *only* marked M.S.I. is that of the metal finger tip against the piano. Thus the film emphasizes the permanent damage to Ada and her music. Perhaps this detail therefore signifies a lasting challenge to the Romantic ideal of sublime music and emotion that might transcend all circumstance:[78] we are made to understand that Ada's unconventionality has come at a lasting price, even if Campion has rewarded her heroine with a new life. In relation to this last point, Bainbridge goes so far as to argue that the metal tip "announces the very fact of [Ada's] castrated status every time she plays the piano" (2008, 162).

---

[78] This is an adaptation of Thompson's description of Romanticism "where the power of emotions and the imagination are privileged with a sense of the sublime" (1999, 65).

In the film's second voiceover which overlaps with her final on-screen performance, Ada tells us that she is now teaching others how to play as she does. With playful flippancy, she says "I teach piano now in Nelson. George has fashioned me a metal fingertip. I'm quite the town freak, which satisfies." Her pointedly casual intonation communicates her drôle enjoyment of being seen as freakish. Further, the fact of her teaching the piano suggests that, despite her marginal position, she has taken on a role of lasting influence over a new generation. Therein lies at least the possibility of some form of power that is greater than the limitations of a metal fingertip. Moreover, the quiet sound effect of birds embellishes Ada's playing, subtly suggesting freedom, or at least suggesting that the noises of her new landscape no longer oppress her.

After showing her at the piano, the final scene cuts to Ada practicing sounds with a black veil over her head because "my sound is still so bad I am ashamed." That Ada has made the choice to speak again is yet another element of the film that may be read in contrary ways: we may view the end as her aural rebirth while also recognizing that her speech means the loss of the self we have come to know, the one that rejected the language of patriarchy. Whichever we choose, Ada's speaking does help distinguish her marriage with Baines from the kind of trap that a "Victorian" marriage might be. In a sequence that was cut from the film, a blind piano tuner speaks about his wife to Baines:

> My wife sang with a bell-clear tone. After we married she stopped. She said she didn't feel like singing, that life made her sad. And that's how she lived, lips clamped closed over a perfect voice, a beautiful voice.[79]

Dalton and Fatzinger argue that, in contradistinction to the tuner's wife, "Ada chooses to speak when she finds a partner who wants her to do so on her own terms" (2003, 37). The veil that Ada wears immediately connotes mourning, but the film also shows George kissing her face through the cloth, before removing it to kiss her face directly. The glimpse of Ada's new present thus ends with more emphasis on her joyful and beloved life. Perhaps we can assume that Ada's choice to learn speech again demonstrates that she rejoices in a new life without losing her power (see Figure 3.23).

In *The Voice in Cinema*, Chion provides several other useful possibilities for analyzing the aural implications of Ada relearning speech.[80] First and most obviously, Chion

---

[79] See Campion's screenplay (1992, 49). Thompson also mentions this original scene as emphasizing that "the snare of Victorian marriage for women bears the death of creativity" (1999, 70).

[80] The original publication of Chion's *The Voice in Cinema* in 1982 obviously predates *The Piano*. However, Chion mentions the film as a key example of using the power of an absent voice (and music standing in its place) in his epilogue for the more recent translation into English by Claudia Gorbman (1999, 168–69).

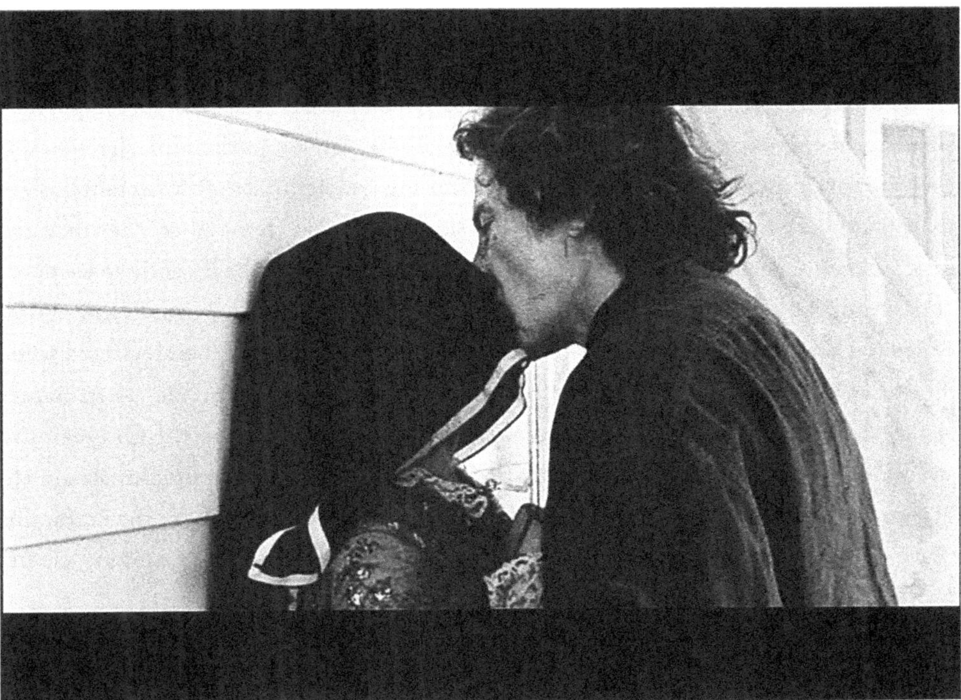

FIGURE 3.23 In the film's final sequence, while Ada practices speaking, Baines kisses her through a black veil.

writes about the authority of mute characters, such as the young deaf-mute adolescent boy in *Out of the Past* (1947). As Chion points out, mute characters are usually peripheral or instrumental to the plot rather than central agents of action. Nevertheless, the mute character is often defined in terms of strange and powerful insight: the mute's eyes "are thought to penetrate deeper," and they are "presumed to harbor the *final word, the key to the quest*" (1999, 97). In other words, says Chion, "the mute is considered the guardian of the secret" (96). If we consider that one of Ada's main piano pieces is called "Big My Secret," his statement takes on special resonance.[81]

Second, for Chion, the wordless authority of the mute is akin to the acousmêtre. The acousmêtre, as we have already explored, is a (usually male) voice that is not positioned inside the film because the source (the body or the mouth) is not seen as we hear it. The acousmêtre is not reduced to the film world for it does not come from a straightforward off-screen place "in an imaginary 'wing'" (1994, 129). *Both* the mute and the acousmêtre possess unearthly possibilities: as Chion explains, "the character

---

[81] In addition, Campion has herself spoken of the power of men being partially answered by the power of women in holding onto their secrets (2005).

who has a body but no voice, or a voice but no body, is taken as more or less all-seeing, all-knowing, often even all-powerful" (1999, 100).

Though Ada is by no means a straightforward instance of the acousmêtre, especially since her voice is narratively connected to her body early on in the film, she is nevertheless mostly imaged without her mouth speaking and her first voiceover emphasizes its beyond-body meaning or more-than-physical emanation (remember "the voice you hear is not my speaking voice"). Ada's inarticulate gasps within the diegetic space never constitute words in *The Piano*. She is never tied down in that sonic sense. The significance of this freedom, which is *similar* to that of the acousmêtre, is emphasized when Stewart demands to know whether Baines ever heard Ada speak: and when Baines shakes his head, Stewart is relieved. Were Ada to speak with Baines, the film seems to say, Baines would have a different claim on her that would be even more threatening to Stewart. So long as she does not speak the same language as either man, she maintains the kind of mysterious stature that Chion writes about and which Campion clearly wanted to emphasize.

Even after Stewart has axed her finger, Ada maintains the power of silence, without uttering so much as a scream. Chion writes that "The screaming point, in a male-directed film, immediately poses the question of *mastery*, of the mastery of the scream" (1999, 78). He then refers to startling instances of men controlling women's voices, notably Kane's attempting to mould and own Susan's voice in *Citizen Kane* (1941), even to the extent that he boasts to reporters "*we* are going to be a great singer" (91, emphasis added). We might also consider the woman's scream in countless horror movies right before the moment her body is claimed by a male predator. Ada's denying Stewart a scream further reinforces the extremity with which she controls her physical (and, by implication, metaphysical) self.

So, by the end of *The Piano* when Ada is learning to speak again, and with a man's help, we have much more than a simply happy turnaround. As Chion writes, with reference to the mute *and* the acousmêtre respectively, "the unveiling of either his voice or his body and his face has the effect of breaking the spell, re-assigning the characters to an ordinary fate, taking away his mythic aura and putative powers" (1999, 100). More specifically, Chion writes that "de-acousmatization" (the stitching back together of voice and body) represents "a sort of enclosing of the voice in the circumscribed limits of a body—which tames the voice and drains it of its power" (1994, 131). We might therefore wonder whether *The Piano* finally plucks out Ada's mystery. We may even read the ending of *The Piano* in terms of what Chion calls the "*ideology* of nailing down" a character, because it restores the unification of Ada's body and voice (1999, 130, original emphasis).

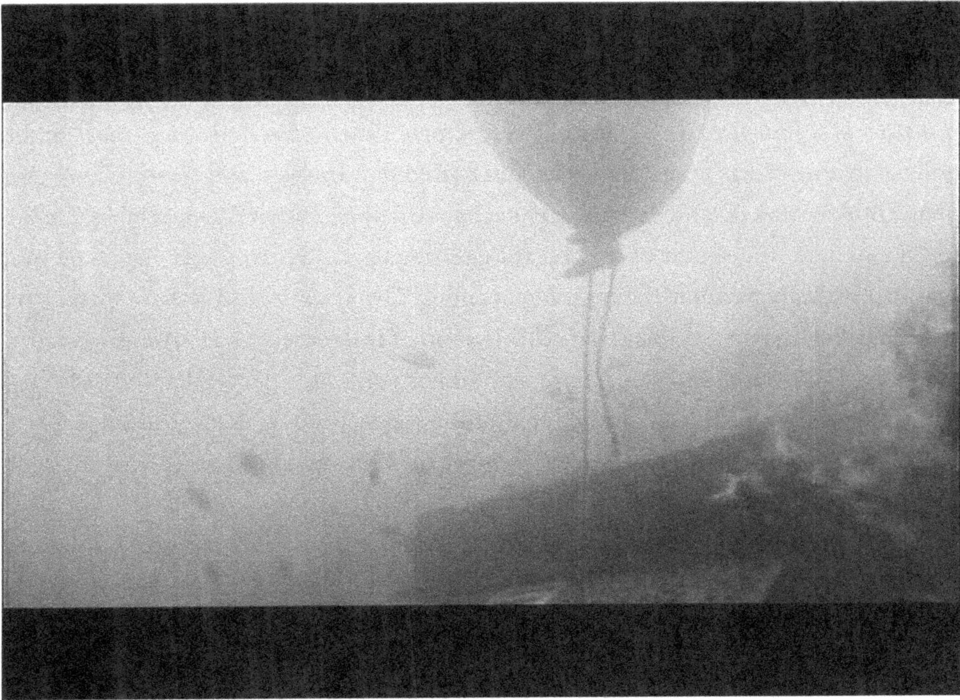

FIGURE 3.24 The final image of Ada floating above, but also tied to, her piano.

Ironically, the final image of Ada neither shows her learning to speak with Baines *nor* playing the piano, but floating underwater, tied to the piano that had (earlier in the film) sunk to its "ocean grave"[82] (see Figure 3.24). Ada's voiceover reveals that this image is from her dreams, but its lasting impact as our final glimpse of her before the credits makes its reality difficult to deny. The image reminds us of Ada's impulse toward suicide even after she is freed by Stewart to make a new life with Baines and Flora. The restoration of Ada's speech in the film's ending is thus juxtaposed with a resonant and haunting image of submerged death.

The complexity of the film, and its sound track in particular, does not even end with its final image. Lest we presume that either of the final possibilities—whether Ada's vocal restoration or her final suppression in death—is the film's statement on her, we should consider the power of Nyman's music for the closing credits. Though Ada's final line is about the silence under the deep sea, her final voiceover also includes mention of the "weird lullaby" that she associates with the submerged piano and which enables her to sleep. When Nyman's music slowly builds over the final credits, it is not much

---

[82] This is Ada's own phrase in the final voiceover.

of a stretch to imagine that we are hearing the lullaby of Ada's dreaming [1:56:40–2:00:49]. The music begins with a version of the final solo piece that Ada plays within the film ("The Silver-fingered Fling"), here further adapted by Nyman and renamed "Dreams of a Journey." The comparatively simple tune suddenly sounds more ambitious: now the strings take it up with a full harmonic variation, and then a piano joins them with another playful variation that echoes the version that Ada played in one lesson for Baines. The sound of the metal fingertip is gone. Next, the strings take over again with a fully harmonized rearrangement of "The Heart Asks Pleasure First" (this version being known as "The Promise"). That other instruments take over Ada's music might troublingly suggest the suppression of her voice *or*, equally, that her voice has been fully answered. These contrary possibilities aside, the overall impression is that of music slowly rising from the deep, taking over the film's end with great buoyancy and without pain.

If we think even beyond the final credits, Nyman's score for the film has had an extraordinary afterlife. Not only has Nyman himself developed the music into a concert suite and a piano concerto, but the original soundtrack CD has sold more than three million copies worldwide. However we read the ending of *The Piano*, then, Ada's "voice" has enough enduring power to extend far beyond the film itself.

SUMMARY

In 1975 Laura Mulvey published an article about tearing down the patriarchal power of mainstream cinema. Mulvey drew particular attention to the patterns of Classical Hollywood, naming *To Have and Have Not* as but one example. Though *To Have and Have Not* clearly follows many of those visual patterns that Mulvey identifies as working in accordance with the controlling male gaze, a close feminist analysis of the sound track reveals it to be a more complex film than it might first appear to be. Indeed, there are many ways in which Bacall's presence as the female lead represents a significant challenge to patriarchal control. She knowingly "freezes the flow of action" through performing several songs, and takes delight in her own aural power. Her deep, strong voice also reinforces her unconventional agency, even if Hawks attempted to control it.

About twenty years after Mulvey's work was published, Jane Campion released *The Piano*, a contemporary, revisionist period film about the importance of an unconventional female protagonist named Ada. *The Piano* ostensibly represents the epitome of female empowerment, most particularly through the music associated with Ada. Ironically, a close feminist analysis of this film's sound track reveals some irresolvable mixed messages when it comes to the power and endurance of a female "voice" in a patriarchal context. Ada's automutism, in particular, may be read as an act of ultimate powerlessness *or* as a choice of empowering resistance.

Such ironies aside, it is indisputable that both Slim and Ada empower themselves through their musical performances. Both *To Have and Have Not* and *The Piano* present us with much more than the spectacle of a to-be-looked-at female lead. And even if the main male characters of both films exert control over the female protagonists' lives, their musical agency repeatedly suggests that which is beyond submission.

WORKS CITED

Bacall, Loren. 2005. *By Myself and Then Some*. New York: HarperCollins Publishers Inc.

Bainbridge, Caroline. 2008. *A Feminine Cinematics: Luce Irigary, Women and Film*. New York: Palgrave Macmillan.

Brozan, Nadine. 1993. "Chronicle." *The New York Times*, August 6, late ed., byline (style desk), 6.

Bruzzi, Stella. 1995. "Tempestuous Petticoats: Costume and Desire in *The Piano*." *Screen* 36 (3): 257–66.

Buhler, James, David Neumeyer, and Rob Deemer. 2010. *Hearing the Movies: Music and Sound in Film History*. New York: Oxford University Press.

Burdick, Dolores. 1981. "Danger of Death: The Hawksian Woman as Agent of Destruction." *Post-Script* 1 (1): 36–40.

Campion, Jane. 1992. *The Piano* (screenplay). London: Bloomsbury Publishing Ltd.

———, dir. 2005. "Interview." *The Piano*. DVD. England: Optimum Classic (2-Disc Special Edition). Includes "Director's Commentary."

Carmichael, H., and S. Longstreet. 1965. *Sometimes I Wonder: The Story of Hoagy Carmichael*. New York: Farar, Staus and Giroux.

Chion, Michel. 1994. *Audio-Vision: Sound on Screen*. Edited and translated by Claudia Gorbman. New York: Columbia University Press. Originally published as *L'Audio-Vision* (Paris: Editions Nathan, 1990).

———. 1999. *The Voice in Cinema*. Edited and translated by Claudia Gorbman. New York: Columbia University Press. Originally published as *La Voix au cinema* (Paris: *Cahiers du cinéma* (Editions de l'Etoile), 1982).

———. 2002. *Eyes Wide Shut*. London: BFI Publishing.

———. 2007. "Mute Music." In *Beyond the Soundtrack: Representing Music in Cinema*, edited by Daniel Goldmark, Lawrence Kramer, and Richard Leppert, 86–96. Berkeley: University of California Press, 2007.

Chumo, Peter N. 1997. "Keys to the Imagination: Jane Campion's *The Piano*." *Literature/Film Quarterly* 25 (3): 173–76.

Columpar, Corinn. 2010. *Unsettling Sights: The Fourth World on Film*. Carbondale: Southern Illinois University Press.

Columpar, Corinn, and Sophie Mayer. 2009. "Introduction." In *There She Goes: Feminist Filmmaking and Beyond*, edited by Corinn Columpar and Sophie Mayer, 1–18. Detroit: Wayne State University Press.

Coombs, Felicity, and Suzanne Gemmell, eds. 1999. *Piano Lessons: Approaches to "The Piano."* Sydney, Australia: John Libby & Co.

Dalton, Mary M., and Kirsten James Fatzinger. 2003. "Choosing Silence: Defiance and Resistance without Voice in Jane Campion's *The Piano*." *Women and Language* 26 (2): 34–39.

Erens, Patricia. 1990. *Issues in Feminist Film Criticism*. Bloomington: Indiana University Press.

Feuer, Jane. (1977) 2012. "The Self-Reflexive Musical and the Myth of Entertainment." In *Film Genre Reader IV*, edited by Barry Keith Grant, 543–57. Austin: University of Texas Press. Originally published in *Quarterly Review of Film Studies* 2 (3): 313–26.

Firmat, Gustavo Pérez. 2008. "Latunes: An Introduction." *Latin American Research Review* 43 (2): 180–203.

Fuller, Sophie. 1996. "New Perspectives: Feminism and Music." In *Analyzing Performance: A Critical Reader*, edited by Patrick Campbell, 70–81. Manchester: Manchester University Press.

Gage, Carolyn. 1994. "*The Piano*: Dangerous Music." *Off Our Backs* 24 (2): 21.

Gillet, Sue. 1995. "Jane Campion's *The Piano*." *Screen* 36 (3): 277–87.

Gorbman, Claudia. 1987. *Unheard Melodies: Narrative Film Music*. London: BFI.

———. 2000. "Music in *The Piano*." In *Jane Campion's "The Piano,"* edited by Harriet Margolis, 42–58. Cambridge: Cambridge University Press.

Hayward, Susan. 2006. *Cinema Studies: The Key Concepts*. 3rd ed. London: Routledge.

Hewitt, Roger. 1983. "Black through White: Hoagy Carmichael and the Cultural Reproduction of Racism." *Popular Music* 3:33–50.

Kael, Pauline. 1963. "Circles and Squares." *Film Quarterly* 16 (3): 12–26.

Kalinak, Kathryn. 1982. "The Fallen Woman and the Virtuous Wife: Musical Stereotypes in *The Informer, Gone with the Wind*, and *Laura*." *Film Reader* 5: 76–82.

———. 1992. *Settling the Score: Music and the Classical Hollywood Film*. Madison: The University of Wisconsin Press.

Kaplan, James. 1994. "'What Becomes a Legend Most': Interview with Lauren Bacall." *New York* 27 (40): 58.

Kassabian, Anahid. 2001. *Hearing Film: Tracking Identifications in Contemporary Hollywood Film Music*. New York: Routledge.

MacKenzie, Suzie. 2003. "What People Don't Know About Holly." *The Guardian*, November 22. Accessed February 14, 2011. <http://www.guardian.co.uk/film/2003/nov/22/features.weekend>.

Man, Glenn. 1993. "Gender, Genre, and Myth in *Thelma and Louise*." *Film Criticism* 18 (1): 36–53.

McCarthy, Todd. 1997. *Howard Hawks: The Grey Fox of Hollywood*. New York: Grove Press.

McGlothlin, Erin. 2004. "Speaking the Mind's Voice: Double Discurvity in Jane Campion's *The Piano*." *Post-Script* 23 (2): 19–32.

Miller, Toby. 2000. "The Nature of the Gaze." In *Film Theory: An Anthology*, edited by Robert Stam and Toby Miller, 475–82. Malden: Blackwell.

Molloy, Maureen. 1999. "Death and the Maiden: The Feminine and the Nation in Recent New Zealand Films." *Signs* 25 (1): 153–70.

Morreau, Annette. 1995. "Introduction" (Chester Music Brochure). The Official Michael Nyman Website, March. Accessed March 9, 2000. <http://www.michaelnyman.org.bioam.htm>.

Mulvey, Laura. (1975) 2004. "Visual Pleasure and Narrative Cinema." In *Film Theory and Criticism*, edited by Leo Braudy and Marshall Cohen, 837–48. 6th ed. New York: Oxford University Press. Originally published in *Screen* 16 (3): 6–18.

———. 1989. "After thoughts on 'Visual Pleasure and Narrative Cinema' Inspired by King Vidor's *Duel in the Sun* (1946)." In *Visual and Other Pleasures*, 14–26. Bloomington: Indiana University Press.

Nyman, Michael. 1974. *Experimental Music: Cage and Beyond*. London: Studio Vista.

———. 2005. *The Piano*. DVD. Directed by Jane Campion. England: Optimum Classic (2-Disc Special Edition).

Parker, Tyler. 1947. *Magic and Myth of the Movies*. New York: Holt.

Radner, Hilary. 2009. "'In extremis': Jane Campion and the Woman's Film." In *Cinema, Nation, Identity: Jane Campion*, edited by Hilary Radner, Alistair Fox, and Irène Bessière, 3–26. Detroit: Wayne State University Press.

Rogers, Bradley. 2008. "The Interpellations of Interpolation; or, The Disintegrating Female Musical Body." *Camera Obscura* 67:89–111.

Rueschmann, Eva. 2007. "Dislocations of Home and Gender in the Films of Jane Campion." In *New Zealand Filmmakers*, edited by Ian Conrich and Stuart Murray, 289–303. Detroit: Wayne State University Press.

Russell, Mark, and James Young. 2000. *Film Music*. Boston: Focal Press.

Scheurer, Timothy. 2008. *Music and Mythmaking in Film: Genre and the Role of the Composer*. Jefferson, NC: McFarland & Company, Inc.

Shakespeare, William. 1988. *Hamlet*. In *The Complete Works*, edited by Stanley Wells, Gary Taylor, John Jowett, and William Montgomery, 653–90. Oxford: Clarendon Press.

Silverman, Kaja. 1988. *The Acoustic Mirror: The Female Voice in Psychoanalysis and Cinema*. Bloomington: Indiana University Press.

Sjogren, Britta. 2006. *Into the Vortex: Female Voice and Paradox in Film*. Urbana: University of Illinois Press.

Smith, Jacob. 2008. *Vocal Tracks: Performance and Sound Media*. Berkeley: University of California Press.

Stilwell, Robynn J. 2005. "Sound and Empathy: Subjectivity, Gender and the Cinematic Soundscape." In *Screen Methods: Comparative Readings in Film Studies*, edited by Jacqueline Furby and Karen Randell, 48–58. London: Wallflower Press.

Sudhalter, Richard M. 2002. *Stardust Melody: The Life and Music of Hoagy Carmichael*. Oxford: Oxford University Press.

Thompson, Kirsten Moana. 1999. "The Sickness unto Death: Dislocated Gothic in a Minor Key." In *Piano Lessons: Approaches to "The Piano,"* edited by Felicity Coombs and Suzanne Gemmell, 64–81. Sydney, Australia: John Libby & Co.

Thomson, David. 1997. *To Have and Have Not*. London: British Film Institute.

Wagner, Laura. 2007. "The Non-Dubbing of Lauren Bacall." Midnight Palace Forums: A Community of Classic Film Lovers. January 2. Accessed January 31, 2011. <http://www.midnightpalace.com/phpbb/nfphpbb/viewtopic.php?t=403&sid=46b76a46d69fc863205be339d100959a>.

Walker, Elsie. 2000. "The Aesthetic Construction of Musical Forms in *Prospero's Books*." In *Peter Greenaway's Prospero's Books*, edited by Christel Stalpaert, 161–79. Belgium: University of Ghent.

Willis, Sharon. 1993. "Hardware and Hard Bodies, What Do Women Want?: A Reading of *Thelma and Louise*." In *Film Theory Goes to the Movies*, edited by Jim Collins, Hilary Radner, and Ava Preacher Collins, 120–28. New York: Routledge.

———. 1997. *High Contrast: Race and Gender in Contemporary Hollywood Films*. Raleigh, NC: Duke University Press.

Wingstedt, Johnny, Sture Brändström, and Jan Berg. 2010. "Narrative Music, Visuals and Meaning in Film." *Visual Communication* 9:193–210.

Psychoanalysis

 # INTRODUCTION

"Looking for the Gaze: Lacanian Film Theory and Its Vicissitudes" by Todd McGowan

Psychoanalysis is broadly concerned with the formation of the self, including the shifting states in which the self is individually and socially defined. It is an important influence on Laura Mulvey's work. However, as we have just explored, understanding "Visual Pleasure and Narrative Cinema" is not necessarily contingent upon a full prior understanding of psychoanalysis. Now we zoom in on several principal psychoanalytic concepts as they have been defined by Jacques Lacan, a psychoanalyst and psychiatrist whose work has far-reaching influence within film studies. We will focus primarily on Lacan's concepts of the Mirror Stage in relation to the Imaginary, Symbolic, and Real orders of subjectivity. We will pay special attention to the Real since it is the most elusive concept. Our focus will then turn to an important example of applying Lacanian principles to film: Todd McGowan's essay titled "Looking for the Gaze: Lacanian Film Theory and Its Vicissitudes" (2003). Lacan's work is widely understood as being visual in emphasis, and this is reflected in most film criticism applying his concepts, including McGowan's work.[1] Much like many film critics have adapted the concepts Lacan developed in the context of psychiatric analysis, we shall use McGowan's reapplication of visually biased Lacanian film analysis to generate new questions for analyzing sound tracks. Then we will apply these questions to *Bigger Than Life* (1956) and *Shutter Island* (2010).

---

[1] For another challenge to the visual bias in most applications of Lacan, see Mladem Dolar's article "The Object Voice" (1996).

The basis of this part of the book is rather different from the others in that our primary Lacanian concepts must be defined from *several* sources. Lacan conceptualized and reworked them in relation to each other at different stages of his professional life, over a period of fifty years, as is faithfully reflected in Dylan Evans's *An Introductory Dictionary of Lacanian Psychoanalysis* (1996).[2] What follows is a series of definitions that are composite summaries drawn from original Lacanian and secondary works. No definition is all-inclusive: we select only the most salient points for each concept, with the goal of using each one for aural analysis. The primary point here is *not* to make an original statement about Lacanian theory or Lacanian concepts in themselves but to establish a strong springboard for our own use of McGowan's article in shaping an original approach to sound tracks. In short, our emphasis is on the original *application* of well-established ideas that have not yet been mined enough for aural film analysis. This redirection of already-established work drives all the parts of this book.

Since Lacan's writing is much-influenced by Sigmund Freud, we should begin with a few fundamental Freudian concepts. First, Freud conceived of three parts to our psyche: the id (the source of uncontrolled yet often repressed urges), the ego (the consciousness which attempts to control the id), and the super-ego (the critical conscience which attempts "to act as a higher-order authority over the id and the ego") (Hayward 2006, 313). His understanding of divided subjectivity is of decisive importance in the work of Lacan. Second, we should consider Freud's concept of the Oedipal complex as it relates to formative development. The Oedipal complex comes after the first mother/child relationship. In order for the child to grow in terms of social order he/she "must be removed from or severed from [his/her] imaginary unity with the mother" (314). Moreover, the father forbids the child's sexual access to the mother. The child perceives that his/her father possesses the phallus and therein has the power to castrate.[3] So, the child "renounces his mother momentarily until it is time for him to find his own female and accede in his turn to "paternal" status which is the reward for renouncing the mother" (314).[4]

In the first Oedipal stage of development as Freud defined it, the child also acquires language. At this stage, the child turns his/her attention to things other than the mother to compensate for the fear of losing her. Freud named this strategy the "*fort-da* game" in relation to seeing his grandson (Ernst) create a game in the absence of his mother. Ernst threw

---

[2] Evans's dictionary is invaluable for those who are not psychoanalysts but who want access to his work. Evans, in turn, cites several useful introductions to Lacan (1996, xiii).

[3] For definitions and discussions of the terms "phallus" and "castration" (from both Freudisn and Lacanian perspectives), see Evans (1996, 140–44, 20–23).

[4] Lacan focuses primarily on the male child, as is reflected in this gender-specific language.

away his toys while uttering "o-o-o-o," a sound which Freud and Ernst's mother interpreted as meaning the German word for "gone" (*fort*). When Ernst played with a spool tied to a string, the game evolved to become "*fort-da*" or "gone" and "there" because he "repeatedly threw away the spool and retrieved it" (Creet 1995, 191). As Freud himself explains, "This, then, was the complete game—disappearance and return. . . He compensated himself for [his mother's disappearance] by himself staging the disappearance and return of objects within his reach" ([1920] 2001, 14).[5] The use of spool and string is a tangible representation of the Lacanian belief that "the child is *born into* the experience of lack and spends the rest of his/(her) life trying to recapture the imagined entity which is the moment he [or she] associates with pre-lack—the imagined unity with the mother" (Hayward 2006, 316, my emphasis). For Lacan, the acquisition of language (including the most basic utterances, such as Ernst's exclamations in the *fort-da* game) is also inextricably linked with the child's awareness of such loss. Now we turn to Lacan's concepts in more detail.

THE MIRROR STAGE

Our first crucial Lacanian concept is the Mirror Stage which, as Evans points out, also translates into English as "the looking-glass phase" (1996, 114). In his essay "The Mirror Stage as Formative of the *I* Function," Lacan describes the young child who, from six months on, is able to lean forward in order to contemplate their image in the mirror. In this action, the child "playfully experiences the relationship between the movements made in the image and the reflected environment, and between this virtual complex and the reality it duplicates—namely, the child's own body, and the persons and even things around him" (2002, 3). Drawing on the research of the French psychologist Henri Wallon, Lacan used the concept of the Mirror Stage to distinguish the human from the animal: whereas the young chimpanzee will quickly realize that the image is illusory and lose interest, the human infant will be fascinated with it (Evans 1996, 115; Lacan 2002, 20). In the Mirror Stage, the child enjoys the gaze that allows him/her "to anticipate and assume an illusory control while lacking this control over her/his real body; the gaze in the Mirror Stage is [thus] a mastering gaze" (McGowan 2003, 45).[6] In other words, the child can perceive an "ideal ego," the "promise of future wholeness" that answers their actual experience of motor incapacity (Evans 1996, 116).

---

[5] Creet (1995) makes the helpful bracketed adjustment to Freud's statement.
[6] McGowan here refers to how the Lacanian concept of the gaze is routinely understood in film analyses. He then explores how Lacan himself redefined the gaze (as discussed more fully below). Unless otherwise specified, all quotations from McGowan come from "Looking for the Gaze" (2003).

Because the child has not "not yet mastered walking, or even standing," it relies on the help of another, or "some prop" (whether human or artificial) in order to "take in an instantaneous view of the image in order to fix it in his mind" (2002, 4). The child thus depends on another's help to perceive this "ideal-I," an image of wholeness that is instantly commanding as well as lasting in its impact (4). Before the Mirror Stage, the child does not perceive their separateness from the mother. However, when the child perceives their own reflection as separate from the mother, even though he/she usually relies on her help to see it, they experience themselves as "a unified being at the center of the world" (Hayward 2006, 317). This is a moment of *jouissance* (jubilation) in the experience of narcissistic identification.

The Mirror Stage is an adaptable concept. It does not necessarily refer to a literal mirror, for even when there is no actual reflection the infant sees its behavior "reflected in the imitative gestures of an adult or another child" (Evans 1996, 190). Equally, though Lacan initially attached the Mirror Stage to a specific developmental phase of a child—from six to eighteen months—he later broadened the concept to represent a "permanent structure of subjectivity" (115). In his article "Some Reflections on the Ego" he gave the concept "twofold value": firstly, as "a decisive turning-point in the mental development of a child," and secondly as "an essential libidinal relationship with the body-image" (Lacan 1953, 14). The subject need not lose contact with the Mirror Stage: indeed, the subject may relive it through modeling themselves on others who appear to be "ideal."

THE IMAGINARY, THE SYMBOLIC, AND THE REAL

The Mirror Stage introduces the child to the Imaginary order, one of the three orders of subjectivity that form the center of Lacanian thought. The other two orders of subjectivity are the Symbolic and the Real, both of which we shall define in due course. With reference to seven separate writings of Lacan, Evans provides a definition of the Imaginary order as "the realm of image and imagination, deception and lure. The principle illusions of the Imaginary are those of wholeness, synthesis, autonomy, duality and, above all, similarity. The Imaginary is thus the order of surface appearances which are deceptive, observable phenomena which hide underlying structure; the affects are such phenomena" (Evans 1996, 82). More specifically, the Imaginary is "founded in the almost hypnotic effect of the specular image" (83), the subject's contemplation of which is inherently narcissistic.

For Lacan, narcissism entails a form of aggressivity because the subject identifies with something "which is outside (and even against) himself" (Evans 1996, 81).

Because the specular image has a wholeness and coordination that contrasts with "the uncoordinated disunity of the subject's real body," it "seems to threaten the subject with disintegration and fragmentation" (120). This "structures the subject as rivaling with himself" (Lacan 2002, 23–24). Therefore, the power of the Imaginary, founded in the specular image, is double-sided: it is both seductive and imprisoning, exciting and potentially self-defeating. Also, the moment the infant realizes his/her separateness from the mother through the specular image, he/she experiences a freedom that also entails a sense of loss. This is the primal moment of sensing lack that, for Lacan, largely defines the human subject. Even the joy of the specular image (or any other image, for that matter) cannot make up for this lack.

Along with realizing itself as separate from the mother, the child enters the Symbolic order that is based in language. The Mirror Stage thus represents a transition between the Imaginary and Symbolic orders. The Symbolic order entails accepting the rules and restrictions over communication and desire that allow one to become part of society. Above all, the Symbolic order is ruled by the "Law" of the Father which is based on language. Lacan writes that "It is in the *name of the father* that we must recognize the support of the symbolic function which, from the dawn of history, has identified his person with the figure of the law" (Lacan 2002, 66, original emphasis). The Law of the Father is also the laws of society and culture, the laws of patriarchy, and/or the laws that are determined by the one who embodies the threat of castration (Hayward 2006, 318). The father represents the authoritative figure of the family who prohibits the child's Oedipal desire for the mother. Desire for the mother does not disappear, however, but is repressed at an unconscious level. Before the Symbolic realm, the child is "pre-lack and pre-linguistic" (Hayward, 2006, 292). Entry into the Symbolic means entry into language *and* lack, especially since the child perceives their separateness from the mother and must repress their desire for her in the Freudian sense. Since the infant's repressed desire becomes part of the unconscious that cannot be voiced in the Symbolic order, speech immediately reflects the denial of the self. In repressing its desire for the mother, the child begins "the unfulfillable search for the eternally lost object" or what Lacan refers to as *l'objet petit-a* (Hayward, 2006, 317).

Whereas the Symbolic order is inextricably connected to language, there is a third order within Lacan's definition of subjectivity that is inexpressible within language: the Real. The Real is the most elusive concept in Lacan's scheme of subjectivity because he not only conceptualizes it in different ways, but he also writes about it less than the other concepts we have discussed. Though the Real is sometimes equated with objective reality, it is also associated with hallucinations and dreams which play out that which cannot be enacted within the Symbolic order (Evans 1996, 160). The Real order is also a state of nature from which we are separated through entering the world of language. Because the Real is "what the subject is unable to speak [. . .] it is like a hole in the Symbolic order" (Hayward 2006, 321). Or, as Elizabeth Wright puts it, "the Real never fits comfortably into any conceptualization. Hence Lacan's point that the Real is impossible to grasp: it must be different from what words say it is" (Wright 1982, 121). Even though we cannot reduce the Real to any form of language or symbolization, as Dino Felluga explains, "it continues to exert its influence throughout our adult lives since it is the rock against which all our fantasies and linguistic structures ultimately fail. The [R]eal [. . .] continues to erupt whenever we are made to acknowledge the materiality of our existence, an acknowledgement that is usually perceived as traumatic (since it threatens our very 'reality')" (2011).

Slavoj Žižek provides an unusually accessible exploration of the Real. Although this realm is not bound by language, and is therefore extremely difficult to pin down, Žižek writes of the ultimate "answer of the [R]eal" in macrocosmically tangible terms. For instance, he argues that it is manifested in the ecological crisis that confronts us today, and in relation to which we cannot but escape our inadequacies in language. Žižek writes that the typical response to the ecological crisis is "I know very well [. . .] but just the same," which he expands as meaning "I know very well (that things are deadly serious, that what is at stake is our very survival), but just the same. . . (I don't really believe it, I'm not really prepared to integrate it into my [S]ymbolic universe, and that is why I continue to act as if ecology is of no lasting consequence for my everyday life)" (Žižek 1991, 35). Another possible reaction is to "read" the ecological crisis as a "sign bearing a certain message," especially as a clear message of punishment for our abuse of nature. The disturbance within nature can thus be read as an "answer of the [R]eal" to the dangers of human praxis, especially the human encroachment upon nature that is organized within a Symbolic order (34).[7] Both possibilities, he argues, are forms of "avoiding an encounter with the [R]eal" (35). In the first scenario we simply dismiss what we know, and in the second we "blind ourselves" to "the irreducible gap separating the [R]eal from the modes of its symbolization" (36). Žižek maintains that the Real cannot be reduced to the Symbolic by our projecting a "message" onto it. Equally, the Real cannot be repaired in the Symbolic order which can never fully represent it.

---

[7] Here Žižek clearly refers to a Lacanian notion of the Real indicated with a capital "R" to separate it from a looser and more general application of the word "real." Therefore, capital "R"s have been consistently added to quotations from Žižek's text to maintain that clear distinction. (The same goes for capitalizing the words "Symbolic" or "Imaginary" to indicate specifically Lacanian understandings of those words.)

After pointing out the irreducible scale of the current ecological crisis, Žižek cites the horrors of Nazi Germany and Chernobyl as occurrences that most spectacularly resist the inevitably reducing process of attempting to encapsulate the Real within language. When it comes to the Real, "no matter what we say about it, it continues to expand, to reduce it to the role of impotent witnesses." The radioactive rays of the Chernobyl disaster, for instance, "are thoroughly unrepresentable, no image is adequate to them" and, equally, all talk about them fails to identify the exact "threshold of danger" (36).

Žižek's approach to defining the Real resonates with our case study films. That nature is in itself already turbulent and imbalanced, as well as resistant to the Symbolic imposition of order is quite literally, and spectacularly, emphasized in *Shutter Island* by a storm that aurally dominates much of the film. The futility of encapsulating the Real is more obliquely implied within *Bigger Than Life*. Both films, however, paradoxically imply the possibilities of that which is beyond their own processes of representation. Moreover, as we shall explore, both films *aurally* situate the realms of the Imaginary and the Symbolic in relation to the deeper power of the ever-elusive Real.

Having defined the Real, Žižek allows for the possibility that it *can* be *"rendered"* even if it exceeds the limitations of language (39).[8] He specifically cites scenes from *The Elephant Man* (1980), in which external sounds are suspended or pushed into the background in favor of strange, uncertain, but rhythmic sounds (part heartbeat, part machine) that relate to the elephant man's subjective experience but which do not "imitate or symbolize any thing": instead, these sounds are "the thing itself" and they "penetrate us like invisible but nonetheless material rays" (41). He argues that the sounds thus allow us to perceive the Elephant Man's Real "psyche" without reducing it to comprehensibility. For Žižek, the film's most impactful content is therefore rendered by its very aural form (43). His comprehension of aural techniques that so affectively render the Real also resonates with our case study films.

To summarize so far, the Imaginary order is the realm of fantasies and perceptions associated with the specular image and the experience of self-identification. The Symbolic is the realm of society and culture based in language, in the context of which the subject articulates (and represses) desire and feelings. The Real is beyond what we can articulate in that it is an essential state of being that precedes language and is infinitely bigger than the limits of language. These concepts are interdependent: indeed, Lacan conceived of them as being inseparable like the intersected rings of a Borromean

---

[8] Here, Žižek draws on Chion's concept of *rendu* (or rendered sound), the notion of sonic access to something bigger and fuller than purely external, or literal, or conventionalized filmic reality. See Chion's "The Real and the Rendered" in *Film, A Sound Art* ([2003] 2009, 237–46).

knot.[9] However, the realms of the Imaginary and the Symbolic are often privileged within film analysis. By contrast, we shall explore some ways in which the sound tracks of both *Bigger Than Life* and *Shutter Island* represent all three Lacanian orders of subjectivity.

APPLYING LACANIAN THEORY TO FILM

Many film theorists picked up Lacanian concepts in the 1970s, especially with regard to conceptualizing film spectatorship. Indeed, such is the powerful influence of these concepts that David Bordwell and Noël Carroll "simply labeled Lacanian film theory '*the* Theory'" (1996, 45).[10] As McGowan and Kunkle write, Lacan's work took on a "foundational role within film studies" because his "insights into the process of identification allowed film theorists to see why film was so effective in involving spectators in its narrative" (2004, xi). In particular, the experience of cinema itself has been frequently conceptualized as a potent and seductive invitation to regress back to the Mirror Stage. For Christian Metz, for instance, going to the cinema holds out such an indulgent possibility. The "inevitable keyhole effect" of film viewing allows the safe possibility of narcissistic identification with, and voyeuristic indulgence in, the image ([1975] 2004, 831). Since film is always a record of what was there but is no longer present, it is a continual experience of lack. However, even though the spectator is aware of this, Metz argues they are able to disavow it and lose themselves in the fantasy or desire of being omnipotent, especially since cinema is only meaningful as the spectator perceives it (Hayward 2006, 325; Metz [1975] 2004, 823). For Metz, films themselves invite the spectator to experience them this way. Much as the child in Lacan's Mirror Stage can enjoy an illusory mastery by gazing at their own body in a reflection that exceeds their own coordination, the film spectator may enjoy a projected fantasy of control by aligning themselves with an ideal protagonist on screen, and without necessarily being self-conscious about it. Even the material setup of a cinema can be seen to support this kind of experience: Jean-Louis Baudry argues that "the arrangement of the different elements—projector, darkened hall, screen [. . .] reconstructs the situation necessary to the release of the 'Mirror Stage' discovered by Lacan" ([1974–75] 2004, 362–63).[11]

---

[9] As Evans explains, a Borromean knot "is a group of three rings which are linked in such a way that if any one of them is severed, all three become separated" (1996, 18).

[10] The italics are added here. Todd McGowan makes this point (2003, 27).

[11] McGowan cites the above works by Metz and Baudry as representative of long-standing applications of Lacanian thought within film theory.

This idea of the cinematic experience providing the opportunity for regression back to a flattering (and deceptive) Mirror Stage was also taken up by Mulvey when she redirected Lacanian theory within feminist analysis. As we have already explored, Mulvey focuses on the ways in which mainstream Hollywood cinema prompts audiences to participate in patriarchy, especially when women on screen are subjected to the male gaze. Mulvey argues that such cinema prompts audiences to narcissistically align themselves with the "ideal-I" of the usually male protagonist, and to enjoy mastery over female characters from that vantage point. Like Baudry and Metz, Mulvey argues that cinema offers the fantasy of regression back to the Mirror Stage while also concealing its own processes. Thus, she argues that cinema often discourages audiences from perceiving their complicity in the dominant Symbolic order.

McGowan's work opens up significant new possibilities for Lacanian film criticism, especially because he presents Lacan's concept of the gaze as more complex than it is often written as being, and as entailing some Real possibilities far exceeding the Mirror Stage or the Symbolic order. His essay "Looking for the Gaze: Lacanian Film Theory and Its Vicissitudes" (2003) is the basis of his more recent book titled *The Real Gaze: Film Theory After Lacan* (2008), as well as a co-edited anthology titled *Lacan and Contemporary Cinema*, a series of essays that use Lacanian theory to explore the "disruptive and radical power of film" (2004, xvii). The essential ideas of McGowan's essay have been cited in numerous other works that therein acknowledge its significance.[12]

"LOOKING FOR THE GAZE: LACANIAN FILM THEORY AND ITS VICISSITUDES"

McGowan begins his essay by noting the profound impact of Lacan's foundational concepts within film studies. Nevertheless, he quickly questions how Lacan's concept of the Mirror Stage has been applied to film. As noted above, those who have most influentially applied Lacanian theory to film have written of fantasy "working hand in hand with the gaze" because "they see the gaze as an illusion of mastery" in connection with the Mirror Stage (2003, 39). Though Lacan conceived of the "mastering gaze" in his essay on the Mirror Stage, McGowan explains that Lacan later conceived of the gaze that marks "the point at which mastery fails," and "the point at which the object looks back" (28–29). This latter conceptualization of "the gaze involves the spectator in the image, *disrupting* her/his ability to remain all-perceiving and unperceived in the cinema" (28–29, my emphasis).

---

[12] For examples, see Manlove (2007) and/or Carlsson (2012).

The key visual example Lacan provides is Hans Holbein's painting *The Ambassadors* (1533). This painting is a famous example of anamorphosis: it requires that the viewer look from a specific vantage point in order to perceive the entire image. Lacan himself thus writes of the painting as a kind of "trap for the gaze" ([1977] 1998, 89). The subject of *The Ambassadors* initially seems clear: two world travelers lean against a table displaying the riches they have gathered. The men stare out from the frame, in postures of apparent confidence. The image of their privilege is, however, soon disrupted by our perception of a distorted anamorphic figure: a skull. We cannot see the skull clearly by looking straight at the painting, but only by looking downward and to the left: it is thus clear to us via a process of "strange contingency" (72). In addition to representing the reality of mortality for the travelers, the skull represents "the site of the gaze" (McGowan 2003, 29).

For McGowan, the skull "says" to us: "You think you are looking at the painting from a safe distance, but the painting sees you—takes into account your presence as a spectator" (29). So, the gaze implies much more than what we can literally see.[13] Because we must view Holbein's painting actively and from a certain angle in order to perceive its whole form and message, we become part of the picture. And the painting also implies the presence of another looking back at us who has anticipated our look. McGowan therefore argues that the experience of looking at the painting becomes far from "an experience of [I]maginary mastery": instead, it becomes "a traumatic encounter with the Real, with the utter failure of the spectator's seemingly safe distance and assumed mastery" (29).

In his context of reconsidering Lacan's reading of *The Ambassadors*, McGowan shifts the gaze from being located within the spectator to being a position adopted by certain objects, especially films, which prompt a certain kind of engagement. As he explains in *The Real Gaze*, "Understood in Lacan's own terms, the gaze is not the spectator's external view of the filmic image, but the mode in which the spectator is accounted for within the film itself" (2007, 7–8). Whereas other critics influenced by Lacan have assumed that the great pleasure in cinema lies in the experience of a "mastering gaze," McGowan argues that spectators actually desire the Real gaze that reveals the "failure of mastery possible in the cinema" (2003, 29). He claims that "rather than seeking power or mastery (the phallus), our desire is drawn to the opposite—the point at which power is entirely lacking" (32). As evidence, McGowan writes of how "no matter how much power one acquires, one always feels oneself missing something" (32).

---

[13] Though, as we have seen, Mulvey literalizes a Lacanian idea of the gaze in terms of visual film techniques, Lacan himself explicitly says "the gaze [is] not the eye" ([1977] 1998, 90).

Here he employs a Lacanian understanding of desire that relates back to the original experience of lack for which there is no solution.

Desire exists because of that which is beyond reach: it is the continuance of some lack that sustains desire. To quote Žižek again, "the [Lacanian] realization of desire does not consist in its being 'fulfilled,' 'fully satisfied,' it coincides rather with the reproduction of desire as such, with its circular movement" (1991, 7). In the film examples explored by McGowan, desire is clearly perpetuated by that which is visually withheld: "The gaze of the object gazes back at the subject, but this gaze is not present in the field of the visible" (2003, 33).

McGowan's leading example is Steven Spielberg's first feature, *Duel* (1970).[14] In this film, a driver is attacked by an unseen truck driver whose motivation for attempting to kill him is not revealed any more than his face obscured by shadow. The film never reduces the identity of the truck driver or his desire to the "field of the visible." Thus, the film shows how "desire emerges in response to the indecipherable gaze" (33). Because the film repeatedly offers the possibility of fully revealing the driver and this desire, only to consistently make the viewer retreat from it, it motivates the desire of the viewer in a Lacanian way: desire sustains itself as desire which entails not encountering the actual object (34). *Duel* "apprehends the gaze indirectly, grasping the way that it disrupts the image" (36) without ever revealing it. For McGowan, the film thus makes us aware of the Real, "the gap within the [S]ymbolic order" and, along with that, "the Real of the gaze in its absence" (36).

McGowan also provides another example from *Schindler's List* (1993), a scene in which we see the Nazi commandant Amon Goeth (Ralph Fiennes) shooting Jews in the concentration camp. Though the scene includes a point-of-view pan of the prisoners from Goeth's position on a balcony above them, the scene also shows him as a blur in the background while he shoots at them indiscriminately: here, "the camera looks up at Goeth, but the shot does not capture his gaze. The spectator cannot experience mastery here but must instead endure [his] indecipherable desire" (37). Herein the film portrays what is most terrifying about Goeth: "why does he decide to shoot those whom he shoots? As one watches, it is clear that no one, not even Goeth himself, could answer this question" (38).

Contrary to such examples of film that represent the indecipherable Real gaze, McGowan argues that "most films do not sustain the logic of desire throughout the

---

[14] It is not the pattern within this book to always mention the director of a film: auteur theory is not the default position here, and we assume the artistic input of many personnel in addition to the director of a given film. Spielberg is specifically cited by McGowan because he reads the auteur's films as representing a consistent "flight from the trauma of the gaze" into fantasy (2003, 37).

narrative. Instead, they retreat from the deadlock of desire—sustaining the gaze in its absence—into a fantasmatic resolution" (36). Such is eventually the case with even *Schindler's List*, for the portrayal of Goeth's incomprehensible desire is reduced by the film when the fantasy father figure" of Oskar Schindler (Liam Neeson) is able to figure out what Goeth wants, and then manipulate him into freeing "more than a thousand Jews from certain death" (38). In other words, Goeth's indecipherability is eventually demystified or, as McGowan puts it, "domesticated" (36). The traumatic and "impossible question" of the Real gaze is here replaced by Schindler's "solution." For McGowan, this is a kind of "fantasy" which allows the audience to "gain a measure of certainty," relieving them from "suffering the perpetual uncertainty of desire" (36).

Ironically, McGowan also argues that such fantasy can allow us to see the vulnerability of the "ideological edifice" within which it makes sense. Even if the turn to fantasy obscures the (traumatic) gaze in the filmic experience, fantasy can ironically reveal that ideology is "in need of support" for it to function: "If ideology and the [S]ymbolic order were not haunted by a Real—that is, if they were self-enclosed structures—there would be no need for fantasy to keep the subjects within them. In this sense, even the most ideological film testifies to the point of failure of ideology, of its need for a fantasmatic supplement" (40).[15] Moreover, "when film employs fantasy but at the same time reveals the limit that fantasy comes up against, it takes us to an encounter with the traumatic Real" (40). With *Bigger Than Life*, we shall experience a film that seems painfully aware of the unspeakable Real that always trumps a retreat into fantasy. And, as we shall explore, the sound track is crucial for relaying this kind of self-consciousness. Equally, we shall explore the retreat into fantasy that is chosen by the main character of *Shutter Island* but from which we are sonically barred. Both films feature strident, non-suturing sound tracks that seem to anticipate our actively perceiving them, much like Holbein's painting anticipates our seeing it from a particular vantage point.[16] In short, both *Bigger Than Life* and *Shutter Island* force us to hear their self-conscious construction, *and* their power in relation to the Real.

---

[15] For a series of similarly subversive applications of Lacanian theory, see the anthology edited by McGowan and Kunkle (2004). Here, Juliet Flower MacCannell's (1994) analysis of the two *Cape Fear* films (the 1962 original and the 1991 remake) as they critically represent the Symbolic order, and as they allude to the terror of the Real, resonates most strongly with *Shutter Island*.

[16] As noted earlier, the term "suture" is loaded in a psychoanalytic context. The term literally means "stitched together" and in film analysis refers to how an audience becomes "stitched into" a film by means of its involving processes that do not call attention to themselves. Though the regular shot-reverse-shot pattern is most often used to discuss suturing, there are many ways in which films "hide" their own constructions, whether we consider all forms of continuity editing, or conventional camerawork, or unobtrusive scoring and conventional sound effects. The "suturing" film experience does not demand that an audience consider how the reality it presents was put together: instead, it allows the audience to ignore

To sum up, Lacanian concepts have had long-standing and much-contested influence within film studies. In using Lacanian theory to argue for the potential political radicalism of mainstream film examples (such as *Schindler's List*), McGowan's work stands apart from the established tradition of applying Lacan's concepts (Ayers 2008, 57–59). Though McGowan's discussion of Lacanian theory is visually biased (in accordance with the primary Lacanian sources), we can open up his arguments to encompass the radical possibilities of what we *hear* in two other mainstream films: the Classical Hollywood, Twentieth Century Fox production of *Bigger Than Life,* and the contemporary, Paramount production of *Shutter Island.* Here are the questions that will govern our psychoanalysis of the sound tracks for both films:

- With Freudian and Lacanian notions of the divided self in mind, how does the film sonically represent its main characters? Do they, for instance, seem coherent or pulled apart by contrary impulses?
- How does the film sonically represent the orders of the Imaginary, the Symbolic, and the Real? How does it ask us to hear its characters in relation to these realms?
- Does the film privilege any realm of subjectivity (and, if so, to what effect)?
- Does the sound track self-consciously represent the possibilities of the Real gaze as defined by McGowan?
- Does the sound track support the fantasy elements of the film?
- Does the sound track open up the possibilities of self-conscious radicalism suggested by McGowan?

---

the very conventions that make it seem like a pre-given or "normal" (because familiarly constructed) cinematic reality. For more on the concept of suturing in Lacanian film theory, see Daniel Dayan (1976), and for a fuller discussion of how the term "suture" has been historically applied in film studies, see Stephen Heath ([1978] 2006).

 # BIGGER THAN LIFE

PLOT SUMMARY

Bigger Than Life revolves around a man whose adverse reaction to medical treatment has near-tragic consequences. The protagonist is Ed Avery (James Mason), a grammar school teacher who struggles to maintain his middle-class family life and who secretly takes a second job at the switchboard of a cabstand (see Figure 4.1). In the exposition, Ed is gripped by more than one debilitating seizure and, after some extensive medical consultations, he is prescribed cortisone treatment. A doctor informs Ed that he will die within a year if he does not pursue this treatment despite its possible adverse side effects. Ed's initial response to the treatment is elated relief, which he expresses through extravagant gifts for his wife and son, despite their relatively modest means (especially with increasing medical expenditures). Ed also shows signs of greater professional ambition not grounded in his actual circumstances: he gives up his work at the cabstand, and uses his position as schoolteacher to authorize his own new, extreme, and dangerous plan for disciplining children. As he becomes seized by his own unreasonable aspirations, he also becomes increasingly alienated from his family and friends, especially his close colleague, Wallie (Walter Matthau). He exerts terrifying control over his son Richie (Christopher Olsen), and this culminates in his plan to sacrifice Richie for his warped sense of the greater good.[17] When his loyal wife Lou (Barbara Rush) shows some resistance to the plan, he literally shuts her away in a closet, only to be confronted by Wallie in a climactic fight that ends with his being defeated and rendered unconscious. The final scene shows Ed waking up in a hospital, and then embracing his wife and son who choose to stay with him in hope of his full recovery.

---

[17] Amy Lawrence provides a more sympathetic, intertextual analysis of Mason's performance as Ed. She argues that Mason repeatedly deconstructed the male authority figures he played, and that he subverted "the illusion of masculinity" by "exposing the agony at the heart of it" (2010, 87).

FIGURE 4.1 Ed Avery, the protagonist of *Bigger Than Life*.

REDRESSING THE CRITICAL BALANCE

Bigger Than Life was critically and commercially unsuccessful upon on its release. Critics of its time found it "too melodramatic and exaggerated" (Andrew 2004, 103), but it has since been reclaimed by American critics as "one of the most radical [though] least-known American films of the 1950s."[18] The film is recognized as an important precursor to contemporary, critical depictions of suburban life.[19] *Revolutionary Road* (2008), for instance, with its subdued palette and highly affective score by Thomas Newman, clearly draws from *Bigger Than Life*. By coincidence, *Revolutionary Road* is set in 1955, the same year in which *The New Yorker* medical writer Berton Roueché published an article that was the original inspiration for *Bigger Than Life*. The article is a true account of a Queens schoolteacher driven to mania after taking the "miracle drug," cortisone. Though the film thus stems from an actual case, it sets the action in the "suburbs of Anytown,"[20] opening up the scale and applicability of its narrative. Indeed,

---

[18] In relation to this point, Scott Foundas notes that the film was never issued on video format in the United States, and only aired occasionally on the Fox Movie Channel until a Cinemascope print was rerun at the Film Forum (New York) in January 2009 (2008). In 2010, Criterion released new DVD and Blu-Ray editions of the film, ensuring its wide availability in restored condition.

[19] Kite also notes that the pattern in Ray's work of "estranging domestic spaces" is echoed by films directed by David Lynch, especially *Twin Peaks: Fire Walk with Me* (1992) (2010).

[20] This is Foundas's phrase and his basis for arguing that the film is focused upon much more than a one-off "mere medical mystery" (2008).

Geoff Andrew argues that where Roueché's article primarily focuses on "the potentially dangerous side effects of cortisone," director Nicholas Ray was "concerned with diagnosing and analyzing the more insidious ills affecting American life in general" (2004, 109). Roueché's article is most compelling for its inclusion of the schoolteacher's wife's statements about her husband's "tyrannical" behavior (1955, 59) and his "colossal self-assurance" (65) following cortisone treatment. This honoring of her perspective is certainly echoed by Ray's film. Nowadays, both the article and film strongly resonate against more conservative and formulaic representations of suburban family life in the 1950s, as typified by the long-running television shows *Father Knows Best* (1954–63) and *Leave It to Beaver* (1957–63). Despite the wave of new critical attention to *Bigger Than Life*, however, the sound track is seldom mentioned. In a representative review, Tom Dawson attributes the film's "emotional force" to the intensity with which Mason "conveys his character's profound torment," without any mention of how much the sound track both amplifies and complicates the impact of his performance (Dawson, 2003). This analysis is about redressing the balance, *listening* to the film along with seeing its subversive psychoanalytic content.

OVERARCHING SONIC PATTERNS

The original score for *Bigger Than Life* was composed by David Raksin, a prolific composer for film and television, best known for his music in *Laura* (1944). Raksin had some formal training with Arnold Schoenberg, a composer who taught and analyzed much tonal music but who is himself best known for breaking experimental ground by favoring atonality and devising the twelve-tone technique.[21] Though Raksin's music for *Bigger Than Life* does not imitate Schoenberg directly, the score reflects his willingness to experiment with conventions of musical form. Near the beginning of his career, Raksin had experience arranging music for radio and film, most notably for Charlie Chaplin's *Modern Times* (1936), a film in which the only spoken voices come from mechanical objects. Thus Raksin had a background in using music to flesh out perceptual possibilities (for radio) and to "speak" what characters do not (on film). His score for *Bigger Than Life* is a strong "voice" that often exceeds what we can see or hear emanating from within the diegetic space.[22]

---

[21] Schoenberg's twelve-tone music is created from sequences of all twelve notes from the chromatic scale without repeating any one of them. It thus avoids being in any particular key. A famous example is *Variations for Orchestra*, op. 31 (1928).

[22] For a fuller discussion of Raksin's work, especially for *Laura*, see Prendergast's *Film Music: A Neglected Art* (1992, 58–67).

Before zooming in on select scenes from the film, we should contextualize them in relation to the sound track's overall patterns of disturbance. These patterns amplify the shaky Symbolic order within the film, especially as it is embodied by the father. Most obviously, the score features numerous stingers, and elongated ones at that. For instance, after light and comedy-connoting music accompanies Ed's trip from his school to the cabstand where he also works, there is a sudden stinger on brass and strings. This stinger marks a moment when he doubles up in pain after changing his clothes [5:30–5:36], amplifying his shifting interior state as well as his different appearance. The combined power of brass and strings is reinforced by several low percussive beats that ominously elongate the effect. Since Ed's work at the cabstand switchboard is a secret from his family, a point that is made explicit in the previous scene, the stinger on an image of his incapacitated body relates to his lone vulnerability as a breadwinner. By marking that moment in which his body becomes less than erect, the stinger accentuates his emasculated role on the switchboard. He soon thereafter takes the place of the only other man working at the switchboard, adding his voice to a chorus of women in the same role, which further emphasizes his gendered vulnerability in taking a job beneath his pedagogical qualifications (see Figure 4.2).

Though the stinger is a commonly used device of Classical Hollywood scoring, Raksin's score for *Bigger Than Life* features so many prominent examples, and elongates them to such a degree, that the overall effect is to keep us almost perpetually on guard.

FIGURE 4.2 Ed takes his emasculated, seated position at the cabstand switchboard.

To give another example, a stinger interrupts the light underscoring of a dinner party scene, along with a cut to show Ed in the kitchen. He is doubled over in pain before the open fridge, spatially separated from his guests and his wife [8:20–8:31]. In yet another example, a montage of doctors treating Ed, oddly underscored by upbeat and comedy-connoting music, is broken by a stinger emphasizing the suddenly silhouetted image of his solitary, nighttime seizures [19:22–19:28]. Both of these latter examples emphasize Ed's sudden separation from those around him and what *they* represent: the complacency of ordinary middle-class living and routine privilege.

In addition to the troubling emphasis on stingers, *Bigger Than Life* denies us the comfort of much developed melodic material. Though the whole film features many cues for punctuating key moments, there are few occasions when we can latch onto a melody for any length of time: most of the music cues are brief, and though many of them provide transitions between scenes and shots, many others cumulatively contribute to an overall emphasis on non-suturing impact.[23] The consequently "broken" form of the film not only parallels the broken identity of the central character, but also points to the fractures within the Symbolic world that he inhabits and embodies.

THE MARRIAGE MUSIC

The film's use of many brief musical cues aside, there are two memorable and oft-used themes associated with Ed's marriage. The first is introduced by woodwind (see Figure 4.3). The first five bars of this theme become a leitmotif that is always attached to defining moments within the marriage of Ed and Lou. The theme has a melancholy and "thin" sound, partly because the harmonies are usually sets of two (rather than three) notes played simultaneously. We first hear it fully stated after their dinner party, a scene in which there is mounting tension between Ed and Lou. During this scene, the music is almost playfully used at two moments where its rests punctuate Ed's movements: first, his switching off lights; and second, his switching off the tap when Lou begins washing up [9:38–10:31]. As the film progresses and we hear it again, however, the same theme

---

[23] Kite writes about patterns of non-suturing *visual* detail in Ray's work, especially his "disrupting smooth sequences with odd interpolations." Here he specifically refers to the shots of Humphrey Bogart's "haggard face" that break up "the steady shot-reserve-shot flow of the first bar scene in *In A Lonely Place*" (1950) and argues such sequences convey "a sense of trying to carve out some place for immediacy and spontaneity inside institutionalized patterns of construction." This positively suggests the subversive energy of Ray's visual techniques which surely parallels the impact of Raksin's cues for *Bigger Than Life* as they repeatedly break up the narrative flow (2010).

FIGURE 4.3 David Raksin's first theme for Ed and Lou's marriage (transcribed directly from the DVD).

takes on more melodramatic and poignant connotations. It becomes associated with scenes that foreground the potential vulnerability of the marriage and those moments where the marriage must be redefined in relation to Ed's increasingly erratic behavior.

This first marriage theme is both repeated and developed when Lou visits Ed in the hospital. During this scene, Ed finally tells Lou about his secret work at the cabstand and she in turn reveals that his suspicious behavior has made her fear his having an affair. Ed affectionately laughs off the possibility and they embrace (see Figure 4.4). The new intimacy that comes with the truthfulness of both characters is reinforced by the restatement of their first marriage theme on woodwind [21:00–21:17]. This theme is then "answered" by an overlapping theme led by strings [21:17–21:43], the main melodic line of which is as follows (see Figure 4.5).

The sonorous development of this secondary marriage theme is suddenly interrupted when doctors enter the hospital room with a dismal prognosis. In later scenes, there are unsettling variations on this theme after Ed's behavior becomes troublingly egocentric, such as when he takes pills while standing before the cabinet mirror [38:41–38:42], and when Lou is unable to reach their doctor for help after Ed becomes despotic [1:06:30–1:06:42]. In its variations, this secondary theme particularly emphasizes threats to the marriage, especially as Ed becomes increasingly pathological. Both marriage themes arrest the ear every time they occur because they are unlike the brief cues

FIGURE 4.4 Ed and Lou lovingly reconcile at the hospital.

FIGURE 4.5 The melodic line of David Raksin's second theme for Ed and Lou's marriage (transcribed directly from the DVD).

and elongated stingers that dominate the film much more often. Despite the importance of the marriage themes, however, the film foregrounds broken and non-melodic cues much more consistently.

Let us think back to Steiner's scoring for *The Searchers* for a strong example of more conventional underscoring in a film released the same year as *Bigger Than Life*. Recall that even the most disturbing scenes of *The Searchers* are modified by music. Recall, also, that even when stingers are used in *The Searchers*, and on more than one occasion in connection with the demonized name "Scar," they straightforwardly reinforce dialogue and are soon superseded by melody-driven music. *Bigger Than Life*, on the other hand, prompts us to feel its stingers much more, and it repeatedly denies us the comfort or reassurances of more traditional musical underscoring. Awkward conversations are left in their awkwardness without musical mediation, and lonely expressions of frustration are not musically answered. The overall result is a film that keeps us not only on the alert, but ever aware of the fractures within its very form as well as the ruptures among and within its characters.

EMPHASIZING THE (BROKEN) SYMBOLIC ORDER

Because *Bigger Than Life* repeatedly foregrounds its own brokenness in parallel to the disturbingly fractured identities of its characters, especially the male protagonist, it works very differently from those other, more conservative Classical Hollywood films critiqued by Mulvey in her feminist application of psychoanalytic concepts. First and foremost, the film discourages us from aligning ourselves with the male protagonist, even though its broken form parallels his troublingly divided subjectivity. Ed is the character around whom the action revolves, and he is present in almost every scene, but the film does not *serve* him. Instead of playing out the dominant patriarchal patterns of its own time, *Bigger Than Life* traps us in our own expectation of them, confronting us with the patriarch's *disturbing* image, and anticipating our look with its Real terror. It therefore resonates with McGowan's readings of subversive possibilities within Hollywood cinema. Raksin's strident and often non-suturing music is a crucial part of this.

That the film denies us the luxury of a fantasy Mirror Stage regression through encouraging us to identify with the protagonist is most obvious in the scenes where Ed sees his own image as a broken reflection. From a feminist perspective (again, with Mulvey's work in mind), it is especially significant that Ed's wife breaks the mirror when she is resisting a role of subservience to him, and that she is the character with whom the film most explicitly encourages us to identity. Lou breaks the mirror after we have seen Ed enjoying his own reflection, fancying the view of himself as a man of leisure. After making several childish demands from Lou that would seem more appropriate from his son (milk, sandwiches, bath water), he catches his own reflection in the mirror and begins to pose before it (see Figure 4.6). He ties a small white towel around his neck like a cravat and becomes fixated with the upper-class ideal-I that he evidently projects onto his own face. While admiring himself this way, he casually demands more bath water from Lou. She becomes enraged, slamming the mirrored cabinet door shut before storming out of the room (see Figure 4.7).

In response to seeing his own broken image, Ed literally grabs himself and the sound track features a stinger of a synthesized chord to amplify his shock [40:09–40:14]. The first marriage theme follows hard upon this stinger, as if to "reassure"

FIGURE 4.6 With his makeshift towel cravat, Ed smugly poses in front of the mirror.

FIGURE 4.7 Lou slams the mirrored cabinet door shut, shattering Ed's self-satisfied image.

the protagonist and us [40:15–40:19]. As Lou re-enters the scene to apologize to Ed, the second marriage theme overlaps with the first [40:20–40:43], and Ed quickly dismisses what he has seen in himself by simply saying they have spent too much time apart. They then passionately embrace, both evidently wishing to "un-see" the brokenness that is all too manifest, and the second marriage theme emphasizes the possibility of (and their hope for) reconciliation. However, the theme is not enough to "answer" what we have just witnessed. Though it dovetails with a fanfare-like flourish as they embrace, this flourish ends on an unresolved cadence and dissonantly overlaps with another synthesized stinger chord as the scene dissolves to show Richie waking up in the night [40:43–40:52]. Richie is awoken by his father's crying alone downstairs, and Raksin's stinger suggests a parallel "waking up" to Ed's instability.

The broken reflection is also reshown, with greater audiovisual emphasis, in the scene where Lou is woken by Richie after he finds his father crying alone, downstairs, in the middle of the night. As Lou leads Ed back up the stairs to their bedroom, we hear a version of the first marriage theme that amplifies the tenderness between them [42:10–42:59]. However, this marriage theme is followed by a sonic shock: after Ed has urged Lou back to bed, phoned the doctor, and picked up an invoice for medical expenses, the paper he holds is injected with sinister life by a *forte* stinger chord that begins right before we see it [43:00–43:08]. As Ed then puts down the phone before even speaking with the doctor, the music becomes more thickly orchestrated, less melodic, lower in pitch, more percussive, and funereal. When he then goes into the bathroom to fetch medication, we hear yet more troubled music that loosely relates to the marriage themes. This music is dominated by descending notes, furtive movements away from the melodic lines, harmonic indeterminacy, increasing complexity with the addition of strings, and some dissonance from the woodwind. Then, yet another strong stinger marks the moment when Ed closes the cabinet door to inadvertently re-subject himself to the broken reflection (see Figure 4.8).

Ed's contemplation of his own split face lasts for several seconds, along with a stinger [44:15–44:26]. At the tail end of the shot and stinger, synthesized upper-pitch notes elongate the moment. The synthesized notes aurally anticipate the most disturbing, climactic scene of Ed's pathology, in which synthesized chords take special prominence as he prepares to kill Richie. Even if Ed all too quickly forgets the warning of his own broken reflection, we are unlikely to, not least because Raksin's music stresses its sinister significance.

After the shot of Ed's re-seen broken reflection, the film fades ominously out to black. It then fades in on a scene with his family physician. Now Ed's blood pressure is being taken and his doctor makes a perfunctory observation—"120 over 80 Ed, it's fine"—before raising a question that is really its own assumed answer—"still no periods of depression?" "Just a little one, first night home" says Ed, returning the doctor's dismissive attitude. What is most aurally striking at this point is the silence around the words of the doctor and Ed, especially following the stretched-out stinger for the

FIGURE 4.8 Ed re-sees his own broken reflection.

preceding shot of the broken mirror reflection, one that aurally anticipates the most horrific action of the film.

This whole sequence (from Ed's crying alone to his seeing the doctor) is representatively powerful in its patterns: the melodic scoring is thrown into relief by sudden aural disturbance and redirection, the stingers reinforce our understanding of Ed's trauma as well as breaking up the sound track in accordance with his broken self, and the sudden quiet in the doctor's office serves to ironically amplify the danger of retreating from the idea that anything is wrong. The silence around Ed's failure to be truthful about the depths of his disturbance, as well as the doctor's pat statements, foregrounds what they both fail to acknowledge: the terrible threat that Ed embodies. Both Ed and the doctor represent powerful figures in the Symbolic order, but the silences of the sound track allow space for our questioning both of them. Here and elsewhere, the sound track features the unnerving power of relative quiet to ironically amplify its critical representation of patriarchal authority.

THE DANGER WITHIN THE FATHER

Perhaps the most shocking element of *Bigger Than Life* is that the greatest threat within the film is *the* quintessential figure of authority in the Symbolic order: the father. Many films contemporary with *Bigger Than Life* represent a benign suburban domestic space against which an outside threat asserts itself. *Invasion of the Body Snatchers* (1956), for instance, shows pristine, cookie-cutter domestic spaces which are menacingly infiltrated by alien pod people who look like replicas of their actual inhabitants. *Invasion* is also a quintessential example of representing a deep threat to the Symbolic order by demonizing those who represent difference and by forcing our alignment with the white, male, heterosexual lead whose way of life is threatened.[24] Similarly, *The Big Heat* (1953) dwells upon the harmonious domestic space of an ordinary middle-class kitchen before an explosion planted outside by gang members makes it a tragic space. By contrast, in *Bigger Than Life*, the greatest threat originates from within the patriarch who lives in the domestic space. The film's emphasis on disturbance caused from within Ed is most visually explicit in a scene showing the X-Ray vision of his body. Shortly after this examination, his doctors prescribe the cortisone that creates those adverse reactions that make him pathological. Ironically, the disturbing X-Ray scene is not underscored. However, the X-Ray scene is preceded by a sequence in which the sound track repeatedly alerts us to that which is most dangerous *in* Ed.

As Ed prepares to go to hospital for a week on his doctor's recommendation, he takes Richie aside to discuss "being head man" in his father's absence. Ed then stops to re-inflate his old football for Richie, an object that symbolizes his physical prowess in the past and which is explicitly connected with memories of his success for a high school team. This memory suggests Ed's lost ideal-I, a time when his body had greater power over itself than it does in the present, thus parallel to Lacan's understanding of how the infant perceives their more-coordinated reflection in the Mirror Stage. That Richie brings him the pump for re-inflation signposts that the boy plays a crucial part in Ed's remembrance of his former self, again parallel to the infant who relies upon some assistance (whether human or a prop) to be able to perceive themselves in the mirror. The football iconographically represents a time in which Ed had a clear and celebrated place within a social context, as well as a time of his physically asserting his masculinity for a clear-cut win. When he gives his re-inflated football to his son, he reveals his reliance on Richie to continue "reflecting" back his lost self (see Figure 4.9). Ironically, there is no music in this scene, nothing to aurally reinforce, sentimentalize, or lament for Ed's former glory.

Right after Ed has given the ball to Richie, thus passing on his power to the temporary "head man," Lou pensively enters the scene. The first and then second marriage

---

[24] See Mann for some further discussion of the reactionary subtexts of *Invasion* in terms of "postwar discourses of difference, namely racial masquerade, alien immigration, and sexual deviance," especially as it dramatizes threats to "hegemonic white patriarchy" (2004, 49).

FIGURE 4.9 Ed gives his treasured high school football, a symbol of his former glory, to his son Richie.

themes briefly resurface to underscore their effort at ordinary conversation [14:53–15:08]. That the music comes with Lou's entrance emphasizes her agony over his, and her comprehension of what presently falls apart over Ed's self-aggrandizing look into the past. The conversation is relatively banal: "Don't look so grim," says Ed, "I think I'm just very tired, you know." "Then a few days rest won't hurt" answers Lou. Here, she makes a verbal effort at ordinary comfort and the music honors the poignancy of that as Ed is leaving. But this music is suddenly interrupted by yet another stinger that is unusually elongated, extending through synthetic sounds that make it last for almost half a minute [15:08–15:35]. This stinger accompanies Ed's sudden fall in the doorway of his home, and his falling against the doorbell, which makes for a doubly emphasized aural warning. As Kite says, here the house "does the screaming for him" (2010), a point that unites the domestic space with Ed as they embody the Symbolic order in crisis.

When the stinger and doorbell ring finish, the second marriage theme is taken up by the strings, echoing the earlier hospital scene where strings provided the musical "answer." But here, the cue sounds much more desperate, especially because it develops into an extended and increasingly poignant variation [15:38–16:45]. After Ed leaves, Lou stands at the doorway, calling after him because he has forgotten his slippers. The theme, first taken up by mid-range strings, is soon reinforced by upper woodwind with *fortissimo* emphasis, but it suddenly dwindles on an unresolved cadence that musically stresses irresolution. The climactic peak of this music comes as Lou sadly turns back into the house [16:30]. The music thus reaches an emotive highpoint *in Ed's absence.* Again, it makes Lou's loss and dread paramount: this is, in itself, a potentially radical step away from the primacy of the patriarch and the associated continuance of the existing Symbolic order.

The very next scene features the X-Ray procedure on Ed. This scene begins in the familiarly artificial light of a hospital room. When the light is suddenly switched off for the procedure, however, the X-Ray suddenly glows in black and red. The colors have hellish connotations in relation to the body of the patriarchal figure, an extreme visual example of the unstable Symbolic order. As part of the procedure, Ed is given liquid by the technician to swallow, and we see the X-Ray clarity of its moving down his gullet and through his body (see Figure 4.10).

The physical bluntness of this image is visually akin to an aural stinger, especially since no underscoring unifies the scene. The bones inside Ed's body appear black while his flesh seems to melt away into light, excepting his face and neck extending out of the machine. Herein the scene visualizes the idea of a man stripped down to his physical essence, and the scrutiny of his body is a visual corollary to the film's self-conscious emphasis on its own "parts," especially since Raksin's cues so often break it up rather than facilitate a smooth narrative flow. The starkness with which we now see the inside of Ed's body, *the* place where the film's ultimate disturbance is housed, is reinforced in the striking *absence* of music. Indeed, this is a most memorable scene for revealing the

FIGURE 4.10 The disturbing image of Ed's X-rayed body, unmediated by music.

power of denying us musical consolation or clarification. Instead of scoring to match the visual disturbance, we only hear more banal conversation: "How's the view down there" asks Ed with some apprehension. "Um-hum" the doctor responds, off-screen. The relative quiet of this scene, like the earlier scenes in the doctor's office, and of Ed giving Richie the football, signal irruptions of the Real: in particular, the unspeakable terror embodied by Ed. The sound track demands we perceive this, even if the characters themselves are incapable of it.

THE DISTURBANCE OF EXTREME AND "VIVID" OPPOSITIONS

The quiet of the X-ray scene is especially noticeable because the sound track reaches an emotive peak right before it. *Bigger Than Life* surely relies upon our comprehension of such aural extremes, and this is part of how the film anticipates our presence. But though these sonic extremes are obvious and sometimes shocking, they are all but ignored in scholarly analyses of the film. Ironically, many critics *have* already noted the extreme moments of color within the *mise-en-scène*'s mostly subdued palette. To cite one memorable example, there is the scene in which Ed forces Lou to try on a series of extravagantly vibrant dresses. Fuelled by his foolhardy divorcement from reality brought on by cortisone, Ed strides into the expensive dress shop demanding service. Lou's subsequent trying on dresses is underscored by non-diegetic music for dancing, including a pleasant waltz that ironically suggests a graciously led partnership even while she must be coerced by Ed [33:04–33:39]. The waltz plays while Lou tries on a bright orange-red gown: like the dress, it is "vividly" opposed to almost everything that precedes it.

Such musical emphasis on extreme contrasts has been ignored by critics to date, though the bright dresses have been frequently mentioned, along with the vibrancy of Richie's red jacket (one that echoes the one worn by James Dean in *Rebel without a Cause* (1955), Ray's best-known film).[25] Lou's orange dress, along with Richie's red jacket, and the bright orange sofa centrally placed within their living room, all signify danger within the otherwise banal household space, as well as suggesting the threat to domestic cohesion that is one of the film's ultimate concerns (and a thematic preoccupation through films directed by Ray). The subdued palette of the *mise-en-scène* allows us to perceive such details more fully in their symbolic power, just as the X-Ray scene is all the more startling for its use of red. What we must now recognize is that the opposing color schemes of the film are paralleled by Raksin's music. Right from the beginning, the music challenges us with extremely opposing ideas and "colors."

---

[25] See Kuersten (2010), and Kite (2010).

Raksin's music for the opening of *Bigger Than Life* immediately presents opposing ideas through contrasting extremes of pitch, timbre, harmony, and texture. The first credits for James Mason and Barbara Rush and the film title are accompanied by thickly orchestrated, minor-key, brass-heavy chords at *forte* [0:31–0:40]. A harp glissando marks the transition into a buoyant secondary, homophonic theme featuring a sprightly major-key line for strings. This music is lightly punctuated by percussive stresses, playful pizzicato, and high-pitched woodwind accents. It is in an immediately accessible ABA structure [0:41–1:38]. This cue accompanies the film's first sights and sounds of children running gleefully out from school.

The film proper opens up after a musical transition and with a long stinger chord abrasively played on brass. This stinger is reinforced by low funereal percussive beats and some synthesized sound [1:47–1:58]. Thus, the melody, harmony, and consonance of the opening music are quickly undercut. Because the film proper begins with a stinger, it immediately imposes upon us an experience of brokenness, being denied stability or rest, and being caught in sudden disturbance. The stinger accompanies the first shot of Ed's hand towards a pocket watch and then up to the back of his head in a gesture of pain. At this point we cannot see his face so, on one level, the music reveals him (or his agony) more fully than the camera. But without our being able to see him or understand what we see right away, the music also emphasizes the ominously unrevealing image (see Figure 4.11).

FIGURE 4.11 The ominously unrevealing first image of Ed.

The stinger subsides, giving way to a suddenly and ironically harmonious chord on strings, before the film cuts to show Ed's position behind the teacher's desk. He is looking at a solitary student in detention. Ed asks the student, "Think you know it?" The first line of the film thus emphasizes Ed's Symbolic power to determine knowledge, a point that later becomes terrifying when his psychosis develops. Most literally, the question "think you know it?" relates to Ed's immediate requirement that the student name the five Great Lakes. But "think you know it?" takes on much deeper meaning in the context of the whole film: through Ed, the film may as well be asking us "think you know what this man will become?," or "think you know where the Symbolic order might lead?," or even "think you can ever comprehend the Real?" A few scenes later, Ed asks his son Richie why he is not bored by westerns because "it's always the same story."[26] In this context, *Bigger Than Life* is self-consciously designed to be the story we cannot predict. The very first stinger alerts us to the danger of becoming too comfortable from the outset. And lest we thereafter presume too much by getting comfortable in a harmonious chord, or a melody, or what sounds like an innocuous line, the film repeatedly assaults us with a sudden shift in aural impact that can rarely be anticipated.

THE POWER OF THE PATRIARCH

From the beginning, *Bigger Than Life* also emphasizes the ease with which Ed asserts control through speaking. The dangerous and potentially far-reaching consequences of his assuming authority comes to the fore in one scene involving many other parents who seem all too easily swayed by his arguments. The scene takes place at a PTA night for Ed's school, shortly after which we see him withholding the truth of his worsening condition from a doctor, a point that encourages our fear of him (or at least our critical distance). Near the start of the PTA scene, Ed witnesses parents being enthralled by their own children's artwork on display at the school, and he then assumes a position at the front of a classroom to declare "100,000 schools like this from coast to coast. Every year whole forests are cut down to supply the paper for these grotesque daubs. And we coo over them as though they were Van Goghs or Rembrandts." When one woman responds by saying Ed "hasn't much faith in the unspoiled instincts of childhood," he quickly responds that "childhood is a congenital disease and the purpose of education is to *cure* it."[27] Another woman enters the room, and looks horrified, but then sits down as if awaiting more of his speech. Then, several more parents take the seats

---

[26] Ironically, as Andrew points out (2004, 105), Ray directed several westerns, including his next film *The True Story of Jesse James* (1957).

[27] This is the emphasis of Mason's delivery.

FIGURE 4.12 Ed "holds court" at the PTA meeting, with many parents sitting obediently where their children have sat.

where we know children have previously sat, also evidently waiting for him to continue his speech (see Figure 4.12).

Ed then continues to decry the celebration of children who moronically indulge their instincts. When one mother objects to his attitude, he claims that her daughter Louise is on an intellectual par with "the African gorilla," a point that prompts a collective gasp of horror but which, amazingly, does not prompt his entire audience to leave. Even when his colleague Wally quickly mumbles to Ed that Louise's mother is the president of the PTA, Ed simply scoffs "oh really?" before resuming his speech.

During this speech Ed is impervious to being undermined or questioned. Ironically, no music accompanies him: indeed, there is quiet around his words, notwithstanding a few interjections and gasps of shock, for over two minutes [46:20–48:27]. Even though other parental characters support his speech, and he ignores the one woman who openly objects to it, the sound track is therefore not straightforwardly "with" him. After his insulting the PTA president, Ed asks for a match to light his cigarette, and another father quickly obliges him. It is a slight detail but one that stresses Ed's dependency on others to complete the performance he is creating. He embodies his own perverse notion of the ideal-I, enabled by other parents whereas he previously relied more on his son Richie. Many of the other parents not only give him attention, but also reflect back his fantasy of power. This makes it all the more important that Raksin's music (even in its absence) becomes the "voice" to undermine his authority.

Ultimately, Ed argues that "we're breeding a race of moral midgets" through "all this hogwash about 'self-expression, permissiveness, development patterns, emotional security'." Creating security for children makes no sense to Ed "with the world ready to blow up." With this last phrase he alludes to global terrors of the film's own time—the Cold War, and the nuclear arms race in particular. His allusion to massive possibilities of destruction amplifies the power of his speech over the on-screen classroom audience but it also surely deepens *our* understanding of his warped logic. Ironically, Ed himself is now most assured and comfortable in his speech, leaning against the teacher's desk with cigarette in hand (see Figure 4.13).

In this context, Raksin's music finally creeps in to underline the danger of his sway [48:26]. The score contains patterns of rising pitches and rhythms of escalating intensity, especially for strings and woodwind. We could say this music underscores the dire state of the world as Ed perceives it, but it primarily reinforces how terrifying *Ed* has become. Upon the climax of Ed's speech, in which he declares "we're committing hara-kiri every day right here in this classroom!," one man excitedly tells Wally "that man oughta be principal of this school." A synthesized stinger chord menacingly

FIGURE 4.13 Ed confidently continues his abhorrent speech at the PTA meeting. His friend Wally (at the door) looks critically but helplessly on while a parent (on the right) gives Ed more serious attention.

FIGURE 4.14 An uncomfortably tight close-up following the climax of Ed's speech.

punctuates the moment, along with a cut to an uncomfortably tight close-up of Ed's self-satisfied face [49:41–49] (see Figure 4.14).

This is the point at which we now understand that Ed fully perceives himself as "bigger than life," and that his Id is in complete control. That his face cannot be literally contained within the frame presses this point home, along with the very next scene in which Wally tells Lou that Ed "even looks bigger" because he considers himself "a bigshot." By contrast, Ed himself critically refers to Lou as the "little woman" in the very same scene.

All this said, there is still a presence that is bigger than Ed's within the film, or at least more expansive. This is the music that sometimes interrogates who he is, thus exceeding his own comprehension and the limits that other characters place on their questioning of him. Before we consider this music further, especially how it gestures towards the expansive domain of the Real, and how it parallels McGowan's definition of the Real gaze in particular, we should pay attention to another important voice of resistance to Ed within the film itself.

RESISTANCE TO THE SYMBOLIC, TO THE FATHER

Though *Bigger Than Life* focuses on Ed's extremely divided subjectivity, the film also represents his son Richie's shifting awareness within the Symbolic order. We perceive the boy's painful separation from his mother, especially in one scene where Ed forces his son to complete mathematical problems in a study separate from the communal family space. Ed's insistence on Richie completing his work means that the dinner Lou prepares for their family is left for hours. Lou sneaks into the study when Ed leaves it for a few minutes to give Richie a glass of milk. The scene resonates with several psychoanalytic principles: the "necessary" separation from the mother in the Symbolic order, the emphasis on forms of language (both words and mathematical symbols) as defining identity within the Symbolic order, the boy's frustration with asserting himself in relation to the father, the child's desire for a return to the pre-lack union with his mother (the milk signifying his life as an infant), and the impossibility of returning to the pre-lack moment (Richie remaining stuck in a room with his father after Lou brings him milk). Throughout this scene there is a notable absence of music. When Lou sneaks in some milk to Richie, the quiet of the scene makes them seem even more vulnerable to Ed.

Because the film emphasizes Richie's vulnerability to his father, it is telling that the first sound associated with the boy is a horse whinnying. We hear this when Ed returns home from work in the film's first sequence and he finds Richie watching a western shoot-out on television. The boy is thus watching a genre of film that is much-associated with defining masculinity through violently competitive control. The sound of a horse whinnying immediately relates to Richie's later protests against his father's many efforts to "rein in" his behavior. Though Richie must succumb to Ed's demands, he also frequently resists them. And it is Richie's rejection of his father's control that leads into the final climactic scene of confrontation, a point that is musically reinforced.

Though Raksin's music is often absent or minimal in those scenes when Ed is most frightening, except to mark culminating moments or transitions, it *does* underscore Richie's desperate search for the cortisone medicine. Richie's search leads into the biggest confrontation between father and son. As Richie frantically rummages around his father's belongings, the music gradually rises in repeated phrases until it reaches a *forte* peak when he finds the incriminating bottle of pills behind a mirrored chest drawer. Though Richie is often visually dwarfed within the frame, the music seems to "enlarge" his actions. Yet another sudden and elongated chord stinger accompanies Richie's slamming the drawer shut so hard it bangs against the wall. He then suddenly perceives his father's face in the mirror above him [1:17:50–1:17:57]. The moment of Ed's appearing where his son's face "should" be, along with the stinger chord and the bang of the drawer, triply marks the psychoanalytic significance of the moment. That Richie's very reflection has been replaced by the father visually indicates his being stuck within the Symbolic order without even the fantasy of a pre-lack state left (see Figure 4.15). Ed's

FIGURE 4.15 A terrifying moment: the son's reflection is "replaced" by his father's image.

taking over the reflection emphasizes the Oedipal power of the father who threatens annihilation. Raksin's music stresses this with terrifying blatancy.

Upon finding his son with the bottle of pills, Ed is immediately horrified by what he perceives to be Richie's betrayal in alliance with Lou. In the argument that follows, during which Ed accuses Richie of being a liar, Richie confronts Ed with having talked up his own football career even though he was "only a substitute" and shouts that he wishes Ed were "dead rather than the way [you] are now!" When Richie then withdraws into the bathroom with a phone to call the doctor, Ed cuts the cord. This action in itself references the moment of physical separation between child and mother, a point emphasized by the film as it shows Lou in a separate room on a different phone, aurally and visually "cut" from her son. "You've done a bad thing, I've got to think about it" says Ed to Richie, a comment made especially terrifying by the quiet around it.

THE REAL

Within the diegetic space, Ed often takes action to control sound: he cuts off the phone, he switches off the television as Richie watches it, he complains about the "jingle-jangle in, jingle-jangle out" of the milkman, and in the final sequence he puts the television back on to cover the sounds of Lou's protests against his sacrificing Richie. However, as we shall explore, the final sequence features a sound track that emphasizes resistance to Ed as well as gesturing towards that which is bigger than him and all of the life in the film. Because the music ultimately demands we perceive the film from a vantage point that far exceeds its characters, it resonates with McGowan's reading of the skull in Holbein's *The Ambassadors*.

After Ed has locked Richie in his room, Raksin's music returns to reinforce the terror of the power he claims. At this point, Ed holds a Bible and quite literally assumes the role of God in his own home. He speaks to Lou about "saving" Richie by sacrificing him, and his "justification" is the near-sacrifice of Issac by his father Abraham as told in the Old Testament. The underscoring for their conversation includes some poignant and subtly foreboding variations on the second marriage theme, emphasizing that the marriage itself is now deeply damaged [1:20:22–1:21:19]. Eventually, some new musical material with prominent low timpani beats pulses underneath the thickening musical texture [1:21:20–1:22:08]. This music is suggestive of a march towards death or a sinister call to arms. It emphasizes the terror of Ed's escalating urgency as well as pressing home the devastating action that he proposes by reading aloud how Issac was laid upon an altar. The music suddenly stops after Lou points out that God intervened and prevented Abraham's death, to which Ed declares "God was wrong!" His declaration is marked by the sudden musical silence around it, followed by *fortissimo*, thick, and dissonant chords on low brass [1:22:10–14]. Ed then restates his plan to sacrifice Richie with a grim insistence on its inevitability. His insistence is punctuated with yet more funeral-connoting music, including more prominent timpani beats and rising strings [1:22:15–1:23:07]. We shall refer to this material as the theme of sacrifice.

In one last attempt to reason with Ed, Lou appeals to him with photographs of Richie as a baby. Along with her effort to engage his eyeline on each image, the music returns to the second marriage theme in a variation that begins plaintively and becomes frantic [1:.23:.08–-1:.23:.29]. "Put it away" shouts Ed, as if consciously shouting over the non-diegetic music. Lou's attempts to protest are further undone by the piercing stinger of the telephone [1:.23:.29]. Soon thereafter, the marriage theme resurfaces only to be interrupted yet again [1:.24:.10–-1:.24:.24]. As the theme is reheard, Lou calls out to Ed, as if in some last-ditch effort to bring him back to her, and then sinks to her knees at his feet. He pulls her up and kisses her passionately before hastening back up the stairs to Richie. But Lou holds him fast and kisses him back before he can push her away. Now the marriage theme is at its loudest and most painfully beautiful. The music thus emphasizes what they have both lost, but seems especially "with" Lou in this. [1:.24:.12–-1:.24:.29]. Her kissing Ed back even seems to *make* the cue last longer, but the theme falls apart into a low, minor-key descending scale when Ed does push

FIGURE 4.16 Richie holds out the football to his father in a tragic moment of compliance.

her away, signifying her dwindling hope [1:.24:.24–-1:.24.:26]. Then the score quickly returns to the theme of sacrifice [1.:24:.30–-1:.25:.09].

Through this entire scene, Raksin creates a musical war between the two characters that amplifies their separation from each other. Eventually their conflict is not resolved but literally closed off and drowned out: when Lou tries to persuade Ed to go on a final walk with her, and he quickly guesses that she intends to walk them past the police station, he locks her in a hall wardrobe. He then switches on the television to block out her screams. The television is playing a fairground scene that is bizarrely and disturbingly evocative of childhood play. The music is in obvious counterpoint to the violence and dangerous delirium of the final sequence: it suggests a descent into grotesque horror [1:25:18].[28]

As Lou screams from her confined space, Ed runs up the stairs with a blade for killing Richie. Upon his entering Richie's room, the boy's back is towards him and he holds out the football to his father in a gesture of heartbreaking submission (see Figure 4.16). As noted above, the football in itself is a loaded object, signifying Ed's hopes in Richie as well as Ed's past, and therein representing the endurance of the existing

---

[28] In sound-track studies, the term "counterpoint" is often used to refer to sound that plays ironically against the visual meaning of the scene: a famous example of this is the use of the upbeat pop song "Stuck in the Middle with You" during the torture scene of *Reservoir Dogs* (1992). This use of "counterpoint" is not to be confused with the purely musical application of the word to mean a texture of interweaving melodic strands.

Symbolic order. Ed's glowering entrance here is marked by two elongated stingers—one synthesized and one brass-heavy—which accompany terrifying, distorted point-of-view shots of Richie from his perspective [1:25:36–1:25:52]. This is the one and only time that the film takes us into Ed's mind alone, for up until now even those stingers that are "with" his action invite some ironic separation from him. Meanwhile, the fairground music continues in its disturbing mania as Wally suddenly arrives, frees Lou, and battles Ed on the stairs. As the two men begin a physical fight, they crash against the stairs, destroying the banister. The sound and sight of the banister breaking represents what now seems to be an irreparably broken home.

Once Ed is overcome by Wally, and eventually rendered unconscious on the floor, Richie finally switches off the television [1:27:07]. The sudden silence is its own sonic shock as well as a relief. The next scene continues the relative quiet as Lou and Richie wait for news at the hospital. Since the film has primed us to understand the danger of its quiet scenes, this aural subsidence cannot represent straightforward relief. Finally, a doctor enters the scene and frankly explains to Lou that Ed may be psychotic. However, the doctor also claims that if Ed can remember and face everything that has happened "it'll be alright." During their conversation, one in which Lou adamantly states (and restates) her "faith" in Ed, the music parallels her emotion through its affective vibrato strings and the strain of wide leaps [1:29:20–1:30:01], and then a variation on the first marriage theme [1:30:02–1:30:47].[29] As Lou speaks to the doctor of having "faith in [her] husband," the second marriage theme also returns [1:30:48–1:31:23]. More disturbingly, the score then segues into the theme of sacrifice, albeit at a quieter and slower (much less overtly threatening) tempo than before [1:31:24–1:31:42]. The return to this theme then leads into a chord that reverberates with the same synthesized elongation that we have heard for numerous stingers earlier in the film, including those moments when Ed was gripped by a most vicious seizure or shown as most terrifying in his psychosis (especially in the climactic moment of his almost murdering Richie) [1:31:44–1:31:48]. The overarching musical message is that, although dire harm has been avoided, the ultimate threat housed in Ed's body is still present.

---

[29] We should frame Lou's assertions of faith in Ed, and her eventual inability to resist his need for her to be "closer, closer" in the context of 1950s American gender politics. When Erich Kuersten unsympathetically pronounces Lou as "perhaps even more at fault for letting denial and fear prevent her from contacting the doctor, putting her own child in danger rather than risking hurting her husband's feelings" (2010), he not only ignores how the film musically prompts our sympathy for her (especially through the second marriage theme) but also the historical context of her entrapment within the effort to be a "good wife." It also matters that Lou vocally stands up to Ed on several occasions, and that she breaks the mirror in which he views his ideal-I, as is amplified by Raksin's stingers.

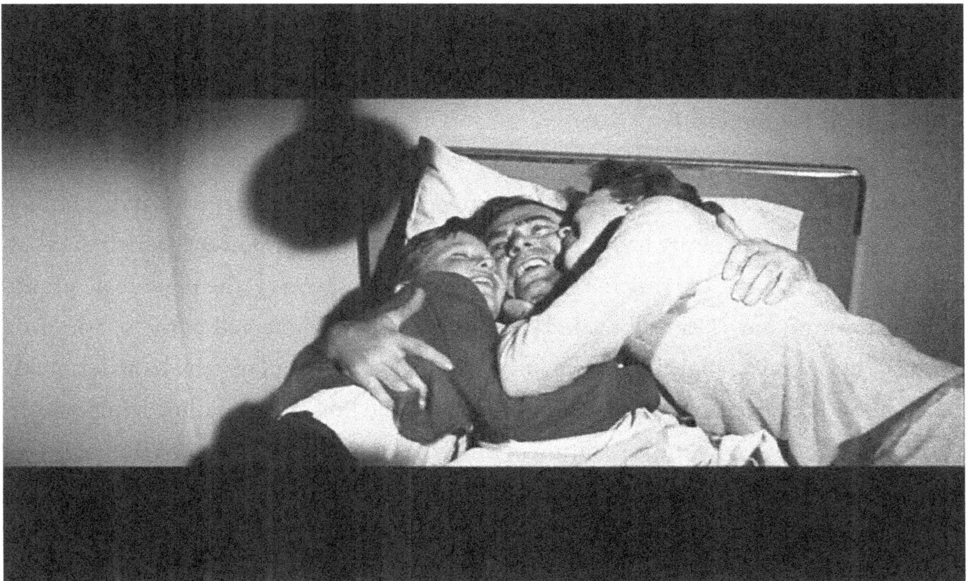

FIGURE 4.17 Ed, Richie, and Lou are united in their final embrace.

The final scene shifts to Ed's hospital bedside and his making a demand upon his waking: in response to the bright light above him, he says "turn out the sun." The line in itself complicates an immediate positive understanding of his gaining consciousness. Then the disoriented and just-conscious Ed tells a doctor "you're a poor substitute for Abraham Lincoln," only to gasp upon seeing his family with the other doctors in the room. He then connects their presence with the name of "Abraham" in its previous sacrificial context. The extreme shift in what "Abraham" means in a matter of seconds aurally emphasizes a sense of uneasy and sudden change. Because Ed is disoriented, Lou kindly says through teary eyes "you sort of fell down the stairs," a selfless effort at ignoring the devastation to the family home that has come with her husband's psychosis. Ed calls Richie over to him, and soon regains his memory enough to ask "did I hurt you?" He asks Richie this with some urgency, clutching his son's arms. The doctor reassuringly emphasizes that "it's important to remember." Upon a cut to the corridor just outside the room, we see a doctor switching off the red light above the door that has been switched on as a signal of medical danger. When Ed then calls his family to him, and implores them to be "closer, closer," there is the last music cue: final phrases from both marriage themes followed by a fanfare for "the end" [1:34:52–1:35:19] (see Figure 4.17).[30]

---

[30] The fanfare fits with what Foundas refers to as the "Production-Code-imposed 'happy' ending" (2008).

INTERPRETING THE FINAL SEQUENCE

The final sequence of *Bigger Than Life* has a sound track that exceeds the comprehension of all its characters. It also communicates a *critically* overseeing perspective. One of the last lines from a doctor—"it's important to remember"—surely connects with how the last musical cues reference many previous moments of pain, tension, conflict, and loss. The final sequence has a cumulatively terrifying sonic power through the escalating arguments, the warring themes of marriage and sacrifice, the perversely prominent fairground music, the elongated stingers of the telephone and of the synthesized chords, the sounds of fighting between Wally and Ed (particularly the banister breaking), the sudden silence after the television is switched off, and the unnerving quiet of the hospital followed by the reiteration of the film's most perturbing as well as poignant musical material. "It's important to remember" everything that precedes the doctor switching off a red light, and the film's final fanfare, especially all that undermines a straightforward sense of resolution. The cumulative impact of the aural elements is akin to the ever-present skull in Holbein's painting, even if we cannot perceive it right away.

At the very least, we must perceive the inadequacy of the final fanfare to answer all the disturbance that precedes it. Kite argues that "the film couldn't possibly resolve itself [. . .] within the confines of Hollywood's Production Code" and that the final scene "of harmonious resolution is resoundingly slurred through dissonance in the staging" (2010). Though Kite uses a musical term ("dissonance"), he focuses on non-musical elements: the "ferocity" with which Rush delivers Lou's lines about "faith" in Ed, even "after the aborted passion play" of almost sacrificing Richie, as well as the shots of Richie underneath the red light just outside his father's room, the shadows of barred windows behind the doctors and family, and the last shot of one doctor's "ghastly, cavernous smile." In contrast to all these details, he argues that "the score heaves toward the heavens," thus ignoring its mixed messages. Notwithstanding the final fanfare (which sounds like stock music more than Raksin's *per se*), the overall sound track certainly stresses the fragility of the final restorative image.

In the context of challenging Mulvey's use of Lacan in critiquing mainstream Hollywood cinema, McGowan argues that the extent to which cinema upholds the status quo of the Symbolic order may in itself point to the fragility of the same order: remember that "even the most ideological film testifies to the point of failure of ideology, of its need for a fantasmatic supplement" (McGowan 2003, 40). McGowan's statement resonates most with the final sight of Ed, Lou, and Richie in an embrace. The final image of the family is itself a willful fantasy, an attempt to obscure the trauma of everything that precedes it. When Ed urges his family "closer, closer," the moment is as desperate as it is sweet: the fractures we have seen in the family are too deep to be healed, especially since the film's sound track has made us feel every moment of literal and figurative pain.

And the source of all deep pain in the film is Ed. Though he is a doubly powerful patriarch as father and teacher, the film is deeply critical of how he exerts control, even to the extent that his urging Lou and Richie "closer, closer" might be interpreted as another form of force. Though the film's music sometimes works for him, especially as it stresses his experiences of physical pain, the score also repeatedly punctuates those moments when he makes declarations and decisions that are questionable or dangerous to others. The music is, therefore, an important regulation of his power, especially since no one in the film world itself is able to exert clear-cut control over him. Because the music is consistently alarmist about or critical of Ed, the final fanfare sounds forced, contrived, and disingenuous. Put simply, the structure of the entire film places a limit on how much we can hear the fanfare "straight." To return to McGowan again: "when film employs fantasy but at the same time reveals the limit that fantasy comes up against, it takes us to an encounter with the traumatic Real" (40).

The final embrace of *Bigger Than Life* can be read as a fantastical attempt to reduce or limit the destructive energies of the film. But this goes against the grain of the overall film experience as it gestures towards that which defies containment. The disturbing implications of the film exceed that which can be contained within a family, a domestic space, a medical profession, or a social order. The title alone also suggests that which exceeds our comprehension, and also leads us back to Žižek's definition of the Lacanian Real. This realm cannot be reduced to words, but it is surely evoked by the traumatic implications of Raksin's score.

/// 12 /// **SHUTTER ISLAND**

PLOT SUMMARY

The action of *Shutter Island* focuses upon Teddy Daniels (Leonardo DiCaprio), a US Marshal leading an investigation into the disappearance of a woman, Rachel Solando (Emily Mortimer). Solando is a patient at Ashecliffe on Shutter Island, a mental institution housing only the most violent of criminally insane offenders. Teddy is accompanied by his new partner, Chuck Aule (Mark Ruffalo), as he questions the head doctor named Cawley (Ben Kingsley), the nurses, and the wardens in charge of Solando's care.[31] During the investigation Teddy is haunted by memories of his dead wife, Dolores Chanel (Michelle Williams) (see Figure 4.18).

Teddy is also haunted by his experiences as a US solider at the liberation of Dachau concentration camp at the end of World War II. He explains to Chuck that Dolores was killed by inhaling smoke after a man named Andrew Laeddis burned their apartment down and that he himself killed many Nazi officers. Teddy thus establishes himself as the victim of a domestic tragedy as well as one who faces his own part in the horrors of war. In the opening scenes, the film places emphasis on Teddy's struggle with focusing in the present, and his letting go of the past, almost as much as his investigation.

When Solando is quite suddenly introduced to Teddy as having returned to the hospital, the narrative changes course: Teddy's investigation of her disappearance segues into his search for Andrew Laeddis at Shutter Island to avenge his wife's death. In the midst of Teddy's searching, Chuck is apparently killed, leaving Teddy alone in an environment that seems progressively (and inexplicably) more hostile: he is attacked by other patients, denied investigative requests by doctors, and chased around the island

---

[31] We use the name Solando to refer to the patient presumed missing as opposed to one of Andrew's children who is also called Rachel.

FIGURE 4.18 One of Teddy's flashbacks, a happy image of his marriage before his wife's murder.

by wardens for no ostensible reason. All the while, a vicious storm is either imminent or taking over the island. Eventually Teddy's searching leads him to the lighthouse office of Dr. Cawley. Then follows a crucial revelatory scene during which Cawley explains that Teddy has invented the story of Laeddis as a fiction to protect him from the truth of his own personal tragedy: he himself killed his wife after discovering she had murdered their three children and invented a new identity for himself (as "Teddy") because he could not forgive himself. As part of this explanation, Cawley points out that Teddy Daniels and Rachel Solando are anagrams for Andrew Laediss and Dolores Chanel, the real names of the protagonist and his wife. In other words, Teddy Daniels and Rachel Solando are but fictional constructs of the protagonist's mind. Cawley then reveals that every scene on Shutter Island up to this point has been "staged" to play out Andrew's fantasy in the desperate hope he will realize the truth once the entire fantasy is finally played out. Chuck re-enters the film at this point, revealing himself to be a psychiatrist at Ashecliffe named Dr. Sheehan, and Andrew is shocked into attempting to kill Dr. Cawley before finally resigning himself to what the two doctors say. Following the revelatory scene, there is the only flashback that we can trust according to Cawley's explanations: here, we see Andrew return home from work to discover Dolores has drowned their children. Shortly thereafter, we see Andrew embrace and shoot Dolores dead in a moment of excruciatingly intimate retaliation. After seeing this tragic memory, presumably as Andrew remembers it, we see him retreat from his life one more time. In the final scene of the film, Andrew apparently chooses to "become" Teddy again, thus shielding himself again from his own tragic reality. He is escorted away by the nurses who will prepare him for a lobotomy that will disable his violent tendencies and destroy who he is. Ironically, as the film ends there is no visible sign of a storm having ever happened on Shutter Island.

For the sake of clarity, we shall refer to the main character as he exists in full awareness of his own actions as "Andrew," and the fantasy self that he creates as "Teddy." We make this distinction purely for convenience and not to suggest that analyzing him is a straightforward process.

THE OVERARCHING PATTERNS

Shutter Island is an adaptation of a novel by Dennis Lehane that incorporates an unusual level of attention to aural detail. Indeed, every key moment of the protagonist's psychological disturbance is sonically marked by Lehane. The soundscape of the novel is dominated by distorted voices, unnerving laughter, shouts, screams, howls, natural disturbances, reverberating echoes, and uncannily shifting acoustics. Sounds take shape and seem to move around Teddy menacingly: he hears patients screaming *as* howls that slide up stairs (Lehane 2003, 98), and he hears the mocking giggles of orderlies floating to his table (108). Sound is also associated with irrepressible memories: the past is like a "gale in his ears."[32] Equally, the stormy sounds of nature take on terrifying anthropomorphic agency: he "could hear the wind find the thick stone wall behind him, pounding on it like fists until he could feel tiny shudders of impact on his back" (145). During the storm he perceives lights going on above him "in a series of liquid cracks that sounded like bones breaking underwater" (246). Most painfully, he perceives the sonic presence of his dead wife: "he could hear her. Even as he couldn't picture her, he could hear her in his brain" (266). Towards the end of the novel, as Andrew finally acknowledges the truth of his having killed her, sound and sight merge most troublingly. When he pulls the trigger on Dolores "the sound of it came out of her eyes" (363), and later "He saw the sound of his gun in her eyes" (366). Sound is a palpable and mobile presence, as well as

---

[32] In another memorable passage, Teddy explains his failure in military service in sonic terms. He tells Chuck he was discharged from the army to radio school where he "blew a decoding" of "enemy position coordinates" (142). Teddy remembers the noise of the radio: "screams, static, crying, static, machine gun fire followed by more screams and static and more static. And a boy's voice, in the near background of all that noise, saying 'You see where the rest of me went?'." This description connects with much of the experimental music in the film that features disturbing fragments of speech and sound (such as Nam June Paik's *Hommage à John Cage*).

a *visual* reality in Lehane's text. Scorsese's film takes the aural emphases of the novel to another manipulative extreme.

Shutter Island is certainly a film that anticipates our hearing it *and* our being trapped by numerous forms of aural signification. Lacan famously stated that "in this matter of the visible, everything is a trap" ([1977] 1998, 93). With *Shutter Island*, this statement should be redirected to everything *audible*. After the revelatory scene with Dr. Cawley, we have to reposition ourselves in relation to everything we have heard up to that point, much like we have to re-see Holbein's *The Ambassadors* from a specific vantage point to perceive the skull. In this sense, the film achieves an aural form of anamorphosis. Much like the viewer must adopt a new angle to fully perceive *The Ambassadors*, *Shutter Island* requires a rehearing after subjecting us to a deliberately misleading sound track. Like perceiving the skull of *The Ambassadors*, this obligation to rehear is deeply disturbing as well as morbidly fascinating: our first sonic impressions have to make way for greater, frightening truths. Moreover, these truths exceed what may be contained within the film's Imaginary or Symbolic orders. In short, the sound track exposes us to an *experience* that evokes the magnitude of the Real.

Right from the outset, the sound track of *Shutter Island* compromises our ability to be sutured into the narrative, or to simply "get lost" in the process of aligning ourselves with the male protagonist. The film's self-conscious obfuscation of truth to the extent that we will knowingly strain to perceive it is there in the very first shot: a fade in on fog [0:48]. For a few seconds there is nothing to see before we can dimly make out part of a ship near the center of the frame [0:52]. Thus, *Shutter Island* immediately emphasizes the indistinct and obscured image. Along with the first sight of the ship we hear Ingram Marshall's *Fog Tropes*, a composition that blends ambient maritime sounds with reverberating brass notes that seem to "belong" to the ship on-screen but which actually come from the non-diegetic space.[33] We are led to logically connect image and sound, or to immediately perceive what Chion terms "added value": the sounds of the ship seem to "naturally" come from what is seen, and [are] already contained in the image itself" ([1990] 1994, 5). What we cannot know is that the film has already duped us into believing a false audiovisual relation. Everything we hear actually comes from the non-diegetic space, a precomposed piece of music beyond the diegetic realm of the film. And so begins the film's pattern of representing a broken reality that reveals itself as such only after the impression of coherence. By the end of the film, the entire narrative has unraveled as a broken reality, forcing us to re-understand everything that seemed

---

[33] In a making-of featurette on the Blu-Ray release of *Shutter Island* (Phillips and Toennies 2010), Scorsese himself says "you don't know quite whether it's a foghorn or it's music."

anchored in meaning. Thus the very form of the film relates to the brokenness of its main character, and this in turn resonates with both Freudian and Lacanian concepts of the divided self.

The music for *Shutter Island* is deeply disturbing and disorienting, and not only because many experimental cues blur the diegetic/non-diegetic distinction (like *Fog Tropes*). The soundtrack also pulls us in different directions because it features extremes, ranging from minimalist or avant-garde contemporary compositions (by John Cage, György Ligeti, Brian Eno, among others), to late Romantic music (by Gustav Mahler), to performances of popular songs from the 1940s and 1950s (by Lonnie Johnson, Kay Starr, and Johnnie Ray). Robbie Robertson, songwriter-guitarist of the Band, was the music supervisor for *Shutter Island*. [34] Instead of commissioning an original score for the film, the director Martin Scorsese asked him to use preexisting music. Though much of the film's visual content seems interdependent with its music to the extent that they seem precisely "matched," it is revealing that none of the music was originally composed for the film. No music here simply serves the film's visuals because every music cue has its own pre-given internal logic. Though the cues are incorporated to complement on-screen action, and are reused enough that several pieces work like leitmotifs because their meaning evolves through the various actions of the film,[35] the music is never a straight accompaniment for what we see. Consider, by contrast, how often Steiner's music for *The Searchers* is tailored to moment-by-moment visual details of the film. Equally, consider that even when the ostensible meanings of Steiner's music work against the grain of the film's visual (or most obvious) emphasis, there is always a direct correlation between what he scored directly for the film and what happens within it.

In further contrast with Steiner's score, *Shutter Island* lacks set themes for individual characters. Moreover, the eclectic cues for different scenes of *Shutter Island* cannot easily (whether harmonically or melodically) blend like Steiner's cues for *The Searchers*. Indeed, *Shutter Island* incorporates numerous blocks of musical sound that compete

---

[34] The Band was an American-Canadian roots rock group that recorded ten studio albums from 1968 to 1998. (Roots rock is a hybrid genre drawing from blues, folk, and country music.) The original band members gave their final touring performance in 1976, which was immortalized in Scorsese's 1978 documentary *The Last Waltz* (see Sarchet 1994). Robertson has a long history of collaborating with Scorsese in various roles: he was composer for *Raging Bull* (1980), music producer for *King of Comedy* (1983), composer for *The Color of Money* (1986), music consultant for *Casino* (1995), executive music producer for *Gangs of New York* (2002), and music producer for *The Departed* (2006). Robertson writes that with *Shutter Island* Scorsese and he deliberately set out to create a sound track "unlike anything we'd ever done before" (Topspin Media 2012).

[35] It is appropriate to speak of the cues being only "*like* leitmotifs" because they are restated rather than presented in various incarnations through the film.

in terms of clashing tonalities, different forms of harmonic and melodic logic, and incompatible structures. The overall result is a profoundly disorienting experience that departs from several fundamental conventions of Classical Hollywood scoring.

Because the musical cues of *Shutter Island* cannot merge easily, when they *do* overlap the result is jarring rather than audibly smooth: it is a sonic experience of brokenness that cannot be forced away. This has particular poignant resonance in relation to the narrative which Andrew creates for himself in order to give "harmonious" reason and coherence to his own life. Much of the *mise-en-scène*, camerawork, and editing reinforces our alignment with Teddy throughout, but the sound track complicates this alignment from the beginning. Many music cues tear away from the film's visual messages or seems problematic in relation to them (again, consider *Fog Tropes*). Robertson's musical choices also repeatedly emphasize rupture, unconventionality, surprise, and ironic contrast: all of which come to the fore in the revelatory scene. It is as if the music always already knows what Teddy, and we along with him, cannot know until Dr. Cawley explains the truth.

THE MIRROR STAGE

Having established some aural patterns of *Shutter Island*, we now zoom in on the foundational Lacanian concepts and some specific music cues in relation to them. First, we focus on those musical elements of the film that bolster our understanding of Andrew's attempted regression to the Mirror Stage. Without being conscious of it (and whether or not it is within his capacity to be conscious of it), Andrew creates the "ideal-I" image of himself as Teddy. *Shutter Island* literalizes this Lacanian concept of self-deception by first showing the protagonist to us as a mirror reflection [1:12] (see Figure 4.19).

We see his reflection after his vomiting into a latrine and his first line is "pull yourself together Teddy, pull yourself together." Thus the film immediately connects the mirror image with an aural emphasis on his physical brokenness. At this point, Teddy's vulnerability seems merely biological, though we *might* also think we see the image of a man confronting his vulnerable self. What we cannot yet know is that at this point Teddy speaks to the specular image of himself, as one who only has the seasickness to worry about. If we have a Freudian understanding of the split psyche in mind, it becomes especially significant that his face literally wobbles as he looks in the mirror. "It's just water," he tells himself. But then, as if dimly aware of his own shifting state, he adds "It's a lot of water." The vocal emphasis on the overwhelming power of water in connection with Teddy's mirror image anticipates how we will learn to perceive his fluid identity.

FIGURE 4.19 The protagonist of *Shutter Island* as he first appears to us, a visual literalization of the Mirror Stage.

Teddy travels towards his initial investigation literally armed aboard the boat, riding the shifting state of water that symbolically parallels his fluctuating internal state. He also has the full authority of being a US Marshal behind him. That he is quickly identified as the lead investigator in the Solando case, as well as a US Marshal, establishes him as one of comparatively high power within the Symbolic realm: we know he has the socially sanctioned power to command, that he is trained for making logical deductions and taking decisive actions, and that he is also authorized to exert the full power of the law. Yet the fact that Teddy must look away from the mirror to be sick on the boat immediately suggests the fragility of his ideal-I (Teddy/the investigator/the US Marshal). In the next shots of the film's opening, Teddy climbs up to the boat deck to join his partner Chuck, and the scene features one of many obvious rear projections used in *Shutter Island*. This visual element most obviously echoes Hitchcock's work.[36] However, we can later understand that such rear projections also anticipate our understanding of how Teddy projects a false notion of the world onto everything around him.

---

[36] *Vertigo* (1958) and *Psycho* (1960) are among those Hitchcock films that make playfully obvious use of rear projections.

CO-CREATING (AND LOSING) THE "IDEAL-I"

As we explored in the introduction to psychoanalysis, the Mirror Stage allows the child to perceive an "ideal-I" who answers their actual experience of motor incapacity or lack of coordination. Equally, we might say that the concept of the Mirror Stage exists as a consoling perception of the self, even in adulthood. The fiction that Andrew creates for himself in being Teddy resonates on this figurative level. *Some* aural cues within the sound track of *Shutter Island* seem to support this fiction, especially because they apparently reinforce Teddy's perceptions. These cues also encourage the audience's complacency through their seemingly obvious, overdetermined, or overstated connotations. One crucial such example is Krzysztof Penderecki's Symphony No. 3, *Passacaglia* (*Allegro Moderato*). Though the film's first scene features the sonic indeterminacy of *Fog Tropes* (in terms of blurring the diegetic and non-diegetic divide, and distinctions between sound effects and music), this soon gives way to the overtly doom-laden connotations of the *Passacaglia* which underscores Teddy's entrance to Shutter Island. Right before this cue, Teddy and his partner Chuck are hypothesizing about the patients who live at Ashecliffe and, in response to Teddy's grim statement that they are "criminally insane," Chuck jokes that Marshals would hardly be needed if the inhabitants were merely "folks running around hearing voices and chasing after butterflies." After this strangely jocular comment the film cuts to the first sight of Shutter Island along with the low, overtly ominous string pulses of the *Passacaglia* [3:51] (see Figure 4.20).

FIGURE 4.20 The first grim sight of Shutter Island.

FIGURE 4.21 The first, overtly ominous string pulses of Krzysztof Penderecki's Symphony No. 3, *Passacaglia* (*Allegro Moderato*) (transcribed directly from the DVD).

Right away, the repetitions of one note (played an octave apart) suggest insistent dread, indicating Teddy's comprehension of great danger (see Figure 4.21). The entire piece is grounded in these repetitions of D. The note repetition in itself suggests that the threat is overstated, almost to the point of parody, especially as it is the musical follow-up to Chuck's strange jocularity. The music is mixed with sounds of wind which rise to the surface after the ship's captain says "storm's coming" [4:22]. Again, the sound track seems overdetermined in that it makes the same point in two ways.

The *Passacaglia* underscores Teddy and Chuck's first arrival at Shutter Island, and then their being met and driven by wardens to Ashecliffe [3:51–6:35]. The visual action alone includes several implied, rather than fully stated, warnings: a warden insists on removing Teddy and Chuck's weapons without providing an adequate justification,[37] the hospital grounds are shown surrounded by high walls with barbed wire which visually allude to concentration camps, and when the gates open at Ashecliffe they reveal garden grounds that seem too "neat" for an institution housing dangerous and criminally insane patients. The warden who confiscates the guns is a signifier of potential threat since he is played by Ted Levine, an actor best known for playing the killer in *The Silence of the Lambs* (more immediately identifiable through his voice than his appearance). This casting decision in itself lends a sense of danger, albeit in an allusively playful way.[38] But the music communicates a much more emphatic and relentless sense of doom than such suggestive visual details.

The *Passacaglia* begins with several sets of repeated low notes (like those in Figure 4.21) that are unpredictably spaced with sporadic rests. The low cellos first

---

[37] The reasoning behind this unarming is not made immediately explicit beyond the warden's citation of a particular regulatory code.

[38] Another senior guard at Shutter Island is played by John Carroll Lynch, the killer in *Zodiac* (2007), a man whose voice is no less distinctive.

carry these repeated notes and are soon reinforced by low percussion and heavy low brass. The deep register is emphatically stated to the extent that when mid-range strings take up the sets of repetition it is a sonic disturbance. The mid-range strings are accompanied by long dissonant notes on brass instruments and lower strings competing for attention. The texture thickens up rapidly, until after a few minutes high strings and piccolos enter with the repeated notes at the upper pitch extreme [6:21]. At this climactic, horror-connoting point, the *Passacaglia* accompanies shots of gates opening onto the hospital grounds. The music creates an impression of danger that escalates with breathtaking rapidity as Teddy and Chuck are driven beyond the gates. Ironically, the gates open onto a seemingly peaceful and pristine garden. Here, right after *Passacaglia* reaches its climactic peak, it suddenly stops [6:35], only to be ironically followed by the sounds of birds quietly chirping and the soft sound of a patient raking the grass.

The *Passacaglia* does not develop in terms of melodic or harmonic development so much as building repetitions and an increasingly layered texture. It is also structured in terms of sudden shifts rather than changes we might anticipate. The music seems fit for a dramatic and exceptionally perturbing climax, not the opening sequence of the introduction to the film's main setting. The music seems overly fatalistic because its *forte* to *fortississimo* build-up has the sonic effect of reaching a dreadful peak without any real musical groundwork being covered. The effect is disturbing enough that it leads us to expect a surprising investigation. But the warning is also extreme enough to suggest nothing will happen without the film's, Teddy's, *and our* over-anticipation of it. Of course, what we are being driven into here (along with Teddy) is not simply the mental hospital, but the beginning of an elaborately staged form of deception. When the film later breaks its own contract of overdetermining anticipation by completely redirecting its (and our) focus, it is all the more shocking.

There is another contract we enter into from the beginning of *Shutter Island*, without our even necessarily knowing it. Just as the infant relies upon the presence of another (usually the mother) in order to perceive their "ideal-I" separateness and wholeness, Teddy relies on us to maintain his "ideal-I" image. Indeed, the whole film leading up to the revelatory scene could be regarded as one that supports his perception of his own specular image. If we follow this logic, the first experience of perceiving *Shutter Island* largely gratifies the narcissistic possibilities of the specular image whereas any subsequent screening would bring the aggressivity associated with encountering the specular image more into play. If we also think back to Mulvey's work, *Shutter Island* incorporates visual elements that commonly encourage our identification with the male protagonist, including obvious point-of-view camerawork, and classical editing which privileges his movements and reactions. However, if we *listen* more carefully to the film, the sound track complicates this psychoanalytically crucial alignment from the start.

The sound track involves us in Teddy's experiences, but it also invites some critical distance.[39] Let us consider how Penderecki's *Passacaglia* is first used from another angle. The cue seems over-obvious but, upon closer analysis, it has a strong dual meaning. Most immediately, the music amplifies a sense of dread related to Teddy's investigation into Solando's disappearance as well as his arrival on the island. However, even if we register those disconcerting elements of the action mentioned above, the music still seems excessive. Because the music exceeds the danger connoted by the film's visuals, it allows the possibility of some critical distance.

Looking back on the first experience of *Shutter Island*, we can reinterpret, and find more than obvious meaning in the *Passacaglia* cue. The piece is, as mentioned above, built from the stressed repetitions of the one note, ranging from sets of two to a climactic point of fourteen stresses in a row. The aural impression is of being battered over and over again with the same point that *begins* at *forte* and only gets louder. The repeated and intermittent stresses on one note create a musical form akin to Morse code: this point ironically resonates with those skills of detection that Teddy reportedly has. But if the music is a form of "code," it is not a puzzle that can be understood according to routine patterns of harmonic progression or melodic development. The music itself therefore emphasizes the concept of that which has meaning but which is not easily decoded. In this way, the music is a sonic representation of Andrew's struggle to understand his own place in Shutter Island as well as aurally suggesting that he must be repeatedly hit with the truth after his many efforts to escape it. The music is, in short, only seemingly a clear-cut representation of the island's danger as Teddy perceives it.

Teddy's first glimpse of Shutter Island retrospectively represents the beginning of a journey into fantasy, one that ends in the rediscovery of *Andrew's* unbearable tragedy. The *Passacaglia* is most associated with the place of Shutter Island, establishing the place as a malevolent character in its own right. Life on the island means being surrounded by water and thus, symbolically speaking, being surrounded by that which is ever shifting. The music associated with the place also shifts in meaning once we understand that it anticipates the horror of what the protagonist will face there. After the revelatory

---

[39] Though we have been primarily focusing on music here, the sound effects of *Shutter Island* are just as alarmingly aligned with Teddy's neurosis, and the dialogue is as misleading as his perceptions: so, the entire sound track gives us no choice but to be drawn into Teddy's experiences as the "truth." Equally, every element of the sound track allows for critical distance because it misleads us, at least up until the revelatory scene.

scene, we can reinterpret the dread suggested by the *Passacaglia* as signifying Andrew's unconscious anticipation of where his story on Shutter Island will end: the annihilation of his regressive fantasy, the rediscovery of ultimate loss, the severance from his own ideal-I, the agony of re-entering a Symbolic order that can no longer allow for his regression, and the final choice to abandon himself entirely. Once we understand the true horror of Andrew's past, the music that seems sardonically overdetermined seems like *not enough*. In this context of re-understanding, the music is at least commensurate with the horror awaiting Teddy rather than an overstatement. Indeed, we might reasonably say no music would be enough to equal the horror of what he will relive by the end of the film. So, the music connects us to *Andrew*, and to Dr Cawley's full understanding of him, before we can even perceive it does so.

MUSIC OF THE IMAGINARY

Those moments when Teddy seems most ironically assured of who he is are also those in which he is most ensconced in the realm of the Imaginary—or at least enmeshed within his own efforts to re-create an ideal-I and to live a fantasy associated with his specular image. The music associated with his certainty about who he is, what motivates him, the truth of his past, and his own morality is the most sonorous, harmonically pleasing, and melodically driven in the whole film. There are two crucial pieces of music that bind us to Teddy in these terms. The affect of these two pieces is worth particular attention: Mahler's Quartet for Piano and Strings in A minor, a composition most associated with Teddy's concentration camp flashbacks; and Max Richter's "On the Nature of Daylight," a contemporary piece repeatedly associated with scenes with Dolores as Teddy perceives her in the past and present. Interestingly, Teddy himself has no "theme": he is, musically speaking, unanchored. So even if the film's visuals clearly focus our attention on his experiences and perceptions, the sound track seems much less restricted in terms of representing him.

We initially hear Mahler's Quartet for Strings and Piano in A Minor in the transition before Teddy and Chuck enter Dr. Cawley's home for the first time in the film [20:15].[40] The music is a kind of "answer" to the storm beginning to dominate the film, and it thus parallels Andrew's own willful effort to inoculate himself from the violent truth of his

---

[40] The cue ends when Teddy and Chuck leave Cawley's home, when it ironically overlaps with the very different, experimental musical logic of Ligeti's "Lantano" [26:19]. The extract from "Lantano," in turn, ironically overlaps with Johnnie Ray singing "Cry" as Teddy dreams of Dolores [27:33]. Such overlapping cues create the superficial impression of suturing between scenes, but this is undermined by the strangeness of the overlaps between clashing forms of music.

life. In the first scene at Cawley's home, Teddy and Chuck meet Dr. Naehring, another character who is doubly powerful within the Symbolic order as a man of medicine. Ironically, Teddy believes he can undermine Dr. Naehring's authority with disdained responses to his probing questions. For example, when Teddy refuses an alcoholic drink, and Naehring asks "isn't it normal for men in your profession to imbibe?," Teddy says he has heard that the psychiatric profession "is overrun with boozers and drunks." Naehring's question alludes to Andrew's alcohol dependency before his family tragedy, a point that retrospectively registers as veiled aggression. The fact that Dr. Naehring vocally expresses admiration for Teddy's "strong defense mechanisms" in this same conversation resonates with the use of Mahler. The music not only smoothes the visual transition from a stormy scene, but it is also an aural mediation of (or "defense" against) the subtextual aggression in Naehring's lines to Teddy.

At first, the Quartet seems to be non-diegetic, but it is soon revealed to be diegetic after Teddy sees Cawley's record player and the LP spinning around. Chuck is the first to comment on the pleasant surprise of this cue: "nice music" he flatly says, revealing his comparative ignorance about it. When Chuck then asks whether it is Brahms, Teddy quickly corrects him: "no [*pause*] it's Mahler."[41] Teddy's pausing before the composer's name throws weight on his identification of Mahler, which immediately connects him to the authority of the canonical music. Such a detail reinforces our impression of Teddy's authority within the Symbolic order: he is superior to Chuck in identifying an example of "high art."

The quotation from Mahler's quartet is the first sustained musical cue of *Shutter Island* that is melody-driven and harmonious, as well as being pleasingly dominated by long, arching phrases and clear call-and-answer patterns among the stringed instruments. Its pleasing sound seems to reinforce an impression of Teddy's relative authority. At the same time, the music also has its own inherent drama through its rising and falling dynamics, rhythmic shifts, and widely escalating ranges of pitch for strings and piano. The initial impression of sonic accessibility, at least compared with most other cues for *Shutter Island*, is displaced as the piece underscores the scene with increasing turbulence.[42] This, in turn, points to Teddy's increasing vulnerability through the scene.

---

[41] The emphasis on the music being attached to Mahler's name might prompt us to consider how the Quartet is used in relation to other filmic uses of his work. For a fascinating discussion of how Mahler's music is repeatedly attached to themes of death, homosexuality, and war on film, see Barham's survey article (2010).

[42] Because *Shutter Island* features so much experimental music, all of which is usefully incorporated within the tie-in double-CD, any melody is its own form of sonic shock. When we hear an extract from Kay Starr's performance of "Wheel of Fortune," for instance, we might well be struck by the melody, even if the sonic comfort of it is ironically complicated by the lyrics emphasizing the arbitrariness of luck, and the need for love. But the song is heard in a distorted, echoing form as Teddy begins his attempted escape

Teddy's connection to the music becomes more complex as his personal perception of it evidently triggers intermittent flashbacks to an image of concentration camp victims, and a scene at Dachau during which he confronts a Nazi commandant [21:06–21:12; 22:20–22:26; 23:01–23:17; 23:48–24:48]. The immediate beauty of Mahler's quartet is a strong contrast with the visual disturbance of the flashbacks: a painting of Hitler on the wall, bodies of concentration camp victims, and the commandant lying in a growing pool of blood with his face horribly disfigured by a gunshot wound. The commandant reaches towards a gun on the floor to commit suicide, but Teddy kicks the gun away, forcing the man to die a slower death. The use of "nice music" with this nasty scene makes the signification of Mahler complicated within the film context: though it is the most aesthetically pleasing sound we have heard up to this point, it is also soon attached to a scene of brutal violence. Moreover, it is the immediately unsympathetic Naehring, one whom Teddy soon identifies as a German Nazi, who in turn identifies the specific piece as Mahler's "Quartet for Strings and Piano, in A Minor." The unpredictably shifting associations of the music—from refinement to nastiness—indirectly point to Teddy's fragility.

The Quartet carries over the cross-cutting of this whole sequence—from the conversation between Teddy and Naehring to the Dachau flashbacks. This sonic continuity is presented in an atypically self-conscious way because the scenes are united by images of a record player with an LP spinning: it seems that the *same* music is playing across time. This detail underlines that Teddy's flashbacks are triggered by the music he hears in the present. Much later in *Shutter Island*, Cawley explains that Teddy "may or may not" have killed any Nazi officers. So, we cannot logically assume that the flashbacks we see are meant to reveal something verifiable beyond Teddy's desires. Thus, the music by Mahler is inextricably connected with Teddy's creation of a past self that lives up to his specular image.

The record player is itself an important prop in relation to Teddy's interior life and his self-deception. The motion of the LP spinning around and around is meant to mesmerize us: in one of the flashbacks to the scene of the dying commandant, a series of four consecutively closer shots show the record spinning around [23:06–23:08]. The visual effect is akin to a repeated musical note being played in slightly different ways, and is thus connected with the many aural patterns of repetition within the film. Teddy is himself a character caught in a spiraling pattern of self-defeating repetition: by the

---

from Ashecliffe [1:37:38–1:38:12]. Moreover, the song's specific and repeated mention of a wheel of fortune connects with the patterns of painful circularity within the film. In short, the film's melodies are like aurally "coming up for air" only to be drowned by the truth again.

end of *Shutter Island*, Cawley has revealed that Andrew has already lived the fantasy of being Teddy over and over before. The needle of the record player spins closer and closer to the center of the turntable but can never reach that center without the music stopping: this pattern of movement is one way of representing a Lacanian understanding of desire, and Teddy's futile circling within a fantasy in particular. The movement of the object itself parallels the idea of circling ever closer to the object of desire without ever being able to reach it. It suggests "the unfulfillable search for the eternally lost object," the *l'objet petit-a* (Hayward 2006, 317) (see Figure 4.22).

The connections between Mahler's music, the protagonist's vulnerable ideal-I, and his entrapment within never-ending circles of desire relates to how Max Richter's "On the Nature of Daylight" is used. This is the most poignant music of the film, especially because it underscores several of Teddy's visions of Dolores. The piece is first connected with a flashback with Dolores that Teddy imagines, one that includes multiple layers of fiction and construction. We first hear this music after she is shown confronting Teddy about his dependency on alcohol. His answer to her concern is simply "I killed a lot of people in the war," a defense that we later learn may or may not be true. Teddy then asks Dolores whether she is real and her response ironically conflates his question about her with an answer regarding Solando: "she's still here. . . she never left." Dolores lightly

FIGURE 4.22 The needle comes closer and closer to the center of the spinning record but can never reach it, a visual representation of never-ending desire.

FIGURE 4.23 The ostinato at the start of Max Richter's "On the Nature of Daylight" (transcribed directly from the DVD).

FIGURE 4.24 The main melodic line rises above the ostinato in Richter's "On the Nature of Daylight" (transcribed directly from the DVD).

smiles as she says this and "On the Nature of Daylight" begins [28:08].[43] The piece starts with an ostinato for strings (see Figure 4.23). There are six phrases like these, with some variation, before the melody finally enters on a violin at higher pitch (see Figure 4.24).

The music communicates the impression of a painstaking, patient but longing wait for the "answer" of a melody that will give the ostinato meaning. The music thus reinforces our understanding of Teddy's perpetual sense of loss. The ostinato and melody repeat together, rising in intensity and volume, but with only modest variation throughout the piece's six minutes. The structure thus emphasizes circling around the same

[43] Silverman explores how Hollywood cinema diegetically contains the female voice (1988, 45), especially through female characters who lose control over their own voices, or whose voices are subordinated to their bodies, or whose voices are lost to male characters speaking for them. In this context, Dolores's speech is unusually controlling. It is also a deeply threatening maternal voice. The maternal voice is interpreted by some, such as Mary Ann Doane, as a "sonorous envelope," a sound that connotes the safety and nurturing of the child, especially as they perceive it from within the womb. (At the cinema, a similar experience of the "sonorous envelope" can be created within the theatrical space (Doane 1980, 45).) Drawing on Chion, Silverman provides a sinister interpretation of the mother's voice that "not only envelops but entraps the newborn infant" (1988, 72). Chion even describes the mother's voice in terms of perverted nature, as "an umbilical web" ([1982] 1999, 61). Within *Shutter Island*, Dolores's voice is an enveloping and entrapping influence on Teddy, prompting him to remain regressed whenever he remembers her, involving him in circling patterns of repetition also represented by Richter's (and other) music.

musical material over and over, another aural corollary to Teddy's circling within a fantasy and around a desire that can never end.

In this flashback scene, the aural pattern of repetition is also connected to nature and disintegration. Throughout the scene, we see and hear ash falling through the room (evoking Dolores's death as Teddy first describes it), as well as hearing sounds of birds, crickets, and waves. Dolores turns to look out the window and we now see that half her back is burning. Teddy, horrified, puts his arms around Dolores and blood streams from her stomach. Here, the music is connected to that which begs belief and that which cannot be rationalized away. The circling structure of the repeated ostinato and melody resonate with Teddy's visualizing his wife's death in different ways, the representations of his unending efforts to make sense of losing her. The scene transitions to a long shot showing them standing together in the middle of the room raining ash (see Figure 4.25).

As the music builds, we can hear the sea moving in and out, and Dolores tells Teddy he has to let her go. "No," he repeatedly sobs in resistance, only to find that she turns to ash in his arms. Finally, the ash "turns" to water, and Dolores inexplicably evaporates, leaving water dripping from Teddy's hands. In the subsequent final shot of the scene, there are sudden fires burning all around him. So it is that the circling music becomes connected with elemental indeterminacy. Flash, ash, fire, water, and blood blend in the body of Dolores who literally slips from Teddy's grasp. The music is here also connected

FIGURE 4.25 Teddy and Dolores stand together in a room raining ash.

to the unthinkability of losing her, a notion visually represented by what is impossible. The scene is an expressionistic representation of how the protagonist not only relives but fails to make sense of their tragedy. The scene does, in this sense, point to the Lacanian Real as Žižek defines it. We see and hear an experience that represents an irreducible trauma, one that exceeds the limitations of language or sense. It comes in the form of a nightmare, as is made explicit in the sudden cut afterwards, one that takes us back to Teddy in a hospital bed as he gasps himself awake [30:20].

Richter's cue is repeated when Dolores re-enters Teddy's mind, such as when she "appears" in another patient's cell [1:14:43–1:16:30]. At this much later point, Teddy has stumbled upon George Noyce (Jackie Earle Haley), one who claims he has himself been attacked by Andrew and who attempts to make Teddy understand who he really is. After Noyce tells Teddy he must let Dolores go, she enters the scene, and Teddy protests, "I can't!" Noyce flatly tells him, "then you'll never leave this island, God help you," and sits down in resignation. Here Richter's music enters with Dolores, aligning itself with Teddy's deliberate refusal to let go of his union with her. The music plays non-diegetically until the scene ends, whereas Dolores's visual appearance is fleeting, further amplifying its lasting power.

Because the film pulls us emotionally into Teddy's narrative through such affective scenes, we have no choice but to be "with" Andrew in the shock of the later revelatory scene when he learns the truth from Cawley. However, when we perceive his deliberate movement away from the truth in the very last scene, we are irresolvably separated from him in our knowledge. In this context, some of the music playing for the film's final credits—Robbie Robertson's mix of Richter's "On the Nature of Daylight" with Dinah Washington singing "This Bitter Earth"—is especially significant. Here, Richter's music obviously recalls earlier scenes showing Dolores with Teddy but it is also made new through the combination with Washington's performance. The combination communicates the fantasy of a reconstituted body: though the pieces were written independently, the fusion of Washington's strong vocal performance with Richter's piece gives the impression of a finished coherent form, a deeply and disturbingly ironic point in relation to the destruction of Andrew's mind that is anticipated by the film's end. In the final credit sequence, this music is clearly heard at *forte* without distortion, interruption, or complication through competing sounds. This is especially striking since so much of the film features fragmented cues and accosting layers of indeterminate sound that seem *either* diegetic or non-diegetic (as in the case of *Fog Tropes*). Equally, the sounds of a hurricane dominate many scenes through the second half of the film. Thus, this music over the final credits communicates a return to relative calm, as well as harmony, fullness, and clarity. Ironically, such full aural connotations of restoration and reconstitution run against the grain of the song's lyrics. The opening verse is especially worth consideration:

> This bitter earth
> What fruit it bears
> What good is love
> That no one shares?
> And if my life is like the dust
> That hides the glow of a rose
> What good am I?
> Heaven only knows.

The song's lyrics allude to Dolores as she bore her children and as she disintegrates in Andrew's hands in the flashback previously discussed. We see Dolores's body destroyed three times in the film—she not only turns to ash and water, but she is also burned next to Cawley's car when Teddy sets it on fire, and finally shot by Andrew in the only true flashback. This makes the sense of reconstitution and wholeness in the film's final music all the more poignant. Before the film's end, Dolores is repeatedly incorporated within flashback sequences that emphasize Teddy's desire to return to her and to the plentitude associated with her: a point reinforced by Richter's music as well as by the exceptionally vibrant colors in these sequences. However, this desire to "return" to Dolores is aurally problematized by the going-nowhere repetitions of Richter's ostinato and melody, as well as the dead-end questions attached to that music through Washington's lyrics at the end. If Dolores represents Andrew's never-ending desire, she also represents his never-ending lack. In the haunting scenes where she appears with Teddy, she is a possibility that quite literally slips through this fingers and disappears. That the music which most fully "speaks" for her plays with the closing credits after Andrew has left our sight hauntingly reinforces their separation. The film's final music also reflects the agony that leads Andrew to his choice for oblivion in the last scene.

As Kathryn Kalinak explains, psychoanalysis often connects the pleasure of music with the pre-birth experience as well as the pre-linguistic state. As she writes, "From our earliest moments inside the womb, we experience the elements of music: the rhythmic patterns of our mother's heartbeat, breathing, and pulse as well as the pitch and dynamics of her voice" (2010, 29). Moreover, the newborn recognizes its mother's voice and first experiences it as "music." With this in mind, perhaps "Music allows us to experience what we are forced to repress in our adult lives: longings for a return to the original state of plenitude and fusion with the mother" (29).

This psychoanalytic exploration of the power of music to enable regression back to an ideal, pre-Symbolic state takes on special resonance in *Shutter Island* and with the representation of Dolores in particular. The primary catalyst for the film's action, as well as the climactic "explanation" for everything that happens to Andrew/Teddy, is the tragedy of Dolores drowning their three children. The children's bodies are ultimately returned to water: the womb becomes the lake where they die. In such a narrative context, no wonder our access to pleasurable music is all too fleeting, complicated, or ironic as it is throughout *Shutter Island*. And no wonder that the music which supports Andrew's regression into Teddy is problematized, or unfixed from stable meanings.

RESISTANCE TO THE SYMBOLIC

Just as Teddy's Imaginary self is aurally represented as ever-shifting and vulnerable, his Symbolic power is eventually stripped away. We are, in turn, meant to experience a loss of power within the Symbolic order of the film that is parallel to Teddy's own. This is most obvious in the revelation scene where Cawley undermines every key assumption we have been led to make through most of *Shutter Island*. Only then do we realize that the very form of the film uses our understanding of cinematic language against us. The "language" of cinema includes all visual and aural messages, and much more than dialogue or verbal elements alone. *Shutter Island*'s cinematic language includes several conventional means of visually aligning us with Teddy, especially point-of-view camerawork, classical editing, and expressionistic *mise-en-scène* (as in the flashback scene with Dolores discussed above). It also uses many music cues that seem to be overtly clear or overstated, as in the case of the *Passacaglia*. The seeming clarity of such audiovisual expression dupes us into becoming unknowing allies with Teddy in a fantasy narrative. However, once we realize that the film has been lying to us, along with Teddy, everything we have seen and heard must be re-understood. In other words, the "language" of the entire film changes in meaning.

Once we understand our own experience this way, we are in a position to fully hear *Shutter Island* better. First, we have to rehear *every* piece of dialogue within the film leading up to the revelatory scene.[44] The subtexts for every conversation Teddy has had within the film up to that point become suddenly manifest. Chuck's very first line to Teddy "You okay boss?"[1:59] is a strong example of a seemingly straightforward line that must be re-understood in terms of a loaded subtext. When we first hear the

---

[44] In "Behind the Shutters," Dicaprio explains that Scorsese directed all his actors to consider how the film would register on a second viewing, so much so that it was like "portraying two different performances." Scorsese adds that with a second or third screening, "every time you hear a line of dialogue it has a different meaning" (Phillips and Toennies 2010).

line, it seems like a banal but deferential enquiry after Teddy has been sick on the boat. The simplicity of the question belies everything we come to understand that Chuck does to preserve the fantasy for Teddy in the hope of helping him. When Chuck uses it again as he enters the revelatory scene as Doctor Sheehan [1:52:34], it communicates his enduring and compassionate care for Teddy: the respectful term "boss" is meant to soften what Teddy is hearing, everything that strips him of authority over the life he has been living.

Another, more heart-wrenching example is in the repetition of the words "why are you all wet baby?" (also rephrased as "Baby, why are you all wet?"). These words are first heard when the haunting presence of Dolores "appears" to be coming in from the storm to see Teddy at Aschecliffe [1:04:03]. We hear these words again at the beginning of the revelatory scene after Teddy desperately swims to the lighthouse in search of Andrew Laeddis only to meet Dr. Cawley who, knowing Teddy's interior life in all its intricacies, poses the question to him as one familiar with the "line" [1:45:47]. Finally, we hear Andrew say these words to Dolores in the tragic scene of his discovering she has drowned their children. Here again, we have a strong example of a line having obvious, trivial meaning, only to be entirely reused within the film so that we have to hear it differently. The words "why are you all wet baby?" first convey Teddy's routine concern for Dolores, but they become inextricably connected to the full revelation of an unthinkable and unique tragedy. The repetition of such words throughout *Shutter Island* parallels the obsessive repetition of music cues throughout the film, and the visual motif of records spinning around turntables. In the revelatory scene, when Dr. Cawley tells Andrew he has repeatedly "reset" himself, or replayed his fantasy, he compares it to "a tape playing over and over on an endless loop." All the aural repetitions of the film are connected to Andrew's compulsion to relive a fantasy as well as the agony of his reliving a tragedy.

Because numerous lines of dialogue within *Shutter Island* shift in meaning in such extreme ways, the entire screenplay suggests a Symbolic order that is vulnerable to change. Similarly, even that which seems most readily understood in terms of musical signification is turned on its head. Without our knowing it, the film primes us to rehear many music cues that subtly anticipate the about-face revelatory scene (the *Passacaglia* being only the first). For another example, there is the music that ominously underscores a scene in which Teddy (accompanied by Chuck) questions the nurses of Aschecliffe hospital in relation to the disappearance of Solando. During this scene [17:00–19:40], the nurses appear bemused by Teddy's urgent questioning, as well as seeming conspiratorially and intransigently unhelpful. The scene creates a sinister impression that the nurses are not only withholding information about Solando from

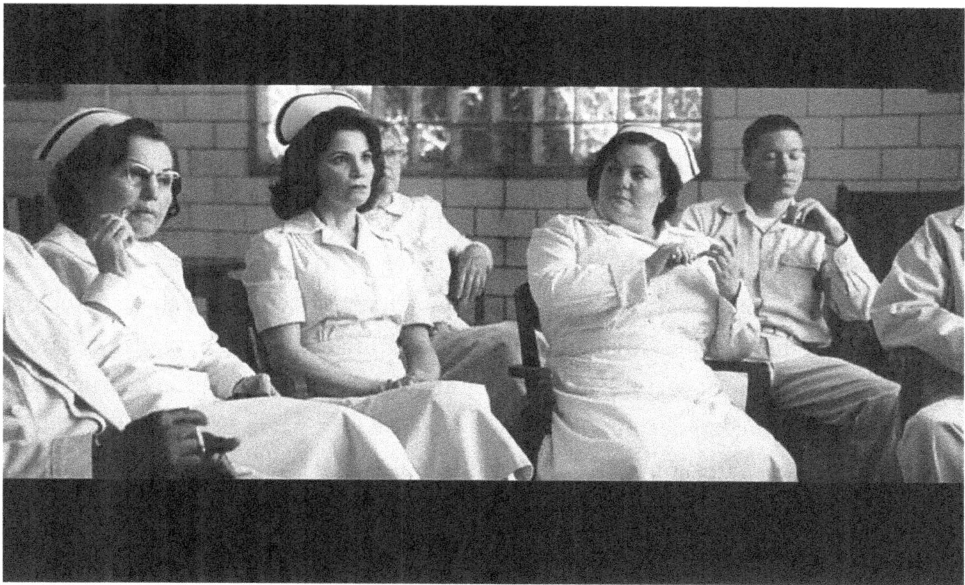

FIGURE 4.26 The nurses seem hostile towards Teddy's investigation, and they are unmoved by his efforts to find Rachel Solando.

Teddy, but also reveling in their power to withhold it from him. This impression is reinforced by their relatively unmoved, amused, or hostile faces in response to Teddy's rising anger (see Figure 4.26).

As Teddy's voice becomes more agitated, higher pitched, and insistent, the nurses' voices are comparatively flat, and devoid of emotional engagement. Most of the conversation of this scene is underscored by *Rothko Chapel 2* by Morton Feldman [17:07–18:04; 18:49–19:34]. The music communicates immediately sinister implications in relation to the nurses' lack of concern. It is structured in terms of wavering and wordless voices, phrases that repeat and rise in intensity without going anywhere harmonically, and sudden rests followed by new phrases. The voices evoke the humming of bees along with increasingly heavy drumbeats: the music's cumulative impression is of a rising threat about to sting. As part of the film scene, the music emphasizes the perturbing unpredictability of the conversation. It reinforces the division between Teddy and the nurses, as well as sonically reinforcing the sinister suspicions we share with him. *After* the revelatory scene, however, we understand that the nurses were participating in the actualization of Andrew's fantasy in the hopes of his returning to himself: the implications of the music are then ironized, and even undone. This is thus another strong example of our having to rehear the film's music after the revelatory scene. *Shutter Island* reframes itself contrarily to all our first audiovisual impressions. Because we live most of the film "with" Teddy, it is difficult to gain a foothold in this newly revealed Symbolic order.[45]

REHEARING *EVERYTHING*

The sound track is a crucial part of our understanding *Shutter Island*'s thematic emphasis on the fluidity of truth. Even the music that appears to have straightforward meaning becomes unanchored, much like Teddy. In connection with this overarching point, the music of the film is repeatedly connected to the shifting states of the sea. For instance, when Teddy and Chuck begin their investigation of Solando's room, after hearing from Dr. Cawley that she has seemingly "evaporated," we hear extracts of Philip Vandré's "Music for Marcel Duchamp" [13:11–13:44; 13:52–14:25]. Many repeated alternating notes on piano immediately evoke the ebb and flow of sea, aurally connecting with the concept of Solando's physical fluidity. A few minutes later György Ligeti's "Lontano" is mixed with the sea as Deputy Warden McPherson shows Teddy and Chuck the shore rocks against which Solando presumably died [15:32–16:59].[46] In being mixed with sounds of the sea, "Lontano" itself seems to hover between being ambient sound from within the diegetic space and non-diegetic scoring. The music also hovers between tonality and atonality, harmony and disharmony, taking melodic shape and resisting it. Minutes after this, when Teddy imagines Dolores, the transition to the scene begins with a portion of Johnnie Ray oscillating between two notes of the popular song "Cry" (as he sings the lyric "if your heartaches seem to hang around too long") [27:33–27:59]. Here the oscillating notes (again, a sonic parallel to the ebb and flow of the sea) relate to the fluid relation between past and present for Teddy, as well as his aching vision of Dolores slipping through his fingers like water. Much later in the film, the sounds of the hurricane on Shutter Island (lightning, thunder, and rain) merge with John Adams's "Christian Zeal and Activity" [55:06–56:19; 56:34–56:54]. This aurally accompanies the onset of Teddy's migraines after a confrontation with Solando, and imposes the disturbance inside his head on us. The piece itself is among those rare cues of the film that are immediately pleasing to the ear in being consonant, tonal, driven by tight harmonies among strings and woodwind, and shaped by sustained notes. In the recording used, the piece includes a Christian sermon about believing in Jesus's presence and His

---

[45] One might argue that the climactic revelations of any thriller entail having to "rehear" or reunderstand everything, but *Shutter Island* takes this to a non-generic extreme.

[46] The use of György Ligeti's "Lontano" is allusively impactful because it is also featured in *The Shining* (1980), a film no less disturbing in psychoanaytic terms.

healing.[47] The sermon is a form of "melody" or leading line supported by a harmonic texture of strings. Within the film, the music communicates faith and compassion which clashes with the hard sounds of the hurricane. At the same time, the music and sound effects are mixed in such a way that they are entangled: the musical emphasis on faith and compassion cannot be separated from the storm which we later learn is yet another outward manifestation of Teddy's broken and ever-changing self.

THE REVELATORY SCENE, AND AFTER

It might seem that, in the revelatory scene, the fluidity of truth ends because the new Symbolic order comes to the fore with authoritative clarity. Dr. Cawley, the most sympathetic as well as authoritative embodiment of Symbolic authority reveals the whole truth of Andrew/Teddy with such attention to detail and emphasis on logic that his words cannot be rejected. Moreover, Ben Kingsley delivers the revelatory speech with unwavering conviction and kindly deliberation (see Figure 4.27).

The revelatory scene seems to move at a rapid rhythm in that it includes many narrative shocks: in just a few minutes we learn that the story of Solando was false, Teddy has been medicated at Ashecliffe as a patient for two years and is suffering withdrawal, Andrew has a severe psychiatric condition which involves living within fantasy to escape the truth, Teddy has been living in his fantasy for two years, Teddy "is" Andrew Laeddis, Andrew has "injured orderlies, guards, other patients," Andrew was at Dachau "but may or may not have killed any guards," he is the "most dangerous patient," he "almost killed" Noyce for calling him "Laeddis," and unless he can be brought back to sanity right away the hospital board has determined he will be lobotomized [1:45:38–1:52:15]. Moments after Dr. Cawley's explanation of all this, Chuck quietly enters the scene, revealing that he faked his own death and that he was a mere role played by Dr. Sheehan who has been Andrew's psychiatrist for two years. At this point, Teddy's eyes begin to water up, a physical representation of his blurred perception of the truth.

---

[47] In his memoir *Hallelujah Junction: Composing an American Life,* John Adams refers to "Christian Zeal and Activity" as the "second panel" in a musical tripytch called *American Standard,* each part of which he intended to be "a deconstruction of a "standard" American musical form" (2008, 74). He refers specifically to "Christian Zeal and Activity" as a dislodged form of the "strict homophony" associated with the traditional hymn structure (75). His score invites the performer to add "extra-musical material." For the first performance, Adams himself added a late-night recording of a radio talk-show host arguing "What is God?" with another man who eventually reveals himself to be a preacher. This version was on the original LP recording produced by Brian Eno in 1973. Later, Adams composed a "tape collage of an evangelical preacher" speaking of Christ's healing the "withered hand," and this version was recorded by the San Franciso Symphony in 1986 (75). The latter version is the one we hear in *Shutter Island.*

FIGURE 4.27 In the revelatory scene, Dr. Cawley tells Andrew the truth with compassionate care as well as authority.

This entire revelatory scene is one of the film's biggest aural surprises in that it is comparatively quiet. After the tumult of so much in the *Shutter Island* sound track (including the *Passacaglia*, the storm, and the cumulative effect of repeated experimental cues like *Rothko Chapel 2*), the comparative quiet of the revelatory scene sets it apart. This quiet not only allows us to take in everything Dr. Cawley says, it gives his words particular weight. There is no music to amplify, mediate, or misdirect us as he finally reveals the truth to Andrew: instead, there are the bald words and incidental sound effects of a diegetic space newly defined in relation to Andrew's true identity. The absence of music or loud diegetic sound amplifies the impact of what happens next: panicked by the unbearable truth that Dr. Cawley reveals to him, Andrew seizes a gun and fires it directly at Cawley. The sound of his shooting works as an extreme stinger as we see blood spattered behind Cawley, obscuring the board of anagram names he has shown to Andrew as part of his explanation [1:55:16–1:55:17] (see Figure 4.28).

When the camera whip pans around and back to Sheehan and then Cawley to show the same board with no blood, we realize the stinger sound of gunfire is an extreme example of aural deception. This is the film's culminating example of sound designed to manipulate us into an experience in accordance with Teddy's perception. The difference in this moment is in the suddenness with which it happens and is, in turn, revealed to be a lie: Dr. Cawley explains that Teddy's gun is itself nothing but a prop, and Teddy subsequently breaks it easily in his hands. Cawley then forces Teddy to look

FIGURE 4.28 Teddy fires his gun, splattering Dr. Cawley's blood over the anagrams that expose his true identity.

at photographs of his dead children—Simon, Henry, Rachel—the last of whom has been seen in earlier flashback scenes involving prisoners at Dachau and Solando's murdered children as imagined by Teddy. Though his forcing Andrew to confront images of his dead children may seem cruel, Cawley's tone of voice always communicates a level of compassion. Suddenly Dolores enters the revelatory scene along with her daughter Rachel (Ruby Jerines). The photographic image seems suddenly actualized. And the uncanny effect of this is reinforced by Dolores's entrance being anticipated by a sound advance of her speaking to Teddy: "I'm so sorry baby, I told you not to come in here."

The sequence that follows includes the only reliable flashback. By implication, "to come in here" means not only entering the lighthouse, but also entering into the danger of the truth. The opening of the flashback features three disparate music cues that meaningfully compete with each other [1:57:47–1:58:51].[48] The first prominent cue is a part of "Tomorrow Night" sung by Lonnie Johnson in 1947, a popular song contemporary with the scene from the past. The song's lyrics are questions, all of which relate to the anxiety of a lost love.[49] Thus, even a fragment of the song is enough to amplify Andrew's loss. The

---

[48] The very beginning of the flashback includes a cue carrying over from the revelatory scene, a fragment of Schnittke's *Four Hymns II, for Cello and Bass*, which clashes with the beginning of "Cry."

[49] The lyrics of the song begin as follows: "Tomorrow night, will you remember what you said tonight?/ Tomorrow night, will all the thrills be gone?/ Tomorrow night, will it be just another memory?/ Or just another lovely song that's in my heart to linger on?"

next musical fragment is from "Christian Zeal and Activity," a piece that (as already noted) combines religious text with harmonious sections featuring strings. The exact fragment we hear from Adams's work includes the words "Take up your bed and walk. Forgive sins. But God?" Overall, this piece emphasizes the miraculous power of Christ to heal, but the fragment used here ends with another question, pointing to the impossibility of perceiving salvation in the tragic scene. This music cue dovetails with yet another piece, a fragment from Alfred Schnittke's *Four Hymns II, for Cello and Double Bass*. This latter fragment includes a strong solo cello line that immediately evokes solitary anguish: it features extreme ranges of pitch, stretching into the upper register of the instrument, and sounds especially impassioned through vibrato. This is the music that underscores Andrew's seeing Dolores rise from a swing chair in their garden and slowly walking towards him in the absence of their children. The fragment from *Four Hymns II* also includes intermittent strumming of repeated low strings that suddenly stops to punctuate the fearfulness in Andrew asking Dolores, "Baby, why are you all wet?" In the ensuing dialogue between Andrew and Dolores, there is a period of no music, foregrounding their words. After Andrew asks where the children are, Dolores simply replies that they are in school. He responds with exasperation—"It's Saturday, and school's not in on Saturday." Here DiCaprio almost spits each word with heavy emphasis, investing the mundane observation with barely suppressed rage. When Dolores smiles at him and simply, quietly says "*my* school is," the horror of what she means by "schooling" is not immediately clear to us, but it seems quickly clear to him. Moments later he is in the lake next to their garden, desperately attempting to save the children who are already drowned there. Both before and after this futile effort, the conversation between Andrew and Dolores is accompanied by nothing more than soft birdsong. Were this culminating action to be underscored by music it might be reduced to clichéd melodrama.[50] That so much music punctuates the horrors and fears of other scenes throughout *Shutter Island* makes the absence of music during this action doubly impactful. The tragic scene of the children in the water is an aurally stark evocation of the Real, beyond that which can be described. Andrew's despair cannot be accompanied or underscored by anything. He is in it alone (see Figure 4.29).

For almost a minute we hear nothing but Andrew's voice and the splashes of water as he finds each submerged child and begins to pull them out with him. With the first manifestly lifeless child, Rachel, Andrew makes a brief effort to apply CPR, a natural knee-jerk reaction as well as a physical effort to undo the truth. His words before and after taking Rachel in his arms are pared down to repetitions that lead nowhere: "Oh my

---

[50] For a more nuanced consideration of the melodrama genre (not in this pejorative sense), especially in relation to *Bigger Than Life*, see Lawrence (2010, 86–87).

FIGURE 4.29 As Andrew embraces his three drowned children, the overhead shot emphasizes his aloneness.

God, oh my God, oh my God, no." The vocal repetition makes narrative sense because it relays Andrew's immediate horror as well as the impossibility of understanding what he has discovered. The vocal repetition also corresponds to the numerous repetitions of musical cues, the many repetitions of individual notes within several of the prominent cues (especially *Passacaglia*), the shots of records circling on a turntable, and Cawley's description of Andrew living like a tape on a loop. In this context, the whole film could be heard in relation to "Oh my God, oh my God, oh my God no" (see Figure 4.30).

As Andrew sits alone with his children, Dolores re-approaches him and suggests a picnic with their children as "living dolls." With her re-entrance in the scene, there is an extract from John Cage's *Root of an Unfocus* that underscores the rest of the flash-back [2:01:57–2:03:47]. This is an experimental piece for piano that involves striking and hammering it in different ways: an instrument traditionally used for creating har-mony and melody is thus used percussively.[51] The sporadic hammering of the piano

---

[51] Cage is probably the most celebrated experimental composer, being especially (in)famous for his com-position titled 4'33" ("Four minutes, thirty-three seconds," 1952), a composition shaped by the appear-ance of a musician who does not play for an audience: the work is the unique sounds created for the specified period of time in the performance setting. This creation is a landmark in terms of challenging assumptions about what constitutes music, performance, and artistic meaning. *Root of an Unfocus* is one of Cage's experimental pieces for "prepared piano," meaning that "objects are placed on the piano strings to alter their sound" (Feldstein 1986, 69).

FIGURE 4.30 Having retrieved his children from the lake, Andrew sits alone with their bodies.

communicates a form of irregular aural violence which "matches" several of the most traumatic moments of *Shutter Island*. The music quietly but insistently brings an end to the quiet around Andrew's voice. Soon thereafter, Andrew's response to Dolores is essentially a need for more quiet: "if you ever loved me Dolores, please stop talking." By this point, we understand that Dolores's voice has become one of the many sounds of *Shutter Island* that confuse, disturb, mislead, and overwhelm him (and, surely, us). Within less than a minute, Dolores has begged to be set free, and they have each expressed love for each other with escalating intensity before Andrew finally shoots her dead. His gunshot, yet another strong stinger, is followed by the continuation of *Root of an Unfocus*, and the soundless movement of blood quickly coursing over Dolores's body while he cries. The blood's movement up Dolores's body is mesmerizing. However, the aesthetic contour of the image is complicated by those hammering sounds from *Root of an Unfocus* which are most memorably connected with Rachel's opening eyes during one of Teddy's earlier, hallucinatory flashback scenes [58:31] (see Figure 4.31).

"See this with open eyes," the music "says" to us, just as Andrew himself must re-see everything. With the subsequent transition back to Dr. Cawley's office, Andrew collapses on the wooden floor with high illumination above him. The effect is much like a theatrical spotlight on a character on stage. It seems that now he can play a new "role," one in which he comprehends the truth of his past. With Cawley's urging, Andrew can

FIGURE 4.31 Rachel's suddenly open eyes, from an earlier flashback scene.

now reduce the past to the simplicity of saying "My name is Andrew Laeddis and I murdered my wife in the spring of '52."

Given everything we have heard up until this moment in *Shutter Island*, such clarity can surely last no longer than a few seconds. In the very next cut after Andrew's simple statement, there is a transition back to the deeply unsettling, and ambiguous, final scene. Here we see the main hospital grounds one more time, but now the gardens are perfectly intact as they were in the opening sequence of the film, even though we have seen and heard the gardens ravaged by a hurricane in several earlier scenes. This conveys an unnerving circularity of form that visually corresponds with many aural patterns of repetition through the film. Then we see Andrew sitting alone on the front steps, and he is soon joined by Dr. Sheehan who gives him a cigarette. Andrew asks Dr. Sheehan what their "next move" will be, a question that evokes their previous, falsely professional partnership. Dr. Sheehan responds in kind with a deferential "you tell me." Andrew's answer then indicates a definite about-face on the previous scene, another regression to living as his fantasy self, US Marshal Teddy Daniels: "we gotta get off this rock, Chuck. Get back to the mainland. Whatever the hell's going on here, it's *bad*." Andrew, now having reverted back to being Teddy, addresses Chuck as "partner," and Dr. Sheehan obligingly returns to calling him "boss." In this context, we understand why Dr. Sheehan then nods to Cawley, Naehring, the warden, and the nurses across the lawn as a signal that Andrew has regressed again. We then see a nurse approaching the front steps with metal surgical instruments wrapped in a white cloth, the clear implication being that Andrew's lobotomy is imminent. The subtle sounds of these wrapped instruments clinking together is as devastatingly powerful as the bombastic noises elsewhere in *Shutter Island*.

Despite this final horror, Andrew himself is granted one last moment of comparative control within the film. Moments before he joins the approaching hospital men who will control the lobotomy procedure, he tells his "partner" that being on Shutter Island makes him wonder "which would be worse, to live as a monster or to die as a good man." He then stands and walks towards the two nurses approaching him, evidently assenting to the procedure rather than being forced into it. Dr. Sheehan's response is a one-word question: "Teddy?" This last word of the film is obviously about Dr. Sheehan literally checking the protagonist's identity. (He may as well say, "Are you Teddy or Andrew consciously choosing to be Teddy?") The film proper closes with a visual emphasis on the sea and the lighthouse,[52] underscored by the final re-entrance of the opening of the *Passacaglia* that is inextricably connected to the malevolent power of Shutter Island [2:10:10]. The sea and the lighthouse (the location of the revelatory scene) are connected with Andrew's shifting perceptions of himself. The music suggests that which is ultimately beyond his control: the Symbolic order in which he must re-understand his place.

THE REAL

Though much of the *Shutter Island* sound track might be readily interpreted, it also repeatedly teeters on the edge of what is perceivable or understandable except in itself as an experience. The sound track provides us with a repeated sense of that which is actually beyond comprehension or putting into words. This is how the film communicates what Lacan might call the stain of the Real in aural form. The sum total of Teddy's Imaginary life with Dr. Cawley's Symbolic explanations of his entire experience are not enough to account for the entire film experience or what it demands that we perceive, even if only in fragments. The film gestures to a world much bigger than the protagonist's *or* the doctor's perceptions, a version of reality that exceeds both of the realms that they represent. It is useful to consider again that all the music for the film was composed before it was made: therein is the sense of a much greater reality controlling Andrew and, by implication, us.

---

[52] The lighthouse inevitably evokes *Vertigo*, along with many other Hitchcockian aspects of the film, which reinforces our understanding of the protagonist's vulnerability.

When the revelatory scene led by Dr. Cawley makes us understand how much we have been misled, to the extent that everything we heard and saw was lying to us, there is another film that might potentially occur to us, one that is truthful about what both men represent but which includes a third all-inclusive perspective. But we can only *imagine* this possibility, the film that we never see. This is the fullness of experience which can never be adequately represented, a possibility of the Real. We must at least dimly perceive this, even as it eludes us. After the revelatory scene, we have to perceive the whole film from this new vantage point. Ironically, it seems as if the sound track anticipates this process from the beginning: from the misleading ambiguities of *Fog Tropes* and the *Passacaglia* on, *Shutter Island* invites us to hear it one way, knowing that we will have to rehear it differently in due course. In this sense we become part of the film: where *The Ambassadors* looks back at us (McGowan 2003, 43), *Shutter Island* anticipates our mishearing it. If the painting forces an "encounter with the Real of the gaze" (43), *Shutter Island* forces an encounter with the Real that can be heard. Our vantage point on the film is cued by sounds that anticipate our reaction to them, only to demand that we reposition ourselves to re-perceive them before the end. Though the principle authority within the Symbolic order, Dr. Cawley, provides answers for everything strange we have seen *and* heard up to the revelatory scene, there is no question of his speech controlling the entire film experience any more than the protagonist can. Put simply, Dr. Cawley's full explanation can never be enough. The film exceeds what anyone says.

CRITICAL RECEPTION

Despite its having been directed by one of the most celebrated American auteurs, *Shutter Island* has received relatively little serious critical attention.[53] And despite its sonic originality, the film has been repeatedly described as generic, whether it terms of being a B-movie schlocker (Quinn) or a derivative psychological thriller (Williams 2010). The influence of Hitchcock's suspenseful films is evident throughout, from the stridency of the music cues that evoke Herrmann's scores for *Psycho* (1960) and *Vertigo* (1958) to the obvious rear projections. Also, B movies were a key inspiration for Lehane's novel which in turn led to the film. Such precursors aside, the impact of *Shutter Island* is far from generic in the pejorative sense of being overfamiliar and clichéd. To call the film "generic" is to ignore that which is unconventional and challenging about it.

---

[53] Such was the overwhelmingly negative critical response to *Shutter Island* that Scorsese could hardly bear to discuss it an interview with Richard Schickel (2011, 282).

The film's reviews also reflect the typical visual bias in popular film criticism. Even when the sound track is mentioned, the reviewer brings it up in passing or writes only of its most startling and obvious effects. Holly Williams, for instance, writes of the sound track as "crashingly overwrought" without mentioning any of its range (2010). Many of the film's subtleties of form and implication have been missed, even in reviews that pay elaborate and sophisticated attention to decoding the film's *mise-en-scène*. Another representative example is Joseph Jon Lanthier's review for *Bright Lights Film Journal* (2010). Lanthier argues that the film displays Scorsese's visual flair to superficial excess. In particular, Lanthier finds "the domestic setting for the tragedy too Elysian." He argues that through the visual strategies of the film (such as "empathetic cinematography"), "Scorsese seems to be in on whatever manipulative put-on the characters are exacting." Finally, Lanthier argues that the "overzealous twist" of Andrew's true identity being revealed "causes the film's plot to collapse in on itself."

There are many problems with Lanthier's analysis precisely because he leaves out all but passing reference to the film's aural dimensions. First, as we have noted, the sound track often pulls in different directions from the visual messages of *Shutter Island*, complicating their superficial immediacy. Even if the film is sometimes arrestingly beautiful, as in the heightened colors of the final true flashback, the sound track provides us with the overwhelming experience of irresolvable trauma. Second, though the film's plot may seem to collapse on itself with the revelatory scene, it is arguably only "complete" at this point. Indeed, the entire film experience is richer if we return to it already knowing the big twist. Cawley's complete explanation of the truth entails a profound challenge to re-understand, or *rehear*, everything. Far from making the plot collapse, this process completes the film experience.

Other popular review responses to *Shutter Island* are similarly mixed. For instance, Peter Bradshaw writing for *The Guardian* simply argues that "everything looks good" and that the film is "engorged with technique" (2010). Anthony Lane for *The New Yorker* writes of the film as a pleasurable "shrine" of clichés (2010). More troublingly, he argues that the Dachau sequences "make aesthetic capital" from "the heaped and frozen corpses in the concentration camp." For Lane, the film does not explore "the wounds of history. They are here for the heebie-jeebies." Finally, Lane argues that there is "nothing" at stake in *Shutter Island*, unlike those other Scorsese-directed films scripted by Paul Schrader that show men painfully confronted with their own reflections: more specifically, he cites the celebrated "are you talkin' to me?" scene from *Taxi Driver* during which Travis confronts his own image, and the final image of *Raging Bull* with Jake La Motta saying "Go get 'em champ" to his solitary reflection. Lane ultimately reads *Shutter Island* as being more in the service of "visual daring" than "moral brinksmanship." Clearly, he misses the deep psychoanalytic significance of Andrew's first line in his mirror reflection—"pull yourself together"—as it relates to the form of the entire film. The complex non-suturing experience of *Shutter Island* cannot be "pulled together" or summed up as a series of arresting visuals without stakes or morality. While the film's visuals do sometimes indulge the audience with aesthetic contours, much like Andrew flatters himself with the ideal-I reflection, the sound track always complicates the beauty we see. Moreover, everything beautiful about the film is problematized by the revelatory scene that unmasks everything up to that point as a projected fantasy of regression. Even the obvious contrivances of the film, such as the flashbacks of Dachau, may be retrospectively understood in this context. Finally, the often experimental and complex sound track repeatedly denies us a straightforward consumption of the image.

SUMMARY

The sound tracks for both *Bigger Than Life* and *Shutter Island* present us with overwhelming experiences of brokenness that cannot be fantastically resolved. In *Bigger Than Life*, Raksin's music amplifies our sense of the patriarch's divided self, as well as paralleling its visual ruptures. The stingers and silences make for a frequently non-sutured experience, one in which we cannot lose ourselves but are prompted to be consistently aware of the film's Real trauma. In particular, the terror of the patriarch's unstable self, one all too easily altered by medical treatment and all too easily sustained by those who uphold his Symbolic power, is anticipated, amplified, reinforced, and critiqued by Raksin's music. The sound track also prompts us to dwell upon the Real that exceeds signification. Thinking back once again to *The Ambassadors*, and McGowan's interpretation of the Lacanian Real gaze, *Bigger Than Life* "looks" back at us, especially through its music. The film anticipates our assuming a vantage point greater than that of any or all of its characters, a view on the action that means questioning the stability of everything they embody.

Similarly, the overall sonic experience of *Shutter Island* is one of loss and trauma. Much of the sound track of *Shutter Island* may be summarized by what it *denies* us. The score emphasizes "lack" in musical terms: many of its cues are extracts from experimental pieces that offer anything but suturing comfort, and those few occasions where we hear a clear melody offer only a brief aural reprieve from the turbulence of the film. In addition, most of the sound track works to undermine the stability or the straightforwardness of what we see, and this undermines Andrew's attempt to regress within the fantasy of being Teddy.

Shutter Island also sonically presents the possibilities of the Real gaze as McGowan defines it: much as we can see the skull of *The Ambassadors* clearly by looking at the painting from a deliberately strange vantage point, we can hear everything in *Shutter Island* anew after the revelatory scene. As soon as we comprehend this possibility, we realize we have already experienced the whole film without knowing what it truly showed us: it escapes our grasp, like the ever-elusive, "impossible" Real that Lacan originally conceptualized. The film also calls attention to itself as a fantasy which we can accept at face value only up to the revelatory scene. Again, recall McGowan's argument that "When film employs fantasy but at the same time reveals the limit that fantasy comes up against, it takes us to an encounter with the traumatic Real" (2003, 40). Rehearing *Shutter Island* means facing the agony of this encounter.

WORKS CITED

Adams, John. 2008. *Hallelujah Junction: Composing an American Life.* New York: Picador.

Andrew, Geoff. 2004. *The Films of Nicholas Ray.* London: BFI Publishing.

Ayers, Drew. 2008. "*The Real Gaze: Film Theory After Lacan* (review)." *The Velvet Light Trap* 61:57–59.

Barham, Jeremy. 2010. "Plundering Archives and Transcending Diegetics: Mahler's Music as 'Overscore'." *Music and the Moving Image* 3 (1):22–47.

Baudry, Jean-Louis. (1974–75) 2004. "Ideological Effects of the Basic Cinematographic Apparatus." Translated by Alan Williams. In *Film Theory and Criticism*, edited by Leo Braudy and Marshall Cohen, 355–65. 6th ed. New York: Oxford University Press. Originally published in *Film Quarterly* 28 (2).

Bordwell, David, and Noël Carroll, eds. 1996. *Post-Theory: Reconstructing Film Studies.* Madison: University of Wisconsin Press.

Bradshaw, Peter. 2010. "*Shutter Island.*" *The Guardian*, March 11. Accessed November 1, 2013. <http://www.theguardian.com/film/2010/mar/11/shutter-island-review>.

Carlsson, Mats. 2012. "The Gaze as Constituent and Annihilator." *Journal of Aesthetics & Culture* 4. Accessed December 4, 2013. <http://www.aestheticsandculture.net/index.php/jac/rt/printerFriendly/19481/24738>.

Carroll, Noël, "Prospects for Film Theory: A Personal Asssessment." In *Post-Theory*, edited by David Bordwell and Noël Carroll.

Chion, Michel. (1990) 1994. *Audio-Vision: Sound on Screen.* Edited and translated by Claudia Gorbman. New York: Columbia University Press. Originally published as *L'Audio-Vision* (Paris: Editions Nathan).

———. (1982) 1999. *The Voice in Cinema.* Edited and translated by Claudia Gorbman. New York: Columbia University Press. Originally published as *La Voix au cinéma* (Paris: *Cahiers du cinéma* (Editions de l'Etoile)).

———. (2003) 2009. *Film, A Sound Art.* Translated by Claudia Gorbman. New York: Columbia University Press. Originally published as *Un art sonare, le cinéma* (Paris: *Cahiers du cinéma* (Editions de l'Etoile)).

Creet, Julia. 1995. "Anxieties of Identity: Coming Out and Coming Undone." In *Negotiating Lesbian & Gay Subjects*, edited by Monica Dorenkamp and Richard Henke, 179–99. New York: Routledge.

Dawson, Tom. 2003. "Bigger Than Life." BBC. 14 November. Accessed December 4, 2013. < http://www.bbc.co.uk/films/2003/11/14/bigger_than_life_1956_review.shtml>.

Dayan, Daniel. 1976. "The Tutor-Code of Classical Cinema." In *Movies and Methods: Vol 1*, edited by Bill Nichols, 438–51. Berkeley: University of California Press.

Doane, Mary Ann. 1980. "The Voice in the Cinema: The Articulation of Body and Space." *Yale French Studies* 60:33–50.

Dolar, Mladen. 1996. "The Object Voice." In *Gaze and Voice as Love Objects*, edited by Renata Salacl and Slavoj Žižek, 7–31. Durham, NC: Duke University Press.

Evans, Dylan. 1996. *An Introductory Dictionary of Lacanian Psychoanalysis*. London: Routledge.

Feldstein, Sandy. 1986. *Alfred's Pocket Dictionary of Music: Terms, Composers, Theory*. Van Nuys, CA: Alfred Publishing Co., Inc.

Felluga, Dino. 2011. "Modules on Lacan: On the Structure of the Psyche." *Introductory Guide to Critical Theory*. Purdue University. January 31. Accessed November 4, 2013. <http://www.purdue.edu/guidetotheory/psychoanalysis/lacanstructure.html>.

Foundas, Scott. 2008. "Nicholas Ray's *Bigger Than Life* at Film Forum: A David Lynch Precursor Gets a Proper Screening." *The Village Voice*, December 31. Accessed November 8, 2013. <http://www.villagevoice.com/2008-12-31/film/nicolas-ray-s-bigger-than-life-at-film-forum/>.

Freud, Sigmund. (1920) 2001. "Beyond the Pleasure Principle." In *The Standard Edition of the Complete Psychological Works by Sigmund Freud, Volume XVIII (1920-1922)*, edited by James Stratchey, 7–66. Translated by James Strachey, Anna Freud, Alix Strachey, and Alan Tyson. London: Vintage.

Hayward, Susan. 2006. *Cinema Studies: The Key Concepts*. 3rd ed. London: Routledge.

Heath, Stephen. (1978) 2006. "Notes on Suture." *The Symptom: Online Journal for Lacan.com*. Accessed November 20, 2013. <http://www.lacan.com/symptom8_articles/heath8.html>. Originally published in *Screen* 18:48–76.

Kalinak, Kathryn. 2010. *Film Music: A Very Short Introduction*. Oxford: Oxford University Press.

Kite, B. 2010. "*Bigger Than Life*: Somewhere in Suburbia." The Criterion Collection Website. March 18. Accessed November 5, 2013. <http://www.criterion.com/current/posts/1412-bigger-than-life-somewhere-in-suburbia>.

Kuersten, Erich. 2010. "*Bigger Than Life*: Nicholas Ray in the Life of the Gray Flannel Darkness." *Bright Lights Film Journal* 68. Accessed October 15, 2013. <http://brightlightsfilm.com/68/68biggerthanlife.php>.

Lacan, Jacques. 1953. "Some Reflections on the Ego." *International Journal of Psycho-Analysis* 34:11–17.

———. (1977) 1998. *The Seminar of Jacques Lacan, Book XI: The Four Fundamental Concepts of Psychoanalysis*. Edited by Jacques-Alain Miller. Translated by Alan Sheridan. New York: W.W. Norton & Company, Inc.

———. 2002. *Écrits: A Selection*. Translated by Bruce Fink. New York: W.W. Norton & Company, Inc.

Lane, Anthony. 2010. "Behind Bars: *Shutter Island and A Prophet*." *The New Yorker*, March 1. Accessed November 1, 2013. <http://www.newyorker.com/arts/critics/cinema/2010/03/01/100301crci_cinema_lane>.

Lanthier, Joseph Jon. 2010. "Outstanding Defense Mechanisms: The Phrenology of Martin Scorsese's *Shutter Island*." *Bright Lights Film Journal* 68. Accessed November 1, 2013. <http://brightlightsfilm.com/68/68shutterisland.php#.UoesiSgvHao>.

Lawrence, Amy. 2010. "A Star is Born *Bigger Than Life*." In *Larger Than Life: Movie Stars of the 1950s*, edited by R. Barton Palmer, 86–106. New Brunswick, NJ: Rutgers University Press.

Lehane, Dennis. 2003. *Shutter Island*. New York: Harper Collins.

MacCannell, Juliet Flower. 1994. "Between the Two Fears." In *Lacan and Contemporary Film*, edited by Todd McGowan and Sheila Kunkle, 47–82. New York: Other Press.

Manlove, Clifford T. 2007. "Visual Drive and Cinematic Narrative: Reading Gaze Theory in Lacan, Hitchcock, and Mulvey." *Cinema Journal* 46 (3): 83–108.

Mann, Katrina. 2004. "'You're Text!': Postwar Hegemony Besieged in *Invasion of the Body Snatchers*." *Cinema Journal* 44 (1): 49–68.

McGowan, Todd. 2003. "Looking for the Gaze: Lacanian Film Theory and Its Vicissitudes." *Cinema Journal* 42 (3): 27–47.

———. 2007. *The Real Gaze: Film Theory after Lacan*. Albany: State University of New York Press.

———and Sheila Kunkle, eds. 2004. *Lacan and Contemporary Film*. New York: Other Press.

Metz, Christian. (1975) 2004. "Identification, Mirror," "The Passion for Perceiving," and "Disavowel/Fetishism." In *Film Theory and Criticism*, edited by Leo Braudy and Marshall Cohen, 355–65. 6th ed. New York: Oxford University Press. Originally published in *Screen* 16 (2).

Phillips, Gidion, and Barbara J. Toennies, prod. 2010. "Behind the Shutters (making-of featurette)." *Shutter Island*. Directed by Martin Scorsese. Blu-Ray. Hollywood: Paramount Home Entertainment.

Prendergast, Roy N. 1992. *Film Music: A Neglected Art*. 2nd ed. New York: W.W. Norton & Company.

Quinn, Anthony. "*Shutter Island*: Shlock and little awe from Marty." The Independent, March 12, 2010. Accessed October 15, 2013. <http://www.independent.co.uk/arts-entertainment/films/reviews/shutter-island-15-1920058.html>.

Rapold, Nicholas. 2006. "Power Mad." *Reverse Shot*. Spring. Accessed October 15, 2013. <http://www.reverseshot.com/article/bigger_than_life>.

Roueché, Berton. 1955. "Ten Feet Tall." *The New Yorker*, September 10, 47–77.

Sarchet, Barry W. 1994. "Rockumentary as Metadocumentary: Martin Scorsese's *The Last Waltz*." *Literature Film Quarterly* 22 (1): 28–35.

Schickel, Richard. 2011. *Conversations with Scorsese*. New York: Alfred A. Knopf.

Silverman, Kaja. 1988. *The Acoustic Mirror: The Female Voice in Psychoanalysis and Cinema*. Bloomington: Indiana University Press.

Topspin Media, Inc. 2012. *Robbie Robertson*. Accessed November 16, 2013. <http://www.robbie-robertson.com/biography/>.

Williams, Holly. 2010. "DVD: *Shutter Island* (15)." *The Independent*, July 30. Accessed November 1, 2013. <http://www.independent.co.uk/arts-entertainment/films/reviews/dvd-shutter-island-15-2038799.html>.

Wright, Elizabeth. 1982. "Modern Psychoanalytic Criticism." In *Modern Literary Theory: A Comparative Introduction*, edited by Ann Jefferson and David Robey, 113–33. Totowa, NJ: Barnes & Noble Books.

Žižek, Slavoj. 1991. *Looking Awry: An Introduction to Jacques Lacan through Popular Culture*. Cambridge, MA: The MIT Press.

Queer Theory

 # INTRODUCTION

"Imitation and Gender Insubordination"
by Judith Butler

Psychoanalytic film criticism often focuses on malleable concepts of identity. Queer theory is more specifically focused on shifting understandings of gender and sexuality, especially as the result of intersecting societal pressures. The term "queer" has been historically used as a pejorative term to refer to gays, lesbians, or "anyone perceived to be different" (Meyer 2007, 15). As Elizabeth J. Meyer explains, the term is now widely used as "a challenge to traditional understandings of sexual identity by deconstructing the categories, the binaries, and language that supports them" (25). Queer theory breaks down conventional, fixed, or normalized concepts of personhood based on such binaries as queer/straight, male/female, masculine/feminine, and proper/improper.[1] Queer theory also complicates "assumptions about continuities between anatomical sex, social gender, gender identity, sexual identity, sexual object choice, and sexual practice" (Martin 1994, 105). It has come to represent an all-encompassing ability to "disrupt and challenge traditional modes of thought and, by standing outside them, examine and dismantle them" (Meyer 2007, 26).

Among other ways of challenging "traditional modes of thought," queer theory often focuses on problematizing "straight" approaches to texts. The term "queering" is meaningfully applied to the practice of reading against the ostensible message of a given text, or against the received notions of its meaning. Queer theory became a prominently subversive approach to literary analysis in the 1990s, during which time queer cinema also became more "visible" in light of the AIDS crisis (Hayward 2006, 330).

---

[1] For more discussion of deconstructing such binaries, see Meijer and Prins (1998).

Judith Butler is recognized as a leading figure in queer theory, and some of her work will be the springboard for our queer approach to sound tracks.

Along with being foundational within queer theory, Butler's work is widely understood as being post-structuralist. The concept of post-structuralism is difficult to define succinctly, not least because it resists closure. For instance, though post-structuralism acknowledges the existence of social hierarchies, it also destabilizes such hierarchies through exposing the dependency of those in power upon those who are subservient to them. In this kind of way, post-structuralism is largely concerned with deconstructing the status quo, and especially those taken-as-a-given truths that produce the illusion of fixed meaning, understanding, reality, or identity. More specifically, the post-structuralist critic deconstructs perceptions of the "self" as a fixed and coherent entity, exposing it as a fictional construct.[2] Equally, the meaning of the text cannot be reduced to a single purpose or meaning attachable to an originating author or creator: instead, every individual reader is a creator of meaning which they identify within a given text. Moreover, the post-structuralist analysis frequently entails that the writer be self-aware about their own subject position in relation to that which they interpret, thus further acknowledging the contingency of how those truths they identify may be perceived.

Butler's work reflects all these emphases of post-structuralism, even though Butler herself resists being associated with any fixed theoretical trend. In terms of destabilizing hierarchies, Butler's work recognizes the relative power of heterosexual normativity, but she also emphasizes the ironic reliance of that power on being defined in relation to homosexual "deviance." In terms of deconstructing dominant perceptions of truths, Butler writes about gender and sexuality as constructs rather than preexistent personal realities. Indeed, Butler writes of sexuality and gender as forms of performance, and of gender, in particular, as a form of "drag" ([1990] 2004, 134). Gender is thus conceptualized by her as a series of performances that reinforce the "*illusion* of an inner sex or essence or psychic gender core" (134, my emphasis). She also defines gender as "the repeated stylization of the body, a set of repeated acts within a highly rigid regulatory frame that congeals over time to produce the appearance of substance, of a natural sort of being" (1990, 33).[3] Finally, Butler frequently calls attention to her own subjectivity as she makes arguments within specific personal experiences and contexts.

---

[2] For some fuller discussion of post-structuralist thought as a primary context for understanding Butler's work, see Rodriguez (2007).

[3] In writing of gender as the effect of something one *does* rather than something one *is*, Judith Butler is influenced by the philosopher J. L. Austin and his writing on performative speech, as in *How to Do Things with Words* (1962). Austin's most cited example is the performative utterance that is the vow "I do" through which a marriage is begun. The term "performativity" is not to be confused with theatricality, performance, or play-acting, for it refers to how we "are constituted in the saying/doing" (Kamitsuka

Our analysis of two films in relation to Butler's work will be self-consciously post-structuralist, admitting its own subjectivity along with exploring the complexity of identity perception in the films themselves. There is no evidence that either film was consciously designed with any of Butler's concepts in mind: the first film, *Rebecca* (1940), was made before Butler began writing and the second film, *Heavenly Creatures* (1994), is contemporaneous with her but makes no reference to her work (nor do all those publicity and marketing materials which surround the film's making). Thus, this final part of the book is an especially self-conscious example of imposing theoretical paradigms on films in the service of opening up interpretive possibilities. Both films indirectly invite such a process, especially because they offer contrary views on their main characters and thus place a particular onus on their audiences to make meaning. In terms of interpreting their sound tracks using queer theory, it is crucial that the lead characters of both films are associated with various aural signifiers of identity that exceed that which can be easily or consistently taken as conclusive, especially with regard to their gendered and sexualized selves. It is thus possible to retroactively identify ways in which both films reward the application of queer theory, regardless of what the filmmakers' original intentions might have been.

We will redirect Butler's work towards sound tracks, just as she has in turn reframed the work of several eminent theorists. Her reflections on the power of language as a form of "control and domination" (and hence her resistance to labeling) draws upon the work of Jacques Derrida, Jacques Lacan, and Michel Foucault. As Meyer explains, though these theorists sometimes clash, they are united in exploring "the power of words as signifiers to constitute a subject and his/her experiences as well as the structures in society that police and reinforce the dominant ideology through discursive practices" (2007, 20–21). The influence of Foucault is especially significant for our purposes because, through his work *The History of Sexuality, Volume 1* (1976), he is credited with having deconstructed the dominant understanding of sexual identity by emphasizing it as "not an essentially personal attribute but an available cultural category" (Jagose 1996, 79).[4] Near the end of this work, Foucault makes an emphatic statement about our obligation to perceive sexuality in relation to power: "We must conceptualize the deployment of

---

2004, 191). Though indebted to Austin in terms of considering speech as action, Butler departs from Austin's idea that the self might be an "autonomous agent that authors performative utterances" (Lloyd 1999, 197). Instead, drawing on the work of Foucault and Derrida in particular, Butler writes of the subject born into and articulating themselves within preexisting cultural and linguistic structures. That the subject is "produced through social discourse does not, however, preclude the possibility of agency" (Magnus 2006, 82).

[4] This quotation is helpfully contextualized by Rodriguez (2007, 286).

sexuality on the basis of the techniques of power that are contemporary with it" (1980, 150).[5] Similarly, Butler conceptualizes identity categories of gender and sexuality as "products" of regimes of power rather than representative of "essential nature" (Jagger 2008, 17). We shall accordingly explore how two sound tracks have been constructed to make us better *hear* queerness in relation to dominant regimes of power.

"IMITATION AND GENDER INSUBORDINATION": THE DANGER OF LABELING

We now zero in on our foundational text for queer theory: Butler's "Imitation and Gender Insubordination" ([1991] 2004). This article first appeared in print a year after her most influential work, *Gender Trouble* (1990), was published. It builds upon several of the main ideas of *Gender Trouble* when it comes to exploring the indeterminacy of sexual and gendered identities, thus challenging the heteronormative status quo. As Sarah Salih explains in her anthology of Butler's writings, both works question "the stability and the value of identity categories, since they invariably operate in the service of oppressive, exclusionary, regulatory regimes."[6]

Butler presented parts of "Imitation and Gender Insubordination" at a conference on homosexuality at Yale University in 1989 but the article itself represents Butler's ambivalence about using the label of "homosexuality." Though she begins her article by identifying herself as lesbian, she soon expresses resistance towards such identity categories because they "tend to be instruments of regulatory regimes, whether as the normalizing categories of oppressive structures or as the rallying points for liberatory contestation of that very oppression" ([1991] 2004, 121). In her anthology, Salih therefore introduces the first paradoxical point of the article: "the undeniability of [Butler's] lesbianism is as important as her assertion that claiming it is insufficient to describe or explain who she is" (2004, 119). Although Butler accepts the term "lesbian" to the extent that she is willing to deliver speeches and write in terms of having that identity, she "would like to have it permanently unclear what precisely that sign signifies"

---

[5] Much of Foucault's work further explores how communities and individuals are regulated through "discursive mechanisms of power," including "discourses of medicine, jurisprudence, sexuality, religion" which determine "the true, the right, the normal" (Kamitsuka 2004, 184). Both *Rebecca* and *Heavenly Creatures* incorporate scenes where queer characters are verbally defined as "sick," involved in prejudicial judiciary proceedings, described in terms of deviant sexuality, and labeled or imaged as sinfully diabolical. Ironically, both films also use the language of cinema to complicate the condemnation of queer identities.

[6] Salih makes this point with regard to most of Butler's work (2004, 119).

([1991] 2004, 121).[7] We shall thus apply the term "lesbian" (and, in one case, "bisexual") for convenience when referring to the main characters from two films without any intention of limiting the possibilities for interpreting who they are.

Because Butler associates the term "lesbian" with the oppressive discourse of heterosexist power, she uses the term as a starting point for resistance.[8] For Butler, any identity category is a "site of necessary trouble" (121). She raises fundamental questions about the meaning of the lesbian-signifier, such as "what, if anything, can lesbians be said to share? And who will decide this question, and in the name of whom?" (122). She also writes about "coming out" as an exposing practice, especially as it is often imposed upon the subject (123).

Both of our case study films for queer theory revolve around characters who might be considered lesbian, but neither film represents lesbianism in a restrictive manner. Neither film ever voices the term "lesbian," and neither film conclusively identifies its lesbian characters as homosexual. In the case of *Rebecca*, this is largely attributable to the Production Code being in effect at the time of its release, along with the term "lesbian" not being in the common parlance of 1940s America. Ironically, because *Rebecca* offers no fixed label for the queer relationship between two of its female characters (Mrs. Danvers and the deceased Mrs. de Winter), the film makes their relationship more potent, implying that it exceeds that which can be named. In the case of *Heavenly Creatures*, we have a film focusing on action taking place during the 1950s, a time when lesbianism was still seldom acknowledged or identified as such in mainstream Western society. There *is* one scene where a psychiatrist unsympathetically associates one of the lead characters with "homosexuality." Yet the film critically represents the moment of his using the word with an uncomfortably extreme close-up on his stuttering mouth [1:01:15–1:01:19] (see Figure 5.1). This close-up not only satirizes his authority as he stutters over the word; it is also meant to make us uncomfortable with the term "homosexuality" itself.

Both *Rebecca* and *Heavenly Creatures* represent, to use Butler's words, "a certain resistance to classification and to identity as such" (123). The lack of labeling in *Rebecca*, and the satirized use of "homosexuality" in *Heavenly Creatures* achieve Butlerian results by different means: both films foreground the power of their main female characters to

---

[7] Unless otherwise stated, all quotations from this section come from Butler's "Imitation and Gender Insubordination" ([1991] 2004).

[8] Here she draws upon the work of Foucault who writes of discourse as an "effect of power" but also a "starting point for an opposing strategy" (121). Also, see Foucault's *The History of Sexuality, Volume 1* (1978, 101) for the basis of Butler's argument.

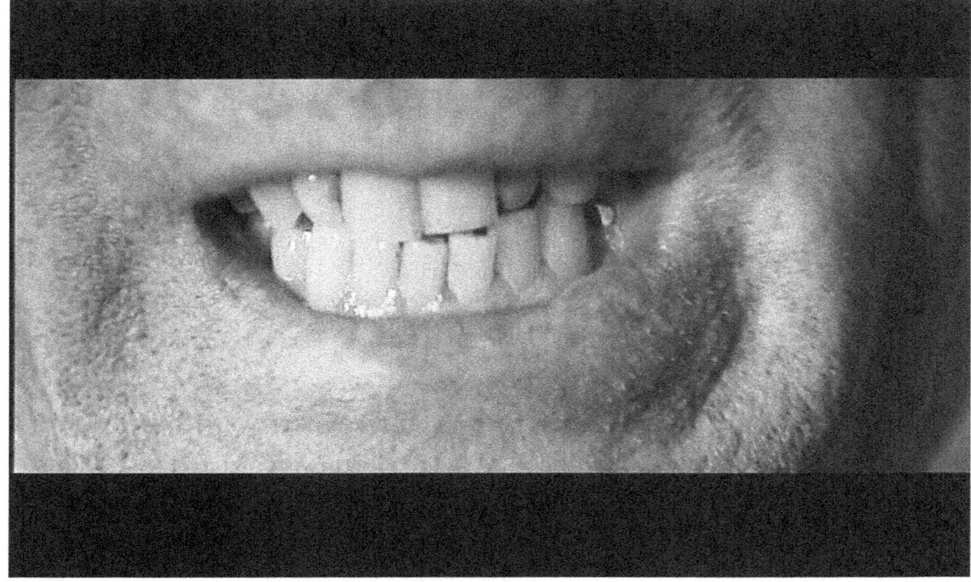

FIGURE 5.1 In *Heavenly Creatures*, this uncomfortably tight close-up on the psychiatrist's mouth makes his damning "diagnosis" of Pauline's homosexuality especially repugnant.

exceed any imposed label in terms of gender or sexuality and, in so doing, undermine the power of the limiting paradigms that bolster heterosexual privilege.

HOMOSEXUALITY/HETEROSEXUALITY ≠ COPY/ORIGINAL

Along with her emphasis on the limitations of the label "lesbian" in itself, Butler interrogates the meaning of homosexuality as it is defined in relation to heterosexuality. She challenges the presumption that lesbianism, in particular, "is an imitation of an "original" heterosexuality" (Salih 2004, 119). Butler argues that lesbian identities do not imitate heterosexual identities; rather, "they panic them by confounding the origin-to-copy/heterosexual-to-lesbian line of causation, thereby exposing heterosexual claims to originality as illusory" (119). Such an argument not only "denaturalizes" the normative concept of heterosexuality, it also disrupts the typical hierarchical distinction between authoritative heterosexuality and subsidiary (or deviant) homosexuality.

Along with her anti-essentialist challenge to straight/gay, original/copy identifications, Butler writes of its being possible to "pursue heterosexual identifications and aims within homosexual practice, and homosexual identifications and aims within heterosexual practice" ([1991] 2004, 123). In other words, Butler ironically argues that it is entirely possible for lesbianism to be at least in part constituted by the very heterosexist power domains that it seeks to displace. She even argues that lesbian sexuality "can be understood to redeploy its 'derivativeness' in the service of displacing hegemonic heterosexual norms" (124). This is another way of overturning "the homophobic construction of the bad copy against the framework that privileges heterosexuality as origin" (124). This line of argument also resonates with both our case study films. First, Mrs. Danvers's love for the late Mrs. de Winter in *Rebecca* is the most consistently compelling, unyielding, intriguing, and passionate feeling expressed in the film. The scenes of heterosexual courtship are anodyne when compared with the volatile desire she expresses for Rebecca. Moreover, the representation of heterosexual marriage is primarily interesting as it is troubled by Rebecca's queer and enduring presence after death. Thus, the hierarchical privilege of heterosexual marriage is undermined. It is also especially significant that Mrs. Danvers's voice (that of Judith Anderson) is the most consistently strong and controlled one in the film. Moreover, the music associated with Mrs. Danvers and her late mistress is, by far, the most complex, dynamic, unpredictable, and varied in the film, further destabilizing the aural presence of the main heterosexual couple played by the film's biggest stars (Laurence Olivier and Joan Fontaine) (see Figure 5.2). The most powerful music is thus associated with the uncontainable desire of a woman whose literal position as housekeeper is subsidiary, but whose importance as a woman desirous of another woman ultimately overturns that of the heterosexual leads.

FIGURE 5.2 The big-name, heterosexual stars of *Rebecca*: Laurence Olivier (as Maxim de Winter) and Joan Fontaine (as the unnamed lead character).

Turning back to *Heavenly Creatures*, we could likewise dwell upon the ways in which both its protagonists (Pauline and Juliet) verbally and musically adopt heterosexual paradigms within the context of their own love affair. This is most obvious in the two moments when the film echoes Classical Hollywood musicals that revolve around heterosexual romance. First, there is a scene when Juliet runs across the New Zealand hills to a rising crescendo of orchestral strings, filmed through a "rotating aerial long-shot" (Elleray 1999, 229). It is a visual echo of Julie Andrews's iconic running across the Swiss Alps in *The Sound of Music* (1965) (see Figure 5.3). Pauline soon runs to Juliet across the hills, leading to their sublime exploration of a fantasy world that quite literally transforms the film (see Figure 5.4). Here, references to *The Sound of Music* only pave the way for a trumping experience of more exciting constructions: giant butterflies, unicorns, and magically materializing gardens transform the space where Juliet runs with

FIGURE 5.3 Juliet runs across the hills, an echo of Julie Andrews in *The Sound of Music*.

FIGURE 5.4 Pauline and Juliet run into a fantasy world together.

FIGURE 5.5 Juliet's glamorous entrance down the stairs, recalling *My Fair Lady*.

Pauline, the power of which is emphatically supported by Peter Dasent's music for their imaginary realm, "the Fourth World" [31:27–34:50].

The second example of echoing a Classical Hollywood musical comes when Juliet descends the stairs at her home: a moment that recalls Eliza Dolittle making her grand stair-descending appearance in *My Fair Lady* (1964) (see Figure 5.5). Juliet wears a gold gown and her fluid motion running down the stairs to meet Pauline is accompanied by the flourishing introduction to Mario Lanza's performance of "The Loveliest Night of the Year" [1:23:33–1:23:41]. The point of view is Pauline's as she watches Juliet in awe. In both these examples, the allusion to a heterosexual female lead in a Classical Hollywood musical emphasizes Pauline's presence. Moreover, each example is followed up with an amplification of musical material that reinforces the transformative power of something *better* which comes after the reference to a heterosexual love story: the girls' togetherness and everything they desire as a couple. In short, *Heavenly Creatures* makes it clear that the love between Pauline and Juliet is much more than a pale imitation of heterosexual ideals.

QUEERING STRAIGHT SOUNDS

In light of Butler's work, it becomes deeply significant that many music cues of *Rebecca* and *Heavenly Creatures* are associable with heterosexual film narratives. Both films use recognizable musical conventions that are traditionally associated with straight stories, but these same conventions are "queered" through the association with lesbian romance. In this sense, both films "dress up" their lesbian characters in the power of what might be reasonably called "straight-sounding" music. We shall therefore consider some music as a form of "drag."

Butler writes about the power of drag in the context of her own suffering through being told that, as a lesbian, she was "a copy, an imitation, a derivative example, a shadow of the real" because "compulsory heterosexuality sets itself up as the original, the true, the authentic," and as "the norm that determines the real which implies that 'being' lesbian is always a kind of miming" (127). As an answer to such powerplay, Butler argues that drag "enacts the very structure of impersonation by which any gender is assumed. Drag is not the putting on of a gender that belongs properly to some other group, i.e. an act of *expropriation* or *appropriation* that assumes gender is the rightful property of sex, that 'masculine' belongs to 'male' and 'feminine' belongs to 'female'" (127, original emphases). In short, drag calls attention to a truth that applies to everyone, regardless of how each him/her represents themselves: *"all gender is a kind of imitation for which there is no original"* (127, original emphases).[9] Here, Butler again undermines a "normative measure of the real" (128) that sets up heterosexuality as being the natural original state.

The use of "straight" music in both *Rebecca* and *Heavenly Creatures* parodies and subverts heterosexual dominance, defamiliarizing the paradigmatic musical constructions associated with more conservative narratives.[10] Both film scores associate their most powerful leitmotifs with queer characters. Of course, the use of leitmotifs has been dominant in mainstream cinema since the Classical Hollywood era, and therefore heard mostly in relation to heterosexual pairings. The musical conventions of both films thus have no single point of origin but are easily recognizable as such. By understanding how such familiar, conventional, "straight" music is self-consciously used as "drag" in both films, we can better understand their queer resonance.

---

[9] Elsewhere Butler has emphasized that drag does not necessarily represent automatic subversion. For instance, she studies the documentary *Paris Is Burning* (1991) in which the drag balls of Harlem are occasions for gay minority men to present themselves in many forms of straight dress. The measure of success in these balls is the gay man's ability to "pass" for being straight or to be perceived as "real" in a straight sense. The categories for these balls, which include "Executive Realness," "Going to School," and "*Dynasty*" (as in the conservative 1980s television show) suggest a strange, ironic celebration of hegemonic heterosexual society. That said, Butler argues that the documentary's subjects are neither completely hegemonic nor completely subversive in their drag. For further discussion of the film and its paradoxical representation of drag, see Butler's "Gender Is Burning: Questions of Appropriation and Subversion" (1993).

[10] This argument is an application of Butler's words: "the parodic replication and resignification of heterosexual constructs within non-heterosexual frames brings into relief the utterly constructed status of the so-called original" ([1991] 2004, 130).

THE "I" IN FLUX

Just as Butler understands sexuality as an unending performance, the repetition of which establishes its instability, she understands identity or that which we mean by "I" as constantly in flux, and as constantly in a process of redefinition. In the context of her identifying herself as a lesbian, she writes that "the 'I' is always displaced by the very repetition that sustains it. In other words, does or can the 'I' ever repeat itself, cite itself, faithfully, or is there always a displacement from its former moment that establishes the permanently non-self-identical status of that 'I' or its 'being lesbian'?" (125). For Butler, the "I" is the "effect of a certain repetition, one which produces the semblance of continuity or coherence" and thus "there is no 'I' that precedes the gender that it is said to perform; the repetition, and the failure to repeat, produce a string of performances that constitute and contest the coherence of that 'I'" (125).

This idea of identity being constituted through repetitions that consistently reshape our understanding to the extent that no final or originary meaning may be reached is especially important for understanding the impact of our chosen sound tracks. First, it is a convention of much Classical Hollywood (and other mainstream) scoring to repeat the music that identifies a character. Though there is an identifiable first instance of their theme (or, typically, leitmotif), that first instance is usually followed by numerous repetitions, including subtleties of variation that demand our constant re-understanding or recontextualization of what that character's identity means. Many scores present such conventional practice without necessarily demanding our conscious attention to the music's repeated redefinition of a character therein. (See our case study of *The Searchers* for examples of how Steiner's score features leitmotifs in numerous revealing variations.) However, in the examples of *Rebecca* and *Heavenly Creatures*, music repeatedly calls attention to identities not only in flux, but *unpredictably so*. In *Rebecca*, Franz Waxman's many different arrangements of the music associated with both Mrs. Danvers and Rebecca reinforce an impression of their queer elusiveness. In *Heavenly Creatures*, Dasent's score features leitmotifs that are associated with the two female leads as they assume different sexualized and gendered identities. The film also features songs performed by Mario Lanza, hymns, and operatic arias which further complicate the various identities that the girls assume. Both films' scores might be said to destabilize characters' identities in a thoroughly Butlerian manner.

It is, of course, unlikely that either score was conceptualized in terms such as these. As we find with every case study in this book, hearing cinema properly means perceiving possibilities that exceed what might be automatically ascribed to any filmmaker's original intent. We gain possibilities by adopting a Butlerian approach: like the sexual or gendered identities which she conceptualizes in terms of ceaseless repetitions that undo the limitations of fixity, these films lend themselves to endless processes of reconceptualization. Both *Rebecca* and *Heavenly Creatures* explore the devastating consequences of queer characters being repressed, and both end in tragic death. Applying Butler's work to both films can, however, help us understand the unconventional *lives* within them as well as appreciating the strength of life which the films themselves represent: the sound tracks of both films represent the kinds of possibility and open-endedness that defy endings and death.

Our focus on sound tracks represents a new, significant extension of Butler's principles. As Lisa M. Walker writes, Butler's work tends to privilege *visual* signifiers of difference when it comes to identifying subversive possibilities, particularly with regard to the potential of drag. Walker herself writes about the experience of "passing" for a straight woman because she did not wear the clothes that would set her apart by signifying her lesbian identity: she specifically recounts wearing cashmere instead of the "ubiquitous flannel-shirts-and-jeans" which were the "lesbian drag of the 1980s" (1993, 866–67). Walker is herein clearly writing about her experience of decades ago. However, her critique of the emphasis on visual signifiers (or absence thereof) remains applicable to Butler's work. Though Walker does not then move on to considering aural indicators of subversiveness, her work logically resonates with the entire purpose of this book as it queers the hegemony of the visual.[11] More specifically, Walker's critique of the visual bias in much of Butler's work resonates with both *Rebecca* and *Heavenly Creatures* because the queer characters of these films could visually "pass" for being straight in the feminine clothes they wear. Because our queer protagonists are visually defined as so-called "femme lesbians"[12] they would be far less noticeably subversive were it not for the numerous queer sonic cues that demand our attention. It is the *aural* dimensions of both films which emphasize that these characters retain their power as "inappropriated others."[13]

---

[11] The "hegemony of the visual" is widely acknowledged to the extent that it has become something of a cliché in sound-track studies. For representative work on recognizing (as well as challenging) this, see the 2012 special issue of *Music and the Moving Image* 5 (2) devoted to teaching sound tracks.

[12] Ironically, and with close reference to Judith Butler, Biddy Martin argues for the subversive power of the "femme lesbian" as follows: "the very fact that the femme may pass implies the possibility of denaturalizing heterosexuality by emphasizing the permeabilities of gay/straight boundaries. In a sense, the lesbian femme who can supposedly pass could be said most successfully to displace the opposition between imitation (of straight roles) and lesbian specificity, since she is neither the same nor different, but both" (1994, 113).

[13] As Walker writes, Trinh T. Minh-ha uses this concept for those who are neither fully assimilated into mainstream heterosexist society nor able to transcend its power because they are "othered" (Walker 1993, 870).

Of course, as Walker points out, Butler has done much to denaturalize relationships between "visible signifiers and the gendered identities they signify" (1993, 883), and to expose "the fiction of heterosexual coherence" when it comes to the visual body in particular. She deconstructs the notion that a "male body should contain a masculine self and the female body a feminine self and that each body's desires will be regulated by the compulsory practice of heterosexuality" (883).[14] As Walker also points out, Butler's frequent "reliance on the trope of visibility" means that "radical consciousness is [often] ascribed to radical appearance" and she "is forced to privilege the butch as the figure that represents the radical discontinuity of sexual and gender identities given that the femme appears to be an integrated, stable subject according to the rules of normative heterosexuality" (884). So it is that the femme lesbian is potentially doubly marginalized because her subversive identity is rendered comparatively "invisible." Walker thus finishes her article with a challenge to "continue to complicate our ideas about what counts as radical self-representation for minority identities" (888). By redirecting Butler's preoccupations towards aural strategies, we pick up from where Walker left off, opening up a hitherto under-researched area of possibility.

In another of her most influential works, *Exciteable Speech*, Butler herself turns attention more towards the subversive possibilities of language, and she suggests ways in which a marginalized subject can resist hegemony by repeating words so that "they enter *new* contexts and develop *new* meaning" (1997, 15).[15] For example, as Kathy Dow Magnus explains, a "word with negative connotations can be assumed in a positive manner and repeated over time in such a way that it attains affirmative meaning" (2006, 88). Such is the case with how the term "queer" has come to signify possibilities for subversion, resistance, and positive self-definition. Magnus argues that within much of Butler's work it remains unclear as to whether such creative power to reclaim words belong to individual subjects or to "language" (88). Or, as Magnus writes (borrowing a phrase from *Exciteable Speech*), "the subject can protest her situation and 'talk back' to socially constructed authorities, but she cannot escape her situation of fundamental subjection [herself]" (Magnus 2006, 84; Butler 1997, 15). Gill Jagger offers a much less fatalistic response to Butler's work. For Jagger, Butler always assumes a basic premise

---

[14] For the original reference, see *Gender Trouble* (1990, 136–37). Butler has also discussed the linguistic vulnerability of the subversive subject who is limited by the norms of speech in terms of making themselves intelligible as well as being exposed or subjected to the language of others (for some discussion of this aspect of Butler's work, see Mills 2007, 142).

[15] See Magnus for a fuller discussion of this argument (2006, 88). Also, see Jagger's section on *Exciteable Speech* (2008, 115–35) for much more analysis of Butler's arguments in that book. (Jagger's entire book is a strong introduction to all Butler's key works.)

that, though we inevitably exist within dominant power systems, we are not necessarily limited by dominant ways of speaking: "we are in some ways linguistically constituted, but . . . it does not follow from this that we are linguistically *determined*" (2008, 115, original emphasis). For the purposes of analyzing two queer sound tracks, we can open up the concept of language to include cinema and its "vocabulary" of dominant scoring practices. Both *Rebecca* and *Heavenly Creatures* place special emphasis on using conventional musical "language" in atypical ways to empower their queer protagonists. Indeed, the music of both films is crucial for representing queer characters as powerful agents of self-definition and subversion beyond subjection.

Here are some questions about sound tracks in relation to "Imitation and Gender Insubordination." The following questions adapt and develop Butler's primary arguments in relation to aural aspects of cinema. We shall apply these questions to both our case studies for queer theory.

- Does the sound track challenge (or reinforce) the heteronormative status quo?
- Does the sound track privilege homosexual or heterosexual characters in terms of their presence and/or narrative and/or emotional life and/or perception?
- Does the sound track reinforce our understanding of any character's queerness?
- To what extent does the sound track encourage us to label the characters of the film in terms of fixed definitions of gender and sexuality?
- Do any elements of the sound track *discourage* us from labeling the main characters of the film in terms of fixed identities? Does the sound track therefore create possibilities for understanding identity (including gender and sexuality) in the open-ended way that Butler advocates?

In another of her widely regarded works, *Precarious Life*, Butler writes:

> Those who gain representation, especially self-representation, have a better chance of being humanized, and those who have no chance to represent themselves run greater risk of being treated as less than human, regarded as less than human, or indeed, not regarded at all (2004, 141).

By applying the questions above, we shall better understand how the sound tracks for *Rebecca* and *Heavenly Creatures* humanize those who are all-too-often dehumanized or ignored.

/ / / 14 / / / **REBECCA**

PLOT SUMMARY

Describing the action of *Rebecca* is far from straightforward since the titular character around whom most of the action revolves has died before the plot begins.[16] Most
plot synopses for the film begin with emphasis on the unnamed character played by
Joan Fontaine, to whom we shall refer to as "Fontaine" hereafter. "Fontaine" is a young
woman who falls in love with a widower named Maxim De Winter (Laurence Olivier),
a man seemingly tormented by the loss of his first wife who apparently drowned at
sea. After a prologue during which "Fontaine" dreams herself back to Manderley, her
husband's estate, the film begins an extended flashback from the time Maxim and his
new wife meet to the night that Manderley burns down. "Fontaine" and Maxim meet
in France while she is a paid travelling companion to one wealthy Mrs. Van Hopper
(Florence Bates). They enjoy a brief courtship and a hasty marriage before settling at
Manderley. Upon arriving at the mansion, "Fontaine" soon meets the housekeeper, Mrs.
Danvers (Judith Anderson), whose authoritative control of Manderley is immediately
established. Soon thereafter, the film makes Mrs. Danvers's obsession with the late Mrs.
De Winter manifest, along with Rebecca's haunting presence. Over the course of the
film, Mrs. Danvers repeatedly asserts her controlling influence over the new mistress,
and manipulates her into believing Rebecca is a peerless predecessor. Well into the film,
a body is discovered, that of the late Rebecca, and Maxim is forced to reveal several
shocking truths: the sham that was his and Rebecca's marriage, Rebecca's affair with
her "favorite cousin," Jack Favell (George Sanders), Rebecca's accidental death during

---

[16] In arguing for Rebecca's pivotal presence we challenge Rey's claim that "it is the man's world around
which the plot revolves" (1999–2000, 151). Were we to pay attention to the big shifts in plot without
full consideration of the film's style, and its sound track in particular, Rey's argument would have more
authority.

a vicious argument with Maxim (in which she declared herself pregnant by Favell), and his burial of her body on the boat which eventually resurfaced. In the ensuing investigation, a doctor reveals that Rebecca was dying of cancer, rather than pregnant as she evidently believed (or at least claimed), and though Favell suspects Maxim's foul play and attempts to blackmail him accordingly, the doctor's diagnosis satisfies the coroner that Rebecca's death was suicide. These findings are related to Mrs. Danvers by Favell and Maxim is left free to return to Manderley. When he arrives back at the mansion he discovers it ablaze: the fire is a suicidal act by Mrs. Danvers, prompted by her need for reunion with Rebecca.

A BRIEF OVERVIEW

As Jack Sullivan writes in his recent book-length study of music in Hitchcock's films, Hitchcock had his first access to a "lush Hollywood score" with *Rebecca* and he used it "to full advantage" (2006a, 58).[17] Sullivan counts seventy-one music cues: six by Max Steiner and two by Johann Strauss, but most by Franz Waxman (59).[18] Music is present in more than ninety minutes of the film's 130-minute run time (Neumeyer and Platte 2012, 17). For Sullivan, the "symphonic lavishness" of the score not only forms a startling contrast with Hitchcock's pared-down scores for his British films, it also "supplies enchantment" for *Rebecca* as "Hitchcock's Cinderella story" (2006a, 60). Sullivan develops his "Cinderella" reading of the film with references to the "haunted hero and heroine" (Maxim and "Fontaine") and the "witch" (Mrs. Danvers) (60). Sullivan is not

---

[17] Sullivan emphasizes David O Selznick's controlling role as producer although the film archives "make it clear that Hitchcock was [still] a strong force behind Waxman's music" (2006a, 63).

[18] A strong introduction to Franz Waxman's life and music is incorporated within Neumeyer and Platte's book-length analysis of the *Rebecca* score (2012, 1–34). A few details from this summary are worth our particular attention. Waxman composed during almost the entire period of the Classical Hollywood studio system. His first break in Hollywood was composing music for James Whale who requested an "unresolved score" for *Bride of Frankenstein* (1935): the film was a significant box-office success and set a new pattern for extensively using music that would be "an integral part of the film's character and style" rather than simply providing mood or accompaniment (6–7). Like Max Steiner, and other Classical Hollywood composers, Waxman mostly wrote music at the postproduction stage (15). That said, each of his scores is designed with such intricate relation to the film's action that it works integrally. He received Academy Awards for his scores for *Sunset Boulevard* (1950) and *A Place in the Sun* (1951). *Suspicion* (1941) is widely considered to be a "sequel" to *Rebecca*, not only in terms of its having also been directed by Hitchcock and starring Joan Fontaine, but also in terms of Waxman's score which he designed to similarly intensify the film's emotional context, dramatic conflict, and characterization (34). Waxman is renowned for the great variety and adventurousness within his music, his intriguing chromatic themes and deep contrasts of musical "color," and for serving many moods of a film by different orchestrations of the same melodies (12, 18–19). The score for *Rebecca* is representative of his work.

alone in describing Mrs. Danvers as a "witch:" she is commonly demonized in critical work about the film.[19] However, as we shall explore, the film's sound track provides us with much more than a good-and-evil fairytale in which sympathies are uncompromised. In particular, Waxman's score demands that we "hear" the comparative complexity of the film's queerest characters: Mrs. Danvers and Rebecca.

While Waxman was aware that the principle of aiming for unobtrusiveness was becoming a cliché of his own time, he argued that subduing music to the point of inaudibility was pointless: indeed, he maintained that "a motion picture score should be noticed just as much as you notice the other elements" (Sullivan 2006a, 77). So Waxman's music was deliberately composed to call attention to itself and this music will be our primary emphasis through this analysis. Though there are some noteworthy sound effects, these are comparatively pared down, in keeping with general Classical Hollywood practice. We will, however, consider some striking sound-effect motifs in addition to the vocal performances and dialogue of *Rebecca*.

THE FILM'S BEGINNING: ESTABLISHING REBECCA'S UNPREDICTABLE POWER

The music of *Rebecca* begins with a timpani roll [0:21–0:24] and tremolo strings [0:24–0:36]. The score immediately establishes a sense of intrigue, dread, and trembling indeterminacy. The tremolo strings rise and fall as mist clears on the screen, establishing a pattern of Mickey-mousing that is often used ironically elsewhere in the film. The woodwinds lead a brief section of chromatically rising and falling notes that are traditionally evocative of wind [0:37–0:40] before the first articulation of the main Rebecca theme, led by strings, over the main credits [0:40–1:28]. This theme rather suddenly materializes, along with the film title, as if out of nowhere: in other words, the furtive opening dominated by tremolo strings does not anticipate the full articulation of the melody. The clear connotations of the Mickey-mousing and the woodwind phrase offset the surprise of the Rebecca theme. These two forms of music establish a push-me-pull-you pattern of relative predictability and unpredictability throughout the film.

The intriguing pull of unpredictably is overwhelmingly towards Rebecca, a character whose name echoes throughout the film and whose identity is impossible to reduce given the varying accounts of her. In terms of queer theory, it is especially significant that this character who is commonly understood as bisexual, and who inspires the

---

[19] See Hepworth (1995, 188) for a representative example.

FIGURE 5.6 The melodic line of "Rebecca's Theme" by Franz Waxman (transcribed directly from the DVD).

lesbian attachment of Mrs. Danvers, is consistently most powerful. [20] The film thus reverses the more usual hierarchy of sexually conservative characters over-and-above sexually "deviant" characters. In its first iteration, the main melodic line of the Rebecca theme is as follows [0:40–1:28] (see Figure 5.6):

The theme is fully orchestrated right away. The parallel phrasing combined with wide and unpredictable melodic leaps evoke the expressive scale of Rachmaninov's melodies. The theme features other strong Romantic patterns: a combination of conjunct and disjunct notes, long arching phrases, and extremes of pitch. The theme therein relates to the several narrative romanticizations of Rebecca which other characters offer before we learn the truth of who she was (or, at least, the truth of who she was for Maxim). The parallel phrasing of the theme (and the harp glissandi that accompany it) surely allude to the ebb-and-flow of the sea that is literally and figuratively crucial to the plot, both in relation to Rebecca's death and her ever-changing identity. The drum rolls as well as the harp glissandi which punctuate the first *forte* iteration of the main theme also create a sense of intriguing, magical, and mighty power. Peter Franklin writes of this theme as "an abandoned roller coaster of abandoned passion and sensuality," sweeping us away "with the expectation of pleasure" (2011, 77).

It is crucial that the main theme is stated so strongly in the film's opening. This not only establishes its aural primacy but also means that even the briefest returns to it are easily recognized thereafter. Because this music is most directly associated with the ghostly presence of the titular character, the sound track thus privileges her presence. Since we can never see Rebecca, the music is atypically crucial for establishing her hold over other

---

[20] For a sense of this collective consensus on the bisexuality of Rebecca see the "Dossier on Hitchcock" section of Creekmur and Doty's *Out in Culture* (1995, 183–306) which includes essays by Hepworth, Wood, and Berenstein.

characters, even before we know who or what she is, and even in her visual absence. In writing music for her, Waxman was well aware of how much his scoring must do:

> Rebecca, the really dominant character of the story, is dead—in actuality she never appears in the scenes, yet the entire drama revolves around her. Through the speech and actions of others, and particularly through the use of music, her character with all its powerful effects had to be revealed to the audience. For this reason in composing the film score I wrote the main theme for the picture representing Rebecca. [...] Whenever a scene involving Rebecca appeared on the screen, it was up to the music to give Rebecca's character life and presence (Neumeyer and Platte 2012, 86).

After the first iteration of the Rebecca theme, as Hitchcock's name appears on the screen, another main theme is introduced [1:38–1:48]. This second theme is for Manderley. The first scene following the opening credits is an introduction to that place and includes four iterations of that theme [1:49–3:40]. Therefore, the Manderley theme is immediately established as being of primary significance too. Though this analysis does not include sustained consideration of the Manderley theme, there is already some substantial discussion of it in the book about Waxman's entire score by David Neumeyer and Nathan Platte. Suffice to say that, since Manderley is inextricably connected with the haunting memory of Rebecca, all its associated music leads us back to her.

Along with the opening Manderley music, we hear "Fontaine's" first voiceover beginning "Last night I dreamt of Manderley." She speaks of the place in anthropomorphic terms, as "secret and silent" with its "staring walls" and "no whisper of the past." Thus the idea of a human presence inhabiting the empty spaces is verbally enforced, as is the concept of the house as a stand-in for Rebecca. "Fontaine's" opening voiceover also emphasizes the importance of what is not spoken in the film. Given that much of *Rebecca* focuses upon a love that dare not speak its name (that is, Mrs. Danvers's infatuation with her late mistress), this has particular queer resonance. "Fontaine" then speaks of sometimes choosing to "return" to Manderley in her dreams, and to "the strange days" which begin, for her, in the South of France where she met Maxim. Upon her mentioning the South of France, the film suddenly cuts from the image of Manderley, accompanied by its theme, to an image and sound of crashing waves [3:41]. Within the ensuing flashback, there is a love theme for Maxim and "Fontaine" [4:19–4:36].[21] The love theme is

---

[21] Some critics, including Sullivan, refer to this character as "I" but this creates a misleading impression that she is the dominant character: though we often view the action as from her point of view, the film prompts ironic detachment from her perspective. Daphne du Maurier's novel *Rebecca*, the well-known primary sourcetext of the film, provides a much more consistent sense of intimacy with the same character

immediately affecting because it punctuates the moment when she interrupts his suicidal contemplation of the sea. However, the relative power of the love theme is undermined by its being relatively short and its being introduced quietly on a solo clarinet, as well as its being heard along with the sound of the sea that is later consistently associated with Rebecca: not only did she allegedly die by drowning, but Mrs. Danvers makes a point of telling "Fontaine" that Rebecca's was the only bedroom at Manderley overlooking the sea. The sounds of the sea stand in for Rebecca's visual presence with implications of elemental ferocity and ever-changing massivity. The power of Rebecca's theme, along with the sudden interruption of the Manderley theme, and the aural motif of waves, all reinforce her sonic primacy. The love theme seems weak by comparison.

Though *Rebecca* ostensibly follows "Fontaine's" narrative, she often operates more as a device for revelation than a protagonist in her own right. She seems like a blank canvas: her plainness is commented upon by Maxim's sister, she attempts to dress as Rebecca, and she imitates the looks of archetypally beautiful women in magazines. Rebecca, by contrast, is described as a singular and unique beauty of the sort that can never be fully known. The film's music consistently reinforces our understanding of Rebecca's comparatively mysterious, *unpredictable* power. For instance, when "Fontaine" asks Maxim's assistant, Frank Crawley (Reginald Denny), many questions about Rebecca, we hear a novachord variation on the first phrase of her theme. Though much of his score was orchestrated by Leonid Raab, Waxman himself chose to use the novachord to make Rebecca's theme often stand out against the "normal orchestra" for other, living characters (Sullivan 2006a, 77). The novachord is a polyphonic synthesizer, and it was first manufactured in 1939, just a year before *Rebecca* was released. As Waxman said, it "has a peculiar sound of unreality—of something that you cannot define" (Neumeyer and Platte 2012, 116). Using this unfamiliar instrument connoting "unreality" reinforces an impression of spooky strangeness at the precise moment that "Fontaine" requires some clear answers about who Rebecca was [52:56–53:09]. In the same scene, "Fontaine" expresses intimidation about being less than Rebecca for Maxim. Frank assures her that her own qualities of kindness, sincerity, and modesty matter more than the past represented by Rebecca. But when "Fontaine" ultimately asks him what Rebecca was like, the statement he makes invites us to run wild with a fantasy never given material form: "I suppose she was the most beautiful creature I ever saw." The first phrase of Rebecca's theme (on novachord) underscores the significance of "Fontaine's" question, along with

---

because she narrates the entire story in the first person. Both Rebecca and Mrs. Danvers are intimidating presences in the novel, not least in terms of their voices (Rebecca's voice being frequently imagined by the narrator), but their combined power is much more palpable in the film's sound track.

FIGURE 5.7 Frank Crawley and "Fontaine" are shown from a distance that makes them appear small in relation to their subject of conversation: Rebecca.

a pregnant pause afterwards [55:12–55:25]. The brief silence allows for the full force of Frank's answer, which is then followed up by the first phrase of the Rebecca theme on strings with harp glissandi at *forte*. At this rearticulation of Rebecca's music, the camera pulls back from Frank and "Fontaine," making them appear smaller while she looks especially defeated [55:30–55:40]. Thus, the music punctuates the moment when others are belittled in relation to Rebecca (see Figure 5.7).

A SELF-CONSCIOUSLY ANACHRONISTIC APPROACH

This study of *Rebecca* is shaped in terms of a theory that has been fully developed long after the film was released. Therefore it is knowingly anachronistic. Certain details within the film are especially, ironically resonant in this context: for instance, "Fontaine" refers to a mysterious old man whom she meets near the sea where Rebecca reportedly died as "a *queer* sort of person" [52:34], and Maxim refers to Rebecca herself as "queer" [1:35:51]. Though the word "queer" means "odd" in the context of the film, rather than subversive in a contemporary or Butlerian sense, its usage still connotes that which cannot be explained and which therefore invites closer analysis.

Rebecca rewards queer theory analysis through its many inherent levels of irony. First, and most obviously, the film overtly challenges the status quo by queering traditional power structures of representation: the heterosexual newlyweds are awkward together for most of the film and, putting it bluntly, they are simply less interesting than the uncanny presences of Rebecca and Mrs. Danvers. The dominant social order is therefore represented as strangely fragile in comparison with the robust, death-defying power of Rebecca and Mrs. Danvers's love for her. Waxman's music repeatedly emphasizes the combined power of Rebecca and Mrs. Danvers at the ironic expense of the heterosexual leads.

Several other patterns of aural irony are particularly noticeable. Almost every scene of the film (up until the investigation sequence towards the end) is punctuated with music. The effect of so much music is to give the film an almost constant feeling of barely suppressed hysteria, mania, or melodrama (a pattern that also, as we shall explore, applies to *Heavenly Creatures*): this in itself invites us to oscillate between ironic extremes of being caught up in and feeling detached from it. The music often works in ironic opposition to the actions and/or words of "Fontaine." This is playfully obvious in her first conversation alone with Maxim at the hotel restaurant. She tells him about her miserable personal circumstances—being forced into becoming the paid travel companion to the overbearing Mrs. Van Hopper due to the death of both her parents—and their conversation is lightly underscored by two pleasant waltzes that are suitable for refined dining rather than her speech [8:42–9:50].[22] Elsewhere, Mickey-mousing frequently punctuates her actions with ironic overdermination, such as when she almost falls in front of her new servants at Manderley, and descending notes for flutes playfully punctuate her clumsiness [37:37–37:38]. The Mickey-mousing emphasizes that she is out of her depth in a dramatically ironic way.[23] There is also the irony that, though we follow "Fontaine's" trajectory through most of the film, she is never named. This does not mean that she has the allure of mystery, however. Indeed, in terms of her dialogue and the music which accompanies her, she represents the dullness of accessibility in comparison with the mysteries of Rebecca in particular.

Though "Fontaine" is nameless, she might easily be labeled a naive girl, ingénue wife, or, as Max uncharitably calls her, "idiot" and "fool." Even as she changes over the course of the film and loses her innocence in the marriage with Maxim (as he, with apparently unwitting condescension, observes), she remains to some extent a blank surface upon which the film writes: the scene in which those home movies projected by Max flicker across her face symbolically reinforces this impression (see Figure 5.8).

---

[22] This portion of the scene (which includes several waltzes) includes two by Johann Strauss, Jr.: "Künsterleben," op. 316, waltz no. 3, and "Rosen aus dem Süden," op. 388, waltz no. 4 (identified as such, along with the other waltzes of the scene, by Neumeyer and Platte (2012, 100)).

[23] "Fontaine's" clumsiness is part of the film's overall emphasis on her childishness and naiveté. Berenstein notes that "even the doorknobs are positioned at a height that make Fontaine look childlike in her attempts to reach them" (1995, 244)

FIGURE 5.8 Maxim's home movies flicker across "Fontaine's" face, reinforcing the impression of her as a blank surface.

In contrast with the limitations of "Fontaine" being labeled and out of her depth, the film repeatedly emphasizes the powerfully intriguing implications, innuendos, and buried truths associated with Rebecca and Mrs. Danvers. And though it never overtly labels Rebecca or Mrs. Danvers as "bisexual" or "lesbian" (as we would expect given the time of its release), these possibilities are repeatedly invoked. Moreover, where the music often prompts ironic detachment from "Fontaine" (whether through counterpoint or Mickey-mousing) it almost always "agrees" with the sinister impressions and truths associated with Rebecca and Mrs. Danvers. Even when the music for Rebecca and Mrs. Danvers communicates the kind of overdetermination that can tend towards parody, it also invokes a wordless power beyond final definition. Rebecca's aural presence is also the most ironically powerful in that she is physically absent from the film.

So, *Rebecca* uses the cumulative power of many aural forms of irony—music that creates dramatic irony and ironic hyperbole, ironic clashes between sound and image, and the ultimate irony of Rebecca's strong aural presence despite her visual absence—all of which invite us to read beyond the film's surface. We can easily use this pattern to "authorize" a queer reading of *Rebecca*. After all, "irony" entails not accepting things at face value. Put simply: *Rebecca* cannot be fully interpreted "straight."

CHALLENGING HETEROSEXUAL (AND PATRIARCHAL) PRIVILEGE

There is another crucial pattern of aural irony within *Rebecca* that rewards queer analysis. The visually dominant, heterosexual pairing at the center of the film—"Fontaine" and Maxim—is repeatedly challenged by music that undermines their experience or the truth of what they say. This is startlingly clear during the climactic scene of Maxim and "Fontaine's" marriage, where they are eventually, lovingly united [1:31:39–1:38:15]. During this scene, Maxim finally reveals who Rebecca was to him and how she died. Before the film's on-screen action begins, Rebecca disclosed her affair with Favell to Maxim, in response to which he struck her and she died falling on a heavy piece of ship's tackle. Maxim buried her at sea on a boat. When Rebecca's body resurfaces (within the on-screen plot), he is forced to reveal the truth to his new wife.

Right after Maxim shocks "Fontaine" with the truth of his hating Rebecca, there is a doom-laden, minor-key variation on the love theme [1:31:27–1:31:37]. The music matches "Fontaine" looking aghast: but this alignment with her is fleeting. Maxim then finally reveals his history with Rebecca, including the circumstances of her death. The music underscoring his speech begins with a slowly developed variation on Rebecca's theme [1:31:39–1:32:32]. Here, the soft mellow sound of an alto flute accompanied by harmonious strings clashes with Maxim's bitter speech about her being "incapable of love or tenderness or decency." The scoring is, as Neumeyer and Platte write, "decidedly anempathetic" (2012, 135) to the on-screen characters because it reflects Rebecca's beauty and her public persona instead of Maxim's bitterness or "Fontaine's" shock. The underscoring for the rest of Maxim's speech about who Rebecca really was includes further variations on her theme, as well as variations on the associated theme of Manderley, that become comparatively menacing and haunting—they are progressively lower in pitch and marked by suspenseful tremolo strings and harp glissandi, as well as the re-entrance of the novachord. Maxim describes Rebecca walking towards him and asking "aren't you going to kill me?"—a question that made him "mad for a moment" before he struck her. There is a heavy silence for several seconds after Maxim remembers Rebecca having fallen, as if the sound track cannot continue without her [1:37:13–1:37:17]. A timpani roll and further variant on Rebecca's theme begin the next cue, suggestive of her rising even after death.

After Maxim's monologue ends, "Fontaine" excitedly argues against his apparent resignation to the condemning power of Rebecca's resurfaced body. She asks Maxim whether anyone else knows the truth, and her question is underscored by a variation on the Manderley theme [1:38:23–1:38:34]. At this point she is turned away from Maxim, but when she soon turns to face him, consolidating her strength and devising a clear plan for Maxim to evade suspicion, the music changes. With uncharacteristic assertiveness she insists that, if Rebecca's resurfaced body is identified, he must simply state he "made a mistake about the other body." By this point in the film, Rebecca's presence has been so strongly emphasized (especially through her theme) that "Fontaine's" assertions—"Rebecca can't speak, she can't bear witness, she can't harm you anymore" [1:38:59–1:39:03]—can only ring hollow. However, "Fontaine's" determination is reinforced by a theme titled "Regeneration," a cue taken from Waxman's score for *The Young At Heart* (1938), which is ironically featured a few minutes earlier in *Rebecca* when "Fontaine" has seemingly been outdone by Mrs. Danvers [1:38:48–1:39:05].[24] "Regeneration" is shaped by surging string phrases that evoke Romantic urgency and match "Fontaine's" desperation in this scene. This music segues into a variation on the love theme [1:39:05–1:39:30] that also reinforces the hope of triumph that she seizes: "No matter what happens now, she [Rebecca] hasn't won!" But "Fontaine's" claim is immediately undermined by the abrasive sound of the phone, some resurfacing music evocative of the sea,[25] a variation on the Manderley theme, a doom-laden, heavy timpani roll punctuating the transition into the next scene of examining Rebecca's body, and a *forte* restatement of the opening phrase of the Rebecca theme featuring low brass [1:39:31–1:40:38]. The phone call in this scene comes from the Constable questioning whether Maxim has made a mistake in identifying Rebecca's body: it thus represents a profound potential threat to the couple's security. Thus, the culmination of the heterosexual love plot is thrown into relief by an emphasis on Rebecca's newly arisen corpse. "Fontaine" is surely wrong that "she hasn't won."

Moments before the constable's call, there is a celebrated "ghostly tracking shot" which moves around in time with Maxim's description of Rebecca's death (Schantz 2010, 7). The camera traces where the movements that Maxim describes took place, and thus "dynamizes Rebecca's absence" (Modleski 1982, 50). The camerawork moves over several objects, specifically those mentioned by Maxim as he describes Rebecca "lying on a divan, a large tray of cigarette stubs beside her. She looked ill, queer. Suddenly she got up, started to walk towards me." Here, Rebecca's capacity to luxuriate in excess, her illness, her queerness, and her threatening demeanor are all combined

---

[24] As noted by Neumeyer and Platte (2012, 139), the earlier use of "Regeneration" comes after the costume ball in which "Fontaine" has unknowingly dressed like Rebecca by following Mrs. Danvers's devious advice. This music underscores much of the ensuing confrontation between "Fontaine" and Danvers [1:21:43–1:22:34].

[25] There are many different cues associated with the sea in *Rebecca*: indeed, though Neumeyer and Platte identity specific melodic phrases associated with the sea (2012, 93), they also mention that this music is "never repeated the same way," which is a "musical reflection of the sea's treacherous unpredictability" (92–93). The power in this elemental unpredictably is, of course, inextricably connected to Rebecca.

in a succinct commingling of concepts associated with "dangerous" homosexuality. The camera's movements, in accordance with Maxim's description, suggest Rebecca's physical actions. The visual emphasis on her agency, even in her absence, matches the dynamism of Waxman's variations on the Rebecca theme: both the camerawork and the music serve our better understanding of her. So, even though this scene represents a climactic, decisive shift in terms of Maxim and "Fontaine's" marriage, the film's stylistic interest remains with Rebecca.

Because the camerawork moves in accordance with Maxim's speech, we could argue that Rebecca exists here only in relation to him (thus undercutting her queer power). Mary Ann Doane, for instance, writes of the camerawork in this scene as enacting "the repression of the feminine—the woman's relegation to the status of a signifier within male discourse" (1999, 71). In this context, Doane also calls attention to how much Maxim speaks for Rebecca in the first person with the following statements from the scene: "I'll play the part of a devoted wife". . . "When I have a child, Max, no one will be able to say that it's not yours". . . "I'll be the perfect mother just as I've been the perfect wife". . . "Well, Max, what are you going to do about it? Aren't you going to kill me?" Doane does observe that the cumulative power of the first-person voice "for" Rebecca, along with the music and tracking camerawork, reinforce the impression of her subjective agency. However, for Doane, Maxim's speaking "for" Rebecca still ultimately allows him to "appropriate Rebecca's 'I.'" By contrast, Tania Modleski points out that the camera movements lead us to experience Rebecca's absence as "an active force," as something more powerful than that which might be contained in a flashback (1982, 41). Equally, for Ned Schantz, the film's visual and musical emphasis on Rebecca's absent presence "exceeds the delimiting power of [Maxim's] narrating voice" (2010, 7). We might also add that Maxim's attempt to take ownership of Rebecca's voice backfires since her first-person agency takes over his speech. Moreover, if we understand the speech as a kind of "coming-out" narrative about Rebecca, the emphasis remains on her identity over Maxim's power.

Whichever way we understand this climactic scene, Rebecca has an aurally overwhelming presence throughout the film. Though the visual elements of *Rebecca* often call attention to her absence, her aural power repeatedly asserts her presence *despite* its being disembodied and unearthly. Even after her body resurfaces, it is important that we do not see it along with those characters who examine it [1:40:40]. During the inquest scene, the camera is positioned so that we cannot see her body: the pattern of alluding to her presence without literally showing her remains intact (see Figure 5.9).

FIGURE 5.9 During the inquest scene, the film maintains its pattern of alluding to Rebecca's presence without literally showing her.

Were we to suddenly see Rebecca at this point, her uncanny power would undoubtedly be reduced. Instead, Waxman's music consistently allows her to exceed the limitations implied by the sight of a mortal body. In the absence of Rebecca's speech (except as she is quoted by Mrs. Danvers or Maxim), her theme works as an acousmatic "voice," one that forever evades what Chion defines as the reducing moment of "real embodiment" ([1982] 1999, 144).

Just as Rebecca's aural presence is the most powerful in the film, the power of "Fontaine" and Maxim is *frequently* undermined. This pattern is obvious early on in the film during their courtship. One of the first scenes of Maxim and "Fontaine" alone together, the so-called "terrace scene," shows "Fontaine" drawing a sketch of Max that is, by her own admission, humorously unimpressive. The underscoring of their conversation begins very lightly, including a comedic cue (a *scherzando*) as Maxim examines her rudimentary portrait of him. This is followed by the sonorous string-led statement of Maxim's theme that ends on a sour note [10:54–11:24]. The sudden change in musical implication anticipates the conversational shift to Manderley and the subsequent, poignant variation on its theme including a stinger [11:28–11:40]. That the music suddenly changes in tenor undoes the frivolity of the scene. Maxim soon abruptly ends the scene himself by offering to take "Fontaine" home.

Upon the cut to the very next scene, "Fontaine" overhears Mrs. Van Hopper gabbling to her nurse about how Max's wife drowned at Manderley.[26] A phrase from Mrs. Van Hopper's speech, "she was the beautiful Rebecca Henrith you know," is then thrice repeated in the next sequence which shows "Fontaine" sleeping restlessly [13:08–18]. The phrase is here repeated with an echoing effect, along with other phrases "Fontaine" has heard from Mrs. Van Hopper in an earlier scene: "they say he simply *adored* her" and "I suppose he just can't get over his wife's death." Thus the emphasis on Rebecca's beauty is restated, as is "Fontaine's" mistaken impression of Maxim's devotion to her. "Fontaine's" distorted impression is underscored by an oblique variation on Waxman's theme for Maxim featuring harmonics, sliding notes, and tremolo strings. We heard this theme clearly in the terrace scene (as noted above) but here it is manipulated almost beyond recognition. The strange power of such music offsets and ironizes the saccharine lightness of much music associated with "Fontaine" and Maxim's courtship before they are married. Moreover, the combination of hearing Rebecca's name often repeated along with the distorted variation on Maxim's theme suggests that, even when she and her music are not present, she still has the power to change who the other characters are.

REBECCA AND MRS. DANVERS'S MERGED POWER

Rebecca's unnerving power is most obviously emphasized by the ephemeral-evoking variations of her theme on novachord.[27] There are several examples of these, in addition to those already discussed. Another variation occurs when "Fontaine" enters Rebecca's morning room and sees all her stationery featuring the prominent letter "R" [39:33–39:51]. The music suddenly ends with the telephone ringing. "Fontaine's" part of the ensuing conversation is as follows: "Mrs. De Winter? Oh, I'm afraid you've made a mistake: Mrs. De Winter's been dead for over a year." No sooner has "Fontaine" awkwardly hung up the phone then she realizes her mistake in failing to identity herself: she

---

[26] The scoring of the scene in which "Fontaine" overhears Mrs. Van Hopper includes "Fontaine's" own theme [12:31–12:40], one that is notated in full by Neumeyer and Platte (2012, 91) but which is not given attention in this analysis except to mention its comparatively understated presence in the overall score. The theme for "Fontaine" includes a leap from F-sharp to B that is played twice, "a musical stammer that mimics our heroine's frequent moments of awkwardness or misunderstanding" (91). The theme for Maxim begins with a leap from F-sharp to B as well, subtly reinforcing a sense of their potential togetherness.

[27] Novachord variations on the Rebecca theme suddenly begin when Mrs. Danvers first shows "Fontaine" Rebecca's bedroom [34:00], and when "Fontaine" happens upon the beach house also used by Rebecca and there is a close-up on the initialed ("R de W") scarf she left there [48:51]. These variations are thus consistently associated with visual signifiers of Rebecca's haunting presence.

helplessly exclaims "Oh I mean. . ." to the person no longer listening, and then starts upon the silent entrance of Mrs. Danvers whose appearance is first registered on "Fontaine's" face, along with the entrance of her oboe-led theme [40:05–40:16]. Mrs. Danvers's theme plays as she explains the phone call was probably from the head gardener wishing instructions. Mrs. Danvers then says she requires instructions for the lunch menu, and another variation of the Rebecca theme takes over from her own theme [40:16–40:59]. By the end of this uncomfortable scene, the novachord has re-entered. Here, the music works against and dominates "Fontaine's" sugary and feeble delivery, and more directly underscores the hard authority of Anderson's lower voice. Yet again, the score emphasizes who holds the power, despite Mrs. Danvers's superficially servile request for her new mistress' "instructions." It also matters that the music for Rebecca and Mrs. Danvers merges in this scene, for this establishes their interconnected sonic power as well as the intimacy of their relationship.

Over the course of the film, it becomes increasingly difficult to separate the power of Rebecca from Mrs. Danvers's obsession with her. (Their inseparability is also emphasized when the men investigating Rebecca's death visit the doctor she saw near the end of her life, and we learn that she saw the doctor under the name of "Mrs. Danvers.") After Mrs. Danvers's exit, rising minor key strings and fragments of the Rebecca theme build in intensity until "Fontaine" accidentally breaks a china Cupid [40:48–41:14]. In the context of a film featuring little diegetic sound, the emphasis on this brittle noise is arresting. A novachord variation on Rebecca's theme soon re-enters [41:18–45], yet again reinforcing our sense of "Fontaine's" defeat as well as her weakness with a sense of Rebecca's irrepressibly resurfacing strength. Right at the end of the scene, after "Fontaine" has hastily hidden the broken Cupid in a drawer for fear of her accident being discovered by Mrs. Danvers, there is a snippet of her own theme [41:38–41:44]. Our only hearing a piece of her music connects her to the brittleness of the broken object and the mythologized cliché of love that it represents. "Fontaine" slumps back into her chair, visually embodying the defeat that the music plays out.

Soon after this action, Maxim's sister Beatrice tells "Fontaine" that Mrs. Danvers must be "insanely jealous of her new mistress" because "she simply *adored* Rebecca," and there is a fragment of another novachord variation on the Rebecca theme [43:32–43:35]. Beatrice's heavy emphasis on the word "adored," with its implication of more-than-Platonic obsession, is followed by this musical fragment along with a memorable shot of "Fontaine" in profile, turning her head towards the camera in a moment of barely concealed terror (see Figure 5.10).

Though "Fontaine's" face barely moves, the visual darkening of everything behind her in combination with the novachord music associated with Rebecca (as well as Mrs.

FIGURE 5.10 After Beatrice reveals that Mrs. Danvers *adored* Rebecca, "Fontaine's" face reveals her barely concealed terror.

Danvers's obsession with her) reveals her overwhelming comprehension. That the scene briefly engulfs "Fontaine's" face in darkness precisely upon the novachord cue suggests that Rebecca (*and* Mrs. Danvers, by implication) has the power to obliterate everything around her. At the very least, the devastating strength of Mrs. Danvers's lasting obsession with Rebecca is visually and aurally marked.

MRS. DANVERS'S MUSIC (AND HER SILENCE)

Mrs. Danvers's own theme is first heard when "Fontaine" first meets her and clumsily drops her gloves [30:33–31:03]. Right before Mrs. Danvers's theme begins, there is music for strings and trumpets that emphasizes the pomposity of the entire Manderley staff presenting themselves to Maxim and "Fontaine" [30:10–30:32] What we hear is a fanfare by Cyril Mockbridge ("Take Me Back to Brighton") from *Stanley and Livingstone* (1939) (Neumeyer and Platte 2012, 114). The awkwardness of the couple in the sudden presence of so many staff is played comically, but the sudden appearance of Mrs. Danvers, and the corresponding shift in music, changes the tone of the scene (see Figure 5.11).

Though there is a hint of playfulness in the extremity of the musical contrast, the power of Mrs. Danvers to "change the music" and, by extension the whole scene, is unmistakable. Her theme is as follows (see Figure 5.12): This theme evokes an

FIGURE 5.11 Mrs. Danvers's first scene immediately establishes her confrontational power.

FIGURE 5.12 "Mrs. Danvers's Theme" by Franz Waxman (transcribed directly from the DVD).

immediate sense of melancholy and a subdued strain. As Neumeyer and Platte note, its emphasis on chromaticism, along with its "opening half-step climb, rhythm, and arch shape" parallel Rebecca's theme. Indeed, they question whether we should assume that it is the thematic origin for Rebecca's theme (given that we hear it first in the film proper) or whether we should consider it an "unnerving variant" on Rebecca's theme (2012, 87). Again, the inseparability of the two themes reinforces the queer closeness of the two characters.

In other scenes of the film, the significance of Mrs. Danvers's presence is also often ironically emphasized through her soundless entrances. One especially striking example occurs in the scene of Favell's sudden intrusion through a window which is loudly announced by Rebecca's dog [1:04:46]. *Moments later,* Mrs. Danvers almost silently enters the same room without being anticipated [1:05:16]. Though the film was made at a time when it was commonplace to leave out unnecessary diegetic sounds given the relative difficulty of adding them, there is an unusual pattern of delayed cuts to show Mrs. Danvers after or upon her noiseless entrances, which reinforces a sense of her stealthy and unnerving command.

As Sullivan writes, Hitchcock knew that silence "could be more sinister than any music" (2006b, 23). Debra Daniel-Richard also cites Hitchcock's emphasis on the effectiveness of silence, making specific mention of the surprising absence of music in much of the climactic crop duster scene of *North by Northwest* (1959) (2010, 58). Hitchcock clearly intended to use Mrs. Danvers's silent entrances for similarly menacing effects. He explained to Truffaut that "Mrs. Danvers was almost never seen walking and was rarely shown in motion. If she entered a room in which the heroine was, what happened is that the girl suddenly heard a sound and there was the ever-present Mrs. Danvers, standing perfectly still by her side. In this way the whole situation was projected from the heroine's point of view: she never knew when Mrs. Danvers might turn up, and this, in itself, was terrifying. To have shown Mrs. Danvers walking about would have been to humanize her" (Modleski 1982, 35). Hitchcock was thus clearly intent on making Mrs. Danvers an inhuman and even monstrous, or spectral, presence. He also evidently intended for Mrs. Danvers's silent entrances to be about emphasizing the subjective experience of "Fontaine." So, in placing emphasis on the mesmerizing power of Mrs. Danvers's silent entrances in terms of her impression on *us* more than on "Fontaine's" experience, we are reading against the grain of what the auteur said. Though recognizing the significance of Hitchcock's directorial role, we nevertheless explore meanings beyond the delimitations set out by him. This is a way of opening up the queer and unfixable identity of the whole film in addition to the identities of its individual characters.

The queer power of Mrs. Danvers's silent entrances is repeatedly marked by "Fontaine's" sudden gasp, or look of shock, such as when Mrs. Danvers is suddenly present in the morning room scene already mentioned [40:06]. (Though Mrs. Danvers's music is included here, her entrance makes no sound in the diegetic space.) Much later, after "Fontaine" tentatively finds her way into Rebecca's bedroom, and after another disturbing variation on the Rebecca theme, Mrs. Danvers again stealthily enters the scene without a sound. Here, though, Mrs. Danvers's sudden appearance is preceded by the "stinger" effect of a window suddenly banging [1:08:30]. The film then cuts to show Mrs. Danvers through diaphanous drapes as from "Fontaine's" point of view. At this point, Mrs. Danvers's body is in complete silhouette and her voice communicates her assured dark power in asking "do you wish anything Madam?" The question is another of her disingenuous offers to assist her mistress. In this scene, it is "Fontaine" who will have to serve the morbidly obsessive Mrs. Danvers by listening to her. The interaction that follows is worth our careful attention since it is here that Mrs. Danvers most fully vocalizes her adoration for Rebecca.

In this whole sequence—from "Fontaine's" wandering into Rebecca's room, and being discovered there by Mrs. Danvers, to her exit—"Fontaine's" facial expressions are characteristically transparent reflections of vulnerability, awe, intimidation, and fear. Her visual transparency is complemented by Mickey-mousing music to match her movements with utmost clarity: a particularly striking example of this comes when she opens the drapes and harp glissandi match the motion [1:07:56–1:07:57]. By contrast, there is much subtextual suggestiveness in the details of Mrs. Danvers's speech: though the words love, obsession, desire, need, and devotion are never used, they are implied in almost everything she says. The powerful pull of both Rebecca's and Danvers's power within the scene is reinforced by Waxman's music: the scoring largely consists of variations on their respective themes "most fully given and developed, not merely cited in fragments" (Neumeyer and Platte 2012, 127).

At one particularly memorable point, Mrs. Danvers pulls out one of Rebecca's old fur coats and brushes it against her cheek (see Figure 5.13).[28] The moment of fur touching her skin is punctuated by a broken celesta chord, suggesting a magically relived moment of touch [1:09:34–1:09:35]. Mrs. Danvers then continues to speak of Rebecca in unmistakably intimate terms. She refers to Rebecca's underwear, to her bathing, and to waiting up for her ("no mater how late"). She speaks of how *everyone loved* Rebecca and how Rebecca "knew *everyone* that mattered." Here, her emphasis on "everyone" thinly conceals her singular attachment. She also quotes Rebecca saying "do my hair Danny" and "good-night Danny." The repeated mentioning of "Mrs. Danvers" being shortened to a male appellation reasserts her queer relationship to Rebecca, even in the context of her also mentioning Rebecca's relationships with men (Maxim and Favell). That Mrs. Danvers wishes to supplant the significance of these men is especially obvious in her calling attention to objects that signify her physical closeness to Rebecca: the brush that she used for Rebecca's hair, the pillow case that she embroidered for her, and the revealing black nightgown which she lovingly pulls out from under the pillow case to show "Fontaine." The black nightgown includes an unusual white collar detail which complements Mrs. Danvers's own white-collared black gown. When she shows "Fontaine" the transparency of Rebecca's

---

[28] Berenstein reads Mrs. Danvers removing the coat from Rebecca's wardrobe as a "humorous form of outing" (1995, 253).

FIGURE 5.13 Mrs. Danvers luxuriates in the feel of Rebecca's fur coat against her cheek.

nightgown against her hand, the film emphasizes the ironic parallel between her own dress and the nightgown as a much skimpier corollary to it (see Figure 5.14). This detail reinforces the impression of merging between Rebecca and Mrs. Danvers, a visual parallel to those aural patterns of merging that we have already explored.

Throughout this scene, Mrs. Danvers does not simply look at or hold such items as the nightgown, or the brush, or the pillow case: she talks almost ceaselessly about each one in turn. The nearly relentless underscoring of the scene also wills us to stay with her in her obsessive attention to detail. Her words allow her to savor the details that represent what was Rebecca's bodily presence and also repeatedly point to those words she cannot say. "Did you ever see anything so delicate?," she rhetorically asks as she holds the nightgown, inviting the dumbfounded "Fontaine" to touch it.[29] "Look, you can see my *hand* through it," says Mrs. Danvers, apparently mesmerized by the visual merging of her hand and that which was once against Rebecca's skin. In contrast with the sexually contained marriage of "Fontaine" and Maxim, this is the most erotically suggestive moment in the film.[30]

---

[29] For further discussion of how Mrs. Danvers physically involves "Fontaine" in her own "lesbian eroticism," see Samuels (1998, 53–55).

[30] This point is most self-consciously represented in the film when Maxim patronizingly tells "Fontaine" that his perfunctory proposal of marriage is probably far from what she imagined and then simply kisses her on the cheek. Even when they share a passionate kiss, right after Maxim has finally told her the truth about Rebecca, their clinch is interrupted by the constable's phone call.

FIGURE 5.14 Mrs. Danvers tenderly holds Rebecca's nightgown, a much skimpier version of her own white-collared black gown.

Soon after this point in the scene, Waxman's music reaches a *forte* peak [1:11:47–1:12:00]. Though "Fontaine" then makes an effort to leave, Mrs. Danvers keeps talking and, with her unnervingly controlled voice, she speaks of Rebecca's enduring aural presence: "Sometimes when I walk along the corridor I fancy I hear her behind me. Just a quick light step. I couldn't mistake it anywhere. It's not only in this room, it's in *all* the rooms in the house. I can almost hear it now." Then she invites "Fontaine" to listen to the "soothing" sea before turning back into the room. "Fontaine" then manages to sneak out but the scene ends with Mrs. Danvers walking back into the space inseparable from Rebecca, mesmerized by the sound associated with her death-defying power.

The scene ends by showing Mrs. Danvers again silhouetted against the diaphanous drapes, dissolving into the image of crashing waves, and then an address book with "R" embroidered in it. The audiovisual power associated with Mrs. Danvers, Rebecca, and the sea is aurally reinforced by a partial, menacing variation on the Rebecca theme led by brass and reinforced by frenetic tremolo strings, harp arpeggios, and glissandi [1:13:11–1:13:40]. This variation carries over into the next scene during which "Fontaine" insists "I'm Mrs. De Winter now!," instructing Mrs. Danvers to forget "everything that happened" in the previous bedroom scene. Mrs. Danvers merely looks at "Fontaine" with a slightly wry smile—there is a hint of surprise but no loss of composure. It seems almost as if Mrs. Danvers knows that she, along with the memory of Rebecca, still controls the film. The sound track only seems to confirm this.

THE UNNERVING POWER OF THE TREMOLOS

In addition to the musical themes obviously connected with Rebecca, Mrs. Danvers, and their merged identities, the use of tremolos is also much associated with these most powerful characters. If we consider that the tremolo is a rapid fluctuation between two different pitches or a rapid reiteration of one note, the pattern relates to concepts of irony or queer indeterminacy. The tremolo is a musical evocation of turbulence: a device we may connect with the challenge that the film represents to mainstream representations of heterosexual love. Such rapid fluctuations within single notes or between two notes also evoke how the film may be read in contrary ways: the "straight" interpretation of *Rebecca* makes "Fontaine" the anchoring point of the narrative and assumes the centrality of her position and her experience; but the queer reading of *Rebecca* hears the film differently, dwelling upon the unconventional power of an absent bisexual heroine and the woman obsessed with her. Tremolos punctuate numerous moments of the film that emphasize the instability of its heterosexual leads, and the strange power of its queer characters, such as when "Fontaine" gasps upon seeing that Mrs. Danvers has soundlessly left a scene [1:06:36]. Tremolos also mark the scene where "Fontaine" happens upon an old vagabond at the beach near Manderley who portentously alludes to Rebecca's enduring memory by asking "she won't come back will she?" [1:24:53–1:24:54]. (The film later implies that he, Ben (Leonard Carey), has witnessed Rebecca's death.) And when Mrs. Danvers makes her final walk through Manderley before the fire (three minutes from the film's end) there are tremolos along with a distorted version of the Rebecca theme. Like the recurring waves of the sea, and the numerous variations of Rebecca's theme, as well as the power of her name being heard more than any other through the film, the tremolos repeatedly point to her unfixed and unfixable, unnerving and uncanny power.

THE WALTZES (AND OTHER PLEASANT MUSIC) OF *REBECCA*

The turbulent-sounding tremolos reinforce the queer power of Mrs. Danvers and Rebecca. By contrast, along with the Mickey-mousing associated with "Fontaine," Maxim and "Fontaine" are often associated with the staid predictability of the waltz. The waltz comes in many forms throughout *Rebecca*. But there is a consistently ironic edge to the familiar triple-time form being used across different scenes. Along with the saccharine love music or light-to-the-point-of-parody music that is associated with their courtship, the waltzes musically communicate that which is ironically safe sounding in terms of rhythmic familiarity. The first waltz of the film is Waxman's cue for the grand hotel lobby where we meet "Fontaine" and the older woman she attends, Mrs. Van Hopper [4:53–7:51].[31] The music here signifies a kind of old-fashioned privilege which clearly intimidates "Fontaine." Several other waltzes lend ironic and strange buoyancy to the later restaurant conversation between "Fontaine" and Maxim when they are first becoming acquainted and she explains that her parents' death means she must earn a living as Van Hopper's companion.[32] A foxtrot serves a similarly ironic function when "Fontaine" and Maxim dance together at the culmination of their courtship, and she drifts into a reverie in his arms [14:45–15:17].[33] Here, the foxtrot signifies her dancing into a new life and her willingly idealistic surrender to that, a detail that is ironized by Maxim's indecorous control of and condescension towards her. Much later on, yet another waltz ("La Prima Donna" by Arthur Lange, from *The Great Ziegfeld* (1936))[34] is even more ironically used against "Fontaine" after she follows Mrs. Danvers's diabolical advice to dress "as" one of Maxim's ancestors for a ball at Manderley, only to discover that Mrs. Danvers has duped her into imitating the appearance of Rebecca [1:20:02–1:21:24]. As "Fontaine" delightedly approaches the ball in the outfit that will cause Maxim immediate outrage, the waltz playfully seems to encourage her mistake and thus works against her. (It is important that music never works "against" Mrs. Danvers or Rebecca in such parodic ways.)[35] As Neumeyer and Platte write, the use of this waltz is "one of the most starkly dissonant and anempathetic moments in the early Hollywood sound cinema" (2012, 131).

VOICES

Listening carefully to the contrasting voices of *Rebecca* further amplifies the ironies of the film and its queer representations of relative power. Most obviously and immediately, there is a striking contrast between the sugary sweet, soft, light, slow-paced, relatively high-pitched tones of "Fontaine" and Mrs. Van Hopper's snappish, aggressive, quick-paced, and lower-pitched voice. Maxim is played by an authoritative exemplar

---

[31] This waltz comes from Waxman's score from *Lady of the Tropics* (1939) and is arranged by Joseph Nussbaum (Neumeyer and Platte 2012, 99).

[32] The waltzes also signify a world of pomp and privilege that does not match "Fontaine's" humble station.

[33] This is Waxman's own slow foxtrot "Yacht Club" from *The Young at Heart* (Neumeyer and Platte 2012, 104).

[34] This particular waltz is identified as such by Neumeyer and Platte (2012, 130).

[35] This fits within a bigger pattern within Hitchcock's work of using the waltz as a "veneer covering impending disaster" (Sullivan 2006a, 69).

of the precision and status of Received Pronunciation: Laurence Olivier.[36] However, Olivier compromises the sway of his own Received Pronunciation by making it sound comparatively harsh. In *Rebecca*, Olivier hits every consonant emphatically, delivers every line quickly, and plays up extremes of pitch and volume to emphasize Maxim's suddenly shifting moods. Even when he uses the full melodiousness of his voice, he often does so as he delivers disconcertingly mixed messages to "Fontaine," such as when he says "I'm asking you to marry me you little fool!" Olivier also uses the beauty of his voice as a strategy for delivering all of Maxim's most condescending lines with the deceptive sound of kindness. The tension between what he says and how he says it is ultimately impossible to ignore: for instance, when he calls "Fontaine" a "little idiot" for fearing the servants after she breaks an ornament, the comparative gentleness of his intonation is undermined by the aggressive impatience of his words. At other points of *Rebecca*, Olivier's Received Pronunciation amplifies the sense of Maxim as a self-parody of Englishness, such as when he sarcastically tells "Fontaine" that she should read a "*thrilling* article" in *The Times* called "what's the matter with English cricket?" In a much later scene, during which Maxim flies into a rage after discovering "Fontaine" has entered Rebecca's beach house, the fearsomeness of which is anticipated with crashing waves against seaside rocks, his calmness suddenly returns in response to her tears. Here he finally acknowledges, "I seem to fly off the handle sometimes." But after this refreshing acknowledgment, one which generates expectations of fuller self-disclosure, he then simply suggests they get a cup of tea and "forget all about it." After the extremity of his rage, this seems like a parodic, more-English-than-the-English solution to a terrifying emotional imbalance. By contrast with Maxim/Olivier, one who is *mostly* able to modulate his voice at will, "Fontaine's" voice is immediately shaky when she is surprised or caught off guard. Her voice becomes especially weak in response to the uncannily silent entrances of Mrs. Danvers. She also flinches at Maxim's shouting, especially when he scolds her for being at Rebecca's beach house.

Yet for all Maxim's power over "Fontaine," and despite Olivier's authority in terms of vocal delivery, the real power of the story is with Rebecca and Mrs. Danvers, *even in their aural absence*. Of course, we never hear Rebecca's voice, but Anderson's voice for Mrs. Danvers is consistently the most controlled in terms of measured tempo, low pitches, and comparative strength. By contrast, Maxim gives in to several rages that

---

[36] Received Pronunciation is an accent originally associated with the private schools and universities of England in the nineteenth century. It is widely associated with the "social elite" and "the Establishment." Olivier as Maxim is partly defined by the prestige and privilege associated with his Received Pronunciation, and his voice is an especially sharp contrast with the regional accent of the vagabond Ben. (For more information on the history of Received Pronunciation, see the British Library Board website, n.d.)

temporarily threaten his ability to remain in control of his voice. (This is especially obvious in the courtroom scene during which only "Fontaine's" well-timed fainting deflects attention from Maxim's uncontrolled rage in response to questioning.) In the climactic scene where Maxim fully describes the way in which Rebecca died, he seems most agitated as he quotes Rebecca in the first person. The dominant impression at this point is her voice resurfacing through his. The cumulative impact of Maxim quoting Rebecca, in addition to "Danny" having quoted her several times, along with the many times her name is spoken and the numerous iterations and variations of her theme, communicates the unearthly possibility of a "voice" in multiple forms, one that is too powerful to be housed in one body.

THE ABSENT MUSIC

That Rebecca and Mrs. Danvers hold the primary aural power in the film is made ironically obvious in their absence for a long portion of the film during the investigation sequence. For our purposes, it is especially significant that there is no music for most of this sequence until the revelation that Rebecca had cancer [1:44:49–2:03:52]. This makes the investigation sequence comparatively flat except for the impish flair of Rebecca's former lover, Favell. The investigation itself is played out with some ironic emphasis on the reluctance of law enforcement to question Maxim—one senior officer even says he looks forward to playing golf with Maxim after everything is over.[37] This reluctance is manifestly connected to Maxim's relative social standing: he is, as Favell puts it, as "a big *noise* around here."[38] Maxim's tendency toward self-righteous anger on the stand makes a noticeable contrast with Ben's fear that he will be sent to an insane asylum in response to being asked about what he saw of Rebecca's death. Through this extreme contrast, the film evidently supports Favell's assessment of Maxim's relative privilege, as well as his ability to abuse it.

Ironically, Maxim's sense of entitlement, or of being a "big noise," is undercut by the scene-stealing, satirical presence of Favell blackmailing him, especially as he munches on some chicken from Maxim and "Fontaine's" lunch during a break from the investigation trial (see Figure 5.15).

---

[37] Favell also accuses Colonel Julian (C. Aubrey Smith) of "not wanting to conduct a thorough investigation for fear of having to forego his dinners at Manderley" (Modleski 1982, 40). Favell's accusation may be taken as a serious attack on the Law as it is represented by the film and, by extension, "the film does not present the men [who control the law] as clear and wholly deserving winners in the battle against feminine rule" (40).

[38] The emphasis on "noise" is inserted here.

FIGURE 5.15 While attempting to blackmail Maxim, Favell merrily munches on some chicken.

Maxim's power is also overshadowed by the intriguing absence of the woman around whom the entire investigation revolves yet whose aural presence remains the strongest in the film. The latter point is ironically emphasized in the sudden absence of the music and aural motifs that are associated with both Rebecca and Mrs. Danvers during the investigation sequence. For Sullivan, this absence places emphasis on what Maxim is confronting, especially his stark isolation and pain (2006a, 78). But perhaps it is more accurate to conclude that the film's real interest lies elsewhere. Certainly, the sudden aural absence of both Rebecca and Mrs. Danvers engenders a desire to return to the aural material that has been most fascinating up to the investigation sequence.

THE FINAL SCENE

The final scene of *Rebecca* culminates in Mrs. Danvers committing suicide by setting fire to Manderley with herself inside it. This shocking action steals attention away from the newly united Maxim and "Fontaine." Mrs. Danvers's suicide comes after Favell is shown telephoning her to reveal that Rebecca had been diagnosed with cancer before her death. In this context, Sullivan reads Mrs. Danvers's final leap into the flames as a consummation of her passionate longing for Rebecca (2006a, 80). The final two minutes of the film are dominated by unnerving variations on the "love" and Rebecca themes, featuring yet more tremolos along with stinger chords and blaring brass upon

Maxim's discovery of Manderley in flames. The overwhelming sounds of fire and falling beams briefly take over the final scene as Mrs Danvers ecstatically succumbs to her death (see Figure 5.16).

Moments later, the final shot of the film shows the embroidered pillowcase that Mrs. Danvers made for Rebecca engulfed in flames (see Figure 5.17). This image is punctuated by the final cue which gathers into a fully orchestrated, *forte* reiteration of the love theme. Sullivan thus reads this ending as a triumph of Maxim and "Fontaine" against Rebecca: for him, the love theme "does *triumphant* battle with the Rebecca motif" in the final moments of the film (2006a, 77, emphasis added). In line with this reading, Rothman argues that the burning of Manderley signifies the burning of patriarchy, thus leaving the possibility of a radically new partnership of equals for Maxim and "Fontaine" (2008, 97).

Such readings of the film's ending downplay the final visual close-up on the signifier of Rebecca, albeit one in flames. To argue for the triumph of Maxim and "Fontaine" is to also ignore the weight of all that precedes the ending: the aural empowerment of Rebecca and Mrs. Danvers, the critical representation of Maxim's threatening behavior, the ironic undermining of his marriage to "Fontaine," and the comparatively little air time given to "Fontaine's" newly empowered position as his wife. In addition, consider that the climactic fire is Mrs. Danvers's creation and that she is not necessarily undone by death: as Modleski writes, "if death by drowning did not extinguish a

FIGURE 5.16 In an ecstasy of grief, Mrs. Danvers willingly succumbs to her own death.

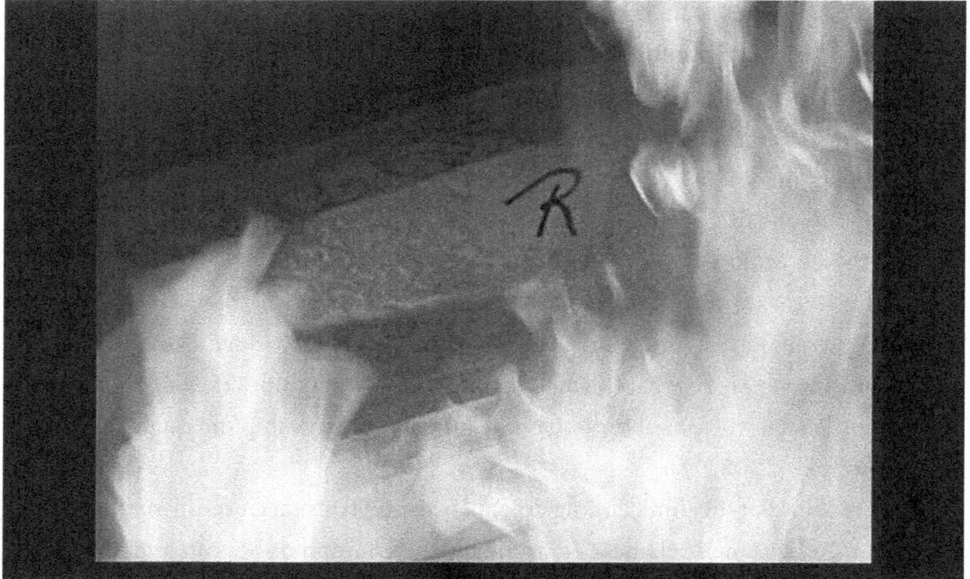

FIGURE 5.17 The final image of *Rebecca*, flames engulfing the pillow case that Mrs. Danvers embroidered for her late mistress.

woman's desire, can we be certain that death by fire has reduced it utterly to ashes?" (1982, 41). And while the final music places emphasis on the love theme, suggesting conventional triumph and a form of restored order, the music associated with Rebecca has still dominated most of the score.[39]

QUEER READINGS OF HITCHCOCK

The queer sound track of *Rebecca* is usefully contextualized in relation to other queer readings of Hitchcock's work. In her book, *The Women Who Knew Too Much*, Tania Modleski identifies patterns of representing ambiguous sexuality and destabilized gender across Hitchcock's films (1988, 5). To give a specific example, Lucretia Knapp reads the main female character of *Marnie* (1964) as one who "opens up possibilities to the lesbian spectator because she doesn't desire a heterosexual life" (1995, 273). Similarly, Sabrina Barton argues that in *Strangers on a Train* (1951) the "masterful" straight male subject position is shown as being "at once produced and continually threatened by its own paranoid homophobic and misogynist plots" (1995, 219). Though Barton does not

---

[39] Although the love theme is reiterated many times throughout the film, especially during defining moments of "Fontaine's" relationship with Maxim, it always seems slight and brief in comparison with the much more developed and consistently dominant melody for Rebecca.

claim that this film (or, by extension, any of Hitchcock's work) necessarily pulls down the privileged position of the bourgeois male subject, "it takes more than perverse pleasure in exposing the mechanisms of, and [the main male character's] complicity in, the displaced violence [against women and gays] required to ensure that privilege."[40] This is an argument that can be equally applied to the main male character of *Rebecca*, Maxim. As we have explored, the film's emphasis on Maxim's fallibility, moral dubiety, propensity for violence, and suppressed rage, especially in relation to his marriages, certainly undermines his patriarchal authority.

By contrast to such queer readings, John Hepworth finds a particularly brutal form of homophobia evident in Hitchcock's work. With emphasis on the two young murderers in *Rope* (1948), Bruno Anthony in *Strangers on a Train*, and Norman Bates in *Psycho* (1960), Hepworth argues that gayness is routinely attached to moral depravity and psychological disorders, if not monstrosity. He persuasively reads the "crazy killer faggots" of Hitchcock's films (especially in *Frenzy* (1972) and *Psycho*) as especially homophobic creations (1995, 190). His dismissal of Mrs. Danvers as a "crazy dike" (188), however, seems like a simplistic reduction of her mesmerizing presence and command in *Rebecca*. Robin Wood, on the other hand, takes a relativist position by arguing that all discussions of Hitchcock's supposedly gay and lesbian characters should be placed "in relation to the deeply troubled heterosexuals and heterosexual relationships that abound in his films" ([1982] 1995, 195).[41] Even if lesbianism is demonized in the form of Mrs. Danvers's maniacal manipulations and the apparent necessity of her violent death as the climax of *Rebecca*, as Doty puts it, "heterosexuality is not made to appear a particularly appealing alternative" (1995, 185).

In addition to these readings of troubled heterosexuality, William Rothman also calls attention to the pattern of troubled marriages within Hitchcock's work: "when married life is glimpsed at all, it is usually glimpsed darkly" (2008, 93). Rothman cites extreme examples like the brief glimpse we get of the Thornwalds in *Rear Window* (1954) before learning that Mr. Thornwald chopped his wife's body into pieces. As Rothman also points out, even the members of the happy couple at the end of *North by Northwest* have knowingly placed each other's life in jeopardy earlier in the film (96). In *Rebecca*, the marriage between Maxim and "Fontaine" is under strain until it is consolidated in the context of a murder investigation and a burning estate: that

---

[40] Alexander Doty provides this summary of Barton's argument in his introduction to the "Dossier on Hitchcock" section of *Gay, Lesbian, and Queer Essays on Popular Culture* (1995, 184).

[41] Wood makes this argument in direct response to Hepworth's reading of Hitchcock in addition to Hepworth's own allegation against Wood that he has been blindsided by the director's talent to the extent of ignoring his prejudice ([1982] 1995).

this harmony only comes in such dire circumstances implicitly emphasizes the vulnerability of the relationship in contrast with the unending desire that Mrs. Danvers holds for Rebecca.

In examining the sound track of *Rebecca*, we have considered how Maxim is critically represented. The film thus poses a threat to heteronormative and patriarchal control. Though Manderley burning down does not signify the end of the dominant order, it nevertheless generates an audiovisual climax at the will of Mrs. Danvers: Maxim and "Fontaine" can only watch the building collapse. They become bystanders to the main action (see Figure 5.18). Soon, the sounds of crackling flames, beams falling, and a partial dark rearticulation of the Rebecca theme transforms into a strong, but *only brief*, final statement of the love theme [2:10:23–2:10:33].

Such a queer interpretation of *Rebecca* could also be usefully contextualized in relation to existing critical work on the film, especially since the sound track is too often given short shrift. The identification of Rebecca as "queer" in the sense of being either lesbian or bisexual is widely accepted in scholarly work. In addition, Mrs. Danvers is frequently referred to as a lesbian (Schantz 2010, 12). Moreover, Berenstein even notes that Favell, the man with whom Rebecca has had an extramarital affair is played by George Sanders, a man whose general performance

FIGURE 5.18 Maxim and "Fontaine" become bystanders to the main action: the fire created by Mrs. Danvers.

suggests "a dandy, a feminized man who bears a striking resemblance to lasting stereotypes of male homosexuals" (1995, 247). Berenstein thus concludes that even Rebecca's heterosexual interests "may not have been very serious or very 'straight'" (247).

Berenstein also emphasizes that Rebecca's queer identity is indisputable even though it is "characterized as unutterable" or unspeakable (246). She notes the pattern in reviews contemporary with the film in terms of acknowledging Rebecca's peculiar power, though reviewers "shied away from enumerating exactly what kind of threat she (dis)embodied" (1998, 17). In her analysis of *Rebecca*, Berenstein thus casts herself as "a detective of sorts, a researcher who has thrilled at capturing and detailing elements of these films that have either remained unseen or rarely acknowledged by others" (33). We follow in her footsteps in terms of dwelling upon those elements of *Rebecca* that "have either remained *unheard* or rarely acknowledged by others" (33, emphasis added).

Despite the fact that many other scholarly works make the relationship between Maxim and Rebecca and/or "Fontaine" and Maxim the center of the film, we have dwelt most upon the queer power of Rebecca and Mrs. Danvers. We have thus focused on those parts of the film which were most immediately controversial and which were designed to escape too much attention. The Production Code administrators were well aware of, and concerned by, the queer meaning of Mrs. Danvers's relationship with Rebecca. Drawing on Leonard Luff's account in *Hitchcock and Selznick*, Berenstein explains that Joseph Breen, head of the Production Code Administration (PCA), was "quite explicit" about his concerns over the film's content. In particular, Breen objected to the representation of a murderer who gets off "scot free" (in response to which the script was adjusted to emphasize Rebecca's death as an "accident" from Maxim's perspective), the repeated references to the illicit affair between Rebecca and Favell, and the "quite inescapable inferences of sexual perversion" which were, for him, allusions to homosexuality (1998, 17). Breen communicated these concerns at the preproduction stage to O'Selznick. He reminded Selznick of that section of the Production Code which states that "sex perversion, *or any inference of it*, will not be allowed" (17). Even though Breen does not explicitly mention "lesbian desires," Berenstein reads the implication of them in his notes about the character of Rebecca which suggest both her homosexuality and bisexuality. For our purposes, it is especially significant that Breen wrote the following: "it will be essential that there be no suggestion whatever of a perverted relationship between Mrs. Danvers and Rebecca. If any possible hint of this creeps into this scene, we will of course not be able to approve the picture. Specifically, we have in mind Mrs. Danvers's description of Rebecca's physical attributes, her handling of the various garments, particularly the night gown" (18). It is puzzling that so much of what Breen objected to remained in the finished film: one can only assume, as Berenstein does, that the "*overt* intimations of perversion were excised" to Breen's satisfaction (18, original emphasis). Whatever limitations were placed upon the film, Rebecca and Mrs. Danvers remain powerfully queer. That the film climaxes with, and soon ends after, Mrs. Danvers's death seems especially significant: after she dies, there is nowhere for the film to go.

 # HEAVENLY CREATURES

PLOT SUMMARY

Heavenly Creatures (1994) is based on the true story of Juliet Hulme (Kate Winslet) and Pauline Parker (Melanie Lynskey), two teenagers who fell in love (see Figure 5.19) and who, when threatened by separation by their parents, murdered Pauline's mother. The action takes place in Christchurch, New Zealand, from 1952–54, from the day the girls met to moments after their crime. When the girls met at Christchurch Girls' High School, they instantly related to each other through having both suffered serious physical ailments as children (Pauline with osteomyelitis, and Juliet with respiratory illness). Their relationship soon became fuelled by an exceptionally full and elaborate fantasy life of their mutual creation. Eventually their parents suspected they had formed an "unhealthily" close attachment and took steps to separate them. When Juliet's father, Dr. Henry Hulme (Clive Merrison), was made redundant as the rector of Canterbury University College and he took a new position in England, their separation became

FIGURE 5.19 The queer protagonists of *Heavenly Creatures*, Pauline and Juliet, dressed in ironically standard school uniforms.

inevitable. Pauline was intent upon leaving New Zealand with Juliet, but her mother, Honora Rieper (Sarah Peirse) put up most emphatic resistance. In response to their fear of being separated, Pauline and Juliet murdered her.

This matricide is one of the most notorious crimes in New Zealand history and it attracted global attention through the ensuing trial. The mainstream New Zealand media demonized the girls for being romantically involved with each other almost as much as committing murder. When the girls were found guilty of murder, they were separately imprisoned for several years and it was a condition of their release that they would never meet again. Though there are many historical writings and representations of the Parker-Hulme case, *Heavenly Creatures* is set apart as an attempt to cinematically represent the psychological experiences of Pauline and Juliet from an overtly subjective standpoint. Our attention to this film is a timely response to other representations of them.

REFLECTIONS OF THE PAST

The most recent filmic representation of the Parker/Hulme case is *Reflections of the Past* (2010), a well-intentioned documentary about how the girls have been perceived historically. The film draws heavily upon accounts from contemporaries and descendants of those who remember when the murder happened. Despite the film's efforts at multifaceted historical accuracy, it features numerous images of newspaper headlines and articles that were contemporary with the trial and which were overwhelmingly critical of the girls and their perceived deviancy. These articles are only intermittently deconstructed within the documentary, so the cumulative impact of seeing many of them on-screen is to give their obvious bias some inadvertent sway. Though *Reflections of the Past* seems to be a concerted effort to understand the Parker/Hulme case from a reasonably sympathetic perspective, most of the speech within the documentary is given over to labeling of the sort that Butler critiques. All the "talking heads" discuss whether the girls were mad or not, whether they were lesbian or not, and whether either of them was the leader in the relationship or not. Though the film critically represents the conservatism of 1950s Christchurch—especially its "Victorian" values and general ignorance about what the term "lesbian" means (several classmates mention having had to look the word up in the dictionary)—the film's own efforts to pigeonhole and sentimentally visualize Pauline and Juliet are problematic.

The oddest moments of the film show two photogenic and prepubescent girls dramatizing scenes of Pauline and Juliet together. These scenes do not include their speech, but only serve to "illustrate" their relationship in a soft-focused and aestheticized way: both girls are conventionally pretty and their interactions are depicted as far from truly adult. There is one especially curious moment in which we see the girls dressed in uniforms, looking young and photogenic, and lying together in a park [1:17:53]. The blond Juliet drops rose petals on Pauline in slow motion, while the afternoon light beams down through the trees, creating a sense of clichéd nostalgia as well as fetishizing the schoolgirls together. The score for this scene features whimsical, airy, light piano music composed by Greg Faust. The music is relatively high-pitched, harmonically light, and predictable: it would not be out of place in a children's story. Thus, the scoring belittles them. Such a representation of Pauline and Juliet dampens their queer identities: they are imaged as familiar pretty young things rather than sexually and psychologically subversive beings who self-consciously defined themselves in terms beyond their own time. Moreover, they are quite literally denied a "voice."

So, although *Reflections of the Past* attempts to bring us closer to some authentic understanding of Pauline and Juliet, the overall impact of the documentary is to push us further away from who they were and how they conceptualized themselves. In its many efforts to pigeonhole them, it is profoundly anti-queer. As we shall explore, *Heavenly Creatures* represents a far more subversively exciting attempt to re-understand Pauline and Juliet on their own terms. If we listen carefully to the film, we can fully comprehend the multifaceted ways in which it demands that we hear its protagonists.

THE FILM'S BEGINNING

The action of *Heavenly Creatures* dates from 1952–54, from the time Pauline and Juliet met to the day they committed murder. In 1950s New Zealand, the colonial legacy of the English Empire lingered, and the film satirically amplifies this. The first speech we hear in *Heavenly Creatures* is a man's Received Pronunciation voiceover for a pretty newsreel of Christchurch [0:35–2:26]. The newsreel is archival footage from the New Zealand Tourist Board, displaying serene images of the Christchurch city plains, parks, streets, the river Avon, cricket pitches, Canterbury University College, Cathedral Square, and other postcard-worthy locations (see Figure 5.20). The voiceover enthuses over each quaint aspect of the city. The pleonastic relationship between voiceover and images immediately establishes a deceptive simplicity of form.

As Fran Walsh (co-screenwriter of *Heavenly Creatures*) puts it, Christchurch has "always been described as a little piece of England; it's considered to be more English than England. It's always aspired to be that, and it still is in some ways" (Lippy 1995). Since Christchurch began as a city modeled on English architectural ideals, the first disembodied voice of *Heavenly Creatures* evokes more than the nation's colonial past; it relates to a conscious effort to manufacture a simulacrum of traditional England and its associated

FIGURE 5.20 A pretty, touristic image of Christchurch Canterbury Cathedral from the opening newsreel in *Heavenly Creatures*.

conservative "values."[42] The quaintness of the footage, along with this voiceover, emphasizes a whitewashed representation of place. There is an implicit disavowal of anything problematic in the process of echoing the Empire: the violence of the Empire's colonial legacy, for instance, is sidestepped. In short, we can quickly perceive that the voiceover offers a biased, pompous, antiquated, conservative, and touristic approach to the city. [43]

Christchurch itself was (and remains) one of the whitest cities in New Zealand.[44] The place is historically associated with cultural and ethnic uniformity, and a way of life unsympathetic to non-mainstream or marginal ways of thinking or being. As Greta Gaard writes, colonization can "be seen as a relationship of compulsory heterosexuality whereby the queer erotic of non-westernized peoples, their culture, and their land, is subdued into the missionary position—with the conqueror 'on top'" (1997, 131).

---

[42] 1950s New Zealand was conservative enough that some nationals even read Honora's death as retribution for her secretly living "in sin" with four children (Glaumuzina and Laurie 1991, 182–83).

[43] The opening emphasis on the legacy of the British Empire is paralleled ironically in Jackson's previously made splatter horror movies *Bad Taste* (1987) and *Braindead* (1992) in which "Horror is directly associated with the colonial experience" (Creed 2000, 62). Creed writes about how these films relish in the ironic destruction of major British icons: "good taste, civilized lifestyle, heritage homes, the Queen and her suburban representative, the Mother" (62). She finds comedy in the disjuncture between how the island suburbs "see themselves as bastions of British civilization" and how Jackson revels in "barbaric events [that] actually unfold on the streets and in the homes" (63). She also rightly emphasizes that Jackson excludes references to Maori people: his focus is on white New Zealand culture.

[44] According to the 1996 census of New Zealand (the one closest to the time that *Heavenly Creatures* was released), Christchurch had 4.1% of the national Maori population (21,462 Maoris out of 523,374 in total) and comparatively few in other minority categories as well (86.2% of the population said they belong to the category of "European"). For more specific details, see the New Zealand Government's statistics website cited below.

With this understanding of colonization in mind, the opening of *Heavenly Creatures* establishes Christchurch as a place of the Empire's heteronormativity. Crucially, this problematic ideal is ironized. First, the place is first presented as something to be sold to an outsider: that the promotional footage interpolates the viewer as a foreigner immediately problematizes access to what it *really* is.[45] Then, one word soon resonates in such a way as to parodically disrupt the film opening as a simple archival curiosity. Within thirteen seconds the voiceover refers to the daffodils which bloom "*gay* and golden in the woodlands of Hagley park."[46] That the voiceover incorporates the word "gay" so near the beginning of a story about two girls who fell in love in the 1950s has the ironically anachronistic effect of defamiliarizing the old footage.

The second section of the first voiceover mentions some specific locations associated with Pauline and Juliet: Christchurch University College (where Juliet's father taught), and the girls' high school (where the girls met). Though the voiceover simply mentions these places without making connections to the girls, those familiar with their story—especially the film's domestic, New Zealand audiences—could quickly identify these places as significant to Pauline and Juliet. Thus the simplicity of the voiceover that "speaks for" tradition, safety, and predictability is again thrown into relief or, in Butlerian terms, queered.

Towards the end of the opening voiceover, the film opening is even further complicated by another incorporation of the word "gay": "In spring, summer, and autumn," the voiceover proudly tell us, "Christchurch gardens are *gay* and colored" [2:15–2:19, original emphasis]. At this point we may perceive the intrusion of Pauline and Juliet's panicked screams on the sound track: the aural overlap is subtle at first. However, by the end of the next voiceover statement—"Yes, Christchurch, New Zealand's city of the plains!" [2:22–2:26]—the girls' screams are prominent. The film then cuts to show Pauline and Juliet running from the scene of the murder, their frenzied panic being emphasized by point-of-view shots, and tracking and handheld camerawork that barely seems able to keep up with them: the scene is a sharp visual contrast with the staid, static camerawork for the preceding newsreel, jolting us into a heightened level of subjective reality.[47] That we hear the girls' screams so soon after the word "gay" further complicates the use of

---

[45] Molloy writes that the "viewer is interpolated first as a foreigner in the opening shots of a 1950s promotional film" (1999, 161). That said, Jackson and Walsh were not primarily aiming for an international audience: the primary goal was to "rectify 40 years of misunderstanding about this case within New Zealand" (Lippy 1995).

[46] The film proper begins at thirty-two seconds, after the very first credits against a black background. The word "gay" is heard seven seconds later.

[47] Shots of the girls running are intercut with black-and-white fantasy images of them aboard a boat. These images are connected to several final images of them farewelling each other, to which we shall return near the end of this analysis.

that word in the archival voiceover. The voiceover obviously uses "gay" in the sense of being simply "merry," but the word resonates anew in the film context. In the 1990s context of the film's release, the term "gay" was (and still is) most commonly used to refer to homosexuality. The word is ironically loaded through the audience's presumed pre-knowledge of Pauline and Juliet having been intimately involved with each other. The intrusion of the girls' screams makes this ironic resonance of the word "gay" suddenly more poignant. The girls' screams are closely miked, creating the illusion of spatial closeness to them, and this sense of intimacy disallows us a prejudicial bias against them. It is especially striking that we experience this closeness to them in a scene showing them just moments after the matricide. This sets the tone for an entire film that demands relative closeness to, or at least strong comprehension of, the girls' psychological and emotional perceptions, even in full awareness of the crime they committed. Also, by aurally cutting from Christchurch to the girls in distress, the film immediately critiques the sort of society that has failed to *hear* girls like Pauline and Juliet. Finally, their voices undermine the archival opening, including its associated conservatism—their aural presence is emotionally much more gripping than the first newsreel voiceover.

HEARING REALITY DIFFERENTLY

The co-screenwriters of *Heavenly Creatures*, Peter Jackson and Fran Walsh, were self-conscious about their reframing of history in terms of demanding such new, compassionate attention to Pauline and Juliet. In their reasonably comprehensive efforts to research the film, they discovered many contemporary instances of attempting to whitewash Pauline and Juliet's story away. Jackson himself explains:

> Christchurch Girls' School had erased these two girls from their history. The yearbook that had the class photograph with Pauline is no longer available. If you go to the school library, they have all the yearbooks available apart from 1953's, which has her photo in it. It's a sort of cleansing of the books. The school didn't recognize what it was we were trying to do, which was to redress the issue. Why wipe these girls off the school records? I mean, they were human beings (Lippy 1995).

In the same extensive interview from which this quotation comes, Jackson and Walsh also speak of attempting to "answer" the numerous inflammatory accounts of Pauline and Juliet. Walsh speaks of deliberately writing the film against "lurid newspaper accounts" and a novel by Tom Gurr and H. H. Cox titled *Obsession* which "takes a very damning view of the girls." Jackson says that the day after the murder the girls' former headmistress stood up at assembly to say "No girl is to discuss a certain matter." Like the "cleansing of the books," such silencing was surely as damaging as the inflammatory accounts. *Heavenly Creatures* is a radical attempt to not only queer history but to restate what happened and to rearticulate the girls' identities for a new time. Maureen Molloy argues that the film "does little to rewrite the 1950s professional and media accounts of the reasons for the murder, except to cast the girls in a more sympathetic light" (1999, 162). Such a claim ignores how, right from the beginning, the film establishes a socio-historical context for understanding the girls. Moreover, she ignores how the film knowingly responds to other accounts.

The overtly emotional and subjective agenda of *Heavenly Creatures* makes it far from a by-the-book attempt to document events. Indeed, the film has met with some criticism due to its obvious artistic license and its manifest lack of strict adherence to many details of the girls' lives. In a comprehensive book about the girls' case titled *Parker and Hulme: A Lesbian View*, Juliet Glamuzina and Alison J. Laurie adopt a usefully clinical approach to defining the social realities of Christchurch in the 1950s, exploring the impact of the crime and trial in New Zealand history, tracing the various reactionary and condemnatory media representations of what the girls did, recapping the main arguments of the trial and the global attention it received, and drawing upon various anonymous responses from the girls' classmates and contemporaries who remember how the entire experience affected them. What Glamuzina and Laurie offer is an important pro-lesbian and feminist investigation of Pauline and Juliet's case, especially in relation to issues of gender and sexuality (1991, 18). They take particular care to place the choices and experiences of Pauline and Juliet in the ideologically limiting social context of 1950s Christchurch, which they define in terms of being extremely class-conscious, politically conservative, and almost completely "white" (31).[48] Like Walsh, they ultimately define Christchurch as "the most English city outside England,"[49] especially in terms of its cultural values as well as its geography and architecture. All of these societal points are of course emphasized by the footage at the very beginning of *Heavenly Creatures*. We shall repeatedly return to Glamuzina and Laurie's book since it resonates so strongly with the film.

Ironically, in her introduction to the United States edition of *Parker and Hulme: A Lesbian View*, B. Ruby Rich dismisses *Heavenly Creatures* as a dazzling display

---

[48] As Glamuzina and Laurie note, the population of the South Island (in which Christchurch is the largest city) grew substantially during the 1950s, but not in terms of diversity: "the total population of the island during the period grew from 625,603 in 1951, including only 4164 Maori, to 676,698 in 1956, which included only 5256 Maori" (1991, 31).

[49] As was literally reported by a British newspaper in 1954 (Glamuzina and Laurie 1991, 29).

of cinematic effects that is not worth the serious attention merited by the book's historical approach. She also argues that the film abandons any identification with the girls during the murder scene, thus "weighing in. . . with the Christchurch elders" (1991, iv). Yet even the snippet of the murder scene which is shown soon after we first hear the girls' screams in the film opening (and after which the film is a flashback leading up to the murder again) is immediately gripping because it throws us into their subjective experience [2:26–3:20]. As Patrick Wen points out, seeing the girls right after the murder scene so early on in the film places compassionate and probing emphasis "not on the *who*, but on the motive—what kind of cultural habitat or deeply repressed demons could have caused such brutal violence?" (2004, 247). By contrast, Rich wrongly argues that the film begins with a "hallucinatory scene" of the two girls covered in blood, thus leaving out the archival opening which we have just explored and thus sidestepping the socio-historical context that is therein quickly established, ironized, and implicitly critiqued.

AURALLY QUEERING THE STATUS QUO

Heavenly Creatures is a consistent effort to understand Pauline and Juliet on their own terms. The film delves into an historical context, albeit quite playfully and often parodically. But its primary emphasis is on the subversive perceptions and identities of the girls as they reacted to the world around them. To quote Rich, once Pauline and Juliet were on trial, the mainstream newspapers wrote for a readership of "white, heterosexual, anti-communist, and firm supporters of fixed gender roles and the nuclear family" (1991, v). By contrast, *Heavenly Creatures* appeals to new, contemporary, and more diverse audiences by assuming their potential complicity in a radical questioning of mainstream ideology.

The sound track of *Heavenly Creatures* frequently *celebrates* the girls' resistance to traditional power structures. Echoing the opening newsreel, the school where Pauline and Juliet are shown first meeting is filled with sounds of control and tradition associated with the Old World: the English accents affected by the headmistress and other teachers, the schoolgirls' regimented steps along corridors and pathways, and the hymns imposed upon the schoolgirls, notably "Just a Closer Walk with Thee" from the first school scene at assembly [3:25–6:02]. This hymn, sung with passionless flatness by the congregated girls, is followed by the headmistress' shrill instruction for them all to "sit!": it sounds like an instruction to disobedient dogs. The disaffection in the schoolgirls' obeisance is aurally emphasized by the sound of their bodies moving in messy collective motion to the floor. The sound when they hit the floorboards is like a rumble of

FIGURE 5.21 At school assembly, Pauline refuses to sing a hymn that signifies unthinking conformity.

human thunder, a nonverbal but nonetheless eloquent implication of possible rebellion [6:05–6:07]. But the fact that Pauline alone refuses to sing the hymn at this assembly singles her out as an embodiment of true resistance (see Figure 5.21). Even when the headmistress looks at her with parodically accusing wide eyes, enforcing her participation in the song, Pauline's response is to move her lips without making a sound. In this scene, her relative silence is as eloquent as the many scenes later in which she and Juliet speak a great deal.[50]

A later scene establishes Juliet's equivalency with Pauline in terms of her rebellious spirit. After the relationship between the girls is firmly established, Juliet is shown proudly delivering her speech about the royal family invented by Pauline and herself [35:32–35:59]. Though their history teacher has meant for the class to prepare speeches on the Windsor family, Juliet proudly delivers a speech about the violent and sexually volatile royal characters she has co-created: "the empress Deborah. . . has to fend off her husband morning, noon, and night and Diello, her son. . . slaughters his nannies whenever the fancy takes him!" She speaks with manic excitement, and

---

[50] One former classmate of the girls remembers how they did not converse much in class in order to set themselves apart: she says "they were making themselves important by being different" (Glamuzina and Laurie 1991, 69). In this claim there is a hint of criticism that is challenged by *Heavenly Creatures* in that it celebrates the girls for their verbal *and* nonverbal acts of defiance.

FIGURE 5.22 Juliet's teacher scolds her for speaking about the rebellious royal family she co-created with Pauline; Juliet herself remains insubordinately gleeful.

anything but English propriety. If we listen hard, we can hear the sound of another student practicing scales on a piano in the next room. Juliet's teacher makes it clear, with her more-English-than-the-English voice, that she is immediately angered by Juliet's making fun of the "Queen and the Empire." Juliet smilingly hears the criticism. But the rigidity of the scales (though subtly heard) underscores the talk of oppressive Old World power (see Figure 5.22).[51]

Overall, *Heavenly Creatures* is certainly not a subtle film, especially since it sympathetically foregrounds the manic hysteria of its main characters and its sound design is in keeping with the parodically overblown style of Jackson's previously made splatter movies (*Bad Taste* (1987) and *Braindead* (1992) in particular).[52] However, in the detail of the quietly underscoring scales, we can perceive subtlety in *Heavenly Creatures*: the piano scales wordlessly and swiftly communicate rigidity, formality, and

---

[51] That Pauline and Juliet are first established as "queer" within school settings is particular resonant since, as Meyer points out, schools have historically "filled an important cultural role of teaching children to learn what has been deemed important by the people in power" (2007, 28).

[52] The sound department for *Heavenly Creatures* included personnel associated with big-scale cinema. Mike Hopkins (one of the two lead sound editors for *Heavenly Creatures*) has primarily worked in sound departments for action-based films and his extensive filmography includes Jackson's manically slapstick splatter-horror *Braindead*. The sound mixer for *Heavenly Creatures*, Michael Hedges, also worked on *Braindead*, along with having mixed sound on all Jackson's major blockbuster films since *Heavenly Creatures*.

closed-mindedness. The scales signify social strictures, whereas Juliet's voice asserts rebellion. That most of the film's remaining sound track is far from subtle has as much to do with the "loud" history that it answers as Jackson's auteur style.

REHEARING HISTORY

Because *Heavenly Creatures* is based on actual events, it is worth our considering its sound track in relation to historical documentation. The impact of the *Heavenly Creatures* sound track resonates with accounts of Pauline and Juliet's real experiences, as well as how they artistically expressed themselves. Pauline and Juliet were prodigiously creative: by the time they were tried for murder, they had reportedly written six novels in addition to plays, poetry, and an opera (Glamuzina and Laurie 1991, 61). In *Heavenly Creatures*, Pauline speaks of the opera as she is preparing the murder weapon. Her short description of a "tragic" story with a three-act structure obviously relates to the form of the film itself which easily divides into three stages of their relationship: the girls' meeting and falling in love, their time apart when Juliet has tuberculosis, and their reunion followed by the threat of their separation that leads to the murder. This structure prompts us to perceive them, or at least understand that the girls perceived themselves, in tragically operatic terms. Pauline's actual diary includes her mention of listening to *Tosca* (73). This point is not mentioned in the film but perhaps inspired the selection of other music by Puccini for the sound track. *Tosca* is well known for featuring scenes of torture, murder, and suicide, in addition to including some of his most euphonious arias. Such contrary elements parallel the film's dwelling upon the beauty that Pauline and Juliet co-created at least as much as the horrific crime they committed.

Puccini's "Humming Chorus" is featured in the final film sequence leading up to the murder [1:39:11–1:42:15]. The chorus comes from *Madame Butterfly*, a tragic opera focused on a fifteen-year-old Japanese bride (Cio-Cio San) who is betrayed by her husband and who kills herself after he marries another (American) woman. The "Humming Chorus" comes at the end of the Second Act when Cio-Cio San waits for her husband to return while their baby son sleeps until morning. The use of this music related to the loyal vigil of a celebrated, young tragic female figure of canonized opera is a surprising and poignant choice in *Heavenly Creatures*. The built-in associations of the chorus reinforce the film's sympathetic interest in Pauline and Juliet, as well as its tragic emphasis on their sense of being trapped into an act of terrible violence. Cio-Cio San becomes the tragic figure who kills herself at the end of her opera, and the implication of using music associated with her is that Pauline and Juliet are committing a kind of suicide when they murder Honora: after all, this act entails the end of their life together. The use of the "Humming Chorus" also echoes an earlier scene of the film, the night before the murder where Juliet is shown singing "Sono Andati" from Puccini's *La Bohème* [1:32:20–1:33:27], another tragic opera in which ordinary people, a seamstress (Mimi) and a poet (Rodolfo) fall in love but are separated by Mimi's death at the end. The fact that both these songs come from Puccini operas focused upon heterosexual romantic relationships is worth dwelling upon: for *Heavenly Creatures* not only grants tragic status to Pauline and Juliet, it also self-consciously grants them the status traditionally preserved for heterosexual lovers alone.[53] Yet again, the film dresses its main characters in "straight" music, a form of drag to ennoble them.

Heavenly Creatures consistently provides a complex and compassionate representation of Pauline and Juliet through its sound track. This is in direct contrast to statements about them during their real trial. Even the defense lawyer for Juliet, Terence Arbuthnot Gresson, argued they were "more to be pitied than blamed" because "their homosexuality was a symptom of their disease of the mind." He then called upon the psychiatrist Reginald Medlicott to present his "diagnosis" of their madness. Medlicott interpreted the homosexual behavior of the girls as being connected with the paranoia that gave rise to what he saw as their *folie à deux* (Glamuzina and Laurie 1991, 89). He then recalled questioning the girls after the murder as follows:

> Each girl would have sudden spells of intenseness. They would, you might say, click into gear, talk so rapidly for a time as to be almost incoherent. . . . On the second visit of the second weekend that I saw them, they really could not be bothered giving up a walk in the sun to talk to me. There was also a very gross reversal of morals or of moral sex. . . they admired those things which were evil and condemned those things which the community considers good. It was obvious that the normal personalities [*sic*] defenses against evil had almost completely gone" (Glamuzina and Laurie 1991, 90).

We should consider what the *Heavenly Creatures* sound track means in relation to such revealing historical accounts. Because Medlicott's account mentions the girls' style of speaking along with what he perceived to be their essential immorality and their capacity for evil, it should prime us to hear them in *Heavenly Creatures* all the better.

---

[53] Though the somber operatic quotations are a "sharp contrast to. . . [the] ebullience of the Lanza music" discussed below (Ribeiro 1995, 37), the film's granting operatic status to Pauline and Juliet has its own strident energy.

The girls were disallowed from speaking at their own trial for fear that they would prejudice the all-male jury against them.[54] This made it easier for their contemporaries to objectify them and for commentators to "describe them as evil, callous, and monstrous" (Glamuzina and Laurie 1991, 98). Glamuzina and Laurie also explain that during the trial itself "the voices of the representatives of the dominant culture, for example psychiatrists and lawyers,... were the ones [most] heard and recorded" (99). Even the reporting of the girls' creative expression was used against them. Ian Hamilton, a social commentator sympathetic to Pauline and Juliet critically commented on the feeling "in the streets and offices: 'It's all this self-expression; get 'em sewing mail bags, that'll teach 'em'." (Glamuzina and Laurie 1991, 146). Because the *Heavenly Creatures* sound track not only privileges the girls' voices, but also repeatedly enforces our understanding (if not alignment with) their perceptions, it "talks back" to such representative responses.

To summarize so far, *Heavenly Creatures* attempts to "answer" how the girls were demonized and socially shunned by aurally recontextualizing their actions, providing a perceptual experience for the audience aligned with theirs, queering straight music to ennoble their characterization, and inviting us to hear their creative experience *and* their tragic experience anew. In terms of queer theory, we should also return to the fact that the girls were demonized and shunned almost as much for their sexuality as for the crime they committed. One historical account after another dwells upon their "deviant" sexuality and explicitly connects it to their ability to murder. Newspapers contemporary with their trial quote extracts from Pauline's diary to support "evidence" of her moral sickness and sexual "abnormality."[55] In their frequently cited book *Famous Australasian Crimes* (1957), Gurr and Cox provide a typically salacious account of the murder, noting that Juliet's tuberculosis was likely connected to her "sexual divergence" (166). Even sixteen years later, similar assumptions prevailed: in a book titled *Queens of Crime* (1973), Gerald Sparrow calls the girls "Satan's children," noting that "unnatural relationships often go hand-in-hand with moral delinquency" (120).[56] Similarly, a 1987

---

[54] For some broader discussion of a Western history of judicial systems that oppress gay people, see Sedgwick's *Epistemology of the Closet* (1990, 67–90).

[55] Such accounts distorted the narrative shape Pauline gave to her own life through the diary. Glamuzina and Laurie emphasize that the extracts from Pauline's diaries that became central in the trial, "as well as subsequent accounts of the case," portray her in a very limited way, giving "the impression that the diaries were filled with violence and murderous fantasies." Glamuzina and Laurie find the diaries emotionally complex in places, and "dull and mundane" in others, concluding that they were "probably quite typical of a teenage girl of the time." They also stress that "the murder entries were not a major part of the diaries" (1991, 81).

[56] Sparrow went even further by connecting other medical challenges of Pauline's family—the blood transfusion needed by her sister at birth and her younger sister being a "Mongolian imbecile"—with Pauline's sexual "illness." He suggested that the defects embodied by her siblings were simply "more secret and malignant" in her (1973, 119).

report for the *Dominion Sunday Times* bluntly states that Pauline and Juliet "battered [Mrs. Rieper] to death so they could continue their lesbian love affair undisturbed" (Glamuzina and Laurie 1991, 116). As Bruce Harding writes, with particular reference to the biased procedures by which Pauline and Juliet were tried, *Heavenly Creatures* constitutes an important "act of cinematic rebellion, a recursion to and radical rethinking of the judicial management of that deeply troubling case" (2012).

AURALLY COMPLEX IDENTITIES

Having already explored how the film's sound track queers historically conservative accounts of Pauline and Juliet, what follows is a deeper exploration of how the sound track prompts a complex understanding of the girls' identities. More specifically, we shall explore how the sound track self-consciously discourages us from labeling the girls according to fixed identities or constructs, and how it complicates the visual signifiers of identity, especially with regard to gender and sexuality.

In keeping with the period detail of *Heavenly Creatures*, the girls are visually feminized by their costumes, so the aural details of *Heavenly Creatures* become all the more crucial for understanding the film's complex representation of gender and sexuality.[57] At the time that Pauline and Juliet were involved with each other, many attempts were made to literally label them in terms of fixed condemnation. By scanning the historical records compiled by Glamuzina and Laurie, we can find a pattern of many damning labels. Pauline and Juliet were called "sexually delinquent," "abnormally homosexual," "precocious and dirty-minded," "either 'mad' or 'bad'," "delusionally insane," and "monsters or curiosities."[58] Contemporary accounts represented them as immoral, cruel, depraved, criminal, eccentric, perverse, or simply evil. Specific contemporary headlines named them "Girl Murderers," "Teenaged Girls," "Gym-Tunic Murderesses," and "Little Girls," as well as calling them personified adjectives like "Hideousness and Ugliness"

---

[57] Despite the conventional outfits worn by Pauline and Juliet (especially school uniforms), the visual patterns of the film are as feminist as its aural strategies. With Mulvey's work in mind, we should note that Pauline and Juliet are not objectified by the camera or made subservient to the gaze of any patriarch. The visuals of the film, much like its sound track, seem primarily at their service in terms of representing their perceptions and emotional reactions.

[58] The specific sources of these labels are as follows: the girls were seen as "sexually delinquent" and "abnormally homosexual" by a committee looking into juvenile resistance to authority created by the government a month after the murder of Mrs. Rieper (Glamuzina and Laurie 1991, 59), "either 'mad' or 'bad'" according to the court trial (84), "depraved," "precocious and dirty-minded" according to Crown Prosecutor Allan Brown (84), paranoid and "delusionally insane" according to the "prominent" psychiatrist who spoke at the trial, Reginald Medlicott (88), and "monsters or curiosities" as represented in various contemporary media reports of their trial (111).

(Glamuzina and Laurie 1991, 113–14). In addition, the decision about whether to label the girls as criminal or insane was the crux of their murder trial. Medlicott, the "prominent" psychiatrist who spoke at the girls' trial, compared them to SS officers in terms of their "senseless and sickening brutality" and he also compared their crime to the 1924 case of Leopold and Loeb, two sons of Chicago millionaires who murdered a young boy and whose case received similar media attention (Glamuzina and Laurie 1991, 88, 127–28).[59] Although Medlicott subsequently admitted having "misdiagnosed" the girls, he simply created a new label for them: "adolescent megalomaniacs" (131).

Rather than attempting to fix either Pauline's or Juliet's identities, *Heavenly Creatures* associates them with a wide range of music, including both male and female voices, verbal and nonverbal scoring, diegetic and non-diegetic cues, and repetitions as well as several one-time iterations of themes without settling on one identifiable piece of musical material to ultimately represent either one of them. Even a cursory scan of the different forms of music associated with them and the range of emotions and implications aurally communicated therein is enough to establish the film's interest in representing their multidimensionality. *Heavenly Creatures* thus places emphasis on the girls' identities in flux. This has radical, Butlerian implications in terms of conceptualizing their gender and sexuality, as well as in terms of redressing a history of heterosexist and homophobic reactions to everything they *were* as well as the crime they committed. Ironically, there is little music associated with other characters, and that which is included is comparatively dull or saccharine, such as the "How much is that doggie in the window?" song associated with Juliet's family beach trip (especially her father's reluctant participation in the song) or the Doris Day record purchased by a boarder at Pauline's house.

DASENT'S ORIGINAL SCORE

The music most heard in association with the girls' moods and dreams is a non-diegetic score composed by Peter Dasent.[60] Dasent's score represents a wide range of stylistic emphases and connotations. However, his musical cues are united in being consistently

---

[59] This case was the inspiration for a play titled *Rope* (1929), the primary sourcetext for Hitchcock's film of the same name.

[60] Peter Dasent is a New Zealand composer and musician. He has played keyboards in several bands and now leads a chamber-jazz group called The Crocodiles. He is currently writing a book on the music of Nino Rota whose film scores are a major influence on him. He also now works for the children's Australian television series Play School with the Australian Broadcasting Corporation. Dasent has composed for several films directed by Peter Jackson, including *Meet the Feebles* (1989) and *Dead Alive* (1992). However, his score for *Heavenly Creatures* is his best-known and most widely distributed work to date.

FIGURE 5.23 The melodic line of Peter Dasent's theme for Pauline and Juliet (transcribed directly from the CD soundtrack). These opening ten bars are used as the dominant leitmotif of the film.

related to Pauline and Juliet's shifting perceptions. In addition, these cues most often refer to what the girls experience together, rather than defining them separately. It is more common for a film focused on a romantic couple to establish separate themes and/or styles of music for each of the two people. Dasent himself says that not only did cowriters Jackson and Walsh require that his music be on Pauline and Juliet's side, they specifically requested a theme for both of them to "emphasize their togetherness in all things." The main "Pauline and Juliet" theme is evocative of light impressionistic music through its playfully shifting harmonies, occasional arpeggios, and rubato rhythm. The melodic line begins as follows (see Figure 5.23):[61]

We first hear the main theme embedded within a cue titled "Bad Chests and Bone Diseases," which accompanies the girls' first conversation and their mutual comfort in sharing stories of sickness. Here the theme is light and whimsical sounding, led by flutes accompanied by strings [13:29–14:00]. Next, there is a more richly orchestrated variation called "The Princess of Ilam," led by oboe and supported by full string orchestra and harp. This variation relates to the pastoral ideal of Juliet's home at Ilam, a tourist attraction in Christchurch at the time she lived there (Glamuzina and Laurie 1991, 35) [14:01–15:05]. This variation also alludes to the string-led, light classical arrangements of Annunzio Paolo Mantovani which were popular on New Zealand radio during the 1950s.[62] The music directly accompanies Juliet's appearance in a self-aggrandizing

---

The quotations from Dasent in this analysis come from his responses to an emailed interview by Elsie Walker on May 17, 2013.

[61] The sound track CD for *Heavenly Creatures* includes an extended version of the main Pauline and Juliet theme on piano, and this is a transcription of the first ten bars. This version is especially reminiscent of *La fille aux cheveux de lin* (or "The Girl with the Flaxen Hair") by Claude Debussy from the *Préludes, Book 1* (1909–10).

[62] Dasent mentioned this, along with the influence of Nino Rota's films scores, in the interview cited above.

princess costume as she runs across the impressive gardens of her parents' residence. It also relates to Pauline's perception of Juliet as the ideal she wants her to be.

Many other cues of the film are derived from the "Pauline and Juliet" theme. A cue titled "The Pursuit of Happiness" includes a variation on the first phrase (mm. 1–4), but with a distorted emphasis. This is heard after Pauline and Juliet have created their plan for murder [1:30:32–1:30:54]. It incorporates the sound of a music box and haunting synthesized growls and bells that interrupt it, complicating the "innocence" suggested by the use of a child's toy. Another cue titled "The Most Hideous Man Alive," which underscores the girls' frantic fantasy with Orson Welles, includes a further variation on the first phrase of the "Pauline and Juliet" theme but at a lower pitch, with heavy emphasis on the hard sound of a harpsichord for its Gothic connotations [1:26:24–1:27:33]. Minor-key variations on the "Pauline and Juliet" theme are also folded into a cue for a "Night with the Saints" featuring light, mid-range and softly played flutes [23:22–23:39]. This cue plays as Pauline and Juliet are shown creating a ritual of the movie stars they deify. This variation gives way to a tremolo stinger on low cello, which playfully exaggerates Juliet throwing away a magazine photo of Orson Welles (whom she proclaims "the most hideous man alive!") [23:40–23:48]. Many of Dasent's cues feature such abrupt shifts. The musical implication of this pattern is that every experience can quickly modulate into its opposite. The overall effect is to involve the audience in the girls' extreme perceptions, commensurate with the full melodrama of first love in adolescence.

The "Pauline and Juliet" theme is the most prominent in Dasent's score, and this matters in several ways. Most important, it reinforces our understanding of the girls' centrality and emphasizes their dominant, fused subjectivity. Dasent uses the first three phrases of the "Pauline and Juliet" as a leading leitmotif, a technique much more associated with "straight" or Classical Hollywood narratives, and which therefore reinforces the subversiveness of *Heavenly Creatures*. The many variations on the theme also complicate any effort to musically "pigeonhole" the girls, emphasizing the power of their identities in flux. Dasent himself cites Nino Rota's scores for the films directed by Federico Fellini as a principle influence: certainly, Dasent echoes the range of tonalities and connotations within Rota's body of film scoring—from the epic sweep of his music for *Nights of Cabiria* (*Le Notti de Cabiria*, 1957) to the lyricism of his score for *La Strada* (1954), to the moody playfulness of his score for *Casanova* (1976).

Dasent's score also punctuates shifts in mood for Pauline and/or Juliet, even when they are fleeting. For instance, we hear extreme musical shifts in the space of two and a half minutes, during a sequence showing Juliet's time in the hospital and a montage of Pauline and Juliet writing to each other "as" their fantasy characters [38:50–41:30]. The sequence features a cue titled "Life in Borovnia," named after a fantasy realm the girls co-created. It begins with strings and woodwind, long phrasing, and unresolved minor-key lyricism. It then shifts between reprisals of the opening of "The Princess of Ilam" (a variation on the "Pauline and Juliet" theme), dominated by a mellow oboe and harmonizing strings, and plodding, playfully ominous, more dissonant phrases featuring the heavier sounds of percussion and brass. The shifts within the cue emphasize the manic energy of the girls' fantasy life and the film's process of drawing us into their contrary feelings.

There are, of course, plenty of film precedents using music to signify/reinforce turn-on-a-time melodrama—a fine example of this is *Bigger Than Life* (1956), as we have already explored. In relation to the terrifying psychosis of James Mason's character in that film, David Raksin's score includes some cues that would be appropriate for a 1950s comedy and many cues that would work for a doom-laden classical film noir. Part of what makes Dasent's score for *Heavenly Creatures* fascinating, however, is its emphasis on helping us understand the extreme and emotional multidimensionality of its subversive protagonists who were all-too-easily labeled monsters in their own time.[63]

MARIO LANZA'S PERFORMANCES

Dasent's score is the crucial non-diegetic barometer of Pauline and Juliet's perceptions.[64] Several of Mario Lanza's performances of songs are similarly, *diegetically* significant, especially as the girls listen to, sing, and/or dance to them. Though the Lanza songs are grounded in the diegetic space, they also cross the diegetic/non-diegetic divide, further complicating our potential responses to Pauline and Juliet. Knowing that Pauline and Juliet were greatly enamored of Lanza and his performances, Jackson speaks of playing Lanza's songs as he cowrote the screenplay scenes: it was the first time he had had "music in advance" and "the music helped [him] visualize" new scenes for the film (Lippy 1995). Thus Lanza's songs had an atypically decisive influence on the entire shape of the film.

We first learn of Pauline and Juliet's mutual admiration for Mario Lanza in one of the early scenes showing them together, in an art class at school. Instead of drawing Pauline as per the class assignment, Juliet draws St. George in the likeness of "the world's greatest tenor, Mario Lanza," which she proudly declares when questioned by

---

[63] Walsh explains her own struggle to understand this demonization in her interview with Lippy: "Reading the diary made me wonder about the huge discrepancies between this young woman [Pauline] and *the monster* who was portrayed in the newspaper accounts and everything else" (1995, emphasis added).

[64] Luisa F. Ribeiro writes of Lanza's music as a "barometer" of Pauline's emotions, especially in relation to her initial captivation with Juliet (punctuated by Lanza's "Be My Love"), her uncertainty about Juliet's flights of fancy (swept aside when Juliet dances with her to Lanza's "The Donkey Serenade"), and her romantic consummation with Juliet (anticipated by Lanza's "The Loveliest Night of the Year") (1995, 35).

the teacher. Pauline expresses her immediate and emphatic delight in the image, despite the teacher's disapproval. Herein Lanza is immediately, visually associated with a kind of deliberate rebellion as well as the mythology which Pauline winds up co-creating with Juliet. The fact that the image of Lanza stands in place of Pauline within Juliet's picture calls our attention to the significance of his music in defining who the girls are, as well as meaning that Juliet's visual understanding of Pauline is far from significant to either of them—what matters most, almost immediately, is the imaginative and creative kinship of the girls. In the next scene, one of the boarders at the Rieper household nervously enters the house with a new Doris Day record: the musical reference immediately suggests emotional and sexual timidity, as well as mainstream conservatism. Mrs. Rieper's inviting him to play the record is interrupted by Pauline as she rushes towards the turntable and begins playing her Lanza recording of "Be My Love" [11:18–12:31]. Buoyed by the vibrato emotion and forte strength of Lanza's singing, Pauline looks up, as if transported to a heavenly space (see Figure 5.24).

The film makes us understand the appeal of Lanza's Italian expressivity, and the warmth of his full voice, especially in contrast with the muted colors of the Rieper household. The lyrics of "Be My Love" tell us about the warmth of Pauline's new feelings for Juliet in particular: "be my love, for no one else can end this yearning,/this need that you and you alone create." When Pauline's father, Herbert Rieper (Simon O'Connor) playfully teases her by speaking of the Irish tenor "Murray O'Lanza," she corrects him

FIGURE 5.24 Lanza's singing transports Pauline to a heavenly place.

FIGURE 5.25 Mr. Rieper teases Pauline by mouthing lyrics from Lanza's song to a mackerel fish.

by shouting "he's Italian Dad!" She then echoes Juliet's declaration that he is "the world's greatest tenor." Mr. Rieper teases her by parodically mouthing lyrics from the song ("be my love, and with your kisses set me burning,/one kiss is all I need to seal my fate") to the mackerel fish he has just purchased from the market (see Figure 5.25). To Pauline, this parodic performance represents the threat of being stuck within prosaic and grotesque normalcy. She responds by physically pushing her father out of the room so that she can enjoy her music again.

Soon after this scene, Pauline's Lanza record is accidentally broken at Juliet's house in a playful tussle between the girls and Juliet's brother. The broken record symbolizes the fragility of Pauline's access to everything that the music represents—emotional freedom, otherworldly possibility, sudden transcendence, and exotic escape. However, we soon see Juliet not only offering to replace the record, but also selecting more Lanza music to play as she fans out her full selection of records on the floor (see Figure 5.26). Juliet's full record collection signifies her relative privilege. It also parallels the confident excess with which she expresses herself.

Robynn J. Stilwell writes about the female significance of record collecting in terms of creating memories and realizing a "different, more internal articulation of the self" (2006, 153). She places *Heavenly Creatures* in the context of other "girls'

FIGURE 5.26 Juliet fans out her full collection of Lanza records.

films" (*A Little Princess* (1995), *The Virgin Suicides* (1999), and *Sen to Chihiro no kamikakushi* (*Spirited Away*, 2001)) which are about "restriction, confinement, even imprisonment" but also about "rituals of transformation, or becoming." She also places *Heavenly Creatures* in the context of other films that feature record collecting. In films like *High Fidelity* (2000) and *Ghost World* (2000), record collecting is male behavior that proves "hunting skills" and provides "opportunities for tales of adventure and conquest," as well as "displays of authority and knowledge" (154). By contrast, Stilwell associates female record collecting with female articulations of self-discovery related to transcending the limitations of literal contexts. She cites several characters who play this out—Enid from *Ghost World*, LV in *Little Voice* (1998), and the Lisbon sisters of *The Virgin Suicides*—in addition to the protagonists of *Heavenly Creatures*. Following on from Stilwell's arguments, Juliet is much more empowered to discover herself and transcend her circumstances than Pauline.

Like the contrast between Melanie Lynskey's recognizably parochial New Zealand accent in contrast with Kate Winslet's polished English voice, the contrast between Pauline's one broken Lanza record and Juliet's full collection markedly distinguishes between Pauline's humble, working class home of cramped spaces and Juliet's comparatively palatial home at Ilam with its spacious rooms and grounds.[65] That Juliet has more Lanza music—and all the possibilities implied by that—reinforces the film's emphasis on her relative privilege. However, the girls' differences in terms of class and wealth seem to matter little when they are brought together in music. This is especially clear in a sequence featuring Lanza's singing of "the Donkey Serenade": it begins as Juliet starts the song on her record player and then quickly, non-diegetically expands into the underscoring for a montage of the girls' leisure time together [17:38–21:25]. Here, the music emphasizes an egalitarian fantasy of playful and transcendent *union*.

"The Donkey Serenade" sequence begins as the camera quite suddenly moves above the girls after Juliet has swept Pauline into a dance at Ilam. The visual implication is that the music suddenly frees them up, a point of particular poignancy in relation to Pauline's restrictive domestic circumstances and humble prospects. Once Juliet places the needle on the record, the camera moves with much more fluidity, in keeping with the girls' movements. The upbeat silliness of Lanza's song, with lyrics about professing love to a donkey when a "fair senorita" is oblivious to him, is matched by the playful camerawork. In the ensuing montage, the camera tracks, pans, dollies, and moves handheld with the girls as they laugh, run, play airplanes, and mould clay figures for their fantasy world. At the climax of the song, the two girls are shown running out from a movie theatre showing a film featuring Lanza, *The Great Caruso* (1951). The girls throw themselves at a theatre poster of Lanza-as-Caruso before Juliet kisses a passing homeless person played by Peter Jackson. From a metacinematic standpoint, one invited by the Caruso reference and Jackson's cameo appearance, the moment suggests that Juliet appreciates *Heavenly Creatures* because of the expressive freedom it allows her.

As "The Donkey Serenade" finishes, the two girls are shown cycling haphazardly along a country road before being run off by an approaching car. After this comically enacted accident, Pauline pretends to die while Juliet theatrically sobs into her neck. Here the music suddenly stops, thus emphasizing the connection between the presence of music and the life of the girls. The music resumes quite quickly, however, when "Paul" scoffs at Juliet's onion breath and the two begin running through the roadside forest

---

[65] Noting the extreme differences between Pauline's and Juliet's backgrounds, Jennifer Henderson argues that Pauline's desire for Juliet is "inseparable from class envy" (45). Michelle Elleray also emphasizes the relative privilege of Juliet, especially in terms of nationhood and class (1999, 224). Where Juliet is the privileged English girl who is introduced to her new schoolmates as one who has "travelled all over the world" (225), Pauline is "marked" in the film as "the New Zealander" through her local accent and the numerous items of kitsch memorabilia (so-called "kiwiana") within her home (225). The divide between the girls' relative social status is uncomfortably, though playfully, emphasized in a scene where Mrs. Rieper affects an upper class English accent at afternoon tea with Juliet. Elsewhere Mrs. Rieper has a more humble Northern English accent mixed with New Zealand inflections.

FIGURE 5.27 The farmer, a typical kiwi bloke, doffs his cap to Pauline and Juliet.

together. At this point, Dasent's score picks up Lanza's song in a synthesized variation. The girls sing "the Donkey Serenade" in time to this non-diegetic music—it becomes their accompaniment as they then gleefully run and strip off clothes down to their underwear. Upon their singing a line that, in the context of this scene, emphasizes the queering of straight lyrics ("her face is a dream, like an angel I saw"), the girls suddenly happen upon a farmer fixing a fence. He is a "traditional occupant of the bush," a masculine stereotype of conservative New Zealand culture: "a bemused man of the land, the prosaic, manual-laboring, taciturn but friendly Kiwi bloke" (Elleray 1999, 232). In his presence the girls suddenly stop singing and the question of how he will respond hangs in the air. However, his surprisingly low-key, friendly response to their down-to-underwear exuberant singing is to simply doff his cap and say "G'day" (see Figure 5.27). In response to this, the girls begin singing again and gleefully run away. Then they fall together (in love) in the bush (see Figure 5.28).[66]

It matters that the empowering of the girls in this sequence takes place on the outskirts of Christchurch. It is as if the girls are temporarily allowed an escape from social limitations. Even the presence of the farmer suggests utopian optimism, for "the farmer" is a representative of traditional conservative values but he makes a gesture

---

[66] Stilwell usefully points out that the girls sing "off-key" during this sequence (2006, 162), a point that subtly emphasizes their everyday humanness and their joyful lack of self-consciousness in each other's presence.

FIGURE 5.28 Juliet and Pauline fall down on the ground, and fall in love, together.

that playfully pays respect to Pauline and Juliet. The use of a song to accompany the idyllic representation of the growing relationship through montage is a technique traditionally reserved for straight cinematic romances. This sequence thus subversively uses a traditional means of economically representing two people falling in love. The playfulness of Lanza's song also matches the playfulness with which the film queers his straight lyrics which are literally taken up by the girls themselves. As they sing in time to Dasent's score, the film self-consciously brings what the girls and the audience hear together. The unusually blurred distinction between diegetic and non-diegetic music is another way of reinforcing our experience of, and alignment with, the girls' perceptions.

All of Lanza's music in *Heavenly Creatures* is similarly used to foster our connection to the girls: when Pauline listens to "Be My Love" after meeting Juliet, for instance, we have access to her unspoken feelings of immediate attraction; when Pauline escapes into a fantasy sequence in Borovnia featuring Lanza's performance of "Funculi, Funcula," we understand it is her desperate effort at joviality during the discomfort of losing her virginity to a man; when Pauline and Juliet are reunited after their parents keep them apart and they dance to "The Loveliest Night of the Year," we understand the fullness of their romantic attachment; and when Lanza's performance of "You'll Never Walk Alone" plays over the film's final captions and credits, the film makes its last bid for us to walk "with" them, even after we have seen their crime enacted [11:18–12:31; 51:33–53:46; 1:23:33–1:25:30; 1:44:39–1:48:26].

Not incidentally, Lanza's life itself resonates with the girls' experiences and aspirations: he was from a working-class family of Italian immigrant parents (a beginning parallel with Pauline's in her comparatively humble status); his star persona was about being intractable, exuberant, and passionate (as Pauline and Juliet decide to be); and he was famous for the power of his voice (a fact of some poignancy with regard to how Juliet and Pauline are often silenced in the film as well as how they were "erased" from New Zealand history after the murder). Lanza made "the image of the opera singer romantic, glamorous, and profitable" during the 1950s, the time when *Heavenly Creatures* takes place (Landy 2001, 246). He was born "Alfred Arnold Cocozza" but changed his name upon signing a contract with MGM at the age of twenty-six. This resonates with the film's emphasis on Pauline and Juliet's attempts to escape the identities they are expected to "perform." On and off the screen, Lanza represented an archetypal fantasy of wish-fulfillment in keeping with the girls' dreams of making it in Hollywood: in *The Great Caruso* he plays the great tenor Enrico Caruso, the film charting his rise from complete obscurity to terrific success in the opera world; and Lanza was himself "discovered" at a Hollywood Bowl Concert by Louis B. Mayer. Lanza was also known for devoting his time to phoning people in hospital and famously gave a young girl victim of leukemia a silver medal as well as an invitation to his home in Los Angeles after her mother only requested a phone call. The young girl was later buried with the silver medal (Landy 2001, 248). Given that *Heavenly Creatures* foregrounds the pain Pauline and Juliet endured in repeated and parallel hospitalizations, this aspect of Lanza's biography also gains new resonance—along with embodying their hopes for Hollywood success, he also represents the possibility of a compassionate star's allegiance with them.

Ironically, Lanza also had a messy fall from grace: he became, as Marcia Landy writes, a "spector of defeat," especially as he battled excessive weight gain, alcoholism, psychic instability, and criticism of his acting to the extent that he was physically replaced by a British actor, Edmund Purdom, who mimed Lanza's singing for *The Student Prince* (1954) (Landy 2001, 250). None of this is referenced in *Heavenly Creatures*, in keeping with the world of hopeful fantasy that the girls associate with his music.

Ironically, following his untimely death from heart failure in 1959, Lanza made something of a comeback in the 1990s when opera stars like Richard Leech and Plácido Domingo acknowledged his influence on them. The fall from grace that Lanzo had embodied was then replaced by a greater recognition of his having risen to become a star from nothing (Landy 2001, 253–54). This romanticization of Lanza is contemporary with the release of *Heavenly Creatures*. This context ironically amplifies the film's knowing representation of how Pauline and Juliet use the star to fuel their fantasy life.

Heavenly Creatures also explores how Pauline and Juliet used their mutual love of Lanza as a displaced form of their mutual infatuation. Lanza has often been identified as a safe heterosexual object of the girls' homosexual desire (Guzik 2001, 60). The same might be said of Orson Welles, as Pauline is shown visually morphing into him for Juliet's pleasure during the most explicitly sexual scene of the film. Similarly, when Pauline and Juliet play-act the royal couple they have co-created (Charles and Deborah) they can safely "maintain and extend their relationship" through the characters of Borovnian lovers (Elleray 1999, 230). That their shared infatuation with Lanza (along with other stars and film characters) allows them to project sexual urges onto straight stories runs parallel to the film's queer use of leitmotifs, as well as its ironic quotations from "straight" musicals and operas.

SELF-CONSCIOUS CONSTRUCTIONS

In queering so much straight music, the *Heavenly Creatures* sound track is an extremely self-conscious construction. That the sound track repeatedly demands that we be aware of its own constructedness is especially obvious when Dasent's score amplifies the girls' shifting and heightened states of emotion. Dasent's score also features many stinger chords which jolt the audience into experiencing the girls' melodramatic perceptions as well as their manic enjoyment of all things dramatic: some such stingers occur when Juliet's brother pounces upon Pauline in a spontaneous game of play-acting [15:43–15:44], after Juliet hysterically pronounces Orson Welles "the most hideous man alive!" [23:15–23:16], and when Pauline turns on the light in her bedroom after an unexpected intrusion from a humorously awkward man [46:17–46:19].[67] As we have already established, the use of stingers was conventionalized in the Classical Hollywood period: we have discussed how *The Searchers* features stingers upon the pronouncement of Scar's name, reinforcing the sense of his being a demonic threat, and how stingers are even more prominent in *Bigger Than Life* as they alert us to the psychological disturbance within the main character. The stingers in *Heavenly Creatures* work for a quite different, much less alarming and often parodic effect. Rather than being used to announce true threats, the stingers self-consciously place emphasis on what the girls *perceive* to be threatening. This is ironically important in that Pauline and Juliet were seen in their own time as threatening figures, for their sexuality *as well as* their crime (Lippy 1995);

---

[67] The man is John (Jed Brophy), the first boarder at her parents' home, and the man to whom she eventually loses her virginity: he *could* have been represented as a threat, but is instead more played for absurd comedy.

where the mainstream media portrayed the girls from an alarmist perspective, the film is much more interested in what alarmed *them.*

Just as the instrumental stingers may playfully catch us off guard, *Heavenly Creatures* also features many sound effects that punctuate the action in terms of the girls' subjectivities, *even in their absence.* For instance, when Mr. Rieper shows up at the Riepers' doorstep to speak about the girls' "unhealthy" relationship, the moment is parodically overstated by the noir-style fedora and trenchcoat he wears and the thunderstorm which punctuates his heavy-handed statements [56:32–56:41].[68] The thunder upon Mr. Hulme's assertion of the Pauline's "wayward fashion" sends up the frequent devaluation of homosexuality in Western culture as "against nature."[69]

Other everyday sounds punctuate what the girls do and feel with similarly overdetermined emphasis: examples include the sound of Pauline bursting through the doors of the hospital when she is finally, gleefully able to visit Juliet [42:19–42:20], or the isolated drops of water which ominously echo in the bathroom as Pauline and Juliet discuss their murder plan [1:29:40–1:30:31], or the crackling fire that burns up the LP records destroyed by Pauline and Juliet when they willfully divorce themselves from their old lives before the murder [1:30:54–1:31:30]. Because many actions of the girls' are amplified by relatively loud sound effects, it is as if their experiences are punctuated with virtual exclamation points, and the film keeps its audience in an almost relentless state of aurally enforced alertness. The combination of stingers and strident sound effects with music which places emphasis on the turbulence of the girls' perceptions makes for an overwhelmingly heightened film experience.

Heavenly Creatures thus not only encourages our complicity with the girls, but also repeatedly calls attention to its own processes of representing them. The film queers a straightforward understanding of Pauline and Juliet's history by thus complicating the sense of objective access to the truth. The representation of history and reality in *Heavenly Creatures* is even further complicated by the use of voiceovers that are lifted verbatim from Pauline's actual diary. The voiceovers reinforce the film's authority as a representation of her experience. However, the use of voiceovers does not simply represent a one-dimensional effort to be historically accurate. There are moments when the film's visual messages communicate the opposite of what Pauline tells us: for instance, right after Pauline speaks of a New Year's resolution to be "more lenient with others," we hear and see her scolding a boarder for attempting to steal part of the morning tea

---

[68] The thunder begins when the film shows Mr. Hulme voyeuristically peering at the girls sleeping peacefully in each other's arms and transitions to his arrival at Mrs. Rieper's doorstep.

[69] For a full discussion of this trend, which dates back to the seventeenth century, see Gaard (1997, 119).

that she has prepared for Juliet [24:29–24:43]; and when she speaks of being "sweet and good" and helping her mother "vigorously" one morning, she is shown sulkily frowning in the back of her parents' car and slowly wiping a clock as her mother moves speedily around with a vacuum cleaner [1:31:33–1:32:01]. Pauline's diary-writing was "*the definitive piece of evidence in the trial*" (Wen 2004, 242). It was used to prove the girls' deliberate intent to murder *and* to support opposing diagnoses of their psychological states. So, it was the most potent means by which the girls could be finally labeled. Because the film sometimes represents a break between what Pauline tells us and what we see, it asks us to question whether the diary always represented truth along with calling attention to her processes of self-definition. In other words, the diary becomes but one of many possibilities in terms of how we might understand Pauline (*and* Juliet, by implication).

AGAINST LABELLING

When Pauline and Juliet were on trial the nature of their relationship was hotly debated. Yet, as Corinn Columpar notes, Jackson has called the question of whether the girls were lesbians a red herring (2002, 325). As Columpar herself adds, "the film mocks any attempt to impose a label on the complex and multidimensional relationship that Pauline and Juliet forge" (325). Along with using various forms of music that emphasize the futility of final labeling, the sound track of *Heavenly Creatures* also obsessively emphasizes the girls' *many* names, especially for each other: "Juliet" is also "Juliet Hulme," "Gina," "Deborah," "Antoinette," "Julietta," and "Julie"; and "Pauline" is also "Pauline Parker," "Paul," "Yvonne," "Charles," and "Pauline Rieper."[70] The film's emphasis on the many different names for the girls is of particular Butlerian resonance because it further implies that neither one of them can be definitively called one thing. The different names for Pauline emphasize her dual identity in terms of gender, and are thus particularly indicative of her identity "continually in flux" (Columpar 2002, 331). *Both* sets of names call attention to the inadequacy of presuming to finally know either girl: the audience has no choice but to identify the girls according to different internal and external perceptions, thus calling any essentialist notion of identity into question. This is, in itself, a radical revisionist tactic since the girls were repeatedly labeled during their own time. Labeling them was an effort to reinforce the very sorts of exclusionary and damaging social practices that Butler critiques.

---

[70] Pauline's two different last names reflect her having taken her father's name though her parents were not married: the surname she was therefore tried with was her mother's.

THE SHOCK OF MURDER

The standard assumption reflected in newspapers contemporary with the girls' trial was that because Juliet and Pauline indulged their lesbian urges unchecked for too long, they gave in to a sickness which led to their being capable of the appalling act of matricide.[71] By extreme contrast, *Heavenly Creatures* avoids judgment of the girls and coercively involves us in their psychological journey to the extent that the final sequence counting down to the murder comes as a particular shock. The murder jolts us out of our necessary compliance with the girls. This experience perhaps parallels the shock the girls themselves experienced upon confronting the reality of their crime.[72]

The lead-up to the murder itself is sonically different from anything that precedes it. First, it is relatively quiet and accompanied by few sound effects. Second, after having spoken so much during the film, Pauline and Juliet say barely anything. In the actual lead-up to killing Pauline's mother, the girls had tea and cakes before their walk through Native bush. In *Heavenly Creatures*, the beauty of Puccini's "Humming Chorus" invests these actions with an ethereal strangeness [1:39:10–1:42:15]. The obvious lack of lyrics within the music transports us to an experience beyond words, one which the real Pauline could not record in her diary. The effect of the music is partly unnerving in that it is unlike any associated with the girls up to that point. This is not to suggest that the aural emphasis is dispassionate; indeed, the music leading up to the murder communicates a kind of lament for what the girls lost through their own tragic belief in there being no other "solution."

Crucially, the music stops right before Pauline strikes the first murderous blow. The first shocked screaming of her mother and the subsequent sounds of blows and screams last less than thirty seconds [1:43:01–1:43:28], but the girls' screaming afterwards lasts longer [1:43:01–1:44:39]. The horror of hearing the violent blows to Mrs. Rieper's head amplifies how much we have been encouraged to hear Pauline and Juliet's story separately from the violence they committed. But the film does not abandon the girls here, even in this horror: instead, it aurally emphasizes the shock of the

---

[71] For full discussion of this assumption, see Glamuzina and Laurie's account of media and other coverage of the Parker/Hulme case (1991, 110–33).

[72] Even Jackson and Walsh had trouble confronting the place of the actual murder. Many of the film's sequences were shot in the original locations: Pauline's visiting the doctor was shot in the office where he actually worked, for instance, and the scene at the tearoom was also filmed at the original location. But Walsh and Jackson decided to film the murder about a hundred yards away from the original site because they felt uncomfortable in the original space: Jackson explains that "all the way down the path you hear the wind and the birds, and suddenly, when you arrive at the spot, you hear nothing." That he here conceptualizes silence as a deep threat resonates with the relative quietness of the film's lead-up to the murder, including the subduing of all diegetic sounds during the "Humming Chorus."

murder, *especially* for them. During the murder itself, the scene cuts back and forth between their attack on Honora and images of them tearfully saying goodbye. The fantasy sequence of them aboard a boat together (as shown near the beginning of the film) has become a scene of Pauline farewelling Juliet aboard the boat without her (see Figures 5.29 and 5.30).[73]

This representation of the girls' fantasy life being painfully transformed to their separation transitions to one last devastating sight: Pauline's bloodied face in full color. Then we hear her final scream, "No!" [1:44:36–1:44:38] (see Figure 5.31). The image is reminiscent of cinematic war footage and is, in that sense, unlike anything else we have seen up to this point in *Heavenly Creatures*. The sudden break from the visual style of the rest of the film (especially the lack of clear resolution) jolts us into a new level of reality, along with Pauline's gut-wrenching scream. Pauline's scream also communicates her inability to understand her own action. This final audiovisual representation of her is the film's ultimate compassionate statement. Although the film does not shy away from the horror of what happened to her mother, it also asks us to dwell upon Pauline's pain.

Heavenly Creatures closes with several captions revealing what happened after the murder, the final point being that "it was a condition of the girls' release that they would never meet again." When we then hear Lanza singing "You'll Never Walk Alone" over the final credits, the lyrics are thus especially ironic. The song comes from the 1945 Rodgers and Hammerstein stage musical *Carousel,* in which it ultimately brings comfort to the female protagonist after her husband has killed himself. Once again, straight music is ironically given to the girls (albeit from a relatively queer musical).[74] The lyrics of "You'll Never Walk Alone" also grimly refer back to the very first hymn of the opening sequence, "Just a Closer Walk with Thee." However, the message remains more compassionate than these levels of neat irony might suggest. Ultimately, *Heavenly Creatures* has asked us to walk with Pauline and Juliet. And even if its self-conscious

---

[73] A third black-and-white fantasy sequence aboard the boat shows Pauline and Juliet running to the latter's parents, and kissing each other while Mr. and Mrs. Hulme look lovingly on. This is shown while Juliet sings "Sono Andati," a somber performance that anticipates the murder [1:32:53–1:33:34]. There is poignancy in the disjunct between the girls' idyllic fantasy and Juliet's singing music from a tragic operatic love story. The sequence ends with a cut showing Pauline waking up, immediately suggesting it is her dream.

[74] One of the queerest aspects of *Carousel* is that the main male character of Billy Bigelow is a criminal on earth but is compassionately treated by a heavenly official, so much so that he is granted a return to the love of his life to make amends to her; in other words, a subversive concept of relative justice is important to the story. This in itself resonates with how *Heavenly Creatures* attempts to do new justice to Pauline and Juliet's story.

FIGURES 5.29 AND 5.30 During the murder scene the film cuts to show Juliet and Pauline farewelling each other.

FIGURE 5.31 The final devastating image of Pauline, directly after the murder.

constructions as well as their final, terrible crime disallow our complete alliance with them, there is a lasting impression of having heard the world as they did.

SUMMARY

Both *Rebecca* and *Heavenly Creatures* invite a Butlerian analysis, especially since they aurally empower their queer characters. The sound tracks of both films make these characters especially complex, multidimensional, and resistant to containment. Both films use "straight" music as a form of drag, protectively clothing their queer characters in the power of well-established aural paradigms more associated with heterosexual narratives. Because these same characters are dressed in "straight" clothing, the musical and non-musical sounds associated with their self-definition, perception, and experience take on particular significance when it comes to interrogating the heteronormative status quo of their time and, by extension, those heteronormative prejudices that endure.

Rebecca and Mrs. Danvers are the most powerful aural presences in *Rebecca*. Ironically, Rebecca's musical power is amplified by her visual absence and verbal silence, just as Mrs. Danvers's musical and vocal power is offset by her silent entrances. Both characters possess complexity and inscrutability in association with the numerous variations of their musical themes. Their power is also reinforced by aural motifs that emphasize their destabilizing impact on others, especially waves crashing and tremolo strings. Music punctuates almost all the main action of the film, and often ironically undercuts the power of the other, heterosexual characters. The sound track's multiple other ironies invite us to read it on several levels, and against the grain of "straight" impressions.

The title of *Heavenly Creatures* appears on the screen as letters on lines that approximate a musical stave (see Figure 5.32). Ironically, there are six rather than five lines that would make a stave, subtly suggesting a queer use of the aural signifier. This visual detail paves the way for an entire sound track that queers the historically dominant impressions of who Pauline Parker and Juliet Hulme were. To apply a term from Rosi Braidotti, the film creates a "counter-memory" of them.[75] Through various forms of music, as well as through numerous details of voiceover, sound effects, and dialogue, the film questions fixed definitions of its protagonists and asks us to "rehear" them.

---

[75] Braidotti uses the term counter-memory in relation to resisting "assimilation or homologation into dominant ways of representing the self." She also uses the term for those "who have forgotten to forget injustice [...] [T]heir memory is activated against the stream; they enact a rebellion of subjugated knowledges" (1994, 25).

FIGURE 5.32 The title *Heavenly Creatures* as it appears in the film across a "stave" of six lines.

Heavenly Creatures ends by emphasizing the tragic conclusion of a lesbian love affair and honoring the significance of that. We could usefully contextualize this in relation to the AIDS crisis which still loomed large at the time of the film's release and during which expressions of grief for same-sex partners was often socially limited. Butler has analyzed how the failure to legitimate gay relationships becomes especially excruciating when a partner dies and "the loss isn't really legitimated as legitimate loss—hospitals don't release the body to the lover, courts don't accept the status of a partner, families do or do not convene to grieve the loss, places of employment struggle to accept whether this is equal to a spousal death [. . .] so I think there is a kind of cultural institution of denial on this issue that raises the question of whether this is a grievable loss" (Bell 1999, 172).[76] Both *Rebecca* and *Heavenly Creatures* focus on the losses experienced by their queer characters. Despite the diabolical ways of Mrs. Danvers, and the terrible crime of Juliet and Pauline, both films are unusual in this regard. Though neither film presents a time when lesbian relationships were "legitimated," both films assume a "grievable loss." This is a form of queer power.

WORKS CITED

Austin, J. L. 1962. *How to Do Things with Words.* Cambridge: Harvard University Press.

Barton, Sabrina. 1995. "'Crisscross': Paranoia and Projection in *Strangers on a Train*." In *Gay, Lesbian, and Queer Essays on Popular Culture*, edited by Corey K. Creekmur and Alexander Doty, 262–81. Durham: Duke University Press.

Bell, Vicki. 1999. "On Speech, Race and Melancholia: An Interview with Judith Butler." *Theory, Culture & Society* 16 (2): 163–74.

---

[76] Recent legislative changes in the United States, especially with regard to gay marriage, now challenge such arguments. However, Butler's words here represent the dominant Western world reality in 1994 when *Heavenly Creatures* was released.

Berenstein, Rhona J. 1995. "'I'm Not the Sort of Person Men Marry': Monsters, Queers, and Hitchcock's *Rebecca*." In *Out In Culture, Gay, Lesbian, and Queer Essays on Popular Culture*, edited by Cory K. Creekmur and Alexander Doty, 239–61. Durham, NC: Duke University Press.

———. 1998. "Adaptation, Censorship, and Audiences of Questionable Type: Lesbian Sightings in *Rebecca* (1940) and *The Uninvited* (1944)." *Cinema Journal* 37 (3): 16–37.

Braidotti, Rosi. 1994. *Nomadic Subjects: Embodiment and Sexual Different in Contemporary Feminist Theory*. New York: Columbia University Press.

British Library Board. n.d. "Received Pronunication." The British Library: Explore the World's Knowledge. Accessed April 13, 2014. <http://www.bl.uk/learning/langlit/sounds/find-out-more/received-pronunciation/>.

Butler, Judith. 1990. *Gender Trouble: Feminism and the Subversion of Identity*. New York: Routledge.

———. (1991) 2004. "Imitation and Gender Insubordination." In *The Judith Butler Reader*, edited by Sarah Salih, 120–37. Malden, MA: Blackwell Publishing. Originally published in *Inside Out: Lesbian Theories, Gay Theories*, edited by Diana Fuss, 13–31 (New York: Routledge).

———. 1993. "Gender Is Burning: Questions of Appropriation and Subversion." In *Bodies That Matter: On the Discursive Limits of "Sex,"* 121–40. New York: Routledge.

———. 1997. *Exciteable Speech: A Politics of the Performative*. New York: Routledge.

———. 2004. *Precarious Life*. London: Verso.

Chion, Michel. (1982) 1999. *The Voice in Cinema*. Edited and translated by Claudia Gorbman. New York: Columbia University Press. Originally published as *La Voix au cinema* (Paris: *Cahiers du cinéma* (Editions de l'Etoile)).

Columpar, Corinn. 2002. "'Til Death Do Us Part: Identity and Friendship in *Heavenly Creatures*." In *Sugar, Spice, and Everything Nice: Cinemas of Girlhood*, edited by Frances Gateward and Murray Pomerance, 323–42. Detroit, MI: Wayne State University Press.

Creed, Barbara. 2000. "*Bad Taste* and Antipodal Inversion: Peter Jackson's Colonial Suburbs." *Postcolonial Studies* 3 (1): 61–68.

Creet, Julia. 1995. "Anxieties of Identity: Coming Out and Coming Undone." In *Negotiating Lesbian and Gay Subjects*, edited by Monica Dorenkamp and Richard Henke, 179–99. New York: Routledge.

Daniel-Richard, Debra. 2010. "The Dance of Suspense: Sound and Silence in *North by Northwest*." *Journal of Film and Video* 62 (3): 53–60.

Dasent, Peter, et al. 1994. *Heavenly Creatures: Music from the Motion Picture Soundtrack*. CD. Auckland, NZ: Mana Music.

Doane, Mary Ann. 1999. "*Caught* and *Rebecca*: The Inscription of Femininity as Absence." In *Feminist Film Theory: A Reader*, edited by Sue Thornham, 70–82. New York: New York University Press.

Doty, Alexander. 1995. "Dossier on Hitchcock: Introduction." In *Gay, Lesbian, and Queer Essays on Popular Culture*, edited by Corey K. Creekmur and Alexander Doty, 183–85. Durham: Duke University Press.

Du Maurier, Daphne. 2006. *Rebecca* (1938). New York: Harper.

Elleray, Michelle. 1999. "Heavenly Creatures in Godzone." In *Out Takes: Essays on Queer Theory and Film*, 223–40. Durham, NC: Duke University Press.

Foucault, Michel. 1972. *Power/Knowledge: Selected Interview and Other Writings, 1972-1977*. Edited and translated by Colin Gordon. New York: Pantheon Books.

———. 1978. *History of Sexuality, Volume 1*. Translated by John Hurley. New York: Random House.

Franklin, Peter. 2011. *Seeing Through Music: Gender and Modernism in Classic Hollywood Film Scores*. Oxford: Oxford University Press.

Gaard, Greta. 1997. "Toward a Queer Ecofeminism." *Hypatia* 12 (1): 114–37.

Glamuzina, Julie, and Alison J. Laurie. 1991. *Parker & Hulme: A Lesbian View*. Ithaca, NY: Firebrand Books.

Gurr, Tom, and H. H. Cox. 1957. *Famous Australasian Crimes*. London: Frederick Muller Ltd.

———. 1958. *Obsession*. London: Frederick Muller Ltd.

Guzik, Elizabeth. 2001. "The Queer Sort of Fandom for *Heavenly Creatures*: The Closeted Indigene, Lesbian Islands, and New Zealand National Cinema." In *Postcolonial and Queer Theories: Intersections and Essays*, edited by John C. Hawley, 47–61. Westport, CT: Greenwood.

Harding, Bruce. 2012. "When the 'Corpus Juris' Meets a Corpus Delicti: The Appearance and Representation of Law's Violence as Purveyed in the Hulme-Parker Trial (1954) and Narrated in Peter Jackson's *Heavenly Creatures* (1994)." University of Canterbury. The Heavenly Creatures Website ("Legal Analysis of the Case"), edited by Adam Abrams, July 2. <http://www.adamabrams.com/hc/faq2/section_10/10.3.html>.

Hayward, Susan. 2006. *Cinema Studies: The Key Concepts*. 3rd ed. London: Routledge.

Henderson, Jennifer. 1997. "Hose Stalking: *Heavenly Creatures* as Feminist Horror." *Canadian Journal of Film Studies* 6 (1): 43-60.

Hepworth, John. 1995. "Hitchcock's Homophobia." In *Gay, Lesbian, and Queer Essays on Popular Culture*, edited by Corey K. Creekmur and Alexander Doty, 186–94. Durham: Duke University Press.

Jagger, Gill. 2008. *Judith Butler: Sexual Politics, Social Change and the Power of the Performative*. London: Routledge.

Jagose, A. 1996. *Queer Theory*. New York: New York University Press.

Kamitsuka, Margaret D. 2004. "Toward a Feminist Postmodern and Postcolonial Interpretation of Sin." *The Journal of Religion* 84 (2): 179–211.

Knapp, Lucretia. 1995. "The Queer Voice in *Marnie*." In *Gay, Lesbian, and Queer Essays on Popular Culture*, edited by Corey K. Creekmur and Alexander Doty, 262–81. Durham: Duke University Press.

Landy, Marcia. 2001. "Mario Lanza and the 'Fourth World'." In *Keyframes: Popular Cinema and Cultural Studies*, edited by Matthew Tinkcom and Amy Villarejo, 242–58. London: Routledge.

Lippy, Tod. 1995. "Writing and Directing Heavenly Creatures." Peter Jackson Online. Accessed July 2, 2012. <http://www.members.tripod.com/peter_jackson_online/interviews/Interview1.htm>.

Lloyd, Moya. 1999. "Performativity, Parody, Politics." *Theory, Culture, and Society* 16 (2): 195–213.

Magnus, Kathy Dow. 2006. "The Unaccountable Subject: Judith Butler and the Social Conditions of Intersubjective Agency." *Hypatia: A Journal of Feminist Philosophy* 21 (1): 81–103.

Martin, Biddy. 1994. "Sexualities without Genders and Other Queer Utopias." *Diacritics* 24 (2/3): 104–21.

Meijer, Irene Costera, and Baukje Prins. 1998. "How Bodies Came to Matter: An Interview with Judith Butler." *Signs* 23 (2): 275–86.

Meyer, Elizabeth J. 2007. "'But I'm Not Gay': What Straight Teachers Need to Know about Queer Theory." In *Queering Straight Teachers: Discourse and Identity in Education*, edited by Nelson M. Rodriguez and William F. Pinar, 15–32. New York: Peter Lang.

Mills, Catherine. 2007. "Normative Violence, Vulnerability, and Responsibility." *Differences: A Journal of Feminist Cultural Studies* 18 (2): 133–56.

Modleski, Tania. 1982. "'Never to Be Thirty-Six Years Old': *Rebecca* as Female Oedipal Drama." *Wide Angle* 5 (1): 34–41.

———. 1988. *The Women Who Knew Too Much*. New York: Routledge.

Molloy, Maureen. 1999. "Death and the Maiden: The Feminine and the Nation in Recent New Zealand Films." *Signs* 25 (1): 153–70.

Neumeyer, David, and Nathan Platte. 2012. *Franz Waxman's "Rebecca": A Film Score Guide*. Lanham, MD: Scarecrow Press.

New Zealand Government. 1997. "Christchurch City (Census '96) (1996 Census of Population and Dwellings)—Brochure." Statistics New Zealand, Tatauranga Aotearoa, July 30. Accessed July 2, 2012. <http://www2.stats.govt.nz/domino/external/pasfull/pasfull.nsf/web/Brochure+Christchurch+City+(Census+96)+1996+Census+of+Population+and+Dwellings?open>.

Rey, Chow. 1999–2000. "When Whiteness Feminizes. . . :Some Consequences of a Supplementary Logic." *Differences* 11 (3): 137–68.

Ribeiro, Luisa F. 1995. "Movie Review: *Heavenly Creatures*." *Film Quarterly* 49 (1): 33–38.

Rich, Ruby. 1991. Introduction to *Parker & Hulme: A Lesbian View*, edited by Julie Glamuzina and Alison J. Laurie, i–xi. Ithaca, NY: Firebrand Books.

Rodrigeuz, Nelson M. 2007. "Queer Theory and the Discourse of Queer(ing) Heterosexuality: Pedagogical Considerations." In *Queering Straight Teachers: Discourse and Identity in Education*, edited by Nelson M. Rodriguez and William F. Pinar, 277–307. New York: Peter Lang.

Rothman, William. 2008. "Blood Is Thicker Than Water: The Family in Hitchcock." In *A Family Affair: Cinema Calls Home*, edited by Murray Pomerance, 91–104. London: Wallflower Press.

Salih, Sarah, ed. 2004. *The Judith Butler Reader*. Malden, MA: Blackwell Publishing.

Samuels, Robert. 1998. *Hitchcock's Bi-Textuality: Lacan, Feminisms, and Queer Theory*. Albany, NY: State University of New York Press.

Schantz, Ned. 2010. "Hospitality and the Unsettled Viewer: Hitchcock's Shadow Scenes." *Camera Obscura* 73 (1): 1–27.

Sedgwick, Eve Kosofsky. 1990. *Epistemology of the Closet*. Berkeley, CA: University of California Press.

Sparrow, Gerald. 1973. *Queens of Crime*. London: Arthur Baker.

Stilwell, Robynn J. 2006. "Vinyl Communion: The Record as Ritual Object in Girls' Rites-of-Passage Films." In *Changing Tues: The Use of Pre-existing Music in Film*, edited by Phil Powrie and Robynn Stilwell, 152–66. Hants, England/Burlington, VT: Ashgate.

Sullivan, Jack. 2006a. *Hitchcock's Music*. New Haven: Yale University Press.

———. 2006b. "*Psycho*: The Music of Terror." *Cineaste* 32 (1): 20–28.

Walker, Lisa M. 1993. "How to Recognize a Lesbian: The Cultural Politics of Looking Like What You Are." *Signs* 18 (4): 866–90.

Wen, Patrick. 2004. "Dirty-Minded Girls Who Wrote Novels Full of Murder: Uncertain Self-Difference and Problematic Representation in the Parker/Hulme Murder Case." *Literature Interpretation Theory* 15 (3): 241–52.

Wood, Robin. (1982) 1995. "Letter to the Editor." In *Gay, Lesbian, and Queer Essays on Popular Culture*, edited by Corey K. Creekmur and Alexander Doty, 262–81. Durham: Duke University Press. Originally published in *Christopher Street* 66:4–5.

CODA

Throughout this book, we have applied various theoretical approaches to sound tracks: genre studies, postcolonialism, feminism, psychoanalysis, and queer theory. We have focused on each approach separately, so as to solidly establish a distinct series of possibilities attached to each one. The next logical step is to *combine* these approaches. Let us briefly examine one film accordingly.

Gravity (2013) was released in theaters just a few weeks before this book was completed. The film exploits numerous experiential possibilities of sound, and it can be meaningfully heard from multiple theoretical vantage points. The following brief analysis was written before the film was released on home video (hence the absence of timings). It is but a preview of how the film might be explored using all the fundamental tools we have used throughout this book.

The plot of *Gravity* revolves around Ryan Stone (Sandra Bullock), a medical engineer on her first space mission aboard the *Explorer* shuttle. The film begins with title cards that emphasize the impossibility of life in space, and the exposition culminates in showing Stone suddenly isolated within this context. The first scene shows her attempting to fix the complex system components of a Hubble telescope in the presence of her more playful coworkers. While she works, Matt Kowalski (George Clooney), an experienced astronaut, coasts through space with a jetpack as he attempts to break the "spacewalk record." Kowalski plays a recording of Hank Williams singing "Angels Are Hard to Find" as he moves. The song's lyrics about longing for love, and appealing to God for another human angel, become poignant in a later sequence when Stone tells Kowalski about the tragic death of her young daughter. Here, however, as it diegetically accompanies Kowalski's spacewalk, the song reinforces the languorous rhythm of his movement and provides a false sense of security through the familiar timbre of Williams's voice singing cadentially predictable country music. In the same opening scene, another astronaut named Shariff successfully replaces some batteries in the Hubble telescope system and then laughingly performs "some version of the Macarena" (as Kowalski derisively calls it). Shariff, attached to the *Explorer* with a long cord, playfully moves about space while Stone continues to work despite her queasiness, high heart rate, and a drop in temperature. Shortly after Kowalski begins to assist Stone, a Russian missile strike causes an unintentional chain reaction, hitting nearby satellites and sending shards of debris hurtling through space. The debris fatally wounds Shariff and destroys the *Explorer*. Ryan and Kowalski are soon perilously attached to each other only, and their repeated efforts to make contact with their commanding officers on earth fail. Kowalski dies after heroically attempting to save Ryan, leaving her to choose survival by herself. The rest of the film follows her solitary efforts to move through space toward aircrafts, to make contact with other human beings, and to eventually return to earth.

A NON-GENERIC GENRE FILM

With genre studies in mind, especially Altman's "semantic/syntactic" approach, *Gravity* knowingly plays upon aural expectations. Though it is readily classifiable as science fiction, it was literally designed to sound different from any film preceding it. The film self-consciously references other films within the genre. The most obvious allusion is to *Apollo 13* (1995): near the beginning, Kowalski jokes with the voice of Mission Control by saying "Houston, I have a bad feeling about this mission." Houston is voiced by the uncredited Ed Harris, providing a strong sonic connection between the films. But after the cloud of debris destroys the *Explorer*, all communication with Houston is lost: it is as if the film says, "hear a connection to something you know, but now hear that connection severed."

The director of *Gravity*, Alfonso Cuarón, was heavily involved in the sound design of the film. In many promotional materials, he stresses that in outer space "sound cannot be transmitted through the atmosphere," but it *can* be transferred through the interaction of different elements: if a person touches something, for instance, its vibrations will travel to their ears, giving them "a muffled representation of that sound" (Coleman 2013). Cuarón therefore only wanted to include those sound effects that the space crew could plausibly hear as vibrations within their spacesuits. Skip Lievsay, re-recording mixer for *Gravity*, explains that the Foley sound was consequently created using transducer recordings of vibrations "rather than regular airborne audio" (Coleman 2013). The pared-down use of diegetic sound effects (especially the absence of exterior sounds) placed a strong onus on the film's composer, Steven Price, to communicate action through his music. Price himself explains that we "don't hear an explosion in the film," but we "might hear some pulsation in the music that reflects it." The relatively limited use of sound effects also allowed Price comparative freedom with instrumentation: "With a lot of action scores, you're competing with a lot of noise," he says. "Say there's a big explosion: the music would conventionally have a lot of Hollywood-style percussion or brass, because that's the only thing that will cut through" (Rosen 2013). By contrast, the score for *Gravity* is atypically prominent, even when it is relatively quiet.

Given the relative freedom of not having to "compete" with sound effects that would potentially limit his choices, Price's score features an extreme range of instrumentation, textures, and dynamics, all of which are clearly designed to be *heard*. The music also includes numerous electronic sounds that reverberate and build upon each other. These electronic sounds merge with acoustic sounds so many times that the distinction between different kinds of instruments becomes blurred. In addition, Price used computer technology to manipulate acoustic sounds, especially voices and classical orchestral instruments, to make them "almost unrecognizable" (Girkout 2013). Instead of recording an entire orchestral performance, he recorded small groups of instruments and solo instrumental lines. This allowed him maximum control as he electronically altered each recording "to create a rich, layered effect that surrounds and constantly moves around the audience" (Girkout 2013). Finally, the score features many musical reverberations, a connection with Cuarón's emphasis on the authenticity of sound effects that are felt as vibrations in outer space. The overall effect of Price's music is to immerse us within an experience unlike any generic precedent.

The cues for *Gravity* are extremely varied in their emotive effects. Several tracks featured on the soundtrack CD feature thick electronic textures of sound that build to a cacophonous peak, only to suddenly stop altogether: examples include "Above Earth," "In the Blind," "Aningaaq," and "Tiangong." This pattern resonates with the power of outer space to take all human life away in an instant. Several other tracks are structurally surprising through extreme internal contrasts: "Parachute," for instance, alternates between sections featuring airily extended pitches at opposing extremes, communicating a sense of time suspended, and sections of suddenly building phrases or note repetitions that strengthen at a frantic pace. There are some tracks that communicate a soft, light sense of transience, such as a relatively accessible and impressionistic piece featuring piano ("Aurora Borealis"), and others that are unsettlingly experimental (such as "Above Earth"). The soundtrack features extremes of texture too: from tracks that emphasize one dominant line (such as "Airlock"), to those that utilize seemingly innumerable layers of acoustic and electronic sound (such as "The Void"). The scoring for *Gravity* is also non-generic in that there is no percussion: Cuarón mandated this with the objective of avoiding any "typical Hollywood clichés."[1]

---

[1] *Elysium* (2013) is a strong, contrasting example of a recent science fiction film featuring heavy percussion, especially in Ryan Amon's underscoring for many scenes of violent combat.

Gravity joins other science fiction films that have extended the repertoire of well-known aural possibilities: the thick textures of the *Alien* (1979) sound track, for instance, which exploit the possibilities of Dolby Stereo though combining Jeff Goldsmith's music with numerous ambiguous sound effects; the famously surprising "classical" music of *2001: A Space Odyssey* (1968), especially Stanley Kubrick's choices of Johann Strauss's *The Blue Danube* waltz and Richard Strauss's *Thus Spake Zarathustra*, which lend ironic grandeur and strange grace to several scenes in space; and the unprecedented range in Vangelis's synthesized scoring for *Blade Runner* (1982), which gives epic and unearthly proportions to the film's futuristic *mise-en-scène*.

A FEMINIST STATEMENT

Gravity is also an important contribution to science fiction in that it revolves around a female protagonist: this remains comparatively rare despite the most influential exception of Ripley (Sigourney Weaver) in the *Alien* series.[2] *Gravity* takes the emphasis on its female protagonist to a polemic extreme because Price's entire score was designed with her subjectivity in mind. Price himself explains how the music reflects her perceptions of outer space around her, especially as it is both "stunningly beautiful" and "massively terrifying" (Girkout 2013). This aural alignment with her extends to the film's many silences too.[3] In other science fiction films, silence often communicates the terror of being isolated in outer space,[4] but Stone tells Kowalski that she takes most pleasure in the quiet of space. In particular, the lack of noise provides an escape from the trauma of her past on earth: during the exposition, she tells Kowalski the story of her four-year-old daughter who died in an ordinary playground accident. It is an everyday occurrence that poignantly emphasizes the ease with which a human life can be lost on earth. Equally, this story throws Stone's own extraordinary survival in outer space into sharp relief. The film initially encourages us to enjoy the quiet as Stone enjoys it, six hundred kilometers above and away from the planet where her daughter died. Only when the quiet of space *becomes* threatening to Stone do we hear it accordingly.

Though a deathly silence sometimes threatens to overtake the film, Price's score ultimately amplifies the meaning of Stone's life, and the grandeur of her survival.

---

[2] The films include *Alien*, *Aliens* (1986), *Alien³* (1992), and *Alien: Resurrection* (1997).

[3] Silence is always an effect in cinema, given that (as Sergi points out), "the complete absence of sound" is impossible to achieve: it is, rather, "a minimal presence of sound" (2004, 161).

[4] This is an important motif of *2001: A Space Odyssey*, for example.

Thinking back to Mulvey's "Visual Pleasure and Narrative Cinema" ([1975] 2004), *Gravity* refrains from objectifying her, especially through this elevating music. Seeing as the camera mostly focuses on her, she could have easily become fetishized, or unsympathetically scrutinized, or made into an icon to be looked at. Instead, the camera consistently moves *with* her, just as the sound track is aligned with her perceptions. Also, the treatment of space is fluid enough that the film rarely features anything like standard shot-reverse-shot patterns, whereby we might expect her to become a subject of the main male character's (Kowalski's) gaze. While many long-tracking shots follow her, the immersive Dolby Atmos sound track gives the impression of moving *with* her across space.[5] Furthermore, as she speaks, she drives the film: since Stone is alone on screen for most of *Gravity*, her voice is the strongest anchoring element of the sound track, especially in contrast with the unpredictable extremes of sound effects and music.

Along with being anchored in Stone's voice, the sound track of *Gravity* is structured so that everything she feels is aurally reinforced. We feel the terror of her endangered life through the many closely miked sounds of her physical aloneness, especially her solitary breathing and her isolated voice. Price wanted the music "to be with her all the time," poetically saying that the score was designed in terms of "where the tempo of [her] heartbeat was" (Ayers 2013). His score thus offsets Stone's lone presence through always being "with" her. The final track titled "Gravity," which accompanies her return to earth, is the most stirring example of this. Up until the film's final sequence, the human voices featured in Price's score often sound far away and distorted, in keeping with the reality of earth being distant from Stone for most of the action. The "Gravity" track, however, features the strongest and clearest female vocal line that rises to *forte* dominance. This track also features the greatest surge in an orchestrally supported melody, further reinforcing the strong impression of the protagonist having reached her ultimate self-actualization. It is the culmination of Price's score, just as it underscores Stone's breathtaking achievement in reaching earthly shores alone. The music communicates an epic sense of scale, even as it accompanies the images of a single woman re-experiencing the extraordinarily ordinary physical sensation of gravity.

---

[5] As Dolby explains on their own website, Dolby Atmos is superior to their other forms of surround sound in that it uses up to sixty-four speakers (including some overhead), to provide the most immersive aural experience possible. Dolby Atmos is designed to match the visual action in precise spatial terms: "Dialogue follows characters. Sound effects track with camera pans. Ambient sounds envelop you. For the first time, you'll hear the whole picture" (Dolby 2013). In *Gravity*, the technology is primarily used to heighten our experience of *Stone's* perceptions.

A QUEER EXPERIENCE

Along with being an important feminist presence, Ryan is also a queer kind of pro-tagonist. She appears through much of the film in spacesuits that hide her womanly body, and even when she strips down she is costumed to appear more androgynous than feminine. Equally, Bullock avoids many clichés of "feminine" speaking, such as high pitches, breathy pausing, "little-girl" intonations, or heavily sexualized huskiness. Instead, her voice is mid-range and surprisingly clear most of the time. Even Ripley, the most iconic female hero of science fiction films, is aurally sexualized and feminized in the last sequence of *Alien* where she sings a version of "You Are My Lucky Star" (a most ironic reference to the final scene of *Singin' in the Rain*). As Ripley prepares to kill the monster, her soft singing and quickening breath become gasps that suggest orgasmic terror.[6] She is aurally reduced to a female victim, reminiscent of countless other horrific scenes that have sexual overtones, especially as women are victimized.[7] By contrast, even when Stone is shown hurtling towards earth in the climactic scene of the film, she almost never loses complete control of her voice. Indeed, she regains enough compo-sure to resolutely tell herself (and us) that whether she survives the descent or not "it'll be one hell of a ride!" In the exposition, when she begins to gasp for air, her sounds of panic are never sexually suggestive. Kowalski repeatedly reminds her to breathe slowly to make the most of the limited oxygen left in her jetpack: we are never allowed to forget that her gasps are for *survival, not pleasure.*

The sound effects of *Gravity* also place emphasis on her strong *human*, rather than gendered presence, in space. When she cries, thus potentially revealing a "feminine" kind of weakness, her tears are imaged and heard as tiny drops of ice that "clink" against surfaces: this aurally emphasized, tangible representation of her emotion mediates any impression of her being simply "soft." Moreover, we consistently hear sound effects as she *and* the other male astronauts feel them: this gives us a sense of their combined aural reality in *human* (rather than gender-specific) terms.

Stone also evades conventionalism in that the music associated with her can-not be said to connote masculinity or femininity. Equally, she does not romantically attach herself to the male lead, nor does she ultimately depend on his presence. After Kowalski is lost in space, one sequence shows him miraculously re-enter the diegesis.

---

[6] Shortly before Ripley begins singing, she is visually sexualized as well: before she changes into a protec-tive spacesuit for the climactic defeat of the alien, she strips down to nothing but a camisole and panties, revealing the fragility of her female body that was mostly concealed up to that point.

[7] Many films foreground the sexualization of women in horrific scenes: *Blow Out* (1981) is a strongly self-conscious example of this, especially through its sound track.

However, we subsequently learn that his re-entrance is Stone's imagining. Although his reappearance, and his urging Stone to attempt survival, might suggest he shares in her triumph, we must understand that everything he says is part of her subjectivity. Because Kowalski only re-enters the film as a facet of Stone's imagination, especially as a manifestation of her own will to live, her consciousness includes male and female voices, pushing the limits of her biologically determined identity in a Butlerian way. In addition, her oft-repeated name "Ryan Stone" sounds male, further queering her female physical presence, just as much as the spacesuits that visually encourage us to read her body as "human" rather than gendered or sexualized. Her queer presence is, in turn, imposed on us insofar as the film uses Dolby Atmos technology to provide the corporeal illusion of moving *with* her: the film thus invites an alignment with Stone that transcends how we might identify ourselves in terms of sex, or gender, or anything else.

A POSTCOLONIAL "CONVERSATION"

From a postcolonial perspective, *Gravity* might seem to be more problematically limited: the one person of color visible on screen (Shariff) is killed within minutes, leaving the two white main characters to dominate. The narrative also implies that the entire future of humankind can be embodied by a Caucasian (Stone). This is clearest in the final scene, which shows her stumble alone onto a shore without any visible signs of civilization. However, there is another important minority presence in the film, albeit one that we only hear without seeing. This presence is the voice of man speaking Greenlandic. Stone accidentally picks up his voice on her radio while repeatedly trying to make contact with her commanding officer on earth. Over and over again, she attempts to communicate that she needs saving, but the man cannot understand her. With unwitting belligerence, she desperately repeats phrases in English, as if their repetition will eventually be understood. She verbally communicates a form of cultural and linguistic arrogance, even though the film sympathetically represents her plight. During this "conversation," neither she nor the man is able to make much sense to the other until she hears sounds that signify meaning beyond language: the noises of dogs, and the man singing a lullaby to his baby. Stone is suddenly comforted by the recognizable sounds that connote a family life, albeit one remote from her American home (Lake Zurich, Illinois). These sounds, along with the man's voice, soothe her into a state of repose. Ironically, none of the earthbound radio voices speaking English to her in the first part of the film create the impression of such a reassuring human connection. This one radio "conversation" emphasizes the need Stone has to truly *hear* another person, even if that person's words are beyond her own linguistic limitations.

Like numerous other science fiction films, *Gravity* explores what it means to be human. The aural contact between Stone and the stranger speaking Greenlandic is a humbling and deeply humane exploration of the power of sound to connect human beings across the greatest possible distances. The film surely respects cultural and ethnic difference: it is not as if Stone can suddenly presume to understand his voice. We know, along with the film, that the world is bigger than what she can immediately understand. However, she values the essential humanness of the stranger's voice. By implication, the film aurally stresses what is worth preserving for *all*, and not just one lone white woman.

The life of this particular scene of just a few minutes has extended beyond the diegesis of *Gravity*. Jonás Cuarón (Alfonso's son, and cowriter for *Gravity*), wrote, edited, and directed a short film featuring the man with whom Stone briefly makes contact. The short, titled *Aningaaq* (2013), is named after the character, and alludes to the one word that Stone and he share during their conversation (aside from "hello"). She repeats his name, guessing that it belongs to him, while he mistakenly identifies "Mayday" as her name. The repetition of his name thus signifies a rare and precious moment of possible understanding across cultures and space.

Aningaaq shows the title character receiving Stone's radio distress call, and represents the opposite side of the conversation that we hear in *Gravity*. Thus, it audiovisually extends the life of Aningaaq's voice, as well as the significance of everything he says. Though Jonás Cuarón says he was careful "to make it a piece that could stand on its own" (Abramovitch 2013), both *Aningaaq* and *Gravity* are only enhanced by our perceiving them side-by-side. Though *Gravity* maintains its focus entirely on Stone's narrative, resisting cuts back to earth until she returns there herself, *Aningaaq* enlarges the *Gravity* narrative from a new, earthbound and culturally remote point of view. The two films together create an experience we could term "interamplification"—hearing the one only allows us to hear the other better, especially in postcolonial terms. In particular, *Aningaaq* calls attention to the absence of minority peoples in *Gravity*, and privileges the voice of a man who embodies cultural difference. When considered alongside *Gravity*, the short film also allows Stone and Aningaaq to become equal participants in the one conversation.

Aningaaq allows us to see a man whose life is an extreme struggle, an earthly parallel to Stone's plight. It prompts us to dwell on the harsh, snow-filled, and windswept plain of Greenland where Aningaaq miraculously picks up her voice. Without knowing it, he shows Stone a great kindness in attempting to speak with her, even if they cannot accurately hear each other, or hear the same way. In the context of *Gravity*, the sound of Aningaaq's dogs' howling brings the comfort of familiarity to Stone, but in his own film

Aningaaq explains that the first dog she hears must be put down. This detail amplifies their cultural difference and the poignant irony of miscommunication through linguistic limitation. The fact that Aningaaq and Stone hear the dog differently is also stressed in that they voice different words for his sound: Stone asks him to make the dog say "woof, woof" again, whereas he insists that the dog's sound is a howl, which he imitates into the radio receiver as "auuuu" [3:37] (see Figure 6.1).

With his howling, Aningaaq painfully anticipates the first dog's death, and the last sound of the film is of his reluctantly shooting a gun. The camera does not show this action, and instead focuses on an expanse of sky beyond Aningaaq while the gunshot reverberates, visually inviting a connection between the sound and Stone's location far above. The sound of the fatal shot comes after Stone tells Aningaaq she is dying and they lose radio contact. This obviously alludes to the brutal possibility of Stone's own immanent death. So, the short film aurally emphasizes what separates, as well as what connects, the two characters. They share a confrontation with death.

A PSYCHOANALYTICALLY CHARGED STORY

In contrast with the sound of death, the presence of the baby in *Aningaaq*—whose voice is another important sound in *Gravity*—initially seems to only mark the difference

FIGURE 6.1 In his conversation with Stone, Aningaaq imitates the sound of his dog—for him, the dog does not "woof, woof" but howls "auuuu."

between Aningaaq's life and the grim reality Stone faces. However, the baby's aural presence in *Gravity* ironically anticipates how Stone will be "reborn" by the end of the film. The final scene where she rediscovers the experience of gravity in her feet suggests rebirth, especially as it comes with her return to earth. Long before this, Aningaaq's lullaby to the baby is especially comforting to Stone, as if returning her to something like the "sonorous envelope" of the womb: this interpretation is visually supported by her being shown confined within a spacecraft while he sings. Aningaaq begins to sing to his baby as Stone is saying "I'm scared, I'm really scared." The baby cries and frets a little, but his song slightly calms him/her, much as it provides comfort to Stone.

The spacecrafts of *Gravity* suggest womb-like confinement in both protective and sinister terms. In connection with this, some of Price's music is so richly layered that its fullness also evokes the pre-lack, and pre-linguistic state. That said, the overall sound track also often evokes the terror of the Real, transporting us to a place we cannot know and that impresses its unconquerable hugeness on us. The action of the film takes place beyond the reaches of the Symbolic realm on earth, and the sound track consistently emphasizes the danger as well as the grandness of being in that space. Moreover, since Price's music distinguishes itself from other scores so strongly, it challenges more familiar examples of symbolization. In parallel to this, Stone must redefine herself as she is torn away from her usual Symbolic space. She largely does this through speaking to us. By speaking, she of course never fully separates from the Symbolic realm, but she also has the power to newly define what matters most: the memory of her daughter, the ordinary pleasures she enjoys at home, and her own will for survival.

BRINGING EVERYTHING TOGETHER: A HEIGHTENED SONIC EXPERIENCE

The sound track for *Gravity* often emphasizes the shocks and threatening moments experienced by Stone through sudden surges of sound, and sonic changes *on the cut*. Such non-suturing patterns ensure that *Gravity* keeps us almost constantly on the alert. Far from inviting a regressive experience akin to the Mirror Stage, the film demands that we perceive, and revel in, its construction. Because the film's entire construction revolves around the physical and emotional experiences of its queer, feminist protagonist, it is a strong example of subversive mainstream cinema.

From *Invasion of the Body Snatchers* (1956) to *The Hunger Games* (2012), science fiction most often focuses on the grim prospect of all humanity under threat. But *Gravity*'s primary focus is the preciousness of just one human life. This is reinforced by every way that the sound track enforces our attachment to this life, and gives us the extraordinary impression of hearing everything in a space beyond our own. The transportive and affective power of the sound track demands an empathetic response to an experience we can never have directly. The same might be said of *all* those sound tracks we have analyzed, all of which awaken us to the ultimate importance of hearing cinema. Such cinematic experiences are only enlarged when we consider their density of meaning from several theoretical perspectives. This brief analysis of *Gravity* is but a glimpse into further possibilities. There is an infinite space for more.

WORKS CITED

Abramovitch, Seth. 2013. "*Gravity* Spinoff: Watch the Other Side of Sandra Bullock's Distress Call." *The Hollywood Reporter*, November 20. Accessed December 21, 2013. <http://www.hollywoodreporter. com/news/gravity-spinoff-watch-side-sandra-657919>.

Ayers, Mike. 2013. "Secrets of the *Gravity* Soundtrack: Composer Steven Price on the Score of 2013's Biggest Movie." *Rolling Stone*, October 9. Accessed December 21, 2013. <http://www.rollingstone. com/movies/news/secrets-of-the-gravity-soundtrack-20131009>.

Coleman, Michael, prod. 2013. "The Sound of *Gravity* (making-of feaurette)." Warner Bros. Accessed December 21, 2013. <http://soundworkscollection.com/videos/gravity>.

Dolby. 2013. "Authentic Cinema Sound by Dolby Atmos." Accessed December 23, 2013. <http://www. dolby.com/us/en/consumer/technology/movie/dolby-atmos-details.html>.

Girkout, Alexa. 2013. "How Do You Score Outer Space? Silence and 'Overwhelming Sound' Says *Gravity* Composer." *The Hollywood Reporter*, October 3. Accessed December 21, 2013. <http://www.holly-woodreporter.com/news/how-do-you-score-outer-638432>.

Mulvey, Laura. (1975) 2004. "Visual Pleasure and Narrative Cinema." In *Film Theory and Criticism*, edited by Leo Braudy and Marshall Cohen, 837–48. 6th ed. New York: Oxford University Press. Originally published in *Screen* 16 (3): 6–18.

Price, Steven. 2013. *Gravity: Original Motion Picture Soundtrack*. CD. Burbank, CA: WaterTower Music.

Rosen, Christopher. 2013. "*Gravity* Composer Steven Price on the Film's Incredible Soundtrack." *The Huffington Post*, October 4. Accessed December 21, 2013. <http://www.huffingtonpost. com/2013/10/04/gravity-steven-price_n_4039455.html>

Sergi, Gianluca. 2004. *The Dolby Era: Film Sound in Contemporary Hollywood*. Manchester: Manchester University Press.

SELECT FILMOGRAPHY

Bigger Than Life. 1956. Directed by Nicholas Ray. Performed by James Mason, Barbara Rush, Walter Matthau, and Christopher Olsen. The Criterion Collection, 2010. DVD.

Brokeback Mountain. 2005. Directed by Ang Lee. Performed by Heath Ledger, Jake Gyllenhaal, Anne Hathaway, and Michelle Williams. Universal Studies Home Entertainment, 2006. DVD.

Dead Man. 1995. Directed by Jim Jarmusch. Performed by Johnny Depp, Gary Farmer, Lance Henrikson, and Gabriel Byrne. Buena Vista Home Entertainment, Inc., 2000. DVD.

Heavenly Creatures. 1994. Directed by Peter Jackson. Performed by Melanie Lynskey, Kate Winslet, Sarah Peirse, and Diana Kent. Buena Vista Home Entertainment, Inc., 2002. DVD.

The Piano. 1993. Directed by Jane Campion. Performed by Holly Hunter, Harvey Keitel, Sam Neill, and Anna Paquin. Artisan Home Entertainment Inc., 1999. DVD.

Rabbit-Proof Fence. 2002. Directed by Phillip Noyce. Performed by Everlyn Sampi, Tianna Sansbury, Laura Monaghan, and Kenneth Branagh. Buena Vista Home Entertainment, Inc., 2003. DVD.

Rebecca. 1940. Directed by Alfred Hitchcock. Performed by Laurence Olivier, Joan Fontaine, George Sanders, and Judith Anderson. Metro-Goldwyn Mayer Studios Inc. (Premiere Collection), 2008. DVD.

The Searchers. 1956. Directed by John Ford. Performed by John Wayne, Jeffrey Hunter, Vera Miles, and Ward Bond. 50th Anniversary Two-Disc Special Edition. Warner Home Video Inc., 2006. DVD.

Shutter Island. 2010. Directed by Martin Scorsese. Performed by Leonardo DiCaprio, Mark Ruffalo, Ben Kingsley, and Max von Sydow. Paramount Pictures, 2010. DVD.

Ten Canoes. 2006. Directed by Rolf de Heer. Co-Directed by Peter Djigirr. Performed by Crusoe Kurdall, Jamie Gulpilil, Peter Minygululu, and David Gulpilil. Madman Entertainment Pty Ltd., 2007. DVD.

To Have and Have Not. 1944. Directed by Howard Hawks. Performed by Humphrey Bogart, Lauren Bacall, Walter Brennan, and Dolores Moran. Warner Home Video Inc., 2003. DVD.

FURTHER PERCEIVING

The questions we have considered at the end of each theoretical introduction could be usefully extended to this list of films. Each example here resonates with the themes and ideological concerns that we have discussed in the close analyses of particular films as well.

GENRE STUDIES (AND THE WESTERN)

Stagecoach (1939)
Broken Arrow (1950)
Dances with Wolves (1990)
Brokeback Mountain (2005)
Meek's Cutoff (2010)

POSTCOLONIALISM (AND AUSTRALIAN CINEMA)

Jedda (1955)
Walkabout (1971)
The Tracker (2002)
Australia (2008)
The Sapphires (2012)

FEMINISM

Some Like It Hot (1959)
My Fair Lady (1964)
Thelma and Louise (1991)
Dancer in the Dark (2000)
Moulin Rouge! (2001)

PSYCHOANALYSIS

Laura (1944)
Vertigo (1958)
Cape Fear (both versions: 1962 and 1991)
Eyes Wide Shut (1999)
Fight Club (1999)

QUEER THEORY

Persona (1966)
3 Women (1977)
The Adventures of Priscilla, Queen of the Desert (1994)
Milk (2008)
A Single Man (2009)

SELECT GLOSSARY

This glossary includes illustrative examples for some of the more complex terms used in this book. Since all the following terms are included within the index, the reader may easily find examples for those that are not immediately elaborated upon here. For another useful glossary to supplement this one, see *Hearing the Movies* (Buhler, Neumeyer, and Deemer 2010, 425–32).

Accent In music, this term most often refers to a "marcato" accent: a note that is given a particular, comparatively loud emphasis. The term can also apply to the stressed beat of a measure, as in a waltz rhythm of *one*-two-three.

Ambient sound This is diegetic sound associated with authenticating the environment or setting shown on-screen. In a restaurant scene, for instance, ambient sounds might include glasses and cutlery clinking, quiet conversations of extras (as restaurant personnel and customers), people coming in an out of the front door, etc. All of these sounds could be mixed to create the background for a conversation at one particular table where the main actors of the scene are seated. This kind of sound does not typically call attention to itself: instead, it creates a sonic context for more prominent sounds.

Anempathetic sound Sounds, especially music, that do not seem sympathetically aligned with one or more characters. Such sound may seem ironic or even hostile towards a character in that it does not "match" their experience. In *Rebecca*, the waltzes that cheerfully play while Fontaine's character reveals her miserable personal circumstances to Maxim are good examples.

Arpeggio A musical chord broken up so that each note is played or sung individually, usually in rapid succession.

Atonal music Music that is not based in a recognizable scale or tonal center. Such music often communicates the impression of "randomness" and/or experimentation because it is not grounded in familiar harmonic and melodic structures.

Aural motif A repeated sonic detail that gathers cumulative, and symbolic, significance within a film.

Cadence A harmonic form of musical punctuation: a progression of chords that finishes a phrase or section within a piece of music. A "final cadence" conveys a sense of musical resolution.

Chromatic Notes that are only a semitone apart are "chromatic." Because major and minor scales, (the basis of most Western music), are built on patterns of semitones *and* tones, chromatic lines of music sometimes create harmonic ambiguity and/or comparatively decorative melodies.

Classical music In a loose or colloquial sense, "Classical" may refer to any chamber, operatic, symphonic, or other music that draws upon long-standing, "serious" musical traditions. In a stricter sense, "Classical" refers to a particular period of composition within the history of Western music: from 1730–1820. The work of Wolfgang Amadeus Mozart falls within this period, and often exemplifies Classical principles of balance, structural discipline, tight harmonic logic, and sharply differentiated melodies within (mostly) homophonic structures.

Consonance Sounds that blend together harmoniously create consonance. In film analysis, both musical and non-musical sounds may be considered in terms of consonance and its opposite, dissonance.

Cue A piece of music composed or chosen to begin and end at particular points within a film.

Diegetic sound Sound that emanates from within a film's world (or diegesis). Characters within the film may potentially hear it because it comes from the same space they inhabit. Diegetic sound may be music, sound effects, or dialogue.

Discordance (see dissonance).

Dissonance Sounds that do not blend together harmoniously. *Shutter Island* often features dissonance through overlapping musical cues that do not mesh together: the overall effect is to emotively amplify a sense of disturbance and rupture.

Dynamics The relative loudness of musical or non-musical sounds. In music, specific dynamics are often written by composers on their scores. The Italian term *forte*, for instance, means "loud," whereas *piano* means soft or quiet. *Mezzo forte* and *mezzo piano* refer to medium-loudness and medium-quiet. Our perception of dynamics is purely dependent on specific aural contexts: for instance, Mrs. Danvers's voice would seem *piano* in relation to the stormy sequences of *Shutter Island*, but in the context of *Rebecca* it usually sounds *mezzo forte* in comparison with "Fontaine's" comparatively weak voice.

Empathetic sound An aural element that clearly aligns itself with the emotional experience of a character (or characters). Such sound usually communicates a sense of subjective investment in that same character, the implication being that we should feel as they do. Stephen Price's score for *Gravity* was written with the primary goal of being empathetic sound for the main character, Stone.

Experimental music Music that overtly plays with its audience's expectations of familiar structures, especially with regard to harmony, melody, rhythm, and/or instrumentation. John Cage is among the most famous of the experimental twentieth-century composers: his works not only feature instruments played unusually or that have been tampered with, but also stretch the bounds of recognizable musical structures. Moreover, many of his works (such as 4'33") challenge fundamental ideas of what constitutes a piece of music in the first place. The term "experimental" refers to a full spectrum of possibilities: whereas Cage represents one extreme, Michael Nyman's music has often been referred to as modestly experimental in that it adapts earlier pieces of music (such as the hymns and Scottish tunes he used for *The Piano*) through combining their melodies with comparatively contemporary harmonies and rhythms.

Expressionistic This term was first coined in relation to poetry and paintings that powerfully express the interior life of their subjects without making an attempt at naturalistic (or pseudo-photographic) representations of reality. Edvard's Munch's *The Scream* (the four original versions of which were created in 1893) is a paradigmatic example: the vibrant swirls of paint indicate the subject's inner turmoil while the painting makes no effort to depict an actual or recognizable face. In other words, Munch makes the emotion of the subject visible. In cinema studies, expressionism refers to those films that favor stylized visions of a character's world with the goal of giving us psychological access to them: a paradigmatic example is the silent horror *The Cabinet of Dr. Caligari* (1920). In this book, we adapt the term expressionism to apply to those moments where sound or music represents the internal life of a character to such an extreme that their internal life is not only made audible but made more important than a sonic representation of "reality." *Shutter Island* features many expressionistic (and experimental) cues and sound effects that communicate the protagonist's internal life in such terms, to the extent that our access to any objective reality is deliberately skewed.

Glissandi A glissando (with the plural being glissandi) is a dramatic sweep or slide from one note to another through a series of consecutive notes between them. Sometimes all individual notes involved in this slide are discernible, as in the many harp glissandi featured in *Rebecca*. In that film context, the glissandi connote unraveling mysteries, especially in association with the titular character. "Sliding note" is a more colloquial term for glissando.

Hard cut Sound that changes *on* the cut, rather than carrying on from one shot to the next. Some hard cuts are relatively unobtrusive, especially when visual elements of continuity editing are still present: for instance, in *To Have and Have Not*, cuts often follow Harry's looking towards another character off-screen to show us the object of his look, but without sounds that carry over the cutting. Some hard cuts are more noticeable and jarring, especially when the sound changes from one extreme to another while images are unpredictably juxtaposed, as is repeatedly the case in *Gravity*: in that film, hard cuts are repeatedly used to foreground the hostile and unpredictable realm of outer space.

Homophonic (see texture).

Legato Notes that are played so that they flow smoothly together. On the piano, a legato technique is easily achieved using the sustaining (or damper) pedal.

Leitmotif A phrase or theme that is associated with a character or concept, and which is typically developed through variable repetitions. The variable repetitions contribute a sense of cumulative significance, as well as a dynamic sense of the characters and/or concepts as they develop meaning through a narrative. The use of leitmotifs is much associated with the operas of Richard Wagner, especially his cycle of operas titled *Der Ring des Nibelungen* (1853–69). Leitmotifs quickly became conventional within Classical Hollywood scoring (as in Max Steiner's numerous original scores). Leitmotifs are still the basis of much Western film scoring.

Mickey-mousing Music that "matches" the on-screen action: for instance, a descending scale that aurally parallels the visual movement of a character walking down some stairs. The term was coined in relation to music for early Disney cartoons that served such a playfully illustrative function.

Minimalism Music stripped down to its "bare bones," often grounded in repetition. The concept was first applied to the visual arts, but was famously adapted by Michael Nyman when he used the term "minimal music" or "minimalism" during his time as a music critic for *The Spectator* (from 1964–76).[1] John Adams, whose piece "Christian Zeal and Activity" (1973) is featured in *Shutter Island*, is well known for his minimalist work.

Modal melodies Modes are created by making a note of a major scale the "first" note in place of the original. For instance, the Lydian mode is eight notes beginning on the fourth note of a major scale. (There are seven modes because there are seven notes in a major scale.) Modes are used in many genres of music, from ancient sacred music, to jazz, to contemporary rock. They are sometimes referred to as "displaced major scales."[2]

Monophonic (see texture).

Musique concrète Meaning "concrete music," this experimental genre combines acoustic instruments with electronic sounds and/or sounds from nature. The term was first associated with the work of the French composer Pierre Schaeffer. Karlheinz Stockhausen's *Hymnen* (1966–67), featured in *Walkabout*, is one celebrated example.

Non-diegetic Non-diegetic sound comes from outside the film world (or diegesis) and its characters cannot hear it. Such sounds often include orchestral scoring (such as David Raksin's score for *Bigger Than Life*) and voiceover (as in the first scene of *Rebecca*).

Ostinato A phrase that is persistently repeated at the same pitches, sometimes incorporating minor variations. Max Richter's "On the Nature of Daylight," featured in *Shutter Island*, is based in a rhythmic/harmonic ostinato, above which a higher-pitched melody rises. Pachelbel's *Canon* (the full title of which is *Canon and Gigue for 3 violins and basso continuo*) features a famous ostinato as the bass line (or "ground bass") that repeats throughout the piece.

Pizzicato Plucking a stringed instrument rather than using a bow (on violins, for instance) or strumming (on guitars, for instance). The effect is usually percussive and clipped rather than sustained or reverberating.

Pleonastic music, or pleonastic sound The word "pleonasm" is used for phrases of words with the same (or similar) definitions ("true fact," for instance). In this book, the term "pleonastic" applies to those moments in a film when the visual details and the sound track communicate the "same" message

---

[1] For more information, see Warburton (1988).

[2] For more information, see Schonbrun (2011, 90–96).

(despite being different forms of signification). Mickey-mousing is the most obvious form of pleonastic music. Steiner's score for *The Searchers* features many examples of Mickey-mousing that provide a sense of narrative clarity because they literally reinforce what we see (a descending scale when Marty is lowered from a rock in the final sequence, for example). By contrast, in *Shutter Island*, the music never Mickey-mouses the action straightforwardly, especially since it was all written before the film's making. However, the music of *Shutter Island* is often pleonastic in that it "matches" what we see in a less obvious, more conceptual sense: for instance, the turbulence of many experimental cues in the film matches the visual emphasis on a storm brewing or raging in many scenes. Ironically, the apparent obviousness of such musical pleonasms only makes the revelatory scene, during which we realize the storm was but an expressionistic representation of the protagonist's experience, all the more surprising.

Polyphonic (see texture).

Rest A moment of intentional silence within a musical composition.

Romanticism In the loose or colloquial sense, Romanticism (or Romantic music) often refers to music that communicates great expressive depth and range, especially in a storytelling context. In the stricter sense, Romanticism refers to a particular period of composing music in the Western world: roughly, from 1800 to 1900. Like any other form of music, there is much variety within Romanticism. However, the specific musical period is associated with soaring melodies, harmonic complexities (especially through chromaticism), complex and shifting textures, variable and extreme dynamics, textures, and pitches. Above all, Romanticism is associated with emotionally affective ranges and the manipulation of Classical structures of music. Many of Ludwig van Beethoven's works are classified as Early Romantic, while Romanticism at its height is much associated with works by Hector Berlioz, Frédéric Chopin, Franz Liszt, and Robert Schumann. Romanticism is also represented by the big-scale, melodically driven, and harmonically rich operas of Richard Wagner.

Rubato *Rubato* refers to the technique of speeding up and/or slowing down the tempo of a piece at the will of the performer. The instruction *rubato* will often be incorporated within a musical score, but the exact interpretation of how much and how quickly the tempo should be manipulated is up to the performer. Michael Nyman's music for Ada in *The Piano* features many *rubato* passages that reinforce a sense of her volatile and unpredictable expressivity.

Sneaking Music (or sound) that unobtrusively enters a film scene. Most cues in Classical Hollywood scores are "snuck" into their respective scenes, only coming to the fore when the scene reaches a climax or a development in the dialogue or action that seems to demand some emotively musical amplification.

Sforzando A sudden accent on a note or chord, often at a comparatively loud (or *forte*) volume. A *sforzando* can create a "stinger" effect, as in many examples within David Raksin's score for *Bigger Than Life*.

Sliding note (see glissando).

Sound advance A sound that anticipates a presence before we see it: for instance, when we hear Lauren Bacall as "Slim" singing of "a lady beyond compare" before a cut shows her in a scene from *To Have and Have Not*.

Soundtrack The music for a film, separated from other aural elements. The term applies to most CDs of music from movies because they do not typically incorporate dialogue or sound effects.

Sound track *All* the aural components of a film, including music, dialogue, and sound effects.

Stinger A musical or non-musical sound that suddenly intrudes upon the sound track, often with sinister or violent implications. The stinger need not necessarily be at *forte*, but it does sound comparatively "sharp." Many stingers are featured in Raksin's scoring for *Bigger Than Life*. Several stingers are featured in *The Searchers*, especially in connection with the demonized character of Scar.

Suturing "Suturing" music or sound carries over cuts, providing sonic continuity that aids a smooth narrative flow. Such practice is so commonplace that it is usually almost imperceptible, except when it is interrupted or repeatedly avoided (as in *Bigger Than Life* or *Shutter Island*).

Syncopation Syncopation is an unexpected rhythmic effect, usually through stressing a beat that would ordinarily be unstressed, and thus making the dominant rhythm less straightforward and/or disrupted and/or playful. Michael Nyman's music for Ada in *The Piano* sometimes features syncopation, reinforcing a sense of the character's unpredictable power.

Texture There are numerous textual possibilities in music. At its most basic, texture refers to the layering of simultaneous sounds: for instance, a thick texture is created by many sounds being mixed together, especially if their pitches are relatively close together; and a thinner texture is created by fewer sounds and/or sounds that are more spread out in terms of pitch. Texture also refers to monophonic, homophonic, and polyphonic forms of music. Monophonic music consists of one dominant melodic line, as in Gregorian chant. In film studies, we might apply this term to any section of a sound track where one sound, whether musical or non-musical, dominates. Homophonic sounds move rhythmically together, as in the traditional harmonized setting of a hymn. In film studies, we might consider any scenes where all dominant sounds rise and fall together as homophonic. Polyphonic music is shaped by interweaving melodic strands that are equally important, as in the fugues of J. S. Bach. In film studies, we might call any scene where different layers of sound "compete for our attention" polyphonic (Buhler, Neumeyer, and Deemer 2010, 50). Melody and accompaniment, as in most popular song, is one further textural possibility. In film studies, we might perceive any scene where one kind of sound rises up over others that support it (as in dialogue that rises over ambient sounds of a city) as a form of melody and accompaniment.[3]

Timbre This term refers to the tone quality of a sound, irrespective of pitch and loudness: for example, the same note at *forte* sounds very different on a piano than it sounds on a piccolo. Timbre will also vary depending on how a single instrument is played. For instance, the timbre of a violin might be softly mellow, warm, and aesthetically pleasing (especially when played with a mute and/or with vibrato and/or legato phrasing) or, at the other extreme, may be sharp, crisp, and disturbing (especially when played roughly enough to generate audible friction between the bow and the strings and/or with staccato (sharply detached) notes).

Trill A musical piece of ornamentation that consists of rapidly alternating between two notes that are close together (usually only a semitone or tone apart). It is not to be confused with the tremolo, as it is primarily meant to embellish the music rather than to create a "trembling" effect.

Tritone A tritone consists of three consecutive whole tones. The tritone is sometimes referred to as the "Devil's interval" for its diabolical associations since Medieval times. Steiner's score uses the sinister associations of the tritone in association with Scar.

Tonal music Music that is clearly grounded in a tonic center: all notes (including chords) are selected with this center in mind. For instance, for a piece of music in C major, all notes and chord progressions would derive from the identifiable scale. Because tonal music is the norm in so much Western music, including film scores, we tend to take it for granted unless it is juxtaposed with atonal music. The sound track for *Shutter Island* features both forms of music, which has a destabilizing overall effect.

Tremolo A rapid fluctuation between different pitches or a rapid reiteration of one note, accentuating the sound for a "trembling" effect. There are numerous examples of tremolos in *Rebecca* that cumulatively communicate a sense of intrigue, mystery, and dread.

Vibrato A controlled, quivering effect achieved by very slight fluctuations in pitch. On a violin, vibrato effects are achieved by gently and rapidly wobbling the fingers as they play individual notes. Vibrato is often associated with heightened emotional expressivity, as in the recordings of Mario Lanza's singing featured in *Heavenly Creatures*.

Voiceover A voice (usually belonging to a character, but sometimes to an omniscient narrator) that comments on the on-screen action from a non-diegetic position. Some films play upon the conventional voiceover: for instance, *Stranger Than Fiction* (2006) has its main character hear a voiceover

---

[3] For more information on textural possibilities, see Buhler, Neumeyer, and Deemer (2010, 47–55).

that belongs to one of the other on-screen characters as she writes her novel about him. This is an extreme example of blurring the diegetic and non-diegetic realms of a film. We typically expect the voiceover to be inaudible to the characters on-screen, and it thus often gives us a sense of privileged access to the truth: for instance, at the start of *The Piano*, Ada's voiceover gives us immediate access to her in a way that she disallows the other characters of the film.

WORKS CITED

Buhler, James, David Neumeyer, and Rob Deemer. 2010. *Hearing the Movies: Music and Sound in Film History*. New York: Oxford University Press.

Schonbrun, Marc. 2011. *The Everything Music Theory Book with CD: Take Your Understanding of Music to the Next Level*. 2nd ed. Avon, MA: Adams Media.

Warburton, Dan. 1988. "A Working Terminology for Minimal Music." *Intégral* 2 (1988): 135–59. Reprinted in *Paris Transatlantic Magazine: Global Coverage of New Music*, edited by Dan Warburton. Accessed April 10, 2014. <http://www.paristransatlantic.com/magazine/main/home.html>.

INDEX